Untouchable

Untouchable

AN INDIAN LIFE HISTORY

James M. Freeman

Stanford University Press, Stanford, California
1979

Stanford University Press
Stanford, California
© *1979 by the Board of Trustees of the*
Leland Stanford Junior University
Printed in the United States of America
ISBN 0-8047-1001-5
LC 78-55319

Acknowledgments

I am grateful to the following institutions for their generous support of my research, of which this book is one result. The American Institute of Indian Studies granted me a Senior Faculty Fellowship for 1970–72, during which time I collected the data on life histories on which this book is based. The Joint Committee on South Asian Studies of the Social Science Research Council and the American Council of Learned Societies awarded me a grant in 1976–77 to edit and analyze the life history materials that I had collected. The Center for Advanced Study in the Behavioral Sciences, with funds from the Andrew W. Mellon Foundation, granted me a fellowship in 1976–77, at which time I wrote this book. And San Jose State University granted me a sabbatical leave during 1976–77 to work on life histories. I am solely responsible for the conclusions and perspectives of this book, which do not necessarily reflect either the opinions or the policies of the institutions mentioned above.

I am deeply indebted to Cora DuBois, my teacher and friend, who guided my first field research in India in 1962–63, and whose emphasis both on fine-grained data collecting and skeptical evaluation of collected data prepared me for my work on life histories. She has followed my work and read and criticized my writings with the dedication of a great teacher.

Over the years, John Pelzel has shown a continuing interest in my work with life histories, and I am grateful for his helpful suggestions, as well as his encouragement of my work.

I am deeply grateful to the Government of India, the Government of the State of Orissa, and Utkal University for graciously permitting me to remain in India and conduct research during the trying times of a war and a national emergency. Dr. L. K. Mahapatra, professor and head of the Department of Anthropology, Utkal University, was not only especially cordial and hospitable, but also gave me many helpful suggestions regarding my research. I thank Gagan Dash for his excellent Oriya language instruction, Dale and Monserrat Harrison for their generous hospitality in Bhubaneswar, and S. M. Gani, whose help and suggestions were invaluable.

While in India, my wife, Patricia Freeman, helped in recording the life history field notes and in taking some of the more than 5,000 photographs that accompany my notes, including several hundred photos of people of the Bauri caste. I am grateful for her help, without which neither the notes nor the photos would have been so complete.

Many other persons have read and commented on portions of my life history study, or suggested leads on topics that I have included in this book, and their suggestions and encouragement influenced the final form of the book: Hilda Kuper, Wallace Chafe, Renato Rosaldo, Gerald Berreman, August Meier, Elliott Rudwick, Eugene Freeman, Ann Freeman, Thomas Freeman, Ruth Freeman, Ronald Cohen, Ved Vatuk, David Krantz, Jack Pierce, James Comer, Michael Kammen, and Sylvia Vatuk.

For typing and editorial assistance, I am indebted especially to Dorothy Brothers, and also to Joan Warmbrunn, Jane Kielsmeier, Mary Tye, Irene Bickenbach, and Heather MacLean, all on the staff of the Center for Advanced Study in the Behavioral Sciences, and to Nadine Willey, of San Jose State University. I am grateful to Meryl Lanning, free-lance editor, for assistance with the final preparation of this book.

No words can adequately convey my debt of gratitude to Harihar Mallia and Muli: this book is the testimony to their contribution. The name "Muli" is a pseudonym, as are all personal names (except Hari's and mine) and many place names used in the narrative. Muli often refers to people by their title, such as Teacher, Doctor Babu, and Sister-in-law. I have followed Muli's usage for certain persons, but to provide variety I have used fictitious proper names for others, such as Dash Babu and Tafulla.

The photos, all taken by the author, depict Bauri and village life styles, but are not of persons in the book. Portions of Chapter 18 first appeared in my book *Scarcity and Opportunity in an Indian Village*, and are reprinted here with the kind permission of the Benjamin/Cummings Publishing Company.

J.M.F.

Contents

Note on Transliteration

Throughout this book, I use several diacritical marks for transliterating the Oriya language. For example:

Length of vowels:	a	(short)	versus aa	(long)
Double vowels:	a-a	(short)	versus aa-aa	(long)
Retroflex consonants:	ḍ	(retroflex)	versus d	(dental)
Aspiration:	th	(aspirated)	versus t	(nonaspirated)
	ch	(aspirated)	versus c	(nonaspirated)

Oriya has three "s" sounds that are distinguished in writing but have become virtually indistinguishable in the speech of people like Muli, who is the subject of this book. To retain the flavor of Muli's speech, I have not distinguished his "s" sounds, or those found in a few footnotes where I give examples of Bauri-caste as well as feminine pronunciations. For proper names such as Shiva and Sankar, which I have not italicized, I have arbitrarily spelled them either with an "sh" or an "s." Caste names such as Oilpresser and Goldsmith are capitalized.

In this book, Oriya words foreign to English are italicized and presented with diacritical marks. I translate these words the first time they are used in each chapter; they are also included in the Glossary-Index. Certain words from Indian languages are now found in Webster's New Third International Dictionary or are otherwise widely used in English. I use neither italics nor diacritical marks for such words, although they also appear in the Glossary-Index; they include anna, babu, betel, dhoti, guru, lungi, paise, rupee, sari, and tiffin.

Part One

Muli: An Indian Untouchable

1. Introducing Muli

During my last visit to India, I came to know an Indian untouchable named Muli well enough to have him confide the story of his life to me. The first time I saw him, he was sitting in the dusty road in front of one of the small thatched roof tea shops in the village, with his glass and saucer placed conspicuously beside him— a silent signal to the shopkeeper that an untouchable wants to buy some tea. Muli was a gaunt forty-year-old with betel-blackened teeth who wore his long hair swept back. His once handsome face was pain-lined, his cheeks were sunken, but his eyes were bold and piercing, not submissive.

Above Muli, sitting on benches in the shop, three men sipped tea, and I heard them gossiping about the marriage feast they had attended the night before. A ten-year-old boy dressed in shorts leisurely refilled their glasses while he studiously ignored the silent man outside. I stopped and watched. After several minutes the boy glanced at Muli; then, in language that deliberately and offensively signaled that he was addressing a social inferior, he called harshly, "*abe saḷaa bauri ṭokaa! tu ka-aṇa nebu?*"* Muli pointed to his glass. From a proper distance, he dropped two coins into the boy's outstretched palm. As the boy bounded up the steps of the shop, Muli poured the tea from his glass into the saucer, then blew on it and slurped it. Suddenly he stood up and shuffled off, crouching to show respect, so that as he passed by the men in the tea shop his right hand trailed in the dust.

Because I was impressed by the untouchable's control, I asked the tea-stall boy if he knew the man's name and address. The boy

*The people of Muli's caste resent these insults: *abe* [hey there], used to call untouchables; *saḷaa* [wife's brother], connoting having sexual relations with one's sister; *bauri*, in the context of this sentence a derogatory use of the name of Muli's untouchable caste; *ṭokaa* [lad or boy], an insult when used to address an untouchable adult male; *tu* [you], the intimate personal pronoun used for children and inferiors; and *nebu* [will take], the verbal form used with the intimate pronoun; the word *ka-aṇa* [what] is not an insulting term.

1. Because he is an untouchable, Muli is prohibited from entering most village shops and tea stalls; sitting outside, he calls in his order and is served on the road.

spoke contemptuously, "His name is Muli. What do you want with him? He's dirty, like all his people. He lives over there." He pointed to a cluster of tiny mud and thatch huts set apart from the rest of the village—one of five such segregated wards for the people of Muli's caste.

Stigmatized from birth as spiritually defiling and therefore potential pollutors of "clean" high-caste people, India's untouchables lived for centuries in segregated hamlets and villages. High castes denied them the use of public wells, as well as entry to schools, shops, and high-caste shrines, and forced them to perform the most despised and defiling jobs of their society: exhausting unskilled physical labor, scavenging, cleaning latrines, and carrying off dead animals.

Untouchability is now officially "abolished" in India. Contemporary Indian laws, as well as the Constitution, prohibit discrimination against untouchables. But nearly 16 percent of India's population, or about 100,000,000 people, are untouchables; and any gains in their situation have been sparse and uneven. Most of them, despite legislation, the expenditure of millions of rupees, and two and a half decades of federal and state efforts to improve their economic and social position, remain desperately poor, semiliterate or illiterate, and subject to brutal discrimination and economic exploitation, with no realistic prospects for economic or social gain.

Muli lives three miles from Bhubaneswar, the capital of the eastern coastal state of Orissa. In Bhubaneswar itself, as in other Indian cities, the different untouchable castes, of which the Bauris are one, experience no obvious public discrimination. But in Muli's village, the old ways persist: although legally permitted to do so, untouchables enter neither shops nor village temples because they fear high-caste reprisals.

The memory of Muli's humiliation stayed with me. I recalled similar incidents in my own country, and I wondered if the responses of untouchables to discrimination paralleled those of minorities in other countries. Was Muli indifferent to the insults he bore in silence? I hardly thought so; but I wondered how an ordinary untouchable like Muli survived economically, socially, and psychologically as a member of a despised group at the bottom of society. What were his joys, aspirations, and triumphs, as well as his humiliations? What would provoke someone like him to question the treatment he received from upper-caste people, to fight back?

I was aware that although many books, articles, and short stories depicted the life styles of India's untouchables, only a handful of untouchables had been the subject of biographies. Fewer still had described their own life experiences in narrated autobiographies or "life histories." Of the few available biographies and life histories, every one had been the story of extraordinary achievers—well-educated, economically successful persons, most of whom held high government and professional positions.* As far as I knew, at

*The best known autobiography of an untouchable is that by Hazari (1969), a remarkable document written in English by an educated man who converted to

that time not a single biography or life history had examined the life styles of the vast majority of India's untouchables, who like Muli had failed to improve their lot. In short, no one had bothered to find out about the life of an ordinary untouchable from the untouchable's point of view.

I determined that as part of my two-year anthropological study of Muli's village, I would collect the first detailed life history of an ordinary Indian untouchable, perhaps Muli's if he were willing. On a gusty March morning in 1971, Hari, my friend and research assistant, who was a native resident of Muli's village, led me along a stony path to the small clearing where Muli's house stood: a windowless, irregular hut of low red mud walls, with a roof of mouse-gray thatch bleached of its once golden color by wind, rain, and scorching sun. At the open well in the clearing, a woman was laboriously pulling up a bucket of water, while six girls sitting on the dusty road were throwing dice. Two men stepped from their houses with pickaxes on their shoulders. Most adults had already left for their daily work of dry season cultivation, stone quarrying, and road building. Except for quarrying and plowing, the women of the Bauri caste work alongside the men.

Muli sat on the narrow veranda of his house. Hari introduced me and then said, "Oh, Muli, we are doing a census of different wards of the village. Could you tell us about your household?"

Since he trusted Hari, Muli described his daily activities. He had lived all his life in his home village, working, like most people of his caste, as a landless unskilled agricultural laborer, earning one-twelfth of the paddy (threshed unmilled rice) he harvested for his landowning masters, unable to save any money, frequently without food when work was unavailable or when he was ill and unable to work. He pointed to his right foot, wrapped in a dirty cloth. He had sliced it with a pickaxe in the quarries. Since he had been unable to walk for a week, his wife had kept him and their son from starving by cutting and selling grass for cattle.

Muli then pointed. "See that house on the other side of the well? The man of that house has two wives. When his first was ill, he

Islam. Zelliot's fifty-page bibliography on untouchability (1972) adds only a few short biographies of Dr. B. R. Ambedkar, the most famous untouchable leader, and one of another prominent leader, Jagjivan Ram. Isaacs (1965[1974]) uses brief selections of life histories of untouchables. All the untouchables mentioned in this footnote are highly educated.

took up with her unmarried younger sister, got her pregnant, and had to marry her. His first wife cursed the new baby with magical spells, and it died. The younger daughter of the next house became a prostitute, so we threw her out of the ward. She wasn't as clever as her elder sister, whom we never caught, although we all knew what she did."

Muli was articulate, detailed, voluble. I asked him if he would tell me the story of his life. He looked puzzled, "What does 'the story of my life' mean?"

"Oh, about what you did when you were a child, the games you played, how you became married, the work you do, your friends, things like that."

"Sure, why not?"

A slender man in his middle twenties sat down next to us. Muli introduced us. He was Muli's youngest brother, Sarala, an automobile mechanic in the nearby city and the first man of his caste from the village ever to buy or own a bicycle.

I asked Sarala how he had become an automobile mechanic and how many other men of his caste held skilled jobs.

He said, "My brother-in-law Bharata, who lives two doors away, got me my job six years ago and trained me. We are the only two skilled workers from our caste. Everybody else does unskilled labor."

I said, "You have one hundred households of your caste in this village, over 450 people. Why do the rest of the men remain unskilled? Other castes, like the Cultivators, have recently become skilled masons, earning high wages in the city. Why have no Bauris become masons?"

Several Bauri men, including Bharata, had come over to listen before leaving for work. A short, middle-aged man named Bagha was the first to reply. "We Bauris do not try to learn because we can afford neither to go through the six-month training period without pay nor to buy the expensive tools. What will we eat while learning? Also, we need contacts who can find a teacher and place us in a job. Who among us has contacts?"

Sarala, Muli's brother, said, "No, skilled masonry is easy to learn. You see it on the job. Some people have natural skills. The clever person who wants to badly enough can learn masonry because unskilled laborers work side by side with the skilled."

Muli disagreed. "If we try to become skilled, we may not do a good job. Then we would be dismissed and starve. I have no faith in our abilities. God has produced us to be like this. Why should we try more?"

I replied, "Yet God also made Bharata, who became an automobile mechanic, and he has improved himself, as has your brother."

Muli shrugged, "We are happy that they have progressed, but we are also happy doing unskilled labor."

I was puzzled. Was Muli telling me what he thought I wanted to hear or what he really believed? If he believed it, did his statement reflect simply a negative self-image, or actual experiences in which aspiring Bauris lost jobs when attempting skilled tasks? I planned to return to this topic when taking Muli's life history.

I also wondered what had enabled Bharata to take the chances that Muli had feared. Had he encountered failures, and if so, how had he coped with them? I asked Bharata how he had become a mechanic.

He replied, "I was born in the village of Jhinti, six miles from here. In 1956, after an argument with my father, I left for Calcutta. I went on my own. In Calcutta, I met some Brahmans from my home village. Because they knew I was interested in mechanical things, they got me a job washing cars. I watched how others repaired the cars and gradually learned how to do it. After two years I returned home, worked as a farm laborer for four years, then moved to this village. I met a temple priest who operated a diesel rice-milling machine. By standing around and watching I learned how to operate it, but because my wages were low, I soon sought work at the garages in the new city nearby. I worked at three garages. The first one failed after four months; the owner of the second one fired me when I ruined some expensive parts. I washed dishes for a year. Then in 1965 a third garage owner hired me, and I have worked there ever since, now earning 120 rupees [U.S. $17] a month."

The men left for work, except for Muli, who remained sitting. He was still on the veranda when we left his ward.

After a few weeks, Hari and I finished the census. Then we began collecting life histories of high-caste villagers. Five months later, Muli suddenly appeared at my doorstep, unshaven, wearing a dirty loincloth. "My father just died," he said. "Would you take his photograph?" He knew I had taken such photos for other families.

I grabbed my camera and we ran to his house. Muli and his

2. Bauri funeral. The corpse is seated on a chair.

brothers propped their father's frail, still warm body on an arm-chair and posed beside him; the women of the house wailed. I took several photographs; then some men of the ward placed the body on a hastily constructed bamboo and cloth stretcher, carried it at a fast walk to the cremation grounds, and placed it on the caste-segregated stones reserved for the cremation of untouchables. Muli, the eldest son, lit the funeral pyre.

Two weeks later, Hari and I returned to Muli's house and gave him the photos of his father. Muli was pale, haggard, and thin. "Something is wrong with me," he said. "I went to my uncle's house to work for a week. I became ill there." Although nearly mid-

3. Bauri cremation on the caste-segregated stones allotted to untouchables.

day, Muli had not eaten since the previous night; his house contained no food.

He was dizzy and unable to walk. We carried him by bicycle to the town hospital. "It's his lungs," the doctor said to me. Medical care is free, but medicines are not; lacking money for food, let alone medicine, most people of Muli's caste do not go to the hospital for treatment. I bought Muli the medicine he needed plus oranges, eggplants, and rice. In gratitude, he offered to tell us whatever he could remember about his life. But harvesting would soon begin. Realizing that Muli could hardly afford to spend days at my house discussing his life without remuneration, I offered him meals, money for marketing, and as much paddy as he would have earned had he labored in the fields.

Little did I realize what he would offer in return. Muli, a masterful storyteller, narrated his life history to me in his native language, Oriya, during a series of almost daily interviews for six months. His account, which Hari and I translated into English from my notes, comes to some 350,000 words.

Muli's life history is one of thirteen I collected that describe from different perspectives the rapidly urbanizing village in which he lives.* Many Westerners have written about India's problems of modernization, urbanization, poverty, population growth, and political stability, usually from Western points of view or from those of high-level Indian administrators and politicians. Few studies of change probe deeply to reveal what ordinary Indians think about their transition to modernity. Surveys and questionnaires without supporting data often provide little more than biased, shallow responses. When investigators ask about change, they receive answers that focus on change. To be polite, Indian villagers often provide answers that they think the investigator wants to hear. Their replies usually bear little relation to the way they live their lives or view the world.†

Many excellent biographies and autobiographies describe the lives of extraordinary, urbanized, highly educated high-caste Indians involved with change, but their views and concerns differ significantly from those of ordinary Indians (Karve and McDonald 1963; Erikson 1969; Chaudhuri 1968; Tandon 1968). When not prodded to answer leading questions by technological missionaries and elites who want to change them, ordinary Indians provide distinctly different views of the problems they consider vital, shattering many stereotypes about the joint family, women's roles, attitudes toward the elderly, religious life styles, sexual mores, and caste rules and rankings, as

---

*Five more life histories will appear in a volume I am now preparing entitled *Five Indian Lives*. These persons, all from one high caste, are: an emigrant to Calcutta who became a criminal terrorist gang leader; a female shopkeeper and ritualist; an irreverent temple priest and old-style leader; a new leader and student revolutionist; and a self-taught drama writer and painter.

†This has been shown convincingly by Mamdani (1972) in his critical evaluation of the Khanna Project, a population control study in western India; his devastating critique shows how an investigator's implicit values and assumptions can predetermine and invalidate his conclusions.

4. Women of a Bauri ward sitting at a well.

well as strategies of adaptation to poverty, new opportunities, and urbanization.

A detailed life history like Muli's provides a way to reach behind the surface answers outsiders often receive, grasping from the insider's perspective what he really values and how he interprets his experiences. Muli does not necessarily represent a typical untouchable or villager, for he makes his own distinctive choices and adaptations; others of his caste choose differently. What Muli shares with the other men of his caste is a limited range of choices of life styles determined by a common physical, economic, and social environment.

Clyde Kluckhohn once rightly observed that an adequate life history study requires not only a comprehensive narrative of a person's life, but also treatment of three other topics: the conditions and ways in which the researcher obtains the life history, including an evaluation of trustworthiness of the data; how the subject's life history integrates with known information about his group; and interpretations of the life history based on a coherent and nonparochial conceptual scheme (Kluckhohn 1945:91). In Chapter 2 I discuss how I collected Muli's life history, and in Chapter 3 I summarize available information on his caste and community. In Chapter 30, I interpret Muli's story using David Mandelbaum's scheme (1973) for the analysis of life histories.

2. Collecting Muli's Life History

Muli began narrating his life history at my house in early November, 1971, and continued intermittently through April, 1972. When I first chose the house I would live in for the two years of my study of Muli's village, I anticipated both the need for privacy in interviews and ready accessibility to the village. Accordingly, I chose a house located in a secluded spot just outside the village limits. About midmorning, Muli would come to my house. After taking tea and breakfast, he would spend from two to five hours narrating episodes, with a break for lunch, which we provided. At first Hari, my assistant and translator, wrote down each sentence in Oriya while Muli spoke. Every few minutes, when Muli reached a stopping point, Hari and I worked out the English translation, which I wrote down. Then Muli would begin again.

I could follow ordinary spoken Oriya, as well as read high-school-level texts. Muli's use of Oriya, however, differed from the cultured, high-caste Oriya that I knew. He used conventional words in unconventional ways, Bauri dialect words, feminine expressions, proverbs, obscenities, and curses. I insisted from the first day that Muli and Hari explain in detail the meanings and uses of any words that were unfamiliar to me. At times we spent as much as one hour examining a single word, phrase, or concept. After Muli left, Hari and I reread the Oriya and English narratives, looking for discrepancies, unclear passages, and topics that needed further development. Muli soon became restless during the periods when Hari and I were translating his narratives. To keep his interest, we let him narrate his story and we translated it after he had left.

I had originally planned to interfere as little as possible with Muli's narrative, letting him choose the topics so that he would reveal his ways of thinking rather than mine. But Muli said he did not know where to begin. I told him to start by describing his daily activities as a child and his relationship to his parents, relatives, and friends. He narrated a brief and altogether inadequate sketch of his childhood, and then turned to elaborate descriptions of his life as a youth. At this point I again tried unsuccessfully to direct the interviews. Despite my numerous requests, Muli never again discussed his childhood, which held no interest for him. Similarly, he omitted describing his own wedding. When Hari and I reminded him of this, he dutifully catalogued a number of dry, lifeless rituals as if he were an outsider to the event. He gave no description of his wife during the ceremony except when we prompted him. He wished to forget the ceremony that had marked the beginning of his unhappy marriage.

Muli was clearly at his best, not when directed, but when allowed to develop his story in his own way. His spontaneously selected episodes are the liveliest and most poignant of his life history. Once he began such stories, he never ran out of words. Our problem was the reverse: he would narrate with repetitious detail how, when, and where each day in past years he had defecated, bathed, brushed his teeth, and eaten breakfast, and to whom he had spoken while performing these activities.* Complicated plots unfolded; stories developed within stories as Muli plodded literal-mindedly through chronological sequences of each day's events. I soon realized that, valuable as his descriptions of minutiae might be, at this pace Muli would require years, not months, to complete his narrative.

I told him to skip those events already described that remained unchanged day by day or those that were less important for his story. Puzzled, Muli said that he was unable to select what was important or to depart from narrating each detail, although he was willing to try. We worked for several days showing him what we considered important; he tried to follow our directions, but with little success. At this point, we told him simply to narrate his story, forgetting our

*Wallace Chafe told me he doubts that a person remembers over long periods information such as the food eaten at dinner or the details of complex anecdotes. Instead, Chafe argues—based on his present research on remembering, as well as on Bartlett's classic investigations (1932[1967])—that what Muli remembered was more a process of reconstruction than an exact recollection, that he imposed an organizational framework on details he had stored. (See Bartlett 1932:197–214; also Rosaldo 1976:121–151.) Norman notes, however, that some persons appear to have better memories than others, although he questions how much is true memory and how much is reconstruction. Experts in particular tasks, he notes, often can reconstruct complex events from very little information, in part because they can rule out implausible happenings (Norman 1969:138).

directions. To save time as Muli spoke, I told Hari what to write down and what to leave unwritten. I interrupted Muli's narratives only to ask him to clarify obscure points and inconsistencies, and to expand his descriptions of customs or rituals and their meanings.

As I had expected, Muli at first described events from the conventional viewpoints that he thought high-status people, nonuntouchables, would prefer to hear. He praised his Brahman employer, as well as other Brahmans of the village. I told Hari in English that I didn't believe Muli's statements. Hari, himself a man of high caste, nodded in agreement.

Looking worried, Muli, who understood no English, asked Hari, "What did James Babu [mister]* say?"

Hari replied in Oriya, "He wants you to tell us what is in your heart. You speak respectfully of Jadu, the Brahman who hired you to work as his farm servant, but throughout our village that man is renowned as a great miser who cheats his employees. Has he never cheated you? Tell us frankly."

Surprised but obviously delighted by this unexpected question, Muli smiled and described an episode in which he ridiculed Jadu in most unflattering terms. Later that harvest season, Muli narrated the unfolding drama that led to his great quarrel with his Brahman employer (see Chapters 28 and 29).

Muli hinted about topics such as prostitution that he said he thought Hari and I might find offensive. He was testing us, hoping that we would be interested. We assured him that he should tell us what he truly believed, as well as the true incidents of his life, and that we would be offended only if he failed to tell us the truth. Emboldened by these words, Muli began describing his life as a pimp, in which he supplied Bauri women to high-caste men. I found out later that he had hoped to draw us into his net as customers of his prostitutes.

As he became more comfortable in my presence, Muli revealed not only his life as a pimp, but also his attraction to transvestite men. Dropping his initial reserve and pretenses, he shifted into Bauri dialect and the feminine expressions of women and transvestites.

We had scheduled our interview sessions daily, but one week

*Babu [mister] is a term of respect used for people of moderate status. Most older Bauris call high-status people and employers *saa-aanta* [master], a term of higher respect than babu. Muli conspicuously avoids using the term "master" when he addresses high-status people.

after we began, Muli failed to show up. After waiting an hour, Hari and I walked to Muli's house. He limped out. I asked, "What happened to you?"

"It's my leg. Look, boils." He had a huge boil on his left leg. "I can't walk. I have to wait until the boil goes down. Then I'll continue my work with you."

I said, "Go to the hospital; otherwise the infection may spread."

His face showed fear. "No! No! They'll cut the boil. It will hurt! I can't stand the pain!"

"The pain will be a lot worse if you don't get it treated," I said.

Hari said soothingly, "They won't hurt you, but just give you medicine. Then you'll be all right."

A Bauri *baistaamba* [hereditary religious leader] standing nearby overheard our conversation. "Don't go to the hospital," he said to Muli. "I've got the cure for you, *guḷucii* [creeper] leaves. This medicine is good and it costs a lot less than going to the hospital. Heat the leaves and put them on your boils along with mustard oil. Leave them on your leg for three hours. The boils then will burst; if they don't, repeat the cure."

Muli asked, "How long before the leg is better?"

The *baistaamba* replied, "Within two days definitely."

"And if it is not?" asked Muli.

"Then I'll eat those eggs in your cold box [refrigerator]," joked the *baistaamba*. Bauris have no money to buy eggs, let alone refrigerators.

We all laughed. Muli looked unconvinced. Hari and I dragged Muli to the hospital.

The doctor grabbed hold of his leg, squeezed, and asked, "How does that feel?"

"Ooah! It hurts. Stop, stop, oh please stop!" cried Muli.

"How long have you had these?" asked the doctor.

"Six days."

The doctor shook his head. "It must be cut. Why didn't you come here immediately when you got them? Treatment will be much harder on you now."

Muli was silent, his face drawn with pain and fear. Why should he come to the hospital when he had no money for medicines? Who would have treated him, an untouchable, had not James Babu and Hari Babu personally brought him?

An orderly told Muli to lie on a table. Suddenly he grabbed

Muli's leg and sliced the main boil with a flame-heated knife. Muli screamed piteously. The orderly squeezed the boil. Muli arched upward; his screams rose; pus oozed. Muli limped out and collapsed forlornly on a bench. The medical compounder, who prepared injections, jabbed Muli's arm with a needle of medicine. Muli winced. I paid for the medicine.

For five days, Hari and I took Muli to the hospital for treatments and medicine. When the boils cleared, Muli resumed narrating his story. A few days later, he had dysentery; after that, a deep cough, then a gashed hand from harvesting paddy—a continuous line of minor ailments and injuries that interrupted our interviews. At first I was annoyed with these delays, but soon I realized that his low resistance to disease, weak stamina, fear of pain and injury, and injury-proneness accounted in great measure for his willingness to narrate his life history: instead of starving while recuperating from his injuries, he earned money by sitting and talking at my house. Furthermore, I realized that his weakness and ill health accounted in part for his becoming a pimp rather than a stone quarry worker.

The interviews with Muli proceeded unevenly. At first he was shy and avoided saying directly what he wanted. Instead, he would pout like Orissan women do, sitting silently, looking unhappy.

During one of his pouts I asked, "What's wrong, Muli?"

"Nothing."

"Come on now—you have a long face. Why?"

"Nothing's wrong. I'm quite all right." He lapsed into silence, occasionally looking up mournfully, otherwise looking down, motionless.

"If you don't tell us, how can we do anything about it?"

Looking up, he said without conviction, "I am not unhappy, Babu, but if I come here to tell you the story of my life, well, how will I eat?"

Hari replied, annoyed, "We already settled that. We'll pay you your daily wage and we'll pay a shopkeeper in the village to supply you with bread, milk, and snacks every day, just as you asked. The shopkeeper won't overcharge you since we are paying him. You told us you were happy with our agreement, so what's the problem?" Since Bauris have little money, they buy oil, spices, and rice in small quantities at much higher rates than do the wealthier villagers, who buy in larger quantities.

Muli replied, "Well, how am I to be paid?"

Hari reminded him of our agreement. "We'll pay you in paddy, which is what you asked for, since the daily wage in paddy is worth more than money wages. I bought you some paddy which I stored at my father's threshing floor. We'll give it to you when you finish your life history."

At that time, we did not realize that Muli would be narrating his story for six months; we later paid him in installments as he finished parts of it.

Muli looked frightened. He wanted more money but feared to ask us. He also wanted assurance that we would pay him. People had often cheated him when he had tried easy or short-cut schemes to acquire money or influence. He said, "But Babu, how do I know that I'll really get the paddy? Look how Jadu the miser has cheated me. If you don't give me that paddy after I work for you rather than harvesting in the fields, what will happen to me and my family? The paddy will feed us for three months. If I don't get it . . ."

I interrupted, "You'll have to trust us, Muli. Take it or leave it. If you prefer to work all day in the fields for a lower wage than I give you, then feel free to do so. I don't want to make you do something you don't want to do."

"Oh, no," he replied quickly. "I'll work for you, except on those days when I must work as a farm servant. On those days I must gather my crop."

I replied, "Yes, of course. We agreed on that several days ago. Between December and the end of January you may miss up to twenty days. On the days you are not in the fields, you work for us. Also, we'll give you money on market days. Right now, though, you should eat lunch."

Muli refused. I knew that this was pretense to show that he wasn't "greedy" for food, even though he wanted it. I said, "You *must* take it." Still he refused. I said, "Okay," and asked no more. His face became unhappy; he pouted. I filled a plate of curry and rice, handed it to him, and commanded, "Here, you eat this."

"Okay, if you order me to, but you start eating first."

I began eating in the customary way for villagers, using my right hand rather than utensils. I hoped this would make him feel more comfortable. With a twinkle in his eyes, he picked up a spoon and effortlessly worked his way through the vegetable curry and a huge mound of rice. Hari, also eating with his hand, asked Muli where he had learned these new city ways. Grinning, Muli described how a gentleman from the city had taught him to use a spoon (see Chapter 14).

Muli's city friends were customers for his prostitutes; hoping still to attract Hari and me as customers, he told several stories about them. His stories became repetitious, and we told him to discuss other topics.

He asked softly, "Wouldn't you like to try one of these women?" He laughed shyly and covered his face with his shouldercloth.

I replied, "I have a wife; Hari has a wife; we don't need your women."

He peered out over the cloth. "Once you try them, you can never leave them."

"I've got pure gold at home," I replied, "so why should I look elsewhere?"

I had wondered what sort of untouchable would tell his story. I now realized with dismay that not only had I selected him, but he had selected me as a way to earn easy money and possibly involve me with his prostitutes. Clearly by his own account, he was a deviant in his culture, a weak, sickly man unable to do men's work, often living entirely on his wife's earnings, constantly embroiled in scandals, a self-confessed liar and scoundrel whose schemes often brought disaster not only to himself but to everybody associated with him.

This was hardly the sort of person I had planned to interview. I had expected to collect several life histories of high-caste and untouchable males and females representing different life styles and ages, and illustrating various adaptations to rapid urbanization. I had expected to find villagers who might speculate on the effects of change in their lives, who might describe their participation at some of the numerous local religious festivals and discuss religious values and beliefs. Muli went to festivals only to solicit customers (see Chapter 26).

I had hoped to collect the life history of a Bauri who would refute the stereotyped images that high castes had of them. A well-educated Brahman woman spoke for many of her caste when she assured me that "the Bauris are lazy and ignorant people. All my life we have hired them to work on my father's estate. They are unreliable. You never know when they will come to work. They never work hard. That's why they are so poor." I now realized that I had inadvertently selected a person who reinforced these very stereotypes. I told Hari that I thought we should pay Muli what we had promised him but terminate the interviews and seek a normal working Bauri male or female.

Hari said, "You won't find anybody else at this time of year. All Bauris who can work are in the fields harvesting paddy. No one else can give you as much time as Muli does. Also, he speaks well, his stories are interesting, and he has given you a lot of information that you cannot get easily from other Bauris. I know that many things he says are true, and we can check the accuracy of any statements we doubt. I think you should keep interviewing him."

I accepted Hari's judgment. I had known him since 1962, when as a fifteen-year-old he had helped me collect census data during my first study of his village. Now, nine years later, he had offered his services again and I had hired him. I needed a translator-assistant, and no untouchables spoke English.

Hari, a robust athlete, was the college-educated, married son of a leader of a high-status landowning caste that hired and often exploited Bauri laborers. Hari himself was a popular youth leader who all his life had received deference from villagers of all castes. While I had expected that I could train him to work well among the people of his own caste, I was unsure if he could effectively interview untouchables, who understandably might resent high-caste persons. Other high-caste youths and men were totally unsuited to the task. Despite their frequent claims of having no caste prejudices, Hari's educated high-caste friends conspicuously avoided untouchable youths and never invited them to their social functions. Hari, by contrast, was the only high-caste villager who by his actions had demonstrated genuine friendship and concern for the untouchables of his community, speaking respectfully to them, eating with them, helping them organize a political group, establishing and running an adult night school for them, and interceding when high-caste landowners and shopkeepers cheated them. Although many untouchables nevertheless distrusted Hari, a few, like Muli, accepted him enough to crack jokes with him about high castes and to reveal their deep resentment of high-caste people.

I thought Hari had the potential to do the job I needed done. Accordingly, for several months I carefully trained him to conduct interviews among the people of his own caste, most of whom trusted him and readily confided in him in my presence. We conducted all interviews jointly. He became sensitive to the kinds of questions I asked. He learned to translate literally, to self-consciously examine ways in which he might have selectively screened or omitted information. He learned to explain to the villagers carefully and in detail what we intended to do with the information we collected, and to inform me about those households from which he could not gather information.* By narrating his own life history to me, Hari learned how to collect the life histories of others.

Hari's most difficult adjustment had come when I told him that he would have to abandon his accustomed role as a leader because such a person often prompts people to give answers that they think will please an authority figure. He had at first enthusiastically tried to extract information from the people of his caste whether or not they were willing. "They are my neighbors," he said, "they *must* tell you the truth." Later, when Muli omitted details, Hari said: "We are paying him; he *must* tell what he knows." I insisted that Hari never order people to divulge information, but rather that he respect their right to offer or withhold it as they pleased. With practice he learned to do this, as well as to ask questions unexpected of persons in authority roles, such as his questioning of Muli's praise of Brahmans.

I came to rely on Hari's judgment. He could spot inconsistencies or errors in responses that escaped me. Using his detailed knowledge of the villagers and their life styles, he followed up leads about topics that I never knew existed. He became a skilled interviewer, and, most important, as a trusted insider he elicited information that an outsider working alone might never have received.

Muli's motivations in confiding to us were more complex than I had at first realized. He narrated his story not simply for money, but also to strike back at neighbors who disliked him and at his parents and brothers, who had thrown him out of the house. He used his life history to recall nostalgically his happy youth, which he contrasted with his unhappy life as a married man. He also took this opportunity to vent his resentment against high-caste men. "To keep their prestige, they avoid us in public, but in private they screw our women, 'hu hu,' panting like dogs." Finally, he wanted people to know what it means to live as a Bauri. "Who has ever cared about us? People should know how we live."

---

*One household unavailable to him was that of his father-in-law where Hari had to observe respect-avoidance relationships (discussed in Chapter 6); another was that of his father's cousin, who was feuding with Hari's household.

5. A higher-caste man whom Muli hopes
to befriend.

Because Muli was dissatisfied with his lot, he dreamed of ways to break away from his starvation-poverty, from his position as a despised untouchable. Although he resented high-caste gentlemen for their double standard, he admired them for their wealth, easy jobs, fine clothes, and jewelry. He wanted to associate with and emulate them, to be *accepted* by them. He imagined that if he provided a service on which a high-caste man became dependent or by which he became compromised—such as supplying him with male or female prostitutes—he would become that man's friend. Prostitution temporarily brought men of wealth and social status to his door, but as customers, not friends. Acting out his hopeless fantasy of friendship, Muli refused to admit the true basis of his relationship with high-caste men and thus often entangled himself in difficulties he had never anticipated. On rare occasions, high-caste men befriended Muli, or at least were polite to him without wanting his women; they often became offended when they discovered that he had befriended them to make them customers.

For days Muli had been telling me that he wanted me to meet one of his customer-friends from the city, a low-grade civil servant (messenger) who had once given Muli a gold ring. Muli said, "He is my best friend of all. Every time I go to his house, he won't let me leave unless I eat a lot of tiffin [snacks]. You must meet him. I'll bring him here on Sunday, his day off, if that's all right with you."

I said, "I would like to meet your friend. Bring him next Sunday."

On the appointed day, neither Muli nor his friend appeared. I thought nothing more about it.

One week later, as the shadows were lengthening in the yard, Muli suddenly appeared with a stocky man dressed in a fine white dhoti [loincloth], long *punjaabi* shirt [shirt worn over trousers or dhoti], and heavy sandals. His face was square, his jaw heavy, and his black hair was oiled. He had a dark-complexioned, clean-shaven face, and a wide smile that displayed white, even teeth. As he minced up to my doorstep, he held the lower folds of his dhoti to avoid the dust. He wore a wristwatch with a wide gold band, and gold rings on three fingers of each hand. Muli, walking a couple of steps behind his friend, was unshaven and wore only a faded lungi [long loincloth] and a soiled undershirt.

Muli introduced us. "This is Madhusudana Babu; this is James Babu." We greeted one another with palms together. I invited them both inside.

Madhusudana Babu appeared perfectly relaxed and at ease; Muli was nervous, disconcerted. Madhusudana Babu, speaking in polite and cultured Oriya, asked me about my research. I told him, and then asked about his work. He said, "I have a cigarette stall near the city market. That's where I met Muli. But I also work in a government office. My home village is a few miles north of the city."

My wife, Pat, served tea and sweets, but Muli refused to take any. Madhusudana Babu quickly ate his, poured tea in his saucer, cooled it, and sipped it. Muli took his sweets and put them on Madhusudana Babu's plate, then poured his untouched tea into his friend's cup. Madhusudana Babu ate some, and then gave the remaining tea and sweets to Muli, who now consumed them. The two men acted like a husband and the wife who serves him. Throughout the visit, Muli served his friend. When they left, Muli, like a dutiful wife, trailed behind him.

Muli's effeminate behavior (by village standards) appeared in many of the episodes of his life history. He shelled peanuts for Madhusudana Babu as they walked down the road; he associated socially with transvestite men; he mixed and talked easily with women and they accepted him among them (unusual behavior unless with transvestite men); he described in great detail the venereal disease of a Brahman customer-friend, including his inspection of his friend's diseased penis; his sexual relations with women were few and usually occurred only when women initiated them; and he was indifferent to his wife—one week after their wedding, he left his bride to solicit men for his prostitutes.

The frustration of Muli's life was that he wanted his customers to treat him as their friend, rather than the pimp who supplied them with prostitutes. Outwardly he was proud, but inwardly he coveted the money from prostitution. He went to devious lengths to deny to himself that he was a pimp, even while he earned money from that work. Usually he refused to accept direct payment from a customer-"friend." The women gave him money, which he interpreted not as payment, but as a donation. Muli construed any attention from gentlemen as "friendship," although their sole aim was to sleep with his prostitutes. Muli's relationships with high-caste men never lasted. He was forty years old, and most of the women he knew intimately were of his age or older. He was unable to mix freely with the younger women of his caste without arousing suspicion. Wanting fresh young prostitutes, the men of the city soon lost interest in Muli.

Madhusudana Babu had been avoiding Muli. Hoping to impress him, Muli had introduced him to me; but since Muli had no new men or women to supply, Madhusudana Babu had turned to other pimps. Muli later said to me forlornly, "I don't know what to do; I don't know why he's no longer as friendly as before. What can I do to make him be my friend again? I'll hire a *guṇiaa* [exorcist-magician] to recite spells to bring him back to me." Muli refused to admit that he could renew the friendship only by supplying a new woman.

While he dreamed and his futile schemes failed, Kia, Muli's hard-working wife, supported their family by cutting grass and harvesting paddy. Increasingly impatient with Muli's introspections, Kia often quarrelled with him and called him lazy.

One morning during the India-Pakistan war over Bangladesh, Muli related a war dream and his wife's typically irritated response to it.

"Last night, I had quite a dream. In it I was a young man at a time when I was very ill. To become cured, I went to a *kaaḷasi* [shaman] near Dhauli hill, about five miles away. The mother goddess entered the shaman's body and then she entered my body. Through this the shaman was curing me. Just at the moment that he called upon the goddess to cure me, two airplanes flew overhead toward the capital city. I heard the sound of bombs and bullets as the planes bombed the city. Suddenly our capital city was in flames.

"Just then the deity left my body. Out of fear I urinated. I knew that I was doing so, but I did not seem to mind. Suddenly I awoke. It was dawn. I was stark naked; I had thrown all my clothes off. I had indeed urinated all over everything. I was lying on my cot, an old door of wooden planks resting on a couple of quarry stones. My urine had seeped through my cotton quilt, through the cracks in the planks, and into some tins below. Ping! Ping! Drops of urine were hitting them. It was those sounds that I thought were bullets and bombs!

"I arose from the cot, put my palms together in a *namaskaar* [greeting], and faced the sun, muttering, 'Well, gods, what a dream you gave me last night!'

"Just then Kia, my wife, entered the room. She had arisen early and had been boiling rice for our noon meal. She does this before going out to cut paddy. When she saw me greeting the sun, she thought I had lost my mind. 'What are you doing there?' she asked.

"I told her the dream and what had happened to the bed. She listened, then stuck out her lower lip and said 'Pfut!', turned the palm of her hand out in a gesture of 'so what,' and walked impatiently out of the room."

On those days during the harvest that Muli worked in the fields, Hari and I accompanied him. Jadu the miser had hired Muli as a farm servant; Muli in turn was supposed to hire day laborers to help harvest the crop and then pay them one-twelfth of the paddy they cut. To keep all the earnings among his relatives, Muli selected his wife, son, mother, youngest brother, and brother's wife. Since he

6. Bauris harvesting paddy.

was the overseer for the day, Muli came to the field attired in a fine dhoti and fancy shirt, while the others came in their working clothes: old saris for the women, a short loincloth for the brother, and short pants for Gopala, Muli's seventeen-year-old schoolboy son. Muli sat on the raised bank of a paddy field and watched. The group was supposed to finish cutting the crop of that field in one day. Muli's wife cut a wide path; the others moved slowly, cutting narrow paths. Although she was working faster than they were, Kia's path was shorter because it was wider. Her son helped her a little, but most of the time he sat and watched, like his father.

Kia talked loudly to herself, making remarks that would embarrass others, "Yesterday I said that we should hire three or four outsiders, but the head of our household said, 'Why get others when all of us in the family can do the work?' So I brought my family out here, but nobody is working hard. This plot of land is small; we should be able to cut it in one day. But the way they work, it will take them two days. Where will the wages come from to pay for two days? If you hire five people to work for two days on such a small piece of land, how much will they take as wages, and how much will remain for us?"

Her son, Gopala, sitting nearby, said irritably, "Why are you opening your big mouth, shouting falsely?"

She shouted, "What, shouting falsely? I'll throw this sickle at your face so that half of it flies away!"

Muli became angry. "Why are you showing off your work? I don't know what work you do except for my prick work."

She replied, "What, you don't know what work I do? Sitting, sitting, speaking big things."

Muli stood up and shouted, "What are you saying? You horse-fucker! Characterless! Younger brother's wife [one who has sexual intercourse with her husband's younger brother]!* Always wanting fucking! Adulteress! Will you bring their wage from your father's house? Why are you shouting like this? Shut up!"

She replied, "Why shut up? For this you are my husband?" Lapsing into Bauri dialect, she used a disrespectful term for "husband."†

Muli raised his fists to beat her. Hari pulled him away, saying, "Why are you scolding your wife? She is right in her way; she is justified."

Muli calmed down. "Yes, she's a very hard worker, and she earns a lot of money. She doesn't depend on my income. But her mouth is very sharp. Nobody can tolerate her language. She's expert in all

---

*The term *saaḷi* [younger sister-in-law] usually refers to the wife's sister, but Muli used it to mean "younger brother's wife," the feminine equivalent of the male insult *saḷaa*.

†The Bauri dialect phrase is *etire ghaita* [for this you are my husband]. The word *etire* is Bauri dialect for *eṭhire*, while the word *ghaita* [husband] is disrespectful, whether used by men or women. A woman is expected to address her husband as babu [mister], *saa-aanta* [master], or with indirect references such as *gopala baapaa* [the father of Gopala]. A man in turn should not refer to his wife by name, but by nicknames or the name of her first child. Muli usually refers to his wife as "my wife," rarely by her name, Kia; but for the purpose of readability, I frequently use her name in the narrative.

7. Too old and weak to work standing, a Bauri grandmother harvests her landlord's paddy.

work. She has been ill for three days, so she is quite angry when my son and younger brother stand around like they have been doing. She can scold my son, but she must not scold my younger brother. He lives in a different household. She has no control over him. That's why she's angry, and that's why she criticized him indirectly."

In his stories, Muli prided himself on being clever and dishonest, an inveterate liar who thought up quick-witted ruses to escape from tight predicaments. Although he also described with ironic detachment how his devious schemes invariably backfired, I became skeptical of the reliability of the life history of a man who claimed to be a liar. Furthermore, some of Muli's stories, like his quarrel with Jadu the miser, sounded so out of character that I could not believe them. Muli claimed that while standing before a tea shop full of patrons he had quarreled with and insulted his Brahman employer. To our knowledge, no Bauri from Muli's village had ever publicly insulted a Brahman.

Unknown to Muli, Hari and I quietly investigated his incident with Jadu, which had occurred during the period of his life history that Muli was presently narrating. Several eyewitnesses including Bauris, Brahmans, and even Jadu's own cousin not only confirmed Muli's description of the confrontation, but claimed that Jadu had truly provoked Muli by cheating him. Both the betel seller and the youth selling vegetables at the market confirmed incidents involving Jadu at the market.

Next we checked Muli's stories about his grandfather Dharma by questioning Muli's paternal uncle, a son of Dharma but no admirer of Muli. He confirmed all of Muli's stories but one. Another Bauri confirmed Muli's scandal involving his second wife, Tafulla. While collecting *paaṭuaa* [a form of song] texts, Hari and I asked several Bauris not about Muli, but about the history of the drama and singing troupes. These persons again confirmed several of Muli's stories of his grandfather Dharma, as well as some of the drama troupe incidents.

Muli's descriptions of Bauri rituals and other activities paralleled those I witnessed, and my own observations of Muli with his prostitutes, customers, transvestite friends, brothers, and wife matched his descriptions of his behavior with them. Whatever his motivations might have been, Muli narrated a life history that was accurate for the most part in its portrayal of Bauri life, including life styles that differed from his.

Muli saw himself as a deviant in his own culture; but far from claiming that all Bauris act and think as he did, he contrasted other life styles with his own without condemning or praising either. Of the thirteen life histories I collected, Muli's was the most pitilessly self-critical. He often described himself in unflattering terms but with neither remorse nor pride.

To be sure, in telling his story, Muli selectively omitted some topics and exaggerated others. Muli was a middle-aged failure with a bleak future. His youthful dreams had failed to materialize. No wonder, then, that he dwelt at length on his idyllic days as an unmarried youth, a time of hopes and dreams, the happiest days of his life.

While he avoided speaking about his childhood, he would sit for hours with his eyes closed, speaking in a low monotone, recalling those days of his youth when high-caste men came to his door, flattered him, and gave him gifts so that he would supply them with women.

Faced with perpetual poverty and frequent starvation, Muli quite understandably overstated the amounts of food and gifts of cloth that his family supplied, and the expenses they met, at feasts and ceremonies. Similarly, he stated that his family paid for the expensive "sin of the fly larvae pollution" ceremony, an unlikely expenditure for an impoverished family.*

To enhance his prestige, Muli exaggerated not only about feasts, but about the leadership activities and skills of his grandfather and his brothers. According to Muli, his grandfather learned wrestling from high-caste villagers, but in fact these persons never allowed the Bauris to practice with them. Muli also embellished the details of his many quarrels with his family and with other families. He claimed that his parents made no preparations for their son Sarala's fourth-night-after-the-wedding ceremony, which is hard to believe, as is his claim that he and his wife paid all the expenses of his brother's ceremony.

Aside from neglecting his childhood, Muli's greatest omission was his refusal to admit that he worked as a pimp for the women of his own ward. Despite much evidence to the contrary, he insisted that except for one woman named Koki, all the women came from other wards and villages, because to use women from his own ward would have been disgraceful. But he frequently associated with the prostitute women of his ward, one of whom, not knowing that I understood Oriya, asked him in my presence if I were a potential customer whom he could send to her. One of Muli's sisters earned money as a prostitute. In Muli's stories, Ananta Babu, Doctor Babu, and other wealthy high-caste customers unaccountably showed great interest in Muli's family, particularly his sisters, whom Muli probably drew into his prostitution business. No wonder Muli's parents constantly quarreled with him and finally threw him out of the house permanently. For months Muli insisted he could not un-

---

*A person infected with fly larvae is considered to be polluted and should undergo a purificatory ritual, but some persons refuse to perform the ritual because of its heavy expenses.

derstand why, and denied that his activities as a pimp might have embarrassed his family.

By April, 1972, Hari and I had collected 350,000 words of Muli's text. We had paid him his paddy, as well as the other things we had promised him. The harvest was over. Muli frequently failed to show up for interviews; he was not working, but wandering about the market with his transvestite friends. We began other life histories.

One day Muli appeared at the door; he needed some money, so he had come for another interview. I agreed to hold one final session. We doubted that he had anything new to tell us, and indeed that day his stories covered the familiar topic of family quarrels. Then suddenly the interview took an unexpected turn. Muli described how he had quarreled for the first time with his favorite uncle Satyabadi, his mother's brother, who criticized him for neglecting his sick father. "What a prick-boy you are!" said Satyabadi. "What kind of son are you, not looking after your father! You are young, you earn well, yet you neglect him. Who will count you as the son of your father? It is better for this kind of son to die before his father does!"

Muli had replied, "Don't tell me about my father. Whenever my father and mother have bad times, they call me for help, but when I am in trouble, they say they aren't my parents. So why does he wait for me now? He's got other sons. Why don't my brothers look after him? I don't like my father. He and his wife are nothing to me; I am nothing to them. I know what kind of people they are. What haven't I done for them when they needed it? But they never looked after me or even talked to me. Rather, they complained to other people that I don't take care of them. I don't need a father like that; I don't want to hear any more about him."

At that point, my assistant Hari interrupted Muli. "Why was your father displeased with you and not with your brothers? You always helped your father and they didn't, so why did he dislike you?"

Muli replied, "My father was displeased with me not once but many times. At first my father and mother liked me, but after my marriage, when I didn't work but spent most of my time with Koki and her lovers, Mother became angry with me and quarreled with me."

Hari asked, "Do you remember the first time your parents threw you out?"

"Yes, it was when my infant son, my wife, and myself became

covered with boils, and my wife and I couldn't earn any money" (see Chapter 18).

Hari asked, "You separated many times because of quarrels over lack of food. Many families do this. But why was your father displeased with you even after driving you out of the house? Did he have other reasons?"

Muli replied, "I don't know why. I always tried to make my father happy whether or not we were separated. I don't know why my father looked at me with a bad eye."

Hari said, "How can you fail to understand? You see, Muli, it is very rare and painful to see a father dislike a son. Even if a son is bad, his father helps him. Did you ever do anything against your father's wishes, something that everybody would dislike?"

"You may ask questions from any side. I am unable to understand anything. You are an educated man. You please point out my faults. Where were they?"

"Did your father ever scold you because people insulted him or complained about your badness? Think about your secret work. Did people find out that you had taken their daughters for bad work? Did they publicly scold you? This would have insulted and humiliated your father. Did this happen?"

"Why not?" admitted Muli. "People insulted Father and me many times because I did things that made everyone hate me. Not only the people of my own ward, but also my mother, father, wife, and brothers found out that I had sold the services of the girls."

Muli then described the first time he was caught. He and another man ran away to Cuttack city with an unmarried girl named Bilasa. The girl had thought they would never return; but after only six days, the men grew tired of her, ran out of money, and returned home. To save Bilasa's reputation, they left her at her sister's house in another village. To deflect suspicion from himself, Muli announced in his own ward that he had seen the missing girl at her sister's house. That night some men secretly went to Bilasa and demanded to know where she had gone, what she had done, and with whom. Following Muli's instructions, Bilasa had lied, "I went to Auntie's house; then I came here."

The angry men replied, "We searched most places and couldn't find you. We'll kill you if you don't tell the truth!"

Bilasa, frightened, replied that Muli and his friend had taken her to Cuttack. The elders, angered, called a meeting at which they fined Muli's father and forced him to give the people of the ward a feast. They said Muli's father had caused Muli's bad behavior by being lax with him. After this public humiliation, Muli's father had scolded him: "A man who does these things—no father should have to look upon a son like you!"

Muli's life history was the creation not of one man, but of three: Muli the storyteller; Hari the native cotranslator and interviewer; and myself the outside cotranslator, interviewer, editor, and analyst. Our combined efforts created something new that none of us had anticipated. I had never expected to collect a 350,000-word life history on the topics covered. Hari never realized how little he had known about Bauri life styles and values. Muli by himself would never have narrated his story, for such oral histories were not part of his tradition; he simply took for granted the details of his existence.

How representative of Bauris is Muli's life history? The details and the manner of telling the stories reflect Muli's distinctive style, but the environment of extreme poverty, social stigma, economic exploitation, and discrimination against untouchables is a reality shared by all Bauris of Muli's community and most Bauris elsewhere. Muli's own life style represents one of only three possible adaptations ordinarily available to Bauri men and women: the life of unskilled laborers; the life of shamanistic faith healers; and the life of transvestites, pimps, and prostitutes. These life styles are neither incompatible nor mutually exclusive, but like Muli most Bauris emphasize one of them more than the others.

Muli was neither my friend nor a person whom I particularly admired. But his life history taught me to understand why, given the limited opportunities available to him, he chose to live his life the way he did.

3. The Setting
of Muli's Life History

Physical Environment

A great portion of Muli's life history deals with the effects of the physical environment on him and his family. Muli lives in a fertile rice-growing alluvial plain in eastern India. Because of population growth during the past century, inherited landholdings in his village have been subdivided and fragmented into parcels so small that even most of the landowners have barely enough to support them. Like Muli, over half the families of the village are landless. Natural disasters aggravate their plight. Striking on the average of six out of every ten years, cyclones, droughts, floods, and epidemics destroy life, crops, and property (Census of India 1961: 11–12, 28).

Natural disasters hit the poor hardest. About 20 percent of the villagers, including Muli's family, live on the brink of starvation, lacking both food reserves and cash to pay for even the cheapest of medicines. If ill and unable to work, they do not eat. About 60 percent subsist at a slightly higher, but still marginal level. Only the highest 20 percent live comfortably, without fearing starvation. Muli describes starving at several times during his life, including his childhood, which he remembers as a time when he was always hungry. Despite the growth of a new city three miles from Muli's home, the starving poor presently have few employment opportunities and little or no chance to improve their economic condition. Although the poor are of all castes, the lowest castes have the highest percentage of persons in desperate economic straits.

Even in favorable years, seasonal fluctuations profoundly affect Muli's life style. During the dry, mild winter harvest months of November, December, and January, with average monthly temperatures no lower than 60°F, Muli and his family, working from dawn to dusk, earn enough paddy as harvesting farm laborers to last them three or four months. These are the only months in which they eat regularly. During the hot, dry spring and summer months, when the

8. Cyclone and fire, June 1972.

average temperature gradually rises to 100°F in May, Muli works as an unskilled laborer to supplement his diminishing paddy. In Muli's life history, most marriages in his family occurred during the summer months, when his family still had some money and food, and the pressure of work was less than during the harvest. In the months of June through September, when the monsoon brings 75–90 percent of the fifty-four inches of annual rainfall for the area, Muli again works as a farm laborer (Census of India 1961:3, 11–12, 28; Sinha 1971:14–20). August and September are Muli's months of greatest hardship. Because food is scarce, prices rise in the market, and the poor are unable to purchase food. During heavy rains, both agricultural and construction work stops, and workers earn no wages. With his food supplies exhausted, Muli takes high-interest loans to buy food but still frequently starves. He repays the loans with the paddy he earns during the subsequent harvest months.

In 1946 the government of Orissa designated the old pilgrimage town of Bhubaneswar the capital of Orissa state. In the following years, the government constructed a new city of stone buildings and wide avenues alongside the old town, with its crowded houses, narrow lanes, and temples half buried in the reddish dirt. By 1971 the population of the new city, the old town, and the surrounding village suburbs was over 100,000 inhabitants (Census of India 1971: 46). With the construction of the city, many villagers seized new economic opportunities. Between 1950 and 1965, Bhubaneswar experienced rapid growth: some villagers like Muli helped build new houses, roads, and public buildings; others became civil servants or businessmen. Many outsiders migrated to the new city, taking up residence in nearby villages such as the one that Muli lived in. After 1965, however, the growth of the city leveled off, and so did employment opportunities for the villagers. Muli, increasingly dependent on the city for employment, was economically worse off in 1972 than he had been in the previous decade.

Muli lives in Kapileswar, a village with a 1971 population of 2,869 persons (594 households) from twenty castes (Freeman 1977a:31). South of the village lie paddy fields and a small river, which villagers use for irrigation and bathing. To the northwest lie the stone quarries where Muli's grandfather and father worked. North of the village lies the old section of Bhubaneswar, a pilgrimage center famous for its ancient temples (Panigrahi 1961).

At the outer edge of the old town, the road to Kapileswar passes through a bazaar with rickety wooden food stalls, as well as a stone building housing a rice mill and a bicycle parts shop, all built since 1966. The bazaar, adjacent to the fishermen's ward, is a favorite meeting place for Muli and his friends. A small stone image of the goddess Chungudei, sacred to the people of Muli's caste, rests in the branches of a banyan tree overlooking the bazaar. The leaders of Muli's caste meet at the banyan tree to arbitrate disputes or preside at purification rites, such as the one Muli's family performed to remove the sin of fly larvae pollution from his grandfather.

The road to Kapileswar leads into a high-caste ward, cramped, crowded and treeless, lined with red mud huts covered with grey thatch, a few single-story dwellings with corrugated iron roofs, and a two-story stone house with elaborately carved balconies. Open stone drains run past an open well, a water spigot, and electric light poles. In 1961, city officials installed these public facilities in the six high-caste wards of the village, which are clustered around the Kapileswar temple, a minor pilgrimage shrine.

By contrast, the isolated, caste-segregated ward that Muli lives in (138 people in twenty-five households crowded into less than an acre) contains no public facilities except an old polluted well. All the houses are of mud and thatch, easily destroyed during fire, cyclones, or floods.

Muli's ward is located at the bottom of a gentle slope, well below the high-caste wards of the village. The open drains from those wards empty into a paddy field near Muli's ward. During the rainy season, the drains overflow into Muli's street, transforming it into a swamp of mud, human excrement, and garbage.

The dominant feature of the village is the sixty-foot-high Kapileswar temple and its adjacent pond, surrounded by stone steps. Muli is allowed to bathe in this pond, but only in one far corner.

The Kapileswar temple is a satellite of the main temple of Bhubaneswar, called Lingaraj. Both the Lingaraj and Kapileswar temples, like others in India, not only provide an income for persons of many castes who take care of the deities and properties of the temples, but also are centers of social, political, and educational activities (Freeman 1977a; Stein 1960; Vidyarthi 1961). Although Muli harvests the crops of temple-owned lands, he has never entered the inner rooms of the Kapileswar or Lingaraj temples because he is an untouchable.

Until the middle of the twentieth century, the Kapileswar temple dominated the economic, ritual, and political life of the village: nearly three-quarters of the villagers received some economic benefit from it. Several castes held tax-free temple paddy lands and tax-free house plots for their performance of obligatory, specialized, interdependent, hereditary services in the temple. The people of Muli's caste trim weeds in the outer compound of the Kapileswar temple, receiving in return a small cash payment plus permission to build their huts on land owned by the deity.

A hereditary trustee and his relatives, from a privileged temple servant caste called Mallia, historically controlled the Kapileswar temple, its endowed properties, and its paddy fields. Found only in

9. The Kapileswar temple, full view.

Kapileswar, the Mallias are the largest caste of the village, with 1,063 persons, or nearly 37 percent of the village population. Their hereditary occupation is service to the deity of the temple. Although nearly half of the Mallias are landless, those remaining are the largest group of landowners and employers of untouchable laborers in the village. Two small but wealthy landowning castes of the village, Brahmans and Oilpressers, also employ many untouchables.

Occupational Setting

Muli's caste, Bauri, is the second largest of the village, with 456 persons (16 percent of the total population). The contrasting economic and occupational responses of the Mallias and the Bauris to

10. Selling sacred food at the Kapileswar temple, a pilgrimage shrine.

urbanization illustrate the widening gap between the affluent and the poor in Kapileswar and highlight in particular the plight of the Bauri poor, who, including Muli, have seen other castes benefit enormously from the opportunities offered by the new city while they have stagnated.

During Muli's adult life, the Mallias have moved into a greater variety of occupations than any other caste group, primarily because the Mallias vary greatly in their levels of wealth and education. The wealthiest are the best educated and have the highest percentage of civil servant clerks; middle-income or less-well-educated Mallias are temple servants, and when that is insufficient for survival, they become unskilled laborers, performing jobs incompatible with their caste status expectations.

Between 1953 and 1971 the numbers of Mallias holding civil service jobs rose from three to sixty-three (25 percent of the Mallia male work force). Educational achievement increased rapidly, as Mallias prepared their sons for government service, which they considered prestigious employment. Correspondingly, fewer of them worked as temple servants: the temple could not support the number qualified for this work (see Freeman 1977a:63–67).

In the mid-1960s, as the growth of the new capital slowed down, government jobs in Bhubaneswar became scarce and difficult to secure. This explains Mallia employment patterns: the government hired thirty-three Mallias during the five peak growth years 1960–1965 but only fourteen during the next five years. Unemployed Mallias with high school and college educations founded small food stores and tea shops. Although less highly regarded than civil service, the tea shop business appealed to many Mallias because it fit their identities as high-caste temple priests who distribute sacred food to pilgrims. Before 1950 Mallias owned eight shops; by 1971 they had started another twenty-nine, including seven that failed because of insufficient capital for extending loans of food to customers.

The growth and decline of city job opportunities also affected Mallia agricultural practices. In 1971, 54 percent of the Mallia households owned paddy land, but only 31 percent worked their own land or even supervised it. Their indifference to agriculture reflected not resistance to new influences but, rather, selective adaptation to them: hiring Bauri laborers or sharecroppers to work their lands, the Mallias themselves became civil servants or businessmen, since both positions carried greater prestige than did cultivation. As government jobs declined, so did Mallia attendance in high school and college. A few youths returned to farming their own lands; others said they would soon follow.

Thus, the Mallias select occupations that conform to high-caste ideals of ritual purity and prestige. The exceptions, such as the seven men (out of a work force of 252 men) who are unskilled construction workers, come from families so poor that their only choice is to work at demeaning jobs or starve.

Bauri workers also hold several different jobs, but unlike the more affluent Mallias, most Bauris have not changed their occupations of

11. Commercial building in the New Capital section of Bhubaneswar.

12. Shops in the New Capital section of Bhubaneswar.

13. Betel and cigarette stall, New Capital.

seasonal agricultural labor and unskilled construction work. In 1971, after over twenty years in an urban setting, only two persons out of a work force of 269 Bauris have acquired new skills. In this impoverished caste, over half the earners are women. By contrast, high-caste women rarely work outside their homes.

The Bauris do not refuse to change jobs; rather, they cannot do so because they are poor. Mallia landowners live off the earnings of their paddy lands while learning new skills, seeking new jobs, or educating their children to new jobs. Bauris lack such an economic cushion: only eight of their one hundred households own land—three and a half barren, unproductive acres.

Six Bauri households have no able-bodied workers; their earnings are from begging and collecting wood and leaves. The remaining ninety-four earn from agriculture: eight are landowning households whose workers are also sharecroppers; fourteen are landless share-cropper households who earn 50 percent of the crop cut; the remaining seventy-two are landless households of agricultural laborers and farm servants who earn 8–12.6 percent of the harvest. From the point of view of the Bauris, the landless sharecroppers are well-off because their share of the rice may last them up to ten months, while the agricultural worker's share rarely lasts longer than four to six months. Muli begs, flatters, and gives gifts of fish and vegetables to prospective employers whom he hopes will hire him as a year-round farm servant.

Since 1962, Bauri landholdings have declined (from four and a half acres to three and a half), as has the number of sharecroppers (from fifty-seven to twenty-seven persons), but the number of agricultural laborers has increased from 203 to 230. In landowning and sharecropping households, the percentage of earners who work as agricultural laborers rather than as sharecroppers has increased from 33 to 93 percent. High-caste landowners have dismissed Bauri share-croppers and farm servants like Muli to avoid the effect of new land laws that enable those who actually cultivate a plot of land to claim it as their own. Many landowners cultivate their own lands, hiring agricultural laborers.* As civil service opportunities decline, more high-caste landowners probably will do their own cultivation, throwing more Bauris out of work.

*On evasion of land laws, see also Bailey 1963:74–75; Sharma 1973:87–92; and Freeman 1977a:133–134.

14. Mallia-caste female shopkeeper.

15. A Bauri sharecropper plowing his master's fields.

16. Bauri women constructing roads in the New Capital.

17. Twelve-year-old Bauri girl carries tar for road construction gang.

Since 1962, the percentage of nonagricultural wage laborers among Bauris has declined from 89 to 81 percent of the Bauri work force because road and house construction jobs in the city have declined. Although a few more Bauri men worked in the stone quarries in 1971 than in 1962, the opportunities for quarry work have decreased: in 1962, men quarried stones every day; by 1971, they found quarry work only one out of every two or three days.

Those who are not able-bodied male adults work at less strenuous jobs. Muli works as a pimp, supplying Bauri women to high-caste men. Many women gather leaves, grass, and bundles of wood. Young children and the elderly and lame fetch or collect coal cinders from the railroad beds and broken scraps of iron and glass, which they sell for a fraction of a rupee. In 1971, 138 persons from 78 households collected fuel and other items for a living. By contrast, the only Bauris with modern skills were the two automobile mechanics mentioned in Chapter 1, who worked in the new capital.

In summary, castes like the Mallias are best able to take advantage of the economic opportunities presented by the new capital economy, often in ways that are compatible with both their caste occupation and their status self-image. The Bauris, by contrast, limited by lack of wealth, contacts, and education, continue to do simple, unskilled labor as their fathers have done for generations. Obviously, the Bauris have gained far less than the Mallias; the economic gap between them has rapidly widened. In some parts of India, including Orissa, untouchables have benefited economically or politically from legal prohibitions of discrimination against them (Bailey 1957:211–227; Cohn 1955:53–77). But in Bhubaneswar, ingrained exploitative aspects of caste, and their economic consequences, remain as strong as they were twenty years ago. Bauris continue to be channeled into unskilled, poorly paid jobs that deny them anything more than basic subsistence earnings.

Distribution of Wealth

In Kapileswar, less than 11 percent of the households (none of them Bauri) own enough paddy land to be supported solely by it. Consequently, most villagers, including virtually all able-bodied Bauris, hold several jobs when they can find them. In Kapileswar, as in Orissa generally, landholdings are unequally distributed (Freeman 1977a:113–116; Sinha 1971:58). One percent of the households

18. Bauri women on the way to work. The woman in the foreground carries a pot of watered rice for lunch.

of Kapileswar own nearly 30 percent of the land, while nearly 60 percent of the households are landless. The range in wealth other than land also is great, from homeless beggars and widows who own nothing to households whose wealth exceeds 100,000 rupees (more than U.S. $13,000) and who own many luxury items. The two Bauri automobile mechanics are the only people of their caste to own luxury items—one transistor radio and one bicycle, both second-hand.

The Bauris are at or near the bottom of the village, not only in landholding and wealth other than land, but also in cash earnings, most of which come from their low-paying unskilled jobs. The an-

19. Exhausted Bauri wood-carrier.

nual income per Bauri household, based on the average number of adults per household (children are averaged as fractions of adults) is barely enough to feed two adults with one meal a day or every two days, with no allowance for clothes, household items, medicines, house repairs, or other basic expenses. All Bauri households subsist marginally at best; some are below starvation level.

Other castes also have low average annual earnings. The Mallias earn only one and a half times that of the Bauris, but in fact they are far better off than the Bauris because they average thirty-five times as much land per household and eight times as much wealth other than land. The Mallias, although more than twice as numerous as the Bauris, have fewer wage earners. Thus Mallia wages per worker are in fact three times those of Bauri workers.

20. Bauris working in the stone quarries.   21. Thatching roofs.

Even the wealthiest caste of the village, the Khuntia Brahmans, have cash income earnings on average only three times as great as the Bauris, but they own sixty times as much wealth other than land, and 200 times as much land per household. (See also Freeman 1977a: 113–124).

Thus the plight of Muli and other Bauris, unlike most other castes of the village, is that they lack all three categories of wealth: they have bare survival or below survival income, little or no additional wealth, and little or no land. Consequently, they have no protection from loss of income resulting from unforeseen though frequent disasters. Muli describes many times in his life when, faced with no food in the house, he and others stole vegetables from wealthy landowners, ate rough grains usually given only to livestock, and still often remained hungry.

Not surprisingly, the impoverished Bauris have the highest number and percentage of households in debt, but their outstanding loans are small, averaging only sixty rupees per household in debt. Other Bauri households are refused loans as bad credit risks. Bauri landowners and sharecroppers with assured employment and income are able to get loans twice as large, on average, as those obtained by agricultural wage laborers. Professional moneylenders and employers, mostly Mallias, give over 80 percent of Bauri loans, charging 25 percent or more annually, payable in paddy or cash. For short-term loans and loans without mortgages, interest rates range from 37 to 60 percent. Significantly, over 60 percent of the ninety Bauri loans are exclusively for food and medicine, as Muli's life history amply attests.

In summary, by village standards, the wealthy and well-to-do households of Kapileswar, who are the primary recipients of benefits from the new capital, maintain high standards of living and are avid customers of new products and luxury items. Their wealth gives them much greater flexibility than the poor, and development of the new capital has provided them with the opportunity to try new occupations, products, and life styles.

By contrast, the new capital has failed to benefit the poor like Muli. Despite twenty years in an urban boom-town environment, 60 percent of the households of Kapileswar, including all of the Bauris, remain poor, virtually landless, without certain income, unable to seize the opportunities that the new capital affords. None of the loans the Bauris take are for starting businesses or furthering their children's education. Most castes, including the Bauris, have sold more paddy lands than they have bought; only the three business castes and one Brahman caste own more land in 1972 than they did in 1950. Although incomes have increased, so has inflation of prices. Few households have made the transition from poor to middle-income or well-to-do status.

The combined economic constraints that prevent the poor from taking advantage of the new capital include, first, an unequal distribution of land, in which a small number of households own most of the land; second, an unequal distribution of wealth other than land, in which only a few households of the village have money for investments in business or education; third, a preponderance of low-income households dependent on occupations with uncertain and fluctuating employment opportunities; fourth, high interest rates on loans that undermine a household's ability to accumulate wealth; fifth, natural disasters that occur at least every other year, hitting the poor harder than the wealthy. The poor have no food reserves. Calamities and crop destruction lead to soaring food prices, to hunger, to widespread emigration from Kapileswar, to selling land and ornaments, and to increased indebtedness. As Muli shows in his life history, the poor spend much of their daily wage repaying loans, at exorbitant rates of interest, that they were forced to take in order to eat.

Faced with such crises, many households become locked into a descending spiral from which they cannot escape and which pulls them below the survival level. Indeed, this was Muli's condition when I first met him. Like others in similar straits, disasters such as drought, food scarcity, and illness hit his household all at the same time. Once ill and unable to work, earn, and eat, weakened by hunger, malnutrition, and disease, Muli, as well as the other poor of Kapileswar, consider themselves fortunate if they survive at all.

Caste

Kapileswar is inhabited by Hindus stratified into twenty local endogamous caste groups, which Orissans, like other North Indians, call *jaati*. High-caste people assert that caste membership is determined by birth. They also claim that castes are ranked on the basis of ritual cleanliness; and that low-untouchable-caste people are born ritually unclean, remain unclean all of their lives regardless of their individual characters, and thus are forever potential polluters of high-caste people. Believing that cooked food and water transfer pollution, high-caste people ordinarily refuse to eat or drink with persons whom they consider lower. Since they consider untouchables to be particularly polluting, the high castes refuse to let them enter temples, shops, or the inner compounds of houses, or to use wells. An untouchable who violates these restrictive rules, whether intentionally or not, pollutes the persons or objects he touches or even comes near. When Muli involuntarily stepped past the open door of the shrine room in the house of his Brahman employer, Jadu the miser, Jadu screamed at him to move away fearing that Muli had polluted the shrine, which would need to be purified.

High-caste persons like Jadu say that untouchables deserve their low status because they must have misbehaved in a previous existence. High-caste people further justify forcing the lower castes to perform hereditary menial occupations that are the least desirable and the most defiling in society on the grounds that lower castes and untouchables are polluting anyway. Sometimes reversing the argument, they claim that untouchables are polluting because of the jobs

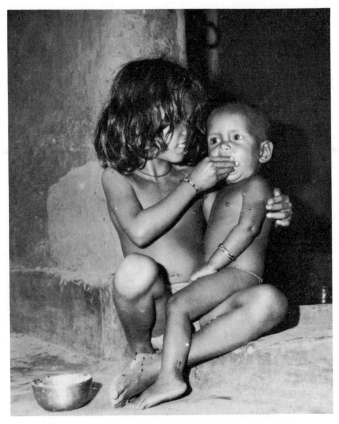

22. A seven-year-old Bauri girl feeds her younger brother while their mother is working in the fields.

they perform. The high castes justify their own less physically demanding but usually more remunerative hereditary occupations, such as priest and scribe, on the grounds that such occupations involve less risk of pollution.

High-caste people also have a low regard for the personal character, integrity, intelligence, cleanliness, and morality of untouchables. Throughout his life history, Muli quotes high-caste persons who talk to untouchables in familiar terms as they do to children; others who address untouchables with terms of abuse such as "uncivilized," "famished ones," "wife's brother," "fool," or "boy"; and still others who use caste names as terms of abuse, saying, for

example, "you act just like a Bauri." Muli's employer, Jadu, de-
grades Muli by telling him that he doesn't know how to shop for
food, save money, or work properly, and that a Bauri does not need
to spend as much money for food as Brahmans do. Muli sees the
word "dirty" written in large letters on the shrine of the untouchable
Sweepers. A high-caste spectator of a Bauri drama practice criticizes
Muli for being dirty and smelling of fish. Construction employers
harass female Bauri construction workers, fondling them, proposi-
tioning them, and directing crude remarks and sexual jokes at them,
rationalizing this coarse behavior by saying that the women like it,
or by telling those women who object that women who want to
preserve their prestige should stay at home.*

Muli, as well as other untouchables, dismiss high-caste explanations of caste rankings and behavior toward untouchables as simply self-serving. "The only difference between the Mallias and ourselves," one of Muli's Bauri friends said to me, "is that the Mallias
have more money than we do. Actually they are lower than we are
because they marry only within our village. That's uncivilized, that's
incest; civilized people marry outside their own village."

The untouchables of Muli's village not only reject the idealized
high-caste notions of clear-cut, immutable rankings of caste, and position accorded them by high castes, and the high-caste view of them,
but they also frequently show great resentment of the ways high-
caste people treat them. In Muli's life history, Bauris complain about
Brahman music and drama teachers who cheat Bauris by overcharg-
ing them for musical instruments. The Bauris of Muli's ward insultingly throw food offered by a Brahman onto the road after the
Brahman insults them. A Bauri insultingly tells a Brahman who cheats
him that if he is so greedy for the Bauri's property, why doesn't he
also eat the Bauri's excrement? After Jadu the miser cheated him,
Muli publicly confronted and insulted him, calling him an uncivilized wife's brother and a man unfit to employ people. Muli mockingly
describes how he forces high-caste men who wish to sleep with
Bauri women to share meals with him and the women—which they
do but only in secret.

The Bauris are one of three untouchable castes in Kapileswar. The
other two are Launderer (fifteen persons in four households) and

*See also Aggarwal and Ashraf (1976:1–25) for a succinct summary of high-caste
discriminatory practices and attitudes toward untouchables.

Sweeper (eighty-five persons in thirteen households). Both of these castes also have expressed their resentment of high-caste discrimination against them. Because they have customers in the new city and thus are no longer dependent on high-caste villagers for their income, the Launderers now refuse to wash the menstrually stained clothes of the village women, historically a polluting but unremunerative ritual forced on them by the high castes. The hereditary occupations of the Sweepers included carrying night soil from the village, carrying off the carcasses of dead cattle (which Sweepers ate), and playing music at village festivals and at the private ceremonies of high-caste people. The Sweepers have become municipal garbage collectors, a polluting job that no other caste will perform. The Bauris, although starving, look with revulsion and scorn on the Sweepers, who have gained secure employment at the expense of perpetuating the stigma historically associated with their caste. Unlike the Bauris, who remain dependent on high-caste village employers, the Sweepers are economically independent of the villagers, and they have used their independence to attempt to raise their status. They have changed their names to ambiguous ones that do not reveal their caste origins. Sweeper youths refuse to patronize shops whose owners will not let them enter, and they refuse to crouch like Bauris when they pass high-caste persons on the street.

For centuries throughout India, many castes not only have disputed their caste ranking, but have attempted to raise their status (Srinivas 1966:1–45; Berreman 1965:115–129; Barber 1968:18–35). Such movements occur usually after aspiring groups have achieved some measure of economic independence. Untouchables frequently attempt to break away from economic and political exploitation by higher castes (Rudolph and Rudolph 1967:36–64). Although the Bauris of Muli's village, fearing immediate reprisal from the high castes, have made no such group attempts, Bauris in other villages of Orissa have attempted unsuccessfully both to wrest land from landowners and to form a political power group to protect Bauris from further exploitation (Freeman 1977a:38–39, 133–134). Elsewhere in India, political and revivalistic religious movements of untouchables have developed into vocal protest groups; and a strident literature of protest has emerged in the western state of Maharashtra (*Times Weekly*, Bombay, 1973; see also Mahar, 1972: articles on Buddhism). These new movements differ from older caste mobility movements in that they attempt not to raise status within the caste system, but to reject caste altogether.

Untouchables thus reveal a great diversity of responses to oppression. Muli's life history, however, suggests that the process of accommodation to or rebellion against oppression is yet more complex. Different landowning masters and other high-caste people treat Muli quite differently one from another, and he responds differently to each of them. In some circumstances, he works as a faithful and subservient employee; at other times he seeks indirect ways to escape his plight; sometimes he cheats his employer; and sometimes he openly revolts against what he considers unfair and excessive oppression. Moreover, the same employer treats Muli differently at different times, and conversely, Muli's ambivalent responses reflect respect for, affection for, resentment of, and rebellion against the same person.*

Religious Life

The religious activities and outlook of the Bauris contrast sharply with those of the privileged high castes, who emphasize ritualism and purification. Many Brahman and Mallia males spend several hours in the morning bathing and praying at various shrines. High-caste women perform daily rituals to purify their kitchens, and on many days throughout the year they fast, pray, and perform purificatory rituals.† No family or individual can remain pure indefinitely, since a person can always become polluted by contact with lower castes or by changes in a family, such as the death of a relative, which requires an elaborate purification ceremony over ten to twelve days. At life-cycle rituals such as weddings and funerals, the high castes utilize the services of family priests, who inherit their position by birth. The procedures for these rites are recorded in palm-leaf manuscripts and printed books which the priests are supposed to follow, although they often depart from the texts.

The Bauris imitate those aspects of high-caste rituals which they have seen and remembered. But the Bauris, affected by the uncer-

---

*August Meier and Elliot Rudwick have called my attention to similarly diverse responses in the master-slave relationships in the antebellum southern United States; see Meier and Rudwick (1976:75–86).

†For a detailed list of religious vows and religious festivals see Kane (1974: vol. V, pt. 1, sect. 1:1–462); see also Babb (1975:47–51) for a discussion of purification in rituals.

23. A *kaaḷasi*-shaman in a trance gives divine advice to his followers.

24. Bauri intervillage council meeting.

tainty of employment and food, rarely have the time or money to perform lengthy daily rituals as do the higher castes. Furthermore, such rituals are not prescribed for Bauris, as they are for castes like Brahmans. In Muli's household, Grandmother Dungi was the only person who performed daily rituals. Each evening at sunset, she lit a tiny earthen wick-lamp and placed a few grains of rice on the doorstep as offerings to deities. She frequently fasted and often visited temples, although she was never allowed inside. The other persons of the house, male and female, approached religion more pragmatically, turning to it for help during crises but otherwise paying little attention to religious rituals or prayers. Unlike the high-caste neighborhood shrines, where people worshiped every day, Muli's ward shrine often remained unattended and unused for months at a time.

Denied the services of high-caste priests, the Bauris have developed their own hereditary religious specialists. The ward leader and assistant leader and their wives have hereditary functions at the marriage and funeral rituals of the people in their ward. The activities of ward leaders figure prominently in Muli's life story. For serious ritual offenses, such as killing a cow or marrying outside of one's caste, leaders from twenty-two wards (called "countries") in several villages meet at the banyan tree mentioned earlier. A hereditary ritual leader, the *baistaamba*, presides over the ritual activities of several groups of Bauri "countries." Muli describes how the *baistaamba*, whom he calls by the high-caste term of *purohita* [family priest], conducted the secret name initiation ceremony for Muli and his bride, imitating high-caste rites. A *mahanta* [abbot] of a monastery located in a village a few miles from Muli's house has authority over *baistaamba*(s) from different regions. The highest religious authority for the Bauris is the head abbot of a monastery in the holy city of Puri, about forty miles from Muli's village. This monastery was founded in the sixteenth century by Chaitanya, a religious leader, whose devotional worship disregarded the barriers of caste. Thus the Bauris are linked in an intervillage caste network embracing hundreds of villages in Orissa.

For the Bauris, however, the most important and dramatic religious event of the year, *panaa sankraanti*, in mid-April, involves not hereditary religious specialists, but shamanistic faith healers called *kaaḷasi,* who, while allegedly spirit-possessed by the mother-goddess Kali, lead their followers over burning coals as a demonstration of their faith that the goddess will protect them.* In some villages near Muli's house, attendants tie Kali-worshipers by their ankles to scaffolds and swing them, hanging face down, through blazing fires. In other villages, devotees pass hot skewers through their tongues, lick boiling milk, or pass hooks through the skin of their backs. During *paṇaa sankraanti,* Bauris in some villages also participate in or listen to a devotional chanting dance called the *paaṭuaa,* which continues for seven days.

While the *kaaḷasi*-leaders of these ordeals usually are untouchables, particularly Bauris, their followers range from educated Brahman civil servants to illiterate untouchable farm laborers. Most followers perform daily rituals at the shrines of the *kaaḷasi* to receive help during crises such as severe illnesses. They believe that a *kaaḷasi* in trance is the living form of the mother-goddess. After walking through the fire while possessed, the *kaaḷasi(s)* drink the blood of sacrificed goats and chickens; then they give divine advice and cures to their believers, who respect the goddess, not the individual she temporarily happens to occupy. Even while possessed, a Bauri *kaaḷasi* remains an untouchable, prohibited access to high-caste temples.†

High-caste priests rarely deal with blood sacrifice, disease, or other impure aspects of Kali, leaving such activities to lower-caste shamanistic *kaaḷasi(s),* who thus can control and earn money from higher castes, if only momentarily. During epidemics and firewalking ceremonies, spirit-possessed *kaaḷasi(s),* free to say or do almost anything because they are considered divine, insult and strike high-caste patients, and also force them to offer expensive goat

---

*The term *kaaḷasi* comes not from Kali the mother-goddess, but from the Sanskrit word *kaaḷasha* [auspicious jar]; devotees carry this jar at auspicious or religious occasions such as weddings, establishing an idol, starting a new enterprise, or firewalking. See Kane (1974: vol. V, pt. 1:280) for a definition of *kaaḷasha.* See Babb (1975:42) for mention of the importance of the *kaaḷasha.* During the procession preceding the firewalking ordeal, devotees carry the auspicious jar of the goddess, which at other times remains at the mother-goddess shrines at which the *kaaḷasi*-shamans worship. The *kaaḷasha* is the concrete symbol of the deity during rituals.
†For a discussion of the symbolism of blood-drinking, plus further details about the firewalking ceremony, see Freeman (1974:54–63); for descriptions of firewalking in other South Asian communities, see Rosner (1966:177–190); and Kuper (1960:217–227).

sacrifices. Terrified of dying, high-caste patrons submit to public humiliation while untouchable spectators grin.*

Despite the importance of *kaaḷasi(s)* for Bauri society, Muli scarcely mentions them in his life history; they represent a religious life style that fails to interest a predominantly secular man like Muli. Men and women usually become *kaaḷasi(s)* only after suffering terrifying experiences. One *kaaḷasi* told me that the mother-goddess first entered his body while he was afflicted with cholera and near death. Another man's first possession occurred after he broke a taboo on firewalking day by eating dried prawns. When he stepped before the shrine of the goddess, he says, she threw him to the ground. "At first nobody realized that the deity had entered my body. They thought that she had just knocked me down to punish me. I stepped forward and again was thrown to the ground. I do not know what happened. When the goddess enters me, I lose all sense of being conscious. Later I was told that when people saw that I became the living goddess, they gathered around me uttering the sacred names and sounds of God."

Although he neglects *kaaḷasi(s)*, Muli frequently describes the activities of people called *guṇiaa* [magician]. In his life history, Muli hires, observes, or reports about magicians who use love magic, perform an abortion on an unmarried Bauri woman, exorcise the spirit of a dead person who enters his wife's body, and cause his paternal grandfather to sicken and die. Unlike the *kaaḷasi(s)*, whose inspiration comes from possession, magicians deliberately learn their craft from books or from other magicians. Muli, like most villagers, greatly fears these exorcist-magicians, as well as the malevolent ghostly spirits of the dead whom the magicians allegedly manipulate.

Social and Family Life

The Bauri family life style differs from that of high-caste Hindu ideals and practices. The high castes of Muli's village have never allowed widows to remarry and rarely allow divorces, since high-caste women are supposed to be faithful to their husbands whether

---

*See Berreman (1964:53–69) for a discussion of the difference between high-caste priests and low-caste shamans. Berreman also contends that low-caste people benefit from these performances. "There can be no doubt that low caste people derive considerable satisfaction, personally if they are practitioners and vicariously if they are not, from the power non-Brahmanical practitioners exercise in overtly manipulating their caste superiors" (1964:62).

alive or deceased.* The only high-caste divorced women allowed to remarry are those without children. By contrast, Bauri widows usually remarry if young, and women frequently divorce and remarry. Because most Bauri women are full-time earners, they are not as economically dependent on their husbands as are high-caste wives. If a Bauri woman dislikes the way her husband or his family treats her, she simply leaves for her father's house, usually no more than five to ten miles away, depriving her husband of her income. One of Muli's sisters is married to her fourth husband, one of his neighbors to his sixth wife. Muli himself left his first wife for another woman, with whom he lived for over a year before returning to his wife. Muli's brother Anadi also lived with a woman other than his wife for more than a year. Muli's account of these events portrays the tensions among spouses and in-laws that contribute to the breakup of Bauri marriages.

Muli extolls the ideals of living cooperatively in a joint family, sharing income and meals with his parents, brothers, and brothers' wives, contributing money, goods, and working time for the marriage ceremonies of his brothers and sisters. In practice, he and his wife frequently quarrel with his parents, brothers, and brothers' wives. For brief periods they live as a joint family; then they quarrel and separate, repeating the process many times.

Muli blames his mother, whom he says quarrels constantly with her daughters-in-law. Muli's father, inarticulate and ineffectual, is unable to control his sharp-tongued wife, and says so publicly when ward leaders and neighbors attempt to settle disputes within Muli's family. Muli is similarly unable to control his own wife. Muli says that wives are supposed to be subordinate to their husbands: a wife should not eat dinner before her husband does; a husband has the right to beat his wife, but she should never beat him. Muli, his brothers, his father, and his grandfather beat their wives. Although the women submit, they openly show their disapproval of their husbands by complaining, pouting, speaking disrespectfully and sometimes cursing their husbands, running away and attempting suicide. The women in Muli's life are physically tough—often stronger than their husbands—as well as strong-willed. When the men of a ward demanded of an unmarried girl named Tafulla that she reveal the

*For a discussion of the disabilities of high-caste widows, see Tyler (1973:135–136); and Harper (1964:175–176).

name of the man who fathered her child, Tafulla loudly and coarsely ridiculed the pretended virtue of every woman in her ward until the men, shamed into silence, walked away with their eyes averted.

Muli lives in a close network of neighbors and relatives who have lived near him all his life. His parents, like most Bauris, arranged marriages for their children with spouses from nearby villages. Muli's mother was born and reared only three miles from Kapileswar, while his paternal uncles live only a couple of doors away from him. Most of his maternal and paternal aunts, married sisters, maternal uncles, and the parental households of his wife and sisters-in-law also are within three miles of Kapileswar. Predictably, much of Muli's social life involves his relatives by blood and by marriage. Muli frequently visits the husbands of his two eldest sisters and the household of his maternal grandfather and maternal uncles, who help him during crises and participate in his family's life-cycle rituals.

Before 1950, almost every ward of Kapileswar had a clubhouse or rehearsal house where men and boys played cards, gossiped, settled disputes, held drama rehearsals, cooked feasts, and took naps. After 1950, the expanding new town provided other leisure activities which replaced those of the clubhouse. Much of Muli's life as a youth focused on the social life of the rehearsal hall. Many rehearsal halls contained libraries of palm-leaf manuscripts on topics such as religion, magic, and medicine. Middle- and high-caste people hired dancing boys, to whom they gave food, lodging (in the rehearsal halls), and small monthly allowances. In return, the dancing boys took female dancing roles in neighborhood dramas and provided nightly dancing entertainment for the men of the ward. In each high-caste ward, youth groups competed in music, drama, and athletic contests, as well as in constructing displays during religious festivals.

Drama and singing troupes provided popular entertainment for villagers from Brahman to untouchable. Many of the drama troupes, including the one in Muli's ward, traveled to other villages during the dry season months, giving performances based on mythological themes taken from Hindu epics and religious books. Although they were paid for performing, the actors and singers rarely earned as much as they spent on the production. Usually within two to three years troupes disbanded due to bickering over money.

Village dramatic performances provided not only entertainment for spectators of all castes, but instruction in the religious traditions and values of Hinduism. Itinerant music masters or directors were in great demand for training the actors and musicians of village and ward drama troupes. Ideally, a music master combined the talents of a poet, playwright, choreographer, and music teacher. In some villages, he auditioned for his position before the actors and other interested spectators. If they hired him, they provided him with food, lodging, and a monthly salary.

The music masters or teachers, usually young high-caste unmarried men, played a particularly important role in educating Bauris to high-caste Hindu traditions and values. The music masters trained Bauri actors to recite their lines in "cultured," literate book-Oriya, not Bauri dialect. Muli first learned high-caste phrases and customs from his music teachers. Because they lived in the Bauri wards where they taught and depended on the Bauris for their wages, high-caste music masters usually dropped the caste restrictions followed in their home villages. Sometimes, as Muli's life history shows, they developed close friendships with Bauri youths, though these usually ceased when the teachers married and moved away. The teachers frequently cheated the Bauris whom they served; but if they were discovered, Bauri leaders unhesitatingly dismissed them.

But Muli's social life includes more than relatives and drama troupe actors. Muli becomes bored sitting in the ward, listening to jealous gossip. He prefers the excitement of the bazaar and the biweekly market, where he wanders about, looks at items for sale, meets strangers, and seeks new experiences. Many episodes of Muli's life history start in the marketplace. He meets and travels with friends from other villages, high-caste men who become customers for his prostitutes, and transvestites who make noisy spectacles of themselves. Although impoverished, Muli lives a life that is varied and full of unexpected events.

Part Two

Youth and Hopes

4. Muli's Childhood, 1932–44

Muli's brief narration of his early years introduces many themes that remain impor-
tant throughout his life, and to which he refers often: poverty and semistarvation;
pervasive discrimination against untouchables; parental sacrifices for children; an
authoritarian father and grandfather; Muli's dislike and avoidance of hard physical
labor; and high-caste sexual exploitation of untouchable Bauri women. Within a few
pages, Muli thus outlines the economic, social, and psychological plight that confronts
most untouchables in contemporary India.

Dharma, my grandfather, had two wives. The first was my grandmother. After she died, my grandfather married another woman,
who quarreled with Hata, my father, and forced him to move out of
my grandfather's household. This happened before I was born.

Grandfather Dharma was very dark, strong, and stout, six feet
tall, and the best-built person among all the Bauris. He was a good
wrestler and gymnast, and also a leader because of his strength and
his ability to settle disputes. My father, slender, shorter, less strong,
and less able to talk about rules of proper behavior, was never a
leader.

Father worked as a *koṭhiaa* [farm servant] for Bhikari Mallia, a
temple priest.* Father's daily wage was one *gouṇii* [about four kilo-
grams] of rice or four annas [one-fourth rupee]. I was the first child.
Soon after me my mother bore three more children—my brother
and two sisters, and much later, she bore a third son and two more
daughters.

When I and my brothers and sisters were less than six months old,

---

*A farm servant is an agricultural laborer hired for an entire year as a full-time
servant—to cultivate his master's fields, dig wells, rethatch his master's house, and
run errands. During the harvest, he receives 12.5 percent of his master's paddy plus
the entire harvest from one-tenth acre of land. In the nonharvest seasons, the farm
servant receives day wages. Although paid less than a *muulya* [wage laborer], Bauris
prefer employment as farm servants because it offers greater security, with guar-
anteed wages in cash or food.

65

Mother fed us barley water, taro water, rice water, and mother's milk; when we were a few months old we ate rice and puffed rice. We were always hungry; most of the time we starved. Father's income alone was insufficient to feed us. Because Mother was usually pregnant or nursing babies, she rarely worked in the fields. We ate whatever we could find: snails from the river, leaves, and rice from the fields. Once a day the adults ate cooked food, mostly *pakhaaḷa* [watered rice], but they gave most of it to us. I remember that when I was five years old we ate hot cooked rice only very rarely, once every two weeks, and it was a great feast for us. We usually ate freshly cooked hot rice too fast. To make it feed more people, we let it cool and added water. We ate this watered rice most of the time.

We suffered most during the rainy season, when we had already consumed the previous year's rice but had not yet harvested the new crop, and the price of rice in shops had risen beyond what we could afford. Sometimes rain fell for three or four days; at other times up to fifteen days. During the rain, Father had no work, and earned nothing. Only those who had some food and fuel in their houses could get by without borrowing. We had nothing. We mortgaged our bell-metal dishes for food; when the food ran out we starved. We often went without food for three or four days. We children could not bear this; we cried for food. My father then would steal taro from the fields, and Mother cooked all of it for us children. My mother and father starved for days on end.

Harvesting began at the end of the rainy season. After harvesting, Father worked in the stone quarries, cutting and shaping building blocks with his pickaxe. When I was six years old, Father carried me on his shoulders to the stone quarry, and later to house construction sites where he worked as an unskilled laborer.

I was eight years old when I helped build a pilgrim rest-house in the temple town near my village. I earned half-wages of two annas. We were starving, so we worked from early morning until evening, with about one hour off for lunch. We ate watered rice which we had brought from home. When we had no watered rice, we bought a light snack of pressed rice in the bazaar.

When I was nine years old, Grandfather told me to attend school. He offered to pay the high tuition fees, six annas per month. I don't know where he found the money. The schoolhouse was a mud and thatch hut located next to the village tank [stone-enclosed pond].

25. Frightened Bauri children walk through a high-caste ward.

The villagers never forgot, nor did they let us forget, that we were untouchables. High-caste children sat inside the school; the Bauri children, about twenty of us, sat outside on the veranda and listened. The two teachers, a Brahman outsider, and a temple servant, refused to touch us, even with a stick. To beat us, they threw bamboo canes. The higher-caste children threw mud at us. Fearing severe beatings, we dared not fight back.

Two months after I started school, the children celebrated *saraswati puuja*, a ceremony for the goddess of knowledge. Most of the students brought coconuts to school and offered them to the goddess; the teachers took the coconuts as payments. Because my family had no money, I brought nothing. Three days after the ceremony, school resumed. That day the teachers beat me so badly that welts formed all over my body. Did they beat me because I did my studies poorly, or because I brought no coconut?

After that, I refused to attend school. Father and Grandfather wanted me to attend, so they beat me with a stick. If I went to school, the teacher beat me; if I stayed home, Father beat me. During school hours I ran away and hid. After Father and Grandfather left for work, I returned home, where my mother and grandmother fed me. I left before father returned and slept in someone else's house at night.

When my father and grandfather found out what I was doing, they criticized the women: "Why do you give him food? If he won't go to school, then he should go with us and learn how to cut stone." One day Father found me sleeping in the *saahi* [ward] clubhouse during school hours. He dragged me home, slapping me and shouting at me. The next morning he led me to the stone quarries. For one month I helped him by carrying away the rubble that he had cut away from the construction blocks. Father then gave me a small pickaxe. I tried to cut the stones, but my hands blistered; I was in pain. After two weeks I refused to cut more stones; I stayed in the ward and played with the other children.

Starvation forced me to return to constructing the pilgrim resthouse. I worked for four months, until the walls became so high that the men prohibited us children from working on the project. They feared that we would fall and hurt ourselves. I returned to playing in the ward. Sometimes I went fishing or collected leaves. Once in a while I went with Father to the stone quarries. After four months I was cutting three stones a day. Father was pleased; he brought me pressed rice and fried rice but never took any himself.

When I was eleven years old, the government started constructing an airfield next to the temple town. Laborers came from many villages for this big project. For five months we cut down a great forest on the site of the proposed airfield. Everybody from my ward worked there: men for sixteen annas [one rupee] a day, women for fourteen annas, and children for twelve annas. Some children of five and six years of age dragged small branches home for fuel, while the government took the large tree trunks. After we cleared the forest, we built the runways. One day we saw an airplane flying overhead. Surprised and frightened, we children ran away screaming in terror,

26. Bauri stone-carriers.

hiding behind trees until it disappeared in the distance. All work stopped. None of us had ever seen an airplane up close, and we wondered, "Will this land here some day?" I was also afraid, but not too much.

Our work group consisted of two skilled masons of higher caste, seven Bauri men from other villages, and seven Bauri women from my village. We Bauris worked as unskilled laborers. Two of the women were young, good-looking, and unmarried; two were young and married, between sixteen and twenty-five years; one was middle-aged, twenty-five to forty; and two were old—over forty years.

A mason named Benu liked me; at the time I didn't realize why. He sent me on little errands to the bazaar, where I bought tea, rice, vegetables, and *biḍi* [inexpensive village cigarettes made of strong tobacco wrapped in a tobacco leaf] for him. He bought me meals. I stayed at the work site all week. On payday each week, I returned home for a day and gave my earnings to my parents.

One day Benu, staring at the breasts of an unmarried woman named Neta, said, "Oh, what big fruits those are!"

She replied, "I have a socket, I hear you have a cylinder. Do you want to borrow my socket for your cylinder?" She tossed her head, and her long hair, tied together, loosened.

Benu replied, "Oh, what a bundle of hair you have! It looks nice. I want to borrow some hair from you." Later I learned that he was referring to pubic hair.

Neta pointed to the *baṭuaa* [betel bag] that hung below Benu's waist near his "gold" [genitals]. The bag contained betel leaves and nuts for chewing. She said, "Give me betel from your bag."

Benu replied, "Oh, in my bag there is a big, big betel. Can it enter your mouth?" He was referring to sexual intercourse.

Near where men mixed cement, water lay on the ground. Pointing to it, Benu called out, "Oh, there is so much excess water that it is running out." This was his reference to semen running out of a vagina.

Neta replied, pointing at his finger, "That peg you've got, can you plug up the leak?"

The four young women laughed, and the men, encouraged by their responses, continued to make their sexual remarks, and jokingly touched the girls on their breasts and bellies. We call this public sexual joking "funny talk." Each speaker tries to be more clever than the other person. Everybody laughed except the three older women. They remained silent, jealous because the men had ignored them.

On the way home that night, the older women called out loudly to each other, "Oh, are you screwing that mason? How is he? Does he give you lots of sweets?"

Neta knew that they were referring to her without mentioning her by name. Angered by these indirect criticisms, Neta spoke aloud to herself, indirectly criticizing the older women, "Some people with dried up tits speak of their prestige, but, screwing everybody on the road, how many hundreds of abortions have they had?"

By the time they reached our village, the women refused to talk with each other. The following morning they walked separately to work. Suspecting that the women had argued over a sexual matter, the men of our ward asked me what had happened. I repeated everything I had heard and seen, unaware that the remarks had a sexual meaning. The young men and the elders of our ward became quite agitated. At the airfield they complained to the contractor who hired both masons and unskilled workers. Surrounded by angry Bauri men, the contractor asked Benu and the second mason, "Why have you misbehaved with these ladies?"

Benu replied, "We never misbehaved, but just did funny talk while working. If anyone has seen us sleeping with these ladies, let that person step forward; then we'll admit it." No one moved. Benu continued, "Then we deny doing it. No one saw us do anything wrong."

The contractor addressed the Bauri men, "You've heard these masons. What's your reply? Nobody cares if fieldworkers use funny talk. People talk to each other like that. How can you prevent them from using mischief words? Besides, they're young, so what can you expect? They enjoy saying these things. Nobody saw them having sexual intercourse. There's no proof of bad behavior."

A Bauri man said, "The prestige of our women is lowered when they become the subject of funny talk."

The contractor replied, "If you are sensitive about prestige, then keep your women at home. That's the only way to prevent funny talk. But right now, work goes on. If you or your women aren't interested in working, then stay home. Others will take your place."

The angry elders returned to the village and prohibited their women from working at the airfield. They enforced their decision for only one week. Every household needed the money; we couldn't afford to keep our women at home. Soon the women were working again, joking with the masons, sleeping with them, and earning extra money in this way. I know because I became their *juṭaaṇiaa* [pimp]. The masons favored me so that I would set up meetings for them after work with the women of my ward. My caste prohibits our women from talking openly with men from a different community, so the women asked me to help them. From the masons I received good food and spending money; from the women I received a part of what the masons gave them. I earned something without working hard. It was a lot better than laboring in the stone quarries!

5. Bauris "Lift Up
Their Faces," 1947–48

In narrating how a Brahman quarry owner became the sponsor of a Bauri musical
drama troupe, Muli introduces us to the complex relationships of high-caste persons
and untouchables. A high-caste patron finances a drama troupe in order to be able to
maintain his secret affair with a young Bauri woman; a high-caste teacher helps the
Bauris to buy musical instruments but cheats them. While focusing on drama troupe
activities, both untouchables and high-caste persons usually act politely toward each
other, masking their real feelings. When provoked, however, the high-caste teacher's
veneer of civility disintegrates as he insults his Bauri employers, revealing his resentful
anger at being the employee of untouchables, and at owing them money which he never
intends to repay. The Bauris, resentful that high-caste persons cheat, exploit, and insult
them, allow themselves to be pushed only so far; then they retaliate with explosions of
angry insults. Gone forever is the myth that untouchables are content with their place in
society and with the treatment they receive from other castes.

Muli also mentions a longstanding factional dispute between two groups of families
in his ward. Such disputes are found throughout India and often become an accepted
part of village life. Although Muli says little about the details of the dispute, it profoundly affected the social life of his ward for many years, leading to the creation of two
competing drama troupes, their refusal to cooperate with rival families when they performed rituals, and consequently the alteration of rituals, as well as a change in the persons who performed them.

Muli also informs us about leadership roles in his community. In addition to hereditary leaders, who have hereditary functions at ceremonies such as marriages and funerals, nonhereditary leaders may emerge on the basis of their abilities to speak well and
settle disputes. Dharma, Muli's paternal grandfather, is a nonhereditary leader, and
we see him in this chapter as a spokesman-leader during the dispute between the Bauris and their Brahman drama teacher.

Finally, Muli refers in passing to a custom called "selling the daughter for marriage." Poor families of all castes, unable to give dowries and find suitable young

72

husbands, marry their daughters to older men who, because of their age, have a hard time finding wives. This custom highlights the flexibility of Hindu marriage patterns and of the Hindu social system generally. Contrary to many stereotyped notions, Indian village life reveals great flexibility. Muli provides examples, not only regarding marriage practices, but also in leadership and ritual behavior as well.

While we were working at the airfield, construction of the new capital began. Due to the heavy demand for building stones, all of our ward people, men, women, and children, received offers to work in the stone quarries. Since quarrying paid more money, we quit working at the airfield. We preferred to cut stones that were underground because they were softer than those exposed to the air. Sometimes the adult women would dig and move away the earth. Then the men cut the stones. Today the quarries are still there, but now they are almost empty.

Many high-caste contractors rented quarries and hired us to work in them. One of the contractors was Dash Babu, a Brahman from a nearby village. He was a strong, stout twenty-eight-year-old man about five and a half feet tall, with a medium-light complexion, long, smiling face, and thinning hair. On market days, Dash Babu paid big advances, as much as ten rupees, for four days of future work.* Even if a man couldn't always pay him back in time, Dash Babu, unlike other contractors, never cut the advance, so the number of his workers increased. Over a hundred people worked for him.

Batua, a man from my ward, was one of Dash Babu's employees. While Batua cut stones, his wife, daughter, and ten-year-old son dug and moved the soil. Dash Babu's wife had died, and he had no one to share his bed. He became attracted to Batua's daughter Koki, a tall, well-built girl with a dark complexion and round face. He gave extra money and vegetables to her family, and often visited their house in the evenings. Gradually, sitting and talking, he showed his affection for the daughter in the presence of the parents. He touched her body, and talked sweetly to her. They played jokes with each

*While older Bauris refer to their higher-caste employers as *saa-aanta* [master], Muli never does—he refers to them as babu [gentleman, sir], a term that, while respectful, does not connote the same distance in status as does one who calls another "master." Masters often refer to their Bauri workers as *saḷaa* [wife's brother].

other. Koki was sixteen years old, while Dash Babu was twenty-eight. Koki's parents certainly knew what was happening, but they never protested—after all, each evening he gave them extra vegetables and tiffin, and he gave Koki two or three extra rupees.

At this time, our ward split into two rival groups, I don't know why. All but three of the households belonged to my grandfather's group. The three rival households were headed by Koki's father Batua, our ward leader Kalandi, and Kalandi's relative Rama. The division occurred before Dash Babu appeared.

When Dash Babu visited Koki's house, people in my grandfather's group spoke indirect criticisms: "Oh, people are becoming highly respected by the upper class by selling their prestige."

The following day, Batua told Dash Babu about the complaints. Dash Babu replied, "Oh, what to do? I like you and your family. But if your ward people dislike my visits, I won't come."

But neither Dash Babu nor Koki forgot their love. Fifteen days later, at the stone quarry, Dash Babu said to Batua, "I have hired a mason for some work, and I need two women, your wife and daughter, to work with him. Why should the others get this money, and not your household?"

Without waiting for Batua's reply, his wife and daughter said, "Yes, we'll go." They didn't even wait for the head of their household to give them permission. The old woman did it for the money; the young one for love.

A couple of stone quarry workers from our ward overheard Dash Babu's offer, and soon the entire ward knew about it.

Actually, Dash Babu had no work for them. He hired Koki's mother to work with the mason, doing make-work. Koki worked at some minor task elsewhere. After a few hours, she slipped away to visit Dash. Her mother knew about it, but didn't do anything. Koki wanted to do what she was doing, and her mother was receiving money for doing nothing instead of working in the quarry.

Dash Babu's family found out about his activities, so he stopped seeing Koki for a month. Then someone hired him to build a house. He built a toolshed for the construction project, and for two or three months "did his work" [sexual intercourse] with Koki in the shed. I heard about this from both of them later on, after I became their go-between.

27. Bauri drummers of a music troupe.

28. Music troupe giving a performance.

Dash Babu wanted to be able to visit Koki at her own house, so he set up a singing-dancing troupe for the households of Kalandi, Batua, and Rama. Dash Babu purchased a harmonium and a tabla drum set, and hired them a teacher. Koki's brother became the lead singer-dancer. Dash Babu hired another dancing boy, plus four background singers, three of whom were Kalandi's sons. Each evening Dash Babu opened the rehearsal; then the youths played and danced, entertaining the people of the ward. While they were singing and dancing in the music hall, they forgot where they were. Then Dash Babu would slip away to Koki and make love to her in her room. Dash Babu went to his "other music hall": her breasts were the tabla that both hands beat; the harmonium was her cunt, and his prick was the finger playing the harmonium. In the meantime, Dash Babu had hired the girl's mother to cook. Dash Babu was very clever; after finishing with her, he returned to his own house before the music ended.

The ten rival families, of whom my family was a member, became jealous of Dash Babu's patronage of Batua's dancing troupe. One evening at a meeting our leaders said, "Why shouldn't we also get such things? Those other three families have a dancing group; so we will do something bigger; we'll start a drama troupe."

Since we did not know how to begin, our leaders asked the help of Bama, a Brahman who was the wealthiest man in the village. He told them that they needed a harmonium and tabla set costing 130–150 rupees, a teacher, and four or five young boys to perform the opening dances. So my Grandfather Dharma and Sadhei Behera set out to collect these things.

At that time our earnings from the stone quarry were high— twenty rupees a week. Since we worked for several contractors, we took loans. Within a week we had 250 rupees. We didn't know where or how to buy the musical instruments, so we asked Bama to help us. He said, "Everything you need is in the city of Cuttack, and I'll help you purchase them."

We paid Bama's transportation to Cuttack as well as his meals at the hotel [restaurant]. He led several men from my ward to a music shop. The owner, an outsider, didn't speak Oriya, but he knew English, as did Bama, and so the two of them bargained for the instruments in English. After returning home, Bama told us to hire

Natabar, a Brahman musician and drama writer from our village. Natabar worked during the days, but he was free in the evenings. We hired Natabar on Bama's recommendation.

Natabar Babu was an intelligent-looking forty-year-old who always wore a fancy-colored *gaamuchaa* [shoulder cloth] and fine, neat and clean dhotis. Each morning he washed his false teeth made of bone in the village tank. He was a braggart, always saying, "I did this, I did that, see how wonderful it was that I did this." He had been married two or three times, sending his wives back to their father's homes because he did not get along well with them.

After one week of instructing us, Natabar Babu asked us how much we had paid for our musical instruments. When we told him, he shook his head and said, "No, the rate is half of that." That's when we knew we had been cheated. We never said anything to Bama because we feared him as the wealthiest man of the village. We feared him greatly.

Natabar introduced a mythological drama, and he gave each of us different roles, with notes to use for practicing our parts. He met us four or five times the first month. After we had learned our parts, he taught us new words; the drama was in the fine language used by high-caste people.

At Natabar Babu's suggestion, we collected eighty rupees from each house of our group to purchase swords, dancing anklets, and costumes for the drama. On the day of the *dasaharaa puuja* festival [tenth day of the bright fortnight of the lunar month Aswin, September-October], our teacher took us by train to Cuttack. Some of the women of our ward also went along to see the *durgaa puuja* [festival of the mother-goddess Durga, ending on *dasaharaa*] displays. Our group consisted of six men and five women. All of us carried some pressed rice, fried rice, salt, and sugar cane molasses. This was my first trip to Cuttack.

Each day our teacher commuted to Cuttack to work at a printing press. Natabar Babu took us to the press and then walked with us to visit the various *durgaa puuja* displays. The city was so big that we could not see everything. Our feet hurt from walking. I was amazed to see such big ceremonies and such large crowds of people going back and forth. We held each other's hands in a line so that we

29. Actors in a high-caste drama troupe of the village.

would not become separated. Late at night we returned to the press. Although we had not eaten, we were so tired, we just fell asleep. Teacher Natabar went somewhere else that night.

Early the next morning, we stood on the roof of the building to watch the men carrying the images of the goddess Durga to be thrown in the river.* The procession lasted for hours. We watched until early afternoon before doing our *nitya karma* [daily (obligatory) work]—defecating, bathing, brushing our teeth. We became hun-

---

*At the conclusion of many ceremonies, devotees discard the images they have worshiped by throwing them into a river or pond, symbolically removing the spirit of the deity from the image. See Freeman (1977a:69–72) for details.

30. Bauri actor recites memorized lines from a musical drama written on a palm leaf manuscript. The actor is illiterate; he uses the manuscript leaves as mnemonic devices.

gry, so finally we ate some of the tiffin we had carried with us. Teacher Natabar did not return until late afternoon.

Several of us walked with the teacher to the same music shop from which Bama had bought our harmonium. We spent a hundred rupees on costumes and equipment. Natia, our cashier, gave five rupees to the teacher for his traveling expenses.

We told the teacher that we wanted to return home. Natabar said, "I'll stay here for a couple of days. You go ahead."

We asked, "How can we get our tickets? We do not know how to do these things." Natabar said, "Okay, I'll buy them at the ticket office in Balu Bazaar."

The price of a third-class ticket from Cuttack to Bhubaneswar was five annas—a lot of money in those days. Teacher collected money

31. Artisan creating a display for the *durgaa puuja* celebrations.

from all of us, bought the tickets, and said, "Go. The road is straight ahead. You know it, you went on it yesterday. Tomorrow or the day after I'll follow."

We started from Balu Bazaar. We were supposed to pass through Choudbury Bazaar to Baxi Bazaar and then turn left. Somehow we missed the turn and went straight ahead, walking along a narrow road past Banku Bazaar to Oriya Bazaar. On the way we asked a young gentleman, "What is the way to the railway station?" He pointed to the right. We walked for an hour. The road curved around. We kept walking. Suddenly we came upon a house that

32. Horse dancers and other participants at the *durgaa puuja* celebrations.

looked like the music shop. It was the shop! We asked, "What are we doing here? We're back in Balu Bazaar where we started!" The gentleman had played a joke on us. Seeing that we were small-caste village people, he had pointed the wrong way.

It was night. We looked around desperately. How could we get to the station? We were exhausted from lugging all that equipment with us. Natia said, "If we cannot get to the train tonight, we can stay where we did the night before." While we were discussing what to do, Natabar Babu passed by the music shop. He asked, surprised, "You people haven't gone yet?"

Natia replied, "We lost our way, and when we asked a gentleman, he pointed to a road which led back here."

Teacher Natabar said, "What happened was my fault; had I gone with you this wouldn't have happened. What do you want to do?"

The men replied, "We don't have enough money or food with us, so we want to go home. Please show us the way; don't leave us until we are sitting in the train."

The women exclaimed, "We cannot walk any more! We will stay here tonight; you go ahead."

Natia said, "Let's find a rickshaw for them." Teacher Natabar then said, "I also need one; I cannot walk all that distance."

We were country people who had never ridden in rickshaws and knew nothing of city ways, so Natia asked the teacher to find rickshaws for all of us. Teacher brought five rickshaws for twelve people, saying that each rickshaw cost ten annas apiece, or twice the price of our train tickets. We didn't speak to the rickshaw drivers; only Natabar did. The distance to the station was three miles, while Bhubaneswar was twenty miles from Cuttack. Now I know that the teacher cheated us a great deal; the rickshaw ride these days, twenty years later, is only twelve annas, and prices of all items are much more now than they were then.

At the station, we found that no train was scheduled for a long time. Natabar Babu said, "You have missed the train for which I bought the tickets. Your old ones are no good. Give them to me and I'll buy new ones for you."

He took our tickets and another five annas from each of us, and went to the ticket office. We stood on the platform. After a short while he returned and gave us our tickets. Although they looked the same as the old ones, we weren't sure, so we said nothing. In those days how were we to know that we had unreserved tickets that could be used for any train?

Teacher Natabar started to leave, but we begged him to stay. We feared trouble in this strange city. He waited with us until the train came. We clambered aboard with all our new drama equipment. Because so many people were packed into the third-class compartment, we had to stand all the way to Bhubaneswar, unable even to turn around. We were exhausted, standing for over an hour in the crowd, holding onto our drama things.

We reached the Bhubaneswar railway station near midnight, and walked home from there. When Natabar returned four days later, he gave our leaders an itemized list of the cost of the goods.

Two months later, Natabar became engaged to a girl from a poor Brahman household in Cuttack district. His engagement was unusual. The girl's father had announced that he would give his daughter in marriage only to a man who gives him 300 rupees. We call this practice "selling the daughter for marriage." Natabar, an old man of forty, unable to find a wife, and desperate for one, agreed to give the girl's father the 300 rupees.

Natabar asked the leaders of my ward for a loan of one hundred rupees to help him pay for his wedding, as well as his future wife. Our leaders felt obliged to lend him eighty rupees for two months' salary plus twenty extra rupees. [Muli may have overestimated the amount, which seems too high.]

A few days later, Natabar told us that he needed more money. Our leaders discussed what to do. If they refused his new request, how would they ever get back the money they had already lent him? He might become angry and leave without repaying us. Since it was now harvest season, we offered to pay him in paddy, fish, wood for fuel, and some cash. Although this was less than he had demanded, the teacher said he was happy to accept. Now he owed us a lot of money.

The following day Natabar Babu told us that he was going to bring the girl to our village, and he asked two of our men to accompany him as conch-shell blowers. The wedding was held the day they returned to the village; no one had bothered to fix the proper date by consulting the astrological book. Because the girl's family could not pay for the wedding and was "selling" her, Natabar held the ceremony at his house.

The wedding occurred happily. Natabar Babu invited us to his wedding feast, but said, "I will be very busy. I won't have time to invite you twice [as is the usual, polite custom]. When I call you at 8:00, please come then. Bring all the men and children." Women are never invited to big feasts.

On the day of Natabar's wedding feast, we dried out an entire pond in the middle of a paddy field by making a hole in the banks, and we collected two large baskets of fish weighing one maund [fifty kilograms]. The fish had come there when the river flooded the fields during the rainy season. We gave all of this fish to Natabar Babu for his feast.

That evening, while waiting for Natabar to invite us, we practiced in the rehearsal hall. By midnight he had not come, and we were quite hungry. We asked our ward leaders whether we should wait for the teacher or eat in our own houses. Our leaders asked, "Hasn't he come yet? Now it is night. Do what you wish, eat or wait. If the teacher comes later, you may go or not go as you wish."

Some of the people returned to the rehearsal hall; others went home and ate. We all fell asleep. About 2 A.M., Teacher Natabar awakened those of us in the rehearsal hall and told us, "Call your people and see *how many* will go to my house."

He had invited all of us; now he was saying, "*how many*." We felt bad. He was trying to reduce the number. We had no desire to call anyone for that kind of feast. We didn't move. Teacher stood there. Finally two or three men crept off to call at each door. No one came; they preferred to sleep. Only those eight of us who had been sleeping at the rehearsal hall went to the feast. Teacher handed us lotus leaves. We put the leaves on the road, and the teacher served us rice, lentils, and curry. We told him, "Give us only a small amount of food. We have already eaten. You have invited us; we have come for courtesy's sake."

Teacher replied, "Why won't you eat? You gave me rice, fish, fuel, and money. My feast could take place only because of you. If you won't eat, who will?" He pushed more and more food on us, more than we could eat.

We refused, saying, "We cannot eat all this."

Still he threw more food on our plates. He came back a third time with food. Seeing that we left everything on the leaves, he exclaimed, "Why are you wife's brothers not eating? Oh, you are a group of *kaangaali* [famished-beggar] Bauris! You left the food on the leaves to take to your own houses. You should eat. If you don't, you shouldn't have it."

"Famished-beggar" and "wife's brother" are great insults. High-caste people call us this all the time, but our teacher shouldn't have; we had paid for his feast. We picked up our leaves, threw the food on the roadside, and left without saying goodbye.

When Teacher Natabar saw that, he shouted, "Since I am in the service of these wife's-brother Bauris, they look at me as though they keep me under their feet. The faces of these Bauri fellows are proudly lifted up." He was insulting us: we Bauri people were not allowed to speak to higher-caste people unless we were spoken to first. When we passed by higher-caste people, we crouched so that one hand touched the ground; we walked by in that position, so that our faces were toward the ground. Now he found fault with us angrily and contemptuously by saying that we didn't keep our faces down or our heads bowed when passing our superior.

We said nothing to these remarks; we simply turned our backs on him.

As we walked away he called out, "Since I am with these small-caste people, they will put their legs on my head, or what?"* Still we said nothing, but kept walking.

Three days later Teacher Natabar came to the rehearsal hall. My grandfather Dharma, who was one of our *murabii* [nonhereditary]† leaders, asked him, "Why did you call us wife's-brother famished-beggar Bauris who lift up our faces? If you think we are low-caste, you should not accept the work of being our teacher."

Natabar Babu replied, "You are a very fearless man to accuse me. You are Bauri-caste people. How should I treat you? Should I give you respect, like my superiors?"

Dharma said, "We don't want respect from you, and you shouldn't want respect from us. According to your own statement, we supplied all the food for your feast, but while we were eating you insulted us. You should realize that you made a big mistake of behavior."

Natabar replied, "What fault did I make? I have the right to talk to my students like this, and to all you Bauris like this. When we order you to do something, we high people always say to you, 'Hey, wife's brother, do this, hey, famished beggar, do that.' Without speaking like this, how could I talk to you?"

We resented his language, and so Dharma replied, "Since you are

---

*According to Hindu belief, the head is the highest and purest part of the body, the feet the lowest and most defiling. To place a person's foot on another's head or to hit a person with a shoe are great insults. See Carstairs (1967:77–79).

†The *murabii* [literally, guardian, protector] becomes a leader based on his abilities to talk eloquently and settle disputes. The Bauris also have a hereditary ward leader called *beheraa* [literally, servant, bearer].

such a big-caste man, you should not mix with small-caste people. You should not return here any more. We don't need a teacher like you."

Natabar Babu said, "If I don't serve here, how can I repay you? I spent all I received at my marriage ceremony."

Dharma said, "We don't care about the money. We don't need your money. We simply want the big-caste teacher to leave this service."

All the money we had lent that man remained unpaid; by insulting us, he had forced us out of self-respect to dismiss him, thus tricking us out of our money. That's how the Bauris ended up paying for the Brahman Natabar's marriage.

6. A Guru for the Bauris, 1948

After the Bauris hire a new high-caste drama teacher, Muli befriends him by supplying him with a young Bauri woman. By using elaborate deceptions, Muli maintains an appearance of respectability for himself, his teacher, and the young woman. Muli's activities thus highlight the contrasts between ideals and unacceptable behavior.

Muli's narrative also provides a detailed account of ordinary activities and folk beliefs: working in a stone quarry; collecting stranded river fish and cooking them at a great feast; going outside at night in groups to scare off ghosts. In these descriptions, he gives us a vivid picture of daily life in his ward, and of his relationships with his parents and friends.

After Natabar's dismissal, we searched for another guru [teacher]. My father's sister informed us that a drama troupe had just dissolved in her village, and its music master, a man named Dinabandhu, was simply sitting idle. We sent a delegation to invite him to our ward, and my father's sister's husband led him to our place. The teacher, a thirty-year-old Militia caste man, did not eat in our houses but in hotels and tea stalls. He was a slender man of medium height, medium complexion, with a long face, long, styled hair, and an everted lower lip with big teeth. We have a proverb about people who look like that: "Big-teeth people are more intelligent."

Dinabandhu agreed to be our teacher for twenty rupees per month plus food. He lived in our ward. Every day we gave him uncooked food and he cooked it. Even though we had finished most of the old drama we had been working on, Teacher assigned us a new drama written by him. His drama, called "Arm Flower," was based on the story of the thirty-two thrones of the king Vikramaditya.

A few days after Teacher arrived, we killed and butchered a pig in my ward. Seeing this, Teacher said, "I am a young unmarried man; I have a hard time cooking and my meals are not tasty, so I will eat pork with your people."

We said to him, "Only the people of our caste eat swine meat; others don't, so how can you eat this meat?"

He replied, "I don't care about caste rules. I am not in my village and no one knows what I do. You cook it; I'll eat it with you. I don't detest you."

Grandfather Dharma then said, "Raji, the wife of Dasia's son, is the best cook in our ward. Will you eat her food?"

He replied, "I'll eat anyone's cooking, just free me from cooking."

So Teacher ate at Dasia's house. Raji and her husband used to call him "uncle" or mother's brother. Her sons and daughters called him mother's father. Whenever he came to their house to eat, they called out, "Mother's Father! Mother's Father!" They played jokes with him, pulling his cloth, talking in a silly manner, and he in turn would say, "Oh, you are my granddaughter; I want to marry you." He said words that are bad if said to a daughter or sister but are all right if said to joking relations. He joked particularly with Raji's eldest daughter, "Oh, you are a nice girl. Why should I give you away for marriage? I'll marry you."

Raji's eldest daughter replied, "Mother's Father, you are an old man. How can you marry me?"

Sometimes when they were alone he would refer indirectly to sexual matters, using "funny language," saying, "Oh, how beautiful you are. If he gets you, he'll be very happy"; but meaning, "How great your tits look; if anybody fucks you, he'll be highly satisfied." Another time, he said, "What a great amount of fruit you have!" meaning "breasts full of milk."

So they acted like joking relatives. We permit this among grandparents with their grandchildren, a husband with his wife's younger brothers and sisters, and a wife with her husband's younger brothers and sisters. If a man dies, his wife may marry one of her husband's younger brothers; if a woman dies, her husband may marry her younger sister. So when a man jokes with his wife's younger sister, he is joking with a potential mate.

Other relatives have avoidance relationships: a wife avoids her father-in-law and even more strictly her husband's elder brothers, who are known as her "one and a half fathers-in-law." She hides her face when her husband's elder brothers are present; she leaves when they eat. They must not touch or talk to each other. Our reasons for this are sexual: we assume that avoidance keeps them from sleeping with each other. When they are absent, a woman refers to her husband's elder brothers not as one and a half fathers-in-law, but as "masters"—the same word that many of our Bauri people use when talking with a high-caste man.

Well, we soon knew that Raji's daughter and Teacher liked each other. When Raji went out for a walk, her ripe seventeen-year-old daughter gave Teacher his food. She understood not only what he wanted to eat, but also the desires of his heart. They joked romantically while he ate his midday lunch. In the evening Teacher taught us at the rehearsal hall, so his love did not interfere with his work.

One day while bathing at the river, several of us saw a two-foot *saalu* fish playing with its thousands of small fish children, turning an area of three or four feet entirely red in color. Higher-caste people don't eat this fish because of its many red and white circles near the tail, which they believe are the wheels of Vishnu, the signs of the deity. Also, they don't like its taste. That's all right; we'll take the fish. We Bauris eat it, as do other untouchables. We sometimes catch the mother fish while she plays with her children, which she does near the riverbank to prevent the river from washing them away. The boys tried to catch the mother fish for Teacher, but failed. However, they caught a huge number of the small fish. All of us took our share and then bathed.

Teacher, seeing Raji's daughter bathing twenty yards away, took some to her for his midday curry. While he gave her the fish, he grabbed her tit. The other boys saw this, but feared to tell anybody because she was the granddaughter of Sadei, the second leader of the ward.

Some adults overheard the children talking about the incident but thought, "It's children's gossip; it might not be true."

Although Teacher ordered us to keep quiet, everyone spread the word quickly. From that day, everybody watched secretly to catch him again playing with her breast, but for many days they discovered nothing.

One evening Teacher led some boys to the Old Town cinema. Five or seven women, including that girl, went with them. The ward leaders sent me and Saraba to spy on Teacher. At intermission, the audience left to urinate and to talk. Teacher went to the women's side of the hall and talked with that girl, then went outside and urinated. During the second half of the film, the girl stood up, said something to someone, walked outside, and didn't return. A few minutes later Teacher told us, "I am going to urinate; you stay here." Saraba and I suspected him: he had urinated only ten minutes earlier. We followed him; he met the girl. After walking a few steps, they turned left at a small lane. It was dark and quiet. Keeping well behind them, we stalked them silently until they reached the Tank of the Three Co-Wives, an isolated tank surrounded by scrub jungle. The couple went into the brush. We reached them just as they had put themselves into position for "work."

I burst out loudly, "Oh, Teacher, you said you went to urinate, but is that what you are doing here? Oh, daughter, why did you come with the teacher?" They remained silent. I said, "Whatever may be, first come to the cinema, then we'll talk to you."

They refused to move. Although we were younger than the teacher, and thus should treat him with respect, we dragged him and his girl back to the cinema, watched the rest of the film, and said nothing to our friends. Our leaders had told us to tell them first before announcing Teacher's misbehavior to others.

The next morning Saraba and I informed my Grandfather Dharma and Sadei, the two nonhereditary leaders of the ward. They frowned angrily but said nothing. That evening, the two leaders called a meeting. When all the men and Teacher had arrived, Dharma said to me, "Tell us in detail what you told me this morning."

I described the incident. The men became angry and murmured loudly, recalling the previous incident at the river, when Teacher had grabbed the girl's breast. They said, "We'll beat him! We'll throw him out!"

But nobody would act until the leaders ordered them to. Teacher threw himself before the feet of the ward leaders, stretched out his hands, and begged them to forgive him. "I promise never to do that again," he cried.

Sadei asked him, "Why are you lying on the ground? Get up." Sadei looked as if he might forgive him, but only said, "Sit down as before." The hall was silent.

Dharma said, "You are a high-caste man. Why are you touching our feet? We are low people." Turning to his people, Dharma asked, "Well, what should we do? He is a higher-caste person. He repents his wrongdoing and begs forgiveness by touching our feet."

Sadei remained silent. Another man said, "This happened because he is a young unmarried man. Let the leaders decide what will be best."

Dharma said, "The girl is not only Sadei's granddaughter, but everybody's granddaughter. All of us are responsible for protecting the prestige and character of all of our girls. What can I tell Teacher? Like our own child he apologized and promised good behavior."

Teacher jumped up and touched Grandfather Dharma's feet and exclaimed, "Oh, you are like God! As I touch your feet I promise I will never again do this sort of thing! If you want to punish me, I shall accept it. You may beat me or kill me, but I don't want to break my relationship with your people."

Dharma replied, "Why should we beat or kill you? From today we prohibit you to enter anybody's house. We will supply food to you, and you do your own cooking."

The next morning I thought about what I had done. He was my teacher; I had hurt him by uncovering him. I tried to talk to him in a friendly way but he was unhappy with me. Anyway, I knew what he really wanted. Over time, I saw more and more of Teacher. We became friends and began to trust each other.

One day Teacher said to me, "Muli, Muli, you once did something to me which should make me your enemy. But now you have become my close friend. Still, I fear to tell you my inner desires."

I replied, "Oh, you are my teacher; I am your student. Earlier, I was not close to you. Now I am your friend, not your betrayer, so you may speak from your heart." I knew perfectly well what he was going to say.

Teacher said, "After you hear me, I fear for my job and life. Still, I'll tell you since you are my faithful friend. I loved that girl you found me with, but due to you I cannot see her. I am very unhappy about this, always thinking and dreaming about her. I want another girl to satisfy my work weapon, my desires. How can I control my work weapon? I need your help to find a girl."

I said, "Not in my ward. Consider what will happen if you are caught again. You must go outside the ward and pay for it. Bring some money and I'll try to find someone."

Teacher said, "I have already talked with Koki of your ward. She's willing and I like her very much. I don't know how to set up a meeting, so you do it for me."

I thought to myself, "Teacher once enjoyed a girl who tasted good; that's why he always thinks about that and is mad with desire. Once before I snatched away his glass of water just as the thirsty man was going to drink. Now he's asking for another drink. He is my teacher, so I should help him."

I said to him, "I'll try, but it will take time."

We each went home and I plotted how to get to talk to Koki. She was from a rival group and was prohibited from talking to us. Also, I heard that the contractor, Dash Babu, was seeing her. I decided to wait for the opportunity.

Two weeks later, I saw Koki walk with her younger sister, who carried a small basket for collecting snails in the paddy field. I followed her, using a different path from hers so that people would not suspect me. The girls went to the curve of the Gangua River where, during each dry season, villagers make a fair weather bridge of bamboo, mud, and thatch. I waded across the river downstream, and followed the curve around until I reached the bridge site. Koki was collecting leaves at the riverbank opposite me. I entered the river, pretending to catch fish, but gradually moving closer to her. How could I talk with her? I didn't usually strike up conversations with girls. So I spoke as if to myself. "Oh, I came for fishing but I found none. Wife's-brother fish, where did you go? I came to take some curry but couldn't catch any fish."

Suddenly she spoke softly, "Oh, Muli, who are you talking to? Why did you come here?"

I replied, "You are from the 'other side,' and also a young girl. How dare you talk to me? If anybody from your group or mine sees us, they will accuse you. So if you talk to me, it's your problem."

She replied, "The leaders of our houses quarrel, but what's that to us? We are the children; I have never quarreled with you or you with me. Some day our groups will reunite, and we'll talk with each other then, so why not now?"

I said, "Well, since you want to talk to me, I'll tell you a secret if you promise to keep it."

"What kind of secret?" she asked.

I said, "You gave your word to a gentleman who now waits for you. How can you promise food to a hungry man and then hide it? Isn't that sinful? If you give that food to him, your food will not become less."

She said, "I'll feed him; who is he? How much money will he pay me?"

I said, "How could I say? He pays the money, not me. He's very desirous; you should satisfy him."

She asked, "Is that man your teacher?"

I said, "How did you know?"

She said, "He's been after me, but I avoided him. If you tell me, I'll do it. Can you find a good place?"

I told her my plan, and she agreed.

The next day, late in the afternoon, Teacher and I received permission from Grandfather Dharma to travel to Balakati village, where Teacher said one of his relatives lived. We needed permission so that we could have an excuse for returning late to the drama rehearsal that evening. Just before leaving, I shouted my teacher's name—"Dinabandhu, we're leaving"—so that Koki knew we were leaving. We started toward Balakati, but turned off a half-mile from our village at the isolated mango grove next to a deserted temple. We waited for Koki.

Koki took another road, pretending to go to the market, but then circled back on a road that led to the mango grove. A small girl accompanied her.

I stayed with the young girl while Teacher and Koki disappeared behind the trees. After they were finished, Koki walked down the road with the small child, while Teacher and I took a different route through the paddy fields to the rehearsal hall.

That night as we lay down to sleep in the rehearsal hall, I asked Teacher, "How did your work go, is your mind satisfied? Did you give her any money?"

He replied, "I did everything happily. I didn't believe you'd help me as much as you did. I can never repay your loan nor forget you. I didn't know your quality before. I hope our friendship, our love, will remain forever."

I said, "We are poor, untouchable. I'll have trouble being your friend because I have no money to spend like you high-caste people. We can be friends only on the face, on the talking level, without exchanging gifts or money."

He replied, "Yes, I also need that kind of friend."

That's how my guru and I became friends.

A few nights later, we were asleep in the rehearsal hall, along with our teacher. It must have been after midnight when Diga, one of the men from our ward, entered and awakened us. Diga likes to fish at night. "If anyone wants to catch some fish," he said to us, "there's a place right now where a lot are available. I just brought back two full baskets. But, if you don't go now, they'll all be gone."

Teacher rubbed his eyes and asked, "Where is this place?"

Diga replied, "The lower earthen dam of the river has broken, but the upper one is intact. The river in between is nearly dry. The fish going upstream are stranded; you can pick them up with your hands."

Teacher awakened all the men and boys in the hut. We rushed to the river, following the light of a lantern, but in our haste we forgot to take baskets to carry the fish. We scooped the fish onto dry land; they piled up on the bank. By morning villagers were astounded by the huge mound of fish. We distributed some to passersby. Children brought baskets, and we carried back to our street what must have been 150 or 200 kilograms of fish. We kept some fish and distributed the rest to every house on the street. After gutting the fish, we cleaned them at the well, then carried them in baskets to the cross-roads near the neighborhood shrine, where we dried them. We took turns watching over them all day. In those days Bauris did not like to sell fish to people of other castes. If a man did so, his neighbors would say, "Oh, you must be a Fisherman-caste man selling fish like that."

That evening we brought the dried fish to the rehearsal hall and covered the baskets with big jute bags. Then I went to the well to wash my shouldercloth. Although I couldn't wash out its fish smell, I threw it over my shoulders and went to the rehearsal hall.

That evening, a high-caste man named Baidyanath, fat and dark with a great beard and long hair, came to watch our rehearsal. Teacher offered him the seat next to him. I sat near the teacher. The bad smell of my shouldercloth spread through the room.

Baidyanath sniffed, turned his face away, and said, "These wife's-brother Bauris, what a bad smell there is! Shouldn't the dancing boys be neat and clean? Are Bauri people qualified to play *pasaa* [a dice game played by kings]?" He stood up and left.

I was angry that he had ridiculed me. I said, "Stop the rehearsal.

Look, this high-caste fellow comes here and tells us anything he likes. Let's go to his ward leader and tell him that Baidyanath came to our rehearsal and insulted us. Who says he can do this?"

Grandfather Dharma said, "I work for the leader of Baidyanath's ward; I'll talk to him about this; you just continue your rehearsing."

By this time, a bad smell came out of the corner where we had put the fish. We tried to continue rehearsing, but the smell was so bad that we had to leave.

That night we ate happily much fish curry. I got the head of a fish. As I was swallowing the meat from that head, a bone caught in my throat. It hurt; I couldn't eat any more. Mother told me to eat a ball of rice to push the bone down my throat. The rice went down but the bone stayed. I drank water; the bone hurt more. The more I talked, the more it hurt. I cried. Mother ran and called the teacher. My stomach was stuffed from eating so much; I was breathless and nauseated.

Teacher said, "Come outside and show me where the bone is. Open up your mouth." I did so. He lifted the lamp and peered into my mouth. Suddenly he stuck his fingers down my throat and pulled at the small bone. I threw up everything. The bone was gone.

"How are you feeling?" the teacher asked.

"Much better," I replied.

I washed up, then started toward the hall to go to sleep when I heard the teacher ask, "Why don't you eat more? It wouldn't be bad—there's nothing left in your stomach now." My mother also called me to eat. I didn't really want to, but since they urged me, I ate another meal.

Late that night I awoke to find that I had to defecate quickly; my bowels were bursting. I raced from the rehearsal hall to the nearest field, defecated, and only afterward realized that I had forgotten to take along any water with which to clean myself. I went home, awakened my mother, and she brought me some water from the well. She always helped me because I was her first son.

The next morning, Mother asked me what I wanted to eat. I told her, "I am not feeling good—my stomach is producing sounds—du du du du—I'll not eat anything today, I'll not go to work today."

She replied, "Well then, take some medicine." She prepared a paste of ginger, limes, and salt which she mixed in a glass of water. I drank the mixture. My stomach made more sounds, and I had to race to the fields once again, but after that I felt better. I was completely emptied out and very weak; I slept most of the day.

Towards evening I stumbled to the rehearsal hall. My friends sitting on the veranda of the hall called to me, "Why do you look so bad, like a person who has been ill for the past six months?" I told them about my stomach trouble. They replied, "Oh, you ate too much fish, that's why you were ill."

I replied, "No, no, it was the fated time to suffer. This isn't the first time I have eaten a lot of fish, but it's the first time I have become ill. It must be my fate, so I am suffering."

The next morning I bathed in the river, then returned home. Mother gave me some watered rice. After eating it, I prepared some betel. We usually do this before starting for work, so Mother asked, "Where are you working today?"

I replied, "I have no work. I may help Father in the stone quarry." I didn't want to, but since she asked, and Father was in the next room, what could I say?

Mother said, "Always try to earn money every day. Afterward you may travel about. Then I won't complain. Our large family cannot eat on the wages your father earns alone."

That day I went with Father to the stone quarry. First I removed the soil from the stone so that Father could start cutting. Then I carried some rocks from the deep quarry where Father was working. Father was cutting a large shaft which he would divide into seven stone blocks. He could not dig them out at once, but had to cut the shaft into two big blocks, one of four future stones, one of three. We lifted the shaft just enough to place a couple of small stones underneath. Then we were able to pry the shaft out of the ground. First we lifted the section of four stones, prying up each stone individually. While pulling up the fourth stone, Father lifted suddenly. I couldn't lift as high as he could, so his side of the stone rose higher than mine, and the stone crushed my fingers. Father scolded me, "Every time you work in the quarry you get hurt. It is due to your laziness. If you would lift the stone like I do you would have no trouble, but you didn't lift up hard enough."

Blood oozed from my fingers. I was in pain. I said to Father, "I am going to rest for a while." I sat under a tree. Then after a while, without telling Father, I slipped away and went home. When Mother saw my injury, she said, "Every day that you go to the stone quarry you get hurt. Was your father working with you?"

I replied, "I was working with my father, and because I didn't lift the stone properly I was hurt."

"You got hurt because you go only once every week or two. How will you learn the work? You must learn it. Now come and eat. I've just finished cooking."

I replied, "How can I eat? My right hand is injured. I don't want to eat with my left." We use our left hand to clean ourselves after defecating.

Mother fed me. Then she took some sap from a tree and rubbed it on my fingers. I left the house and went to the rehearsal hall, where I took a nap. Several days passed; my crushed fingers healed.

Late one afternoon, four or five men and women walked to the river to catch fish by hand, and I went with them. While fishing, an old woman named Ranga passed remarks, pretending to talk to herself, but speaking loud enough for all of us to hear. "Every day the women in the Fisherman's ward pound rice into flour with the *ḍhenki* [husking pedal]. Now the husking pedal sounds daily in our own ward, thumping 'dhaka dhaka' as it goes up and down."

The husking pedal is a large log with a peg on the end that falls into a hole, crushing or pressing rice. By referring to the movement of the husking pedal, old Ranga had made a criticizing pun, first, that Teacher and I were always going up and down, wandering aimlessly back and forth, and second, that we were involved with sexual work.

The father of the girl caught with Teacher at the cinema hall heard Ranga's remarks and snapped, "Why are you talking like this?"

Ranga replied, "Our people spent money for the teacher. He came four months ago. During all this time he has failed to teach our boys the entire drama. How can he? He always spends his time with lovely Muli, and three months' work takes six months. Our people wasted their money."

The girl's father said, "What! All the men are interested in the rehearsal and pay its cost. Nobody thinks it's useless. Why do you make such statements? It is not your duty to talk like this!"

Old Ranga shouted, "My husband gives money; it goes to the teacher by being deducted from our stomachs!"

I said to Ranga's husband, who was fishing nearby, "Your wife speaks like this, but you say nothing. Well, she should prove that your money is wasted! What does she mean that the pedal goes up and down, 'dhaka dhaka,' in our ward? If she gives me proof, then we'll accept whatever the people decide. If she doesn't, then I'll complain to our leaders that she's passing nasty remarks!" I walked off angrily.

I didn't fear because I was the grandson of a ward leader; no one dared accuse me openly unless they had real proof. People suspected what I was doing, and so they gossiped and passed remarks of indirect criticism. But they didn't have proof. I knew that if I made their complaints public I could force them to back down and stop complaining, at least for a while.

That night, I lay in the rehearsal hall, trying to sleep. Teacher had gone out to defecate, accompanied by two boys. After a few minutes the three of them returned. I was still awake. I said to the boys, "Oh, you're here already? Come with me while I urinate." They went outside with me, talking loudly, and we returned together.

People fear to go out alone at night; that's why they go in groups. If you see a shadow that looks like a man, maybe it's a *bhuutaa* [ghost, evil spirit]. The moment we go out, we talk loudly and make sounds to make it appear that many people are together. That way we do not fear *preta* [dead spirits] or ghosts. Our hearts are weak, we fear that someone may hurt us. We believe that if two or three people stay together, the spirit will leave us alone. Sometimes we look at our own shadows and startle ourselves. We fear to walk alone and hear our own footsteps. A ghost is the spirit of a dead person who never married and cannot go to heaven. Instead, it wanders about and hurts people. So we fear.

7. Koki's Abortion, 1948

In describing the induced abortion of Koki, an unmarried Bauri woman, Muli introduces us to an aspect of Indian life rarely discussed. In Muli's village, a pregnant unmarried high-caste woman brings disgrace on herself and her family. If her lover is discovered to be of a different caste, she is usually expelled from her village. Some women have drowned themselves in wells rather than be publicly humiliated. Although more flexible than the high castes, the Bauris also believe that the sexual behavior of a woman affects the prestige of her family. Ideally, an unmarried woman should not have lovers, and when married, she should remain faithful to her husband. In practice, Bauri women often have lovers; if discovered, the lover may be beaten by the woman's irate relatives, and the woman herself married off quickly to a family that lives too far away to have heard of the scandal. If an unmarried woman becomes pregnant by an unmarried male of her own caste, the woman's family and ward leaders sometimes force the two to marry. Usually the leaders try to find a compromise that will enable the woman and her family to maintain their prestige. If, however, the biological father is believed to be a man from another caste, the Bauri woman often is expelled from her community and thus is forced to become an openly acknowledged prostitute. Fearing this fate, Koki desperately sought an abortion, no matter what the danger.

Muli acts as a facilitator, an indispensable go-between who locates and hires an abortionist and convinces Koki's two high-caste lovers to pay the abortionist's fees. Throughout his life, Muli takes such roles to make high-caste men dependent on him in the hope that they will become his friends and give him gifts and money. Usually they give him less than he expects. A such moments, Muli portrays himself and his Bauri women as victims exploited by high-caste men.

Muli provides a glimpse of the strange activities of powerful exorcist-magicians who both cause and cure demonic possession, as well as perform abortions. He also shows how women use gossip as a powerful means of controlling behavior.

Dash Babu regularly came to Batua's house to sleep with Koki. Teacher also enjoyed Koki sometimes. For a couple of months one woman kept two men in her palm. Koki's household flourished happily from their own earnings, Dash Babu's gifts, and an occasional rupee or two from Teacher.

With this new money, Batua built a new room made of mud and thatch, while Koki bought new saris, scented oil, and soap. Everybody in the ward looked jealously at their prosperity. "Where did they get such money?" people asked.

But three or four months later, Koki became pregnant. She hid this at first, so nobody knew, including her two lovers. After one or two months the women of the ward knew it. Menstruating women bathe in a separate place at the Gangua River, apart from others. Those women who usually menstruated when Koki did noticed her absence at the isolated bathing spot, and whispered that she must be pregnant. Koki knew of their whispering. Feeling ashamed, she avoided them.

She also worried because she didn't know which of her two lovers was the father. She told Dash Babu that the child was one month along, instead of three, because she feared he would ask her why she hadn't told him earlier. Then she said, "If you don't do anything to help, I'll announce your name, and I'll stay with you. Everybody will discover your character and all your prestige in Brahman society will disappear. But so will mine in Bauri society. To stop this, try to get me an abortion."

He agreed to help, but wondered who could do it. Where could he find the necessary medicine? Both Koki and Dash thought about this for some days.

One morning, Koki saw me near the Gangua River. She said, "Oh Muli, once you introduced me to that man [Teacher]. You have not seen me since then. But that man bothered me, every other day, sometimes every day. I fell in love with Dash Babu two years ago, but nothing ever happened until now. I think your teacher did it to me."

I asked, "What happened to you?"

She replied, "If you can help me cross the river, I'll be very grateful to you. Two months ago I became pregnant. If people spread this news, I'll remain unmarried forever. I think of nothing except how I can cross this danger."

I became deaf, unable to move or talk. I lost my wits. If they were discovered, I would be dragged down with them. Finally she said,

"Why have you become silent, saying nothing? Find someone to clear it from my belly."

I mumbled, "I'll try."

We parted; I thought about nothing else, but knew of no person in whom I could confide. Four days later, I remembered that a spirit sent by *guṇi* [magic] once had attacked the wife of my neighbor, Diga. Her grandfather, a magician, had cured her. I went to Diga's wife. We weren't related, but out of respect I addressed her as a relative, "Oh elder brother's wife, I came to ask you something. If you'll agree, I'll ask."

She said, "What thing, good or bad?" She thought I wanted something bad [sex], so she said, "You are a male; I am a young daughter-in-law. If you come to tell me a good thing, let your brother also listen." She was referring to her husband. She assumed I was there for bad because of my reputation.

I replied, "Don't tell Brother Diga; I would feel ashamed. You are [like] my elder brother's wife, like my mother. I never think of you in that other way. Please listen. One of my friend's wives is suffering from magic and needs a magician to cure her. She becomes senseless and silent for long periods, looks at others with red eyes, and angrily shouts at them. I heard that your grandfather, who knows magic, cured you of an attack of magic. I'd be grateful if you would call him to your house so I could talk to him."

She replied, "Oh, for this thing you ask me! Why didn't you just say so? Going round and round, saying 'I came to ask you something.' I thought you meant for bad. Since you didn't, let your brother come. Tell him this. Then he may bring the magician. I am a young woman and daughter-in-law of the house, prohibited from traveling about."

Diga agreed to help me, so two or three times each day for the next fifteen days I went to Diga's house to hear when the magician would come. No magician came. The people in the ward suspected me and Diga's wife, a beautiful young woman. Complaints reached my father, who sternly forbade me to enter Diga's house.

I said to Father, "All that you heard is false. The grandfather of Diga's wife is a magician, and I need him. Since you have prohibited me from going to Diga's house, please bring that magician for me."

Father was angry, "Why does a small boy like you need a magi-

cian?" Perhaps he thought I needed to arrange an abortion. He suspected me because people gossiped that I was always around women.

I replied, "Teacher beats me every day. If I do things correctly he
beats me; if I do things incorrectly, he beats me. Every day I cry at
rehearsal. I don't want to go there any more. Why does he always
beat me? If I get a magic talisman for my arm or waist, he won't beat
me any more."

He said, "That wicked, wife's-brother uneducated teacher! All
right, we'll arrange a magician." But he didn't sound entirely convinced.

A few days later he invited a magician to come to our house on
market day. I went to Teacher and said, "I need some money to
bring a magician here."

He replied, "I don't have any; I'll give you some when I get paid."

I said, "The magician is coming because of you and your work.
You did such work to that girl that she became pregnant and badly
needs an abortion. She needs money; you had better get some, or
she will announce your name, and you will lose your job."

On market day, the magician came to our door. He was a gaunt,
toothless man with a piercing look. He and I walked to an isolated
field where no one could hear us. He asked, "Why do you need
me?"

I said, "What my father told you is completely wrong. You are
[like] my grandfather. I'll tell you the complete truth, hiding nothing. But you must promise before the lord Kapilanath that you won't
tell anyone else."

He replied, "We are magicians. We go various places, see many
things; we don't disclose the secrets of others. But how can I treat
you without knowing what's wrong?"

I said, "Don't tell anyone else. I fell in love with a young unmarried girl. By chance she became pregnant two months ago. How can
we cross this dangerous border? Others should never know of our
love, or both she and I would be in trouble. That's why I called you.
If you can help, I'll give you whatever money you need."

He said, "I can do abortions up to five months, but it harms the
girl. She must remain in bed for seven days after the abortion."

I led him back to the house, gave him betel and a tiffin, and he
agreed to do the job.

The next morning I told Koki what the magician had told me and urged her to persuade Dash Babu to find a place to perform the abortion. Not long after, Dash Babu sent me a message to meet him at the construction site the following day. I told Father, "Oh, Father, I want to go to my maternal uncle's house and look about."

Father said, "If you'll work in the stone quarries, you'll earn some money. What will you earn at your uncle's house? No, you cannot go."

I felt bad. After Father ate, Mother gave me food.

I refused to eat. Father, waiting outside, called me to go to work. I said, "Oh, Mother, please tell Father I'll not work today but go to Uncle's house."

She said, "No, I can't say that to your father."

I sat like a statue without eating. Mother called out, "Why are you just sitting? Why are you pouting? Eat!"

I said, "If you'll tell my father that my uncle invited me and that you may go with me, *then* I'll eat and go to work."

Father, under Mother's chain, does what she says, while Mother is under my chain—if I pout and refuse to eat, she grants my desires. Mother said, "Yes, go to work with your father. When you return, I'll tell him."

That noon, Mother said to Father, "Why does Muli's uncle want him? You may tell Muli to go alone or you may go with him."

Father said irritably, "I have no time; he may go alone."

I was happy. Like most afternoons, instead of returning to the quarry I rested, then attended the rehearsal that evening. The next morning, carrying Teacher's money, I walked to Dash Babu's construction site. Dash Babu called me inside a room and whispered, "I hear you know a magician."

I said brightly, "Yes I know him, but he's from a distant village. I rarely see him."

He said, "I've got some work for a magician. Can you bring him?"

I pretended I didn't know what he wanted. I hoped to avoid Dash Babu's noose, but make him fall into mine. I said, "How can I go? The people of my house may be displeased with me, wondering why I should be calling a magician. Tell me what work you need, and I'll tell you if he can do it."

Suddenly he said imploringly, "Oh Muli, please, bring that magician! I'll satisfy you. Please help me; I'm in a lot of trouble."

"Okay, I'll try to get him, but he lives far away."

He understood what I was asking for. He gave me 10 rupees for travel expenses and the magician's advance payment.

As I was leaving, Dash Babu ran after me, handed me another five rupees, and said, "Give this to your household if anyone is displeased with you. Or take it for your own *aṇlaa* [waist money: people tuck money in their waists]." He accompanied me to the bazaar and bought me tiffin. When I went home, Teacher saw me and asked what had happened.

I said, "Everything's fine. Tomorrow I'll get the magician. Now I'm going to transfer the basket from our head to Dash Babu's head."

The next morning I said to Mother, "I'm going for a job where I'll be paid and also learn how to become a mason! Oh, Mother, listen, when I came from my uncle's yesterday, I got this thing. Can you identify it?" I pulled out the five-rupee note. Father said, with much excitement, "Show me! Show me!" I held it up. He said, "Hey, this is a five-rupee note! Give me!"

I gave him the money and left. They were satisfied with me; they would never ask questions as long as I brought home money. I walked to the magician's village, and told him the whole story.

The magician asked, "What'll I get?"

I replied, "Dash Babu is a rich man. He'll give you what you demand."

It was already dark. The magician said he would go in the morning. I didn't want to remain there, but to ensure that he accompanied me the following day, I stayed overnight.

The next morning, we walked to Bhubaneswar. Near the construction house, the magician hid behind a tree while I went ahead to find Dash Babu. Many people knew the magician, and he wanted no one to see him.

Koki and her mother were working there, while Dash Babu was sitting nearby. I told him that the magician was waiting for him.

Dash Babu said to Koki's mother, "Ma, go back to your house. If anyone asks about Koki, tell him she went to your sister's house to take care of a sick relative. No one will work here for the next eight days."

Dash Babu gave Koki's mother some money and warned her, "Don't tell anyone that Koki is staying here! Nobody should know anything. You are a woman. You realize how difficult and bad this work is. If anyone finds out, my prestige will be lost. Go now, be careful."

Koki's mother stepped out slowly, just like a cat. She feared what they would do to her daughter. From time to time she looked back at the compound where her daughter would have her abortion.

I brought the magician and started to leave.

Dash Babu said, "Oh, no, no. Stay. If you go we cannot do this thing."

The magician pulled from his bag four or five different-colored roots, and a small grinding stone. He ground the roots into a paste, mixed it with water, and told Koki to drink it. She drank it down.

About an hour later she began to scream. "I've died! I've died! My stomach will burst!" For an hour she howled in pain, rolling back and forth on the ground. We stood nearby. The magician told us to hold her tightly. We refused. She continued screaming. After another hour Dash Babu said, "Hold her, she may die. We'll give her some water. She might be thirsty."

I grabbed her from behind, hands around her breasts. I held her for some time. A round, bloody ball came out, a tremendous amount of blood! Just like somebody urinating! After that she stopped screaming; she became unconscious. Dash Babu threw some water on her face; she awakened, drank some water, and fell asleep. I dragged her a little distance from the pool of blood.

I asked Dash Babu to let me leave. He told me to stay and clean up the pool of blood, so I had to. He gave me some canvas. I swept out the bloody mess, dumping it in a corner of his pond. While mopping up the rest of the blood, Dash Babu said, "You look after Koki. I'm taking the magician to my house."

They walked away. What could I do for Koki? Blood oozed without stopping. She slept, and the blood kept coming out. When enough blood accumulated, I mopped it up with the canvas.

In the evening Dash Babu returned to check on Koki's condition. I told him, "The bleeding goes on and on; she is too tired to sit up."

He looked worried. He left, returned soon with two nurses and a doctor from the Old Town hospital. He told them, "This woman was three months pregnant. Two evenings ago, while sitting under a mango tree, she saw ghosts moving and became greatly frightened. Yesterday her body temperature increased and remained high today. Suddenly this afternoon it happened. Can you help her? Please look at her."

One of the nurses examined Koki's vagina and cleaned it. I don't know what she saw. Dash Babu asked me, "Have you told your father you are staying here?"

I replied, "No, I told them I was going to work."

He said, "Look, take five rupees, give it to your family, and return here this evening."

I said, "I'll stay home; otherwise my father will be angry."

Koki shouted from the other room, "Muli! Muli! Without you, how can I survive? Please return."

While the doctor and nurses remained with Koki, I went home. I said, "Mother, please give me some food."

Mother was quite angry, "Where will food come to you? One man earns. How will all eat?" I had refused to work in the quarries with my father, I had been absent, and suddenly I appeared, demanding food.

I handed her the five rupees, saying, "Oh, I came from work; take this advance wage." Her anger ceased; she smilingly took the money and gave me dry toasted rice. I ate, went to the rehearsal, then returned home. Mother gave me dinner. I said to Mother, "Bou, I may or may not sleep at the rehearsal hall tonight, but don't wonder where I am."*

Then I went to Dash Babu's house, where he invited me to eat. I said, "I've already eaten and can't eat more."

He replied, "What can be done? You must eat here." He put some food before me on the outside veranda. After I ate and washed my hands, I carried some food to Koki.

She ate, then she said, "Why is my body shivering? I'm so cold! Can you make a fire for me?"

She was still bleeding. I collected a huge quantity of dried leaves and made a fire. I warmed my hands by the fire, then placed them on her body. I kept this up until she fell asleep.

The next morning I cleaned Koki's room, changed her clothes, and started off to my home to bathe. I met Dash Babu, bringing me breakfast tiffin. He told me to return to Koki's side. Reluctantly, I said I would. After bathing, I ate the tiffin, and then visited Teacher.

---

*Bou is a contraction of *bohuu* [son's wife]; a small son hears his *jeje maa* [father's mother] call his mother *bohuu* and tries to repeat the word.

I told him, "Oh, God! My bad fortune dragged me into difficulties for these past three days. I brought the magician, helped in the abortion, and watched overnight. I've done every kind of service she needed. It's finished now."

He asked, "How much did it cost?"

I said, "Dash Babu paid for everything. You may take back your money." Of course I never expected him to take it, since I had saved him from the consequences of his fun with Koki.

He said, with a wave of his hand, "No, no, keep it. If I get that money, I'll automatically spend it."

I said, "It's not good if your money stays with me. Take it." I didn't want to appear greedy for the money. I handed it to him, he put it in his waist. I had thought that he would tell me to keep it as a reward. Instead he took it back, without giving me a single rupee, my generous teacher!

I returned to Koki. Dash Babu and the magician were bargaining over the payment. The magician said, "Why do you keep me sitting here? Why don't you let me go [pay me]? Here I'm simply getting food. If I go home I'll work and earn something. Give me what you want, and let me go."

Dash Babu said, "Why don't you state your demands?"

He replied, "I did a big job for you. You may fix the rate approximately."

Dash Babu said, "You say what you want."

The magician said, "I'll take fifteen rupees."

Dash Babu replied, "Yes, you helped me a lot. I can never repay you throughout my life. But I have only ten rupees. Take that and return happily."

He accepted the money and left. I went inside, I washed Koki, washed out the room, and arranged her bed. Dash Babu gave her three types of tablets, instructing me how to administer them to her. So the days went.

Each evening Dash Babu gave me two or three rupees, which I gave to Mother, keeping her happy with me. Since I attended the rehearsals, Teacher was also pleased with me.

On the ninth day, when Koki's bleeding stopped, my service stopped. Dash Babu gave me five rupees, which I kept with the ten rupees he had given me for travel expenses.

I stayed with Koki for another two or three days, until her mother came to bring her back. Dash Babu gave Koki new cloth, roasted rice, and some sweets, just as if a relative had come to visit. They walked home.

Koki, weak and listless, had lost a lot of weight. When the women of the ward saw her, they asked, "What happened to you? Why are you so thin?" Of course they thought they knew; that's why they buzzed, like flies on a sore.

Koki replied, "I became quite ill at my aunt's house."

The people nodded, but smiled inwardly.

8. "I Like You
Sixteen Annas' Worth," 1948

At the age of sixteen, Muli becomes the pimp of a young Bauri prostitute named Hara. Typically, Muli claims that Hara recruited him rather than the reverse, but he does acknowledge that Hara sought him because of rumors about his association with Koki and her lovers. Muli frequently portrays himself as reluctantly involved with Bauri women who want him to find them rich high-caste men. As in Chapter 6, Muli describes his elaborate ruses to keep his illicit activities secret; but as before, other Bauris suspect him of supplying women, although they fail to catch him at it.

Hara represents Muli's view of Bauri prostitutes: sexy women who enjoy their work as well as the remuneration it brings. In an incident not included in this book, Muli's teacher says of Hara, "She's not a real human; she's a demon with some magical or god-given power. She was not satisfied by one discharge; she wanted more, and wouldn't let me go until I discharged a second time. She satisfies you so much that you want her more and more."

Muli pretends reluctance, but in fact enjoys his role as Hara's pimp and occasional lover. But on a deeper level he resents both Hara and her high-caste lovers because he sees them as using him. Hara earns more money than he does, and she manipulates him to bring her customers. He also manipulates her to benefit his high-caste friends. Hara's customers flatter Muli and pay him a pittance, only to reach her. They gain her favors because they have money, while he stands outside, a poor Bauri boy who watches as they enjoy her. One man patronizes him by sharing a meal in private with him and Hara. Another wealthy customer expresses his contempt by taking Muli's only shouldercloth to lie with Hara; Muli angrily refuses to take it back, but he nevertheless continues to work as Hara's pimp until the day she suddenly deserts him.

While returning home one evening, a beautiful eighteen-year-old woman named Hara called to me, "Hey Muli, I've heard something about you." She was five feet tall, and bulky, with a medium complexion, long eyebrows, a round face, and a wide smile. Unlike most women of my caste, who wore only short, knee-length working saris, Hara wore a sari, blouse, and underskirt. She lived in another Bauri ward of our village.

I said, "What do you know about me?"

"Do you go to Dash Babu's house?"

"Yes, he's our contractor. We are his laborers."

"No, no, not about that. I know he used to go to Koki, but has stopped, right?"

I said, "How would I know? I've got no contact with Koki; she's in a rival group. What do I care what she does."

She persisted, "I hear that you are their mediator, that you made everything possible."

I denied knowing anything. She wouldn't quit. "I want to tell you something that you shouldn't disclose. I trust you. I want you to go with me on a job at the railroad station bazaar, but don't ask why. Yesterday the stone mason came to my ward to recruit unskilled laborers for a two-year job. Why don't you come along?"

The next morning she led me not to a work site but to a guest house near the station. We sat on the veranda. I asked, "Where's the work? Why are we sitting here?"

She said, "Just sit."

After a while a fat, black man appeared. He was about thirty-five, five feet five, and he wore a dhoti, a long *punjaabi* shirt, and an old-style landlord's jacket. He had a grave and fearsome face with a long, thick mustache, high forehead, and a full head of hair. When he spoke, his voice was deep and commanding. "Oh, did you come? My old consumer!"

Hara said, "Yes, we've been here a long time." They whispered together. She came back and said, "Work begins tomorrow."

That man motioned to me: "*abe ṭokaa* [hey, boy], here's a rupee; bring some tiffin."

They went inside the guest house. I bought tiffin and waited for them on the guest house veranda. Three hours passed. I became angry; I wanted to return to the village. But how could I leave her? We expect our women to return accompanied by those who had worked at the same site. If she arrived alone people would gossip about where she had been. Suddenly they appeared.

She exclaimed, "Oh, Muli! You are sitting here?"

I said, pouting, "That gentleman gave me money. I've been sitting here with the food. Take it."

She asked, "You've not eaten?"

I replied, "How could I know who it was for? How dare I eat a rupee's worth of food without working?"

She said, "Now you can eat it."

I said, "How can I eat alone? Take some." While we both ate, I asked, "What sort of work did you do inside while I sat outside?"

I wanted her to admit it openly; instead, she said, "A little work, not very hard."

The dark, fat man appeared and handed her five rupees. She said sharply, "Why only five rupees? Two people were here."

He said, "Come back tomorrow and I'll have more. And you'll have rooms to wash."

I asked again, "What sort of work is this? He pays you five rupees plus another rupee's worth of food—three times the daily wage for two people."

"Why worry? Sitting, sitting, you get paid every day, so what's your complaint? Would you rather work in the stone quarries?"

I asked again, "Well, tell me what you did, and what we should tell people we did—we don't look as if we did any work; we're not tired, dusty, and sweaty."

She said, "I didn't do much, just swept one room, sat with him, talked sweet talk, and laughed. Tell others that we washed the rooms of the railroad guest house. People won't question that."

When we reached the village, Hara gave me two rupees and kept three. She told me to meet her tomorrow at the same spot outside the village.

The next day, I again asked her, "What exactly do you do inside? Why not let me see?"

She replied, "You are younger than me; I address you as brother, so you should not see my work."

I said, "Wherever you go, I'll go." She shrugged and led me into the room.

The dark man was angry. "Where are you going?"

I replied, "Where my elder sister goes, I go."

He angrily turned to Hara and said, "Who is this boy, always following you around?"

She said, "He is my neighbor; I call him brother."

His eyes were red with anger. I was scared, but I said, "I can't leave my sister; I'll go with her."

Hara said, "Let him sit outside the room; we'll go inside. When we joke with each other, he'll leave automatically. Don't worry about him. He's a good boy. Even if he sees, he'll not tell anyone."

I sat on a bench. They went inside a room, sat on a bed, talked, laughed, played. In front of me they came together. He kissed her. Now I knew why he paid us so much. I was angry with him. I went outside. Afterward the dark man came outside and gave me a rupee for tiffin.

Hara came out and we started back. I was silent.

She noticed and said, "Eh, Muli, do you feel bad? I like the work I do. I get not only pleasure, but money. From that I pay you. Why should you think it bad?"

I said nothing except "Yes, yes." She kept on trying to convince me. She gave me three rupees and told me to meet her at the same place the following day.

I said, "Tell me his name and address or I won't go."

"His name is Bihari Babu," she said, "He's a wealthy Militia-caste landlord."

That evening after the rehearsal, Teacher asked me about Hara, whom he had seen walking with me. "She doesn't look like the working type," he said. "In your caste a girl like this is uncommon. I am your teacher, so tell me the truth. Who is she? Promise by touching my body. If you lie, the sin for falsehood will be on you."

I feared sin, so I told him everything. He immediately said, "Well, I like this new one a lot. I'm hungry; if someone brings food to a hungry man, God will bless him. You have my food. I'm your teacher, begging you. See, I hold your hand, so you *must* do this. What a solid [hard] heart you have!"

I was surprised to hear this. I said, "I'll try to get her."

Teacher was pressing me too much. If he had seen me with Hara, who else had? I thought to myself that I should stay away from Hara. If anyone in her ward found out what I had been doing with her, what they'd do to me I didn't want to imagine! I remembered Koki's abortion and who was stuck with all the trouble. I was angry; I decided I wouldn't go with Hara any more.

I avoided her for several days, but one morning she found me near the river and said, "You have caused me to starve. I was living peacefully, earning and eating regularly. Simply by sitting you earned good food and two or three rupees a day instead of the usual wage of one rupee. Why did you stop?"

"I saw what you do; I don't like it."

She said, "Muli, I like you, sixteen annas' worth [100 percent]. When I saw you my hopes increased. Then you talk like this. Aren't we old enough for that kind of work? I've been mature three or four years now. My mother and father have not given me a wedding. If I am not attracted to that sort of thing at my age, do you think I'll be attracted when I am older? Why do you feel bad? I'll give you money, food, cloth, and a beautiful girl—my own wealth and property—to enjoy a lot. So please agree to come with me."

Money, cloth, food, the girl herself. How could I turn this all down? I said, "We'll start tomorrow."

When we met the next day, Hara said, "Today I'll arrange a nice, beautiful girl for you. You don't know; you are a small boy. Once you enjoy her; you'll never be able to forget her. You'll forget everything else—food, sleep, everything, and you'll say, 'I'll marry that girl; I'll not leave her.' "

I became silent.

At the guest house, Bihari Babu said, "Where have you been all these days?"

Hara answered, "This boy was ill; we couldn't come."

He called Hara inside to "sweep the room." Hara said to me, "Sit here; come inside when I call you."

I sat outside and waited, lonely, my mind swirling, full of many things. After an hour, Bihari Babu came outside and said, "Your sister is calling."

Hara gave me two rupees for sweets. I bought them and carried them back. She called me inside the room, and told me to sit on the cot and eat. I told her she should take food first. She pulled my hand to eat, saying, "Come, we'll both eat. From today you are not small; I am not big. We are the same." We ate. Then she said, "You see, Muli, I like what Bihari Babu does with me, but I want it three times a day. He can only do it once a day. While he stayed in my body he grabbed me and kissed me; I liked that a great deal, oh, a great deal!"

I became like a statue, unable to talk. She saw this and called, "Eat, eat, eat." She fed me.

I said, "By listening to what you say, I've become mad. I have no appetite to eat."

She fed me with her right hand, but her left hand ran over my body. She touched my "gold" [penis]. She said, "Oh, Muli, I really like you. I told you about Bihari Babu only to get you to change your mind. We ate in one pot today. You are not small, I am not big." She pushed her breasts against my body. "I know you don't think about me, but I like you, sixteen annas' worth." She touched me in different ways. Lastly we enjoyed each other. In the face I was shy, but in the heart I really liked it. That was my first time. I'd had money, food, enjoyment. I became greedy. I never disliked it again.

One morning Hara arrived a little late. I pretended to be angry, looking grave and silent. She asked, "Why do you look so dried up?"

"I'll not tell."

"Come on, tell me."

"No, well, I want to tell you something, but I'm afraid to."

"Why don't you? We're equal now. Tell me."

I told her about Teacher's request to enjoy her, that he was upper-caste and young, but not good for much money. I asked her to screw him as a favor to me.

She was unhappy. "I'll give him one chance, not more; no long-term work."

We arranged the time and place.

At the guest house that day, Bihari Babu said, "I've got some news to tell you."

I asked, "What is it?"

He said, "Not you—your sister. Why should I tell you? Why do you want to listen?"

I said, "If you don't tell me, my sister won't go in. If I say so, you won't get her again."

Bihari looked toward Hara, and she said, "Why look at me? He knows everything. Tell him."

He spoke softly, "You see, my good Brahman friend here wants to talk with you. What do you say? You'll earn a little more, and get more enjoyment. That's not bad."

I said angrily, "Do you like to offer your food to others? We've never gone to anyone else besides you. Today you recommend her to one of your friends. Tomorrow he'll recommend her to someone else. Well, if that's what you want, okay, distribute. I don't care."

Bihari said, "He's my friend, so I don't care."

On the way home, I said to Hara, "You got two hunters today. I think you must feel good." Nodding, she asked about the following day's program.

I told her that we would meet Teacher, not for money, but as a favor to me.

The following day, I introduced Teacher to Hara at an isolated place, and they went to do their work. When they were done, they bathed, and we all went home: three people, three paths.

That evening, Dash Babu came to his singing group in our ward. When nobody was looking, he called me over and said, "Eh, Muli, I saw that girl who came along the road with you yesterday, laughing and playing jokes with you. Who is she; where does she live?"

I replied, "I don't know, just a friend from the road. I made some remarks that satisfied her mind, so she replied. But she's a *nice* girl."

He said, "No, no, you know who she is."

I said, "Who cares? You have permanent goods, so don't think about others."

He said, "No, no, a man needs a variety of tastes. Give me her address. I can't live without her!" He placed his palms together imploringly. When I remained silent, he said, "I demand that you give an oath before the goddess of your ward. I am a Brahman. Touching my body and that of the goddess, you *must* tell me the truth about her."

I trembled with fear. Because of the oath, I couldn't refuse him. I told him all about her and promised to introduce him to her.

He left me, grinning widely.

The next day I met Hara at our special meeting place. She looked unhappy; I asked her why.

She said, "You see, the man you sent me yesterday, your teacher, is not a good man. He gave me no money, saying you would pay me; and his work was very rough."

I said, "Well, I'll pay you by borrowing from others." Hara didn't like my reply at all. We reached the railway guest house hardly speaking to each other. We sat outside for hours, waiting for Bihari Babu, wasting the whole day.

Late in the afternoon, Bihari Babu arrived, handed me money to buy tiffin for them, and entered a room with Hara. After loitering for a long time, I entered her room, shouting, "Hara! Hara! Sister!"

She shouted angrily, "Don't come in! I'll take tiffin later, later. Get out of here!"

Perhaps they were in the middle of their work. I went outside. After a while Bihari Babu called me. I carried in Hara's tiffin and put it down. She was alone. I said nothing to her because she had shouted at me before. I stood near her with a drawn and unhappy face.

Hara looked up at me, "Why, Muli, is your face so sad? Why aren't you eating?"

I said, "I've already eaten. The food here is for you." I looked away from her as I spoke, pouting. Trying to cheer me up, she pulled my hand and chucked my chin, "Come, come."

I said, "No, I've already eaten. I pushed my arm out at her and pushed her away. She caught hold of my hand tightly, fell back, tried to balance herself, and fell forward onto me. My open palm touched her chest.

She said, "What's this, Muli, once you got a taste, you're not forgetting eh? You want it every day?"

I replied, "It's in your mind, not mine. That's why you put my hand on your chest."

Like this we talked back and forth. She pushed me; I pushed her. She pulled my cloth; I pulled hers. Finally she took my cloth, grabbed hold of my *baanda* [prick] and exclaimed, "See Muli, I see you've got sixteen annas' willingness with me! Look. Why do you say you don't?"

I said, "No, no, it's due to your behavior. You tempted me, so I like it."

She said, "If you're tempted, come and enjoy it!"

She pulled me. I sure wanted it, but in the face I said, "No, no, no!" But when she came closer I lay on her. Afterwards, I went to clean my body at the well. Bihari Babu saw me there.

He said, "What! Have you been eating tiffin all this time, or were you dreaming inside the room?"

I said, "We rested after eating, talked, just idle gossip in that room. We..."

He interrupted, "No, no, you *did* something in that room. You eat first. If you don't eat, who does? Without it we can't get it. Why do you deny it before me?"

I simply laughed.

On the way home we met Bihari Babu's friend. He called me to him, while Hara sat at some distance on the platform of a nearby temple. He said, "Since eating your goods, I think of nothing else, only your goods. I really want your goods."

I asked Hara. She said she had no further desire that day. The man was so agitated and hungry that Hara finally gave in. They went off together behind a clump of bushes. When they returned, he gave me five rupees, and promised more the next time.

That evening, Teacher called me aside and said, "Can you get her now? I don't know why, my mind can't forget her."

I said, "Forget Hara. Your *taanku* [animal leg] won't remain attached to your body if you show yourself in her ward. The only thing you'll get will be some blows, a real beating. If you want to go, go!"

Teacher remained silent. I went home to eat dinner. Then I slept in the hall.

Teacher wouldn't leave me alone. That night he awakened me and said, "I'm very greedy for her. I'll give her all my pay. Please bring her." I said nothing. The following day he kept after me. Finally I gave in and arranged for him to meet her a second time. I promised her I'd pay for it. Even then, Teacher wouldn't leave me alone; he wanted me to arrange for his third free enjoyment.

I said, "Do you think what you want is roasted rice that we can simply take and eat? She's annoyed with you. You never pay her. What can I do? Quit nagging me."

The following morning, the watchman at the station said that Bihari Babu would arrive late in the afternoon. Hara refused to wait. Near the bazaar, I told Hara that I wanted to eat; she said she had no money. When I asked her what she did with all the money she earned, she replied that she gave some to her parents, used some for herself, and put the rest in a clay box in a corner of her room.

I said, "Oh, you must have a lot of money! Can I see your bank?"

She said, "You have already seen my *real* bank [body]. Why shouldn't I show you the other? When you come to my house, I'll show you."

I had no money to take home as wages, so I asked her for some. She went home and brought back three rupees, which she gave to me. I did not go to her ward; two out of sixteen annas' worth of people already suspected us and were gossiping about us.

The next morning I went to defecate near the river. I was still angry with Teacher because he had never paid Hara and she had become angry with me. When defecating, we clench our teeth and speak to no one. If we open our mouths, the bad smell enters and weakens our teeth. When I saw Teacher, I immediately squatted down. People avoid those who are defecating so that they do not embarrass them. Teacher went further into the field. I quickly washed and hurried home, preventing Teacher from talking to me on the road. Outside the village or late at night he could whisper secrets concerning the girl, but not in daylight in the village.

Later that day, Hara and I walked to the railway guest house. When Bihari Babu ordered me to bring tiffin for Hara and me, I replied, "Will only Hara and I take tiffin, not you?" I wanted to see if he would eat with untouchables.

Hara was waiting for him inside the room; he replied impatiently, "I already had some tiffin; I don't need any more."

I said, "Why won't you take tiffin with us? Hara told me that you would eat with us today." I was lying, of course.

Bihari Babu replied, "Hara has become more than my own wife, so she might desire that and have said that. Okay, I'll eat with you." His hunger for sex was stronger than his caste prohibitions on food.

I went to the confectioner's stall and brought back tiffin for the three of us. By the time I returned, Bihari Babu had gone inside. I entered the guest house shouting Hara's name to warn them of my presence. They didn't notice; they both sat on a cot playing with each other as I entered.

Bihari said to me, "Why are you standing? Sit behind us." I sat behind them.

Bihari Babu said, "Why delay? Let's all start tiffin as we said we would." We ate out of the same plate. Bihari ordered his servant to bring us water and betel, which we took. I started to leave so that they could make love. Bihari Babu said, "Stay, why are you going away? You told me we should eat all together, so let's do this." I sat. After a while he said, "Tell me the truth. If you don't, you won't escape from here. If you tell the truth, I'll be very happy."

I became afraid because I had told him that Hara wanted to eat with him. I thought he might suspect this, and wondered what to do if he decided to kill me inside the room. I decided, if God wishes, I'll die in this room; if not, I'll live. Finally I said, "What do you want to know?"

He replied, "Did Hara request that she wants to eat with me or did you?"

I said, "I did, but first listen to something."

"Okay, say what you want." He spoke gravely. He hardly ever used sweet talk. He was a taciturn, silent man who sounded angry all the time, never laughed, and never revealed his heart. He used the same tone ordering people around, whether or not he liked you.

I trembled as I spoke. "Since the man of great caste raises the feet and legs of the untouchable-caste girl on his own shoulders [while sleeping with her] why won't he take food from her plate? I tested you to see if you would mix freely with us."

Taciturn Bihari Babu remained silent. I trembled. Suddenly, Bihari threw his arms around me—was I about to be crushed by an angry bull? No, he was smiling! He said, "What a good argument! How intelligent you are! Yes, I accept your friendliness; I'll mix with you. But we will act as equals only when we are in a private place like this room. In public, I must keep my prestige. Outside, we should not act as we do here. You must keep your distance. This girl may break off with me, but I will never break my friendship with you. Four wards of your people live in my village, but I never found anybody like you or this girl. Later, she may marry and leave. But you will find another girl for me. In this way you will retain your friendship with me."

After this *maalaankali* [mixing of both hearts; exchange of confidences], he praised me and I praised him. I said, "Because of you I get a daily wage without working hard. No one treats me as well as you do. You are my master, a wealthy, great man."

We each used sweet talk with the other. Then Bihari said, "Go, I'll see you in a moment."

I went outside. They remained inside. Bihari Babu's friend came by; he wanted Hara. After Hara finished with Bihari Babu, she did her sexual work with Bihari's friend, and after that I took her to meet Dash Babu at the construction shed. She wanted Dash Babu. When she saw a good-looking man, she would try to get him by finding a man like me to bring him to her. At this time she was only seeing Bihari Babu, Bihari's friend, me, and Teacher, and was just beginning with Dash Babu; but not long after, many men of our village would visit her, Brahmans, Mallias, Cultivators, and many others, including Bauri men.

In those days, when I was sixteen years old, I was a little shorter than now, but in good health and good-looking, with long hair swept back. Look at me now, with my hair shaved from my father's death four weeks ago, my cheeks sunken, my ribs showing. Now I have decreased much from disease.

The construction shed was a long room divided with a bamboo screen through which one could see if one looked carefully. One side was a storage place containing a bench made of two planks of wood. The other side was a sitting room with a cot, sheets, and pillow. Hara and I went to the storage side and waited for Dash Babu, who had gone to the bazaar for sweets.

Dash Babu came in and whispered to me, "I'd like some of your sweets if you'd like some of mine. Have you told her yet? Is she willing?"

I nodded. They went to the sitting room side and talked softly for a moment. At first I couldn't hear them. Then I heard her say, "Wait, if you want to fuck me, wait. I need another sari. If you get semen on this one, you will ruin it."

Dash Babu said, "I have nothing to give, no extra cloth."

Hara said, "Then borrow a shouldercloth from Muli. His is long."

Dash Babu called out, "Give me your shouldercloth, Muli."

I reluctantly handed it to him. For Dash Babu, what does a single shouldercloth matter? He can afford lots of them, but my starving family cannot. It was my only one. I sat there with a long face while they grunted, fucking on the other side of the screen. When they finished, Dash Babu handed me my cloth, wet with semen. I said, "It's dirty, I don't want it; throw it away."

Hara washed it in a small pond and handed it to me, but I threw it on the ground and left it there. As we left Dash Babu's toolshed, Hara handed me four rupees from her earnings and sighed, "If anybody else wants to mount me today, I may die!"

I accompanied Hara for many months on her visits to different gentlemen. One day, as I was walking down the road with Hara, "Uncle" Dhania, actually Hara's cousin, appeared. He was very black and stout, about twenty-five years old, and he carried a small stick in his hand. He asked me, "Where are you going?"

"To the station," I replied.

"What kind of work do you have there?"

Hara replied, "We are going to our work. Why should you worry about that?"

Uncle said, "Are you really going for work, or for another kind of work? Tell the truth."

Hara said, "Whatever may be, we are going for one kind of work."

Uncle said, "If you mean the other kind of work, tell me, and I'll go with you."

When he said this, my ears perked up, and I said angrily, "You shouldn't ask such disrespectful questions. What other work do you think we do?"

Hara said, "Let him know; it is nothing bad."

I said to Uncle, "If you talk freely to each other about such things, do you work [sleep] together?"

He replied, "It may be we are related in every sense. I'll go with you to the station. If work is unavailable, I'll see what happens." He laughed at his pun.

I was unhappy at this turn of affairs. I said, "I feel sick." I left and they went off together.

Not long after, Hara and Uncle Dhania ran away together to Calcutta. She had been my first full-time prostitute. Later, I found others to serve the high and wealthy men of my community.

9. Grandmother Dungi's Death, 1948

After the death and burial of his paternal grandmother, Muli and his relatives per-
form twelve days of ceremonies designed to purify themselves of death pollution, break
the ties of the living with the dead, and prevent the dead spirit from returning to Muli's
house or village (see Appendix A for further details).

According to Muli, the Bauris historically buried their dead rather than cremate
them like the higher castes. Muli's explanation is economic: with barely enough money
for food, they had no money to buy firewood for cremations. In 1952, acting on com-
plaints that dogs and jackals were digging up Bauri corpses, high-caste leaders, without
concern for the economic consequences, forced the Bauris to cremate their dead.

Muli describes not only the burial rituals for his grandmother, but also daily activ-
ities during the period of the death-pollution rituals. He gives memorable portraits of his
own clumsiness in the stone quarries, his father's criticisms of him at mealtime, and
his frustrated teacher's beatings of drama students after Muli refuses to find him a
woman.

One night, Grandmother Dungi, my father's stepmother, began
shouting; she was shivering with fever. She pleaded for someone to
throw mats or cloth over her. After placing some mats on her, I lay
on her body to keep her warm. After a few minutes, when her temperature lessened, I massaged her body. Then, feeling tired, I slept
at her feet.

The following evening, I skipped the drama rehearsal because
Granny was ill. I slept next to her that night. She suffered much, and
in the early morning she died.

To take her corpse to the burial ground, my family needed the
help of the *kuṭumba* [brother's families], the relatives on my father's
side. Four men served as pallbearers for the stretcher we made to
carry her; four more carried various articles. In those days, we buried our dead in the forest near the Rai Bahadur's house [a Bengali
gentleman], just a few yards behind one of the Bauri wards of our
village.

33. The Bauri funeral ceremony is similar in most respects to those performed by higher-caste persons, as is shown here. In both ceremonies, the eldest son gives offerings to the deceased father's image, formed from the mud of the river.

34. The funeral party returns from the river to a spot outside the ward where three lines will be drawn to prevent the spirit of the deceased person from entering the village.

The relatives took the corpse to the burial ground. I accompanied them. All of us were crying. We had all liked Granny; she had taken care of us when we were young and had told us many things. When we had cried, she had paid attention to us so that we did not cry. Granny was thin and tall, with a medium complexion disfigured by smallpox scars. She was lame, from the time Grandfather Dharma had beaten her and broken her leg. I remember Granny as a smiling, peaceful, gentle person, and very religious; every evening, she set out her clay oil lamp for deities, and offered them rice. She often fasted for the deities and visited many temples to worship deities, even though she was not allowed in. From outside the temple she watched, and gave her greetings. For four or five years during the Shivaratri festival [birthday of the deity Shiva] she went to the Dhabaleswar temple, which stands in the middle of the Mahanadi River, and burned a clay lamp full of oil. She also went to Puri every two years or so to visit Lord Jagannath, but she never went inside the temple. I myself went into the outer compound of the Jagannath temple for the first time only in 1970. I didn't go into the inner room; I have never seen anybody of my caste enter the temple compound before this time.

My male relatives carried Granny Dungi to the burial ground, while my father, Granny's eldest stepson, called out, "*raama naama*" [the name of Rama (God)]. High castes prohibit us from carrying a corpse on a high-caste road, so we carried her by circling outside the village. The women went only as far as the end of the ward. Usually they don't go with the corpse, although they may if they wish. The men dug the hole one or two feet deep. Then they carried the body around the hole in a clockwise direction three times, and we uttered the name of the deity Rama to get him to excuse the deceased in the heavenly court of judgment. "*Raama satya ho*" [truth through Rama]. Then we called Granny's name three times, "Are you alive, Dungi, Dungi, Dungi?" If a person is not dead, but asleep, he might awaken at this time; if he gives no answer, we assume he is dead.

At Granny's burial spot one of the men asked my father, Hata, to witness that Granny didn't answer the call and was therefore dead. Father nodded. The men lowered her into the ground, face down, straight, and facing north, I don't know why. Father lit a wick and put it on Granny's head, to indicate our promise that we would perform a *sraaddha* [ancestor ceremony] for her later. We threw some of her old cloths in the hole, as well as her thick sleeping mat. Then Father threw a handful of dirt, symbolizing sadness, on her. The men of the ward covered her up.

These days, we no longer bury our dead; we cremate them. This change occurred in 1952, soon after construction of the airfield. One night, jackals and dogs pulled out the corpse of a recently buried old woman from my ward, dragged it into the Rai Bahadur's compound, and ate it. The Rai Bahadur was in Calcutta; his caretaker telephoned him and told him what had happened. The Rai Bahadur left by train immediately. When he arrived the next morning, he found the half-eaten corpse at his front gate. He angrily demanded to know who this dead body was. When he found out that she was a Bauri, he walked through all the Bauri wards until he found out who had buried her. He shouted that if they didn't take the corpse out of his compound, he would call the police. We feared the police. The family carried off the corpse and buried it again. When the Rai Bahadur saw that they had again buried the body near his compound, he wrote out a complaint.

Government officials came to our ward and warned us never to bury bodies again. Instead of burying our people next to the Rai Bahadur's house, we buried them elsewhere, near the road between the village and the airfield. Three years later, the Government sold that hollow plot of land to someone. Then we had trouble; we requested the Mallias, who rule our village, to allow us to bury our people at the cremation grounds since other places were not available. For two years the village leader allowed us to bury our people there. Then many Mallias complained that they found half-eaten bodies of the Bauris strewn around the cremation grounds, and that the bad smells prevented the Mallias from using the grounds. They told us that we must cremate our dead from that day.

We used to bury the dead because we were poor and had no money to buy firewood. Now we are forced to cremate them even if we have to starve to do it.

If a man cannot afford to cremate a body, the people of the ward help him out. When we buried the dead, the *bhaaiali* [brotherly] family ate two feasts, on the tenth and the eleventh days after the burial. Now that we cremate the dead, the helpers take three feasts, on the tenth, eleventh, and twelfth days, because they have to give more labor at the funeral. Cremation is a high-caste custom, as is that of holding three days of feasts.

After burying Granny, we walked to the Gangua River, where we waited until another man from our ward brought us some oil. After putting on the oil and bathing, we returned to the house where Granny died. We could not go inside directly. Old Saphini, who knew more about rituals than anyone else, prepared a cuplike thing made of cow dung. He placed it right in front of the door and poured water in it. On the left side he placed a pot of water. People had carried some digging tools for the burial. They had cleaned the tools at the Gangua River. Again at the door of the house they threw some cow dung water on these tools with the fifth finger of the left hand. Then they cleaned the tools with the water from the pot. All of us dipped our fifth left fingers in the cow dung water, which we consider holy, and spread the stuff on our fingernails and toenails. Then we dipped all our fingers in the cow dung water. After washing off our fingers with the water from the pot, we entered the house. We had become impure by touching the dead body, whose spirit lies with the people. We purified ourselves of the dead spirit by washing with cow dung water.

The women of the house cleaned Granny's room, washed some of her cloths, and spread cow dung on the floor of the room where she had died. The persons who carried and buried her sat in the house. The male household members supplied the helpers with puffed rice in a winnowing basket. They threw some water and salt on the puffed rice and mixed it. From that they placed an offering of puffed rice next to the tools used for digging the grave. Then they divided the rest of the puffed rice. The five outsiders got half of it to take home and the family took the other half. On that day of the funeral the relatives of the deceased must not eat cooked food. We ate dry food only; I don't know why.

Twenty-four hours after Granny's death, the women resumed cooking. We ate a special curry called *biri daali*, which is not fried and has no spices, but contains *pitta*, a strong and bitter substance. We make the curry bitter because the dead spirit likes it, and it makes us forget and leave the deceased.

Before cooking rice and bitter curry for the people of the household, the women cooked rice, lentils, plantain, potato, and taro, which they put in a small pot for the dead spirit. Then we ate a little of the bitter curry from the larger pot. Father carried the dead spirit's pot to the edge of the ward on the Gangua River road, placed it on the road, and threw some water on the ground, so that the dead spirit could wash her hands and drink after eating the meal set before her.

Until the son offers this pot to the dead spirit, the relatives do not eat a full meal, but only take a small taste of the bitter curry. For ten days after a funeral, starting twenty-four hours after the person's death, the relatives must eat only one cooked meal a day.

That night, I dreamed that somebody grabbed me and tried to kill me. That day Granny had died. We believe that her spirit moves back and forth in the house for some time. I woke up, frightened. Nothing was in the room. I went outside to urinate and saw two silent people standing near the well. I thought it might be the spirit of Granny. Suspiciously, to see who they were, I lit a match to smoke a village cigarette. I called out in the dark, "Who are you?"

I heard someone say, "I am."

I asked, "Are you a man or a spirit?"

"We are men."

"Who are you?" I went toward them. I lit another match. I saw a young woman of my ward with a man who turned his face away before I could identify him. They stood under a gloomy tree, lovers caught by surprise. I returned to my house.

The next morning, I awoke late. Mother said to me, "Your father and grandfather already have left for the stone quarries. We need the money; we've got none, and no food in the house except for a little watered rice for this morning. We spent everything on Granny's funeral. So you must work in the quarries with your father."

I ate some watered rice. I didn't want to go to the quarries. I quietly slipped out of the house and went to the bazaar, where I traveled about until evening, when I returned home. Neither Father nor Grandfather had returned from the quarries. Mother was cooking the evening meal. When Father came home, he carried a new clay pot for Granny to the edge of the village. He would offer food to her each day for ten days.

After that, Father and Grandfather ate. I disliked eating in the presence of my father because he always criticized how I ate. Whenever I dropped grains of rice on the ground, Father would shout angrily, "Why are you taking rice like this? Are you unable to see how we eat? Are you a man or a cow?" I usually ate rice from the heel of my hand; Father would tell me to take it with my fingers to prevent it falling down my arms. I slurped the rice with a sharp intake of breath. It often went down the wrong way and I would cough. Father yelled at me whenever this happened. I avoided eating when he was around. Knowing this, Mother usually called me before or after Father had eaten. On this day, I waited until Father had finished eating.

Later, Teacher followed me out to the field where I went to defecate, bothering me about his sexual desires. I said, annoyed, "If you want a girl, find one yourself." When we returned, I saw Father carrying Granny's cooking pot to the road. Father moved aside to let me pass. Nobody should touch the person holding the pot because he is *karttaa* [ritual master or performer] for the deceased, the only one designated to give food to the deceased. Only men should offer this food, although sometimes women do it.

When I entered the rehearsal hall that evening, Teacher looked at me gravely. Since other people were present, he couldn't say what he really wanted. When my turn to rehearse came, I made mistakes. For the first time in my career, Teacher scolded me, telling me how to act for the drama. I felt bad and made more mistakes. Teacher beat my back with a cane. I remained silent. An eight-year-old child named Bagha, a stutterer, made a mistake; Teacher beat him furiously. Blood appeared on Bagha's back, welts formed, and he cried. Bagha's father screamed, "Why do you beat the children? Instead of teaching them, you beat them blindly. Be careful. We pay your family a wage, we feed you, and you beat our children. We beat our children sometimes, but never like that. You'd better not do it again."

A man named Dasia said, "Oh, Teacher, if you beat the children bloody they won't attend the drama."

Teacher replied, "If you won't let me beat the children, I'll leave! Without beating them, three months of training will take six months. If that's what you want, I'll not beat any child. But then they won't respect me, listen to my words, or care for my instruction; they won't learn properly."

Dasia said, "If you have to beat them, do it so that the children can tolerate it."

I had another turn for practice coming up, and I had been wondering how badly he would beat me. With the rehearsal now disrupted, we all dispersed for home.

The next morning, Father said to me, "You aren't working now, so help me at the stone quarry. Yesterday I cut the lines for many stones. Today I need your help to cut them out and load them."

I disliked quarrying, but since Father ordered me, I had to go. Father wanted me to work with him, but I didn't know how. He told me to separate the stone from the ground. I feared I would ruin the stone block, so I asked him how to do it. Father told me instead to collect the stones in one place. Then a cart man came, and the two of us loaded stones. When he joined the bullocks, the front of the cart was overweighted, as usually happens. If the weight is not balanced front and back, the bullocks cannot pull it. The cart man told me to shift the stones back a bit. I jumped on the cart. While moving the stones back, I dropped one on my left fingers and smashed them bloody. Father told me to take the sap of a tree and put it on the fingers to stop the bleeding. Disgusted with my poor performance, he told me to go home, and I did.

When Mother saw my hand she exclaimed, "What happened to your fingers?" I explained. I wanted to lie down. Mother said, "Eat first." Since my hand was hurt, I couldn't wash, so Mother washed my hand. I felt cold in my body; I lay down to sleep. It was midday. I dreamed that Granny came, wildly scratched my body, jumped on my back, and choked me. I became afraid and awoke with a start. When I told *bou* [Mother] my dream, she mumbled unhappily to herself, scolding Granny, "Granny is not alive, why is she coming to my house and disturbing my sleeping child?" Then she said to me, "Go outside, Muli, don't stay here right now." This was the ninth day after her death.

The next morning I said to my Mother that I wanted to go wandering. Father overheard this and said, "You cannot go anywhere today. We have plenty of work for you. Since today is the tenth day of Granny's death [the first day is death day], we must buy food, cloth, and all other things required for the funeral ceremony. You'll help with this."

Although unhappy, I went to the bazaar, bought the food, returned home, then went with Father to Iswer the merchant and bought cloth. The day passed slowly. That evening I went to the rehearsal hall. I was on bad terms with Teacher; he wanted me to find him a girl, and I refused to talk about it. I sat with the other rehearsal players. One of my paternal uncles asked me for some ghi [clarified butter] to put on his cracked lips. Although we rarely had this expensive item, he knew we had bought some for the funeral ceremony. I went to my house and brought back a small clay dish of clarified butter.

The next morning, all of us in the family cleaned out the house. We spread cow dung on the floor and wet red mud on the walls inside and outside, but inside especially. We hurried to finish by 10 A.M. Then we went to the bathing place for the ceremonies that purified us [summarized in Appendix A].

10. Koki's Marriage, 1948–49

As in earlier chapters, Muli serves as a mediator between Koki and her lovers; this time, however, he persuades and cajoles her lovers to give expensive gifts at her wedding. Muli's teacher is portrayed as a miser who reluctantly gives Koki a gift only when Muli forces it out of him. By contrast, Dash Babu, the Brahman contractor, appears both generous and deeply devoted to Koki. Predictably, Muli resents Dash Babu when, thanks to Muli's efforts, Koki returns Dash Babu's affections.

Muli portrays himself again as a quick-witted liar—a clever man who manipulates people with words. The one person whom he cannot sway is his father, who constantly criticizes him. Muli easily handles his mother. When she criticizes him for coming home late, he deflects her anger by pretending to be ill, refusing to eat, and then protesting with mock anger when she tries to force him to eat. Muli's account of his relationships with his parents is consistent with descriptions by others in India who present the same general themes: authoritarian fathers, indulgent mothers, sulking sons, and pampered daughters.

One evening, as I sat on the outside veranda of my house, Koki passed me and whispered, "Oh, Muli, I must tell you something, but not here." She kept on going to her house without breaking stride; I wondered what she wanted to say.

I took the path that led from my house around to the back. Koki meanwhile stepped out the side entrance of her house, taking a path that also led to the back. We met at the taro field of Lingaraj the Brahman.

Koki whispered, "Dash Babu gave me luxuries; he likes me a lot. I cannot meet him now but I cannot forget him. He is angry at me because I no longer give my body to him very much. But I fear I will conceive, like I did once before. With great difficulties I got rid of the child. If I conceive again it would be very bad. Tell Dash Babu that I think of him and his love, but that my parents have arranged my marriage for next month. I may not be allowed outside for work because I will be busy traveling to my relatives' house for my last stay as an unmarried girl. But tell him that I want to see him once or twice before I'm married, and that I'll see him regularly after I'm married."

I asked, "After your marriage, how will you see him?"

She replied, "One month after my marriage, following our custom, I'll return home for one year, and each year for the next five years, I'll come home for one to three months. During my visits I can continue with Dash Babu. If I become pregnant then, nobody will think of it, because they'll assume my husband did it. So tell Dash Babu."

I replied, "Will I always be engaged with your work, always as a messenger, without enjoying you myself at least once? Will you keep me like this? I too want to enjoy your body." I said this in a joking manner.

"Sure," she joked back, "if you want, why not?" We joked about it at first, but before the evening was over, I had done my work with her.

I went to the rehearsal hall and sat down. Teacher saw me and said, "Where did you go? Why are you breathing so rapidly?" He knew I had followed Koki. He joked with me, pushing his stick against my foot.

I replied, "Why are you interested in that matter? I was doing some other work; that's why I'm tired."

He said, "No, no, tell me what you really did; were you with someone else?"

I replied, "It may be, it may not be." When I said this, he knew what I had really been doing.

The following morning, I went to Dash Babu's house, where I told him about Koki's upcoming marriage, and her desire to continue seeing him. I also told him that I had tasted his fruit last night, stolen his property. He didn't seem to mind. He said he would meet her that night.

That evening, I took Koki to meet Dash Babu at the construction site. I stood a few feet from them. Dash Babu asked Koki to tell him everything that had happened the night before. She told him about the marriage negotiations, and her desire to continue seeing him— everything except that she had slept with me. Then she asked him for a gift for her marriage.

Dash Babu replied angrily, "I may give something; I may not. It depends on your fate. If I have enough money at that time, I may give a good thing. If I have no money, I may give nothing, or a small thing. I can't say definitely." We don't deny requests directly, but she knew this meant he wouldn't give anything. She saw he was angry, and she walked away upset.

She walked over to me and asked, "Why is Dash Babu angry with me? He asked me to tell him everything about last night, and I did, using no lies, half-words, or strong words."

I said, "You left one thing out; what we did behind your house. He knows about this because I told him, and he asked you about this. You told him a lie and he knows it. He likes you a lot, and has given you most of the money he earns. He gives you whatever you ask, so why ask him for a dowry? Let your brother and father take care of that. Ask Dash Babu for your own expenses—cloth, and food. Tell him you didn't tell him about us because you were shy, since it involved your personal prestige."

She asked him to forgive her, but he remained angry. I said, "Oh, Dash Babu, you are angry at her because I told you what she and I did. So it's my fault, not hers; I got her to do it. Without me neither of you can do anything. I helped her get an abortion, so both of you are obligated to me. When I wanted her, she couldn't refuse my request. I told you because I thought you would forgive me. Now you're angry at her, and she's angry at me because I told you. My fortune is like that. I am the way I was born. Remember the proverb, 'At the time that mother and father join together [in sexual intercourse], the creator, the god of fortune has written that fate on my forehead.' According to the proverb, we are all running according to our character. My fate is the way it is, yours is the way it is, Koki's is the way hers is. So I am the guilty person, not Koki. You shouldn't dislike her; she likes you, more than a husband, and not only for the money. If you want to say or do anything to someone, do it to me."

When he heard this, Dash Babu praised me, "Where did you get this sort of language, and proverbs? How is it that you are so intelligent?"

I replied, "We are *choṭa* [small] caste people; you are high-caste people, the king of castes. Before you we should not talk. However that may be, my grandfather is a leader, and I used to go with him to various meetings at which he settled disputes. I learned something from my grandfather." I spoke a bit proudly here. Since he had praised me, I felt more courageous to speak out, so I now told him, "Now go inside the room and make sweet talk."

Dash Babu remained silent. Koki grabbed his hand and pulled him into the shed. I don't know what they said to each other. I stayed away. After a few minutes I went nearer, but when I saw them playing with each other's bodies, I felt shy and stayed outside. Some time later they both went to the tank to clean themselves and wash their clothes, which were wet since they had forgotten to change their clothes while "working" with each other.

When they returned from the tank, Dash Babu said, "Muli, what should I do? How can I walk on the road with a wet cloth? What will people think? Give me your dhoti to wear. Wear your shouldercloth till my dhoti dries, then put it on and go home."

I said to him, "You are the king of castes; yet again you ask to wear my dhoti. This is not good. We are low-caste people. If I give you my cloth, it will be a great fault, and sin will come to me. While wearing my dhoti since this morning, I have urinated many times; and bad air has come from my body, so my cloth is not too good. Take my shouldercloth instead; it has only been on my shoulders. I'll take your cloth, dry it, and then go home."

Koki now approached, wearing a wet sari, and asked, "What will I wear? How can I go on the road? The lower half of my sari is wet. What will people think?"

I thought that I ought to give my cloth to Koki; her sari was very thick and wouldn't dry without sun. I wrapped my shouldercloth around my waist and gave her my dhoti. Seeing this, Dash Babu said, "Each and every time you cross me; I am unable to cross you."

I replied jokingly, "Why will I cross you? Give me some money and I'll buy another dhoti for you, and another sari for her. Then you can go home easily in your new cloth. Koki will have a new sari, and I can take your old dhoti."

He said, without laughing, "Money does not come from the *bela* tree at my back. I'll wait 'til my dhoti dries. Can you say how much I spend on Koki each day she comes to me? Not less than ten rupees. How much will I earn, and how much will I keep?"

Koki, standing some distance from us near a pillar of the house, started crying. Dash Babu said to me, "Everything went well with us; ask her why she is crying."

I walked over to her and asked her. She cried without replying. I scolded her, "A while ago you were quarreling with Dash Babu;

I reunited you. Again you are crying. Why are you unhappy with Dash Babu? Do you know how much profit you have gotten from your relationship with him? Because of him you eat in brass and bell-metal pots; your father was able to build two more rooms; you live luxuriously. The saris you wear are so expensive that no other women of our society can afford ones like them. If Dash Babu said something you don't like, forget it; you should be submissive and correct your behavior to accommodate him."

She stopped crying; Dash Babu remained silent. She tried to leave without saying anything. When two people quarrel, intermediaries are used to establish contact; otherwise the two people might not talk to each other. So I followed her out of the work compound. She turned to me and said, "I am not unhappy about money; I cried because I want to keep my friendship with him forever. Each year I'll be returning home after I am married. Dash Babu lives near my village. I don't want him to forget me after I am married; that's why I am crying."

I told Dash Babu. He told me to tell Koki he would remember her. We parted and went our separate ways.

When I met Dash Babu later, he said he would buy Koki ornaments and bell-metal dishes for her wedding. But Teacher wanted to avoid giving her anything. He said, "Where will I get money to give to her? How much can I give? I might wish to give her some money, but not things. All my money comes from your people in this ward; and the next month my own marriage will take place."

I said angrily, "What, you enjoy her without giving her anything! And now, at the last time she will be home before her marriage, you say 'I *want* to, I *might wish* to'? These words are not acceptable. Prepare what you will give to her. You *must* give something to her."

He was silent.

It was late afternoon. We were sitting on the rehearsal house veranda when Koki passed by on her way to defecate.

Teacher said, "Well, then, we'll go to defecate too."

We waited a few minutes to give her a head start. Then we walked down the path. I tried to steer Teacher away from the girl. Teacher followed me. On our way back, we saw her defecating. She was about fifty hands away [twenty-five yards]. When Teacher saw her, he pointed at her and exclaimed, "See, see, what a beautiful ass she has!"

I was quite annoyed. I said, "You should not play like this. She is not a harlot. She has some prestige, and so do you. Why are you so delighted with her beauty? You enjoyed her, so you need not be greedy or jealous over her. If you behave like that again, I'll never go out with you again."

That night, Koki passed me in the ward and whispered that she wanted to meet me in the taro field. When we had sneaked into the field, Koki said, "Oh, Muli, do you think that on account of you I should be thrown out of my house? Because of you, I'm being treated as no more than a prostitute. That man, your teacher, treats me like a whore. Why does he follow me when I bathe or defecate, and then pass comments? He has enjoyed me many times only because of your requests, and now in your presence he dares to make remarks and point at me while I am defecating! If he did this to your mother or sister, would you put up with it? In a few days I will be married. If someone discloses something bad about my character, my marriage will be stopped. You should think about my prestige."

I said, "I am sorry, I didn't realize you felt so strongly about Teacher's behavior. Please forgive him, and I'll see that he doesn't do that any more."

She said, "Okay, but I must tell you that my marriage will not be next month, but next week, seven days from now. Tell Dash Babu to prepare my gifts and bring them to my house within four to five days. Then the people of the ward can see my dowry."

We parted. On the way back to the village I started to pass through a narrow passageway near Uncle Kedar's house. He was just coming out to wash his hands after having eaten, and he said, "Who are you?" He peered into the darkness.

I replied, "Muli." I was still on the far side of the passageway.

He asked, "Why are you going to a dark taro field?"

I replied softly, "Oh Uncle, I went to steal some taro. We have no curry today. Mother told me to go and get some taro. I went there, but I was afraid—what if somebody sees me digging up taro? So I returned without any."

He said, "If you have no curry, go and dig; I'll watch for you."

I had to go back to the field and dig up some taro. I brought back two bunches and gave one to Uncle Kedar. He asked, "Why are you giving it to me? We have already eaten. Take it for your curry."

I said, "Oh, one bunch is sufficient for my family. Mother won't take any. Only Father, Grandfather, and I will eat it. So you take the rest."

He took it. I carried the taro inside and hid it in a dark corner. Mother suddenly appeared and asked, "Where did that taro come from?"

I said, "I went to urinate behind Uncle Kedar's house. Since I saw Uncle Kedar bringing back many bunches of taro, I asked him for one. He didn't want to give it, but I forcibly took it."

She asked, "Why did you bring it? It's better to give it back to him. If your grandfather hears of it he will scold me."

I said, "Keep the taro; we'll eat it tomorrow. Nobody will know we stole it."

Later that evening, I told Teacher that Koki would be married within seven days, and that he should give her a gift. He agreed, but said we must fake a postcard from his father asking that he bring money for his own marriage negotiation ceremony: then the people of my ward would give him an advance.

The following morning I brought a card into the ward, saying it was for Teacher. That evening, the men of the ward met, and Dharma asked Uncle Kedar to read the card. He read the letter aloud; then Sadei said, "You all listened; now tell us what should be done."

The men agreed to give him twenty-five rupees.

That night I convinced Teacher to order a ring made of gold for Koki. He ordered it from a Goldsmith whom I thought was honest, but whom I later found overcharged people. But I took my cut, too. I told Teacher that the ring cost seventeen rupees when it cost fifteen.

The next morning, after returning from our bath, Teacher found a real letter waiting for him. His father wrote him that his marriage was going to be held on a particular day, and that he should collect some money and come home two days before the wedding, which was scheduled on the same day as Koki's!

Teacher's jaw dropped. "What can I do? I cannot approach the ward elders for more money. How can I tell them that my marriage negotiations have already been completed? I have no idea what to do!"

I shrugged, "I don't know either. How can I say what you should say? With my people, the negotiation ceremony takes place near the altar, just before the marriage. Maybe you should tell our elders that because of lack of money, your family will do the same thing—that the letter, although sent long ago, was delayed at the post office; since you couldn't meet the expense of the negotiations ceremony, they stopped it."

That night, the ward men met again to hear Teacher's new request, but they were not pleased. Sadei frowned and said, "This is very strange. It is not likely to be true. Yesterday a letter came for negotiations; today we find a second letter for marriage. We cannot give more money than we promised you yesterday. If we hadn't already promised it to you, I would say we shouldn't give you anything."

Teacher was unhappy, but he got no more money.

The following afternoon, I went to Dash Babu's construction site and waited for him. He arrived several hours later. I went with him as he bought big, heavy ornaments, more expensive than those owned by any woman of my ward; then he bought heavy bell-metal dishes and a brass water pot. Dash told me to carry them to my village, but I said I couldn't be seen carrying them for her family. Certainly he couldn't just carry them either, so I carried the items back to the construction shed. After all, since Koki's family was getting these gifts free, they could go and pick them up.

Dash Babu then offered to give me a ride back to my village. I hid my face as I rode on the back of his bicycle. What would people think if a Brahman were seen carrying a small-caste man? This simply was not done. And people would have been suspicious if they had seen us together like this. On the way we stopped for tiffin, and I ate a lot. Just outside the village I jumped off and we parted. I went to the rehearsal hall, while Dash Babu went to his beloved's house. He stayed there a long time. When he left, I followed him and met him near the edge of the village. I asked him why he was so late.

He said, "Today's matter is a happy one. When I went to her house, Koki's mother greeted me with a sullen expression; she wouldn't talk to me. I told her I had bought some things for Koki's marriage, that she should bring them back from the construction shed, and that she should hurry before someone else steals them. When Koki's mother heard this, her expression changed to one of interested excitement. She said, 'Oh, son, I am very sorry that being a lower-caste person and you being a higher-caste person we are unable to treat you to food, betel, or tea. You come here so often, so how would you like it if I offer you a betel?' She had never offered betel before, but now she did; just a minute ago she was sullen, and refused to talk to me, now she used sweet talk. So I said, 'Bring the betel bag; I'll take some before going home.' Koki's mother said, 'The betel bag is in the back room. You may go and prepare it yourself.' Koki's mother said to her son, 'Hold the kerosene lamp and come with me while I go to get water.' Both son and mother left the house and went to the well. 'Go get the betel,' she called to me. So I went from the outer guests' room to the back room of the compound. Koki was preparing betel, but I didn't know if it was for her or me. I went to take a betel leaf from the bag. Koki prevented me. I said, 'Your mother told me to take the betel. Why are you stopping me?' She said, 'I'm not stopping. If you have the power, you may take it.' So I pushed my hand toward the bag and she grabbed my hand. I pulled her shoulder with my left hand, fingers just touching her breast. She looked into my face and laughed. I lifted up her chin with one hand and playfully slapped her, saying 'chi chi.' Then we started our work. We finished our first show, but still nobody had come back. We began our second show; still nobody came. We had time even after that to talk. I asked if she would continue with me after her marriage. She said, 'Don't ask me questions like that. If you like me, then how can I leave you? If you forget me, then there is no value to discussing the future. I'll surely never forget you during my life. But while I'm away, think over what you'll do to arrange our meeting again!' We talked like this.

"Then her mother called in, 'Koki, why aren't you taking the rice pot in the room?' I replied, 'Why aren't you bringing it?' I went to the inner courtyard and sat there. Koki's father came in. When he saw me he frowned and said nothing. He went into the back room without even greeting me. Koki's mother hurried in after him. I heard them whispering, but could not tell what they said. But when Batua came out of the room, he smiled broadly at me and said, 'Oh, son, when did you come? I had no time to talk to you. I am sorry!' He turned to his wife and talked sweetly, 'Oh, Kokibu [Koki's mother], have you treated Dash Babu well? At least give him betel leaf and nut; he can prepare it himself.' Kokibu replied, 'That son does not take betel in our house because his caste will go away [he will lose his caste].' Batua then said, 'If he won't take betel, will nobody talk with him? He is sitting alone!' So I said, 'I have no need to sit here more. I came to inform you that someone should go to the construction shed and bring the things for Koki.' I stood up to leave, but before I stepped out of the house, I gave Koki two rupees and said, 'Take these two rupees in your dowry box. It's all I've got now. If I see you later, I'll give you more.' Koki cried. I left. I never got such an opportunity since I have been going to their house!"

I said to Dash Babu, "Today you have become the groom! Betel is coming from your father-in-law's house. What else happened?"

He replied, "Nothing more. I got more satisfaction today than at any other time. I am quite happy."

I felt quite jealous and bad. I had been sitting out on the veranda while he was having a good time. I said to him, "You ate too much in the feast. People like you and give you plenty of food. But I am only a poor messenger who is always hearing and hearing, looking and looking, while others are enjoying and enjoying. No one cares for the starving fellows."

Dash Babu replied, "Why are you so worried? You got some once; you'll get some many times. You'll get plenty of opportunities when she comes home from her husband's house. Now it is not possible. Wait. Later you'll get the chance. If you still cannot, I'll arrange it for you."

I said angrily, "You'll arrange for me? When I once told you that I had worked with her, you got angrier at her than anybody would dare to be with their own wife. Now you say you'll arrange her for me? I know your character. Go and leave me alone!" I left him at the temple and walked away.

At home, everyone had already eaten. Mother, who had been waiting for me, said, "Everybody came from the rehearsal hall to eat long ago. What were you doing that took so long? Are you rehearsing more than anybody else?"

I spoke very softly, "What should I do, Mother? This afternoon I ate too much tiffin and my stomach is upset. I've been out defecating. I left the rehearsal with Teacher's permission, and I've just returned. I don't want to eat." I didn't really feel this way. I knew that Mother would make me eat something. "By the way," I said, "what is there to eat, cold watered rice or a hot meal?"

Mother said, "We have watered rice and hot food. I will make you some hot watered rice, with lemon and ginger. You should take some for your stomach."

I replied with mock anger, "For this reason I don't want to come to my house! I know that you'll *compel* me to eat. I would have stayed at the hall without coming to the house, but I needed to pick up my bedding. Okay, give me a small quantity of hot watered rice. Really I don't want it, but for your sake I'll eat."

I protested, knowing that Mother liked it if her son ate much. She liked me so much that unless I ate, she would not eat. Many mothers and wives are like this. There is no rule that says mothers must act this way, but it just happens. Mother often tried to get me to eat so that she could eat. When I wouldn't, she would say, "Eat a small amount! Then I will eat." In fact I was hungry that night, but by refusing food, I distracted my mother from her anger at me for being late and put her on the defensive.

Mother placed some hot watered rice before me. I ate a little and then went to the hall with my bedding. I fell asleep. Teacher shook me awake and asked me about Dash Babu's activities. I told him what had happened.

Teacher was very jealous that Dash Babu had enjoyed Koki in her own house, just like a wife. "How was Dash Babu able to do this thing? How good he is at this sort of thing! He got inside the house and nobody objected. She never gave me that sort of opportunity to go into her house!"

I said, "What reason do you have for entering her house? He is our master, our employer. He can enter anybody's house. Nobody can oppose him. He has sufficient reason to show if anybody asks why he went in. What would you reply to that question? He spends a lot of money on her; you always make credit accounts, saying you want to pay later. Give the money tomorrow, I'll bring the ring from the Goldsmith, and we'll give it to Koki. After that, we'll enjoy her to our maximum satisfaction." We fell asleep.

Dash Babu enjoyed Koki in her house on a Sunday night. Koki was to be married on the following Wednesday. On Monday I went to bring the ring, but could not find the Goldsmith. Time was running out. Late on Tuesday afternoon the husband's party would come to take her to their house, an act called *talaakanyaa* [collection of the daughter as free goods]. Both high and low castes do this. If the bride's family is not wealthy enough to pay for the marriage ceremony, they simply send their daughter to the groom and perform the wedding in his house. Koki's father was sending her early to the groom's house for the ceremony. Among us Bauris, the groom's family should pay for the expenses at the altar on the marriage day. The bride's family should bear the cost of the altar expenses on the fourth night. The first-day ceremony may be held at the bride's or the groom's village. If the bride is poor, it is held at the groom's village. The fourth-day ceremony should be at the groom's house. Anyway, we had little time before Koki would leave.

On Tuesday morning I brought the ring from the Goldsmith. Then I saw Koki drawing water from the well. I quickly grabbed a water pot from Uncle Ghania's house and hurried to the well. She was about to leave when I said, "Spill the water." She pretended to drop the water pot, and while she drew some more water, I whispered my plan to her, telling her about Teacher's request, and that he had a ring for her.

"What kind of ring is it?" she asked, "Silver or gold?"

I told her it was gold, and that since she was leaving later in the afternoon, she had to meet Teacher sometime during the day.

A few minutes later she started off to the river, accompanied by Kalandi's granddaughter, aged six. Teacher and I followed about a hundred hands behind [fifty yards]. When the girls reached the river, Koki told the little girl to stay on the bank. She waded across the river and went to a grove of trees. We crossed the river further down. I stood guard as Teacher went to Koki.

Half an hour later, Teacher returned and said, "Koki is asking for you. Go there."

I said, "Why should I go there? I have no work with her. Tell her she should not wait for me."

I was angry and jealous because Teacher had just enjoyed her. I didn't want to follow after him. I shouted, "Oh Koki, oh Koki, come, the child on the bank is crying. What are you doing over there?"

Then she came out running. When I saw her, I angrily turned and left the two of them and went back home alone. Dash Babu had her, Teacher had her, but I spent all my time arranging for them, not me. I felt angry and not in the mood for her. Teacher called after me to wait, but I did not turn back. I waited at the hall.

When Teacher arrived, he asked me why I left in such anger, when Koki had wanted to satisfy me.

I said, "You are like my father. It is not good for me to do work in your presence. Is the same thing available both to the father and to the son? Is what's available to the mother also available to the daughter? Why should everyone hide themselves before each other? Out of respect. So how can I dare to do work in the presence of you who are like my father?" I didn't want to tell him I was really jealous, so I said this thing about respect.

Teacher said, "I thought you got angry because I went first and told you to enjoy her after I finished. I did not know that you came back here speedily for this reason. Being a small boy you are very courteous. You are always teaching me a lesson. Thank you."

I thought to myself, "Such a greedy man. Until he is satisfied, he is bad; when he is satisfied, he is very good, makes sweet talk, and praises me."

Later that day, Teacher left the village to attend his own wedding.

11. Doctor Babu, 1949

When Muli injures his foot, a doctor from the hospital treats him and pays all medical expenses so that Muli will provide him with a Bauri woman. Muli plays up to him and hooks another customer. He intersperses his narrative with a description of his home life and family crises that vividly reveal the Bauri life-style. Muli's mother bewails the loss of a shattered pot full of rice. Muli's father, frustrated because the quarry stones he cut were too soft and broke into worthless fragments, beats and kicks his wife, who screams at him and refuses to cook that evening. Muli's father, a proud wage earner, angrily refuses to eat food paid for by Doctor Babu because he is embarrassed to accept charity.

At the end of the chapter, Muli remarks ironically that he and Doctor Babu have reversed roles: the respected doctor begs a Bauri boy for favors. Although Muli laughs uneasily about this, he obviously enjoys the turnabout. He tries to maneuver all of his customers into depending on him. In a sense, I, too, became his customer, not for his women, but for his life history.

The days passed. One morning, while walking along the road, I saw a mongoose. I ran after it; but instead of catching it, I stepped on a thorn, which went through my foot. I limped home in pain.

Mother asked, "What happened to your foot?"

I said, "When I went to get a short-handled spade to move some soil at the quarry, well, I stepped on an old iron nail. A lot of blood came out. I thought Father might be angry, so I didn't tell him; I just came back."

Mother charred some cloth and pushed it into the puncture wound. Then she took me to the well to give me a bath. She gave me a little bit of rice to eat—she hadn't finished cooking. I slept on the inside veranda.

Father arrived, saw me, and scolded me. Mother told him what I had told her. He scolded me more. Mother now became angry. "He's just a small boy. He goes out and works every day. Now he got hurt. What do you want from him?"

I lay there, pretending to sleep, listening to every word. Father looked at me, now showing concern. "How did he get hurt? If he needed the spade, why didn't he tell me? Every time he goes to the stone quarry he gets hurt."

Father went to bathe and returned carrying some red castor plant, the sap of which we use for medicine. He cleaned the root, broke it open, and heated it in a round-bottomed metal pot. Mother pressed that heated root to my foot and bound it tightly. I shouted a great deal. But when I saw Father, I stopped shouting. I was unable to move; I lay on the veranda.

When Grandfather came home and saw me lying on the veranda, he said, "Why are you sleeping?"

I showed him my wound. After inspecting it anxiously, he scolded me. "Why did you do such a stupid thing? Why don't you look where you are going? If you'd look down once in a while this wouldn't happen."

Mother cooked me *saagu* [sago], which we give to small children and to people who are ill. I ate it, then fell asleep again.

The next day, I sent Dasia to inform Dash Babu that I was injured and had to go to the hospital. Mother overheard me, and said, "Why are you mixing with that Dash Babu fellow? It's not good; he supports our rivals."

I said, "What's that to me? Still he's our master at the stone quarry where we work. Without mixing with him, how will we live? Tell Father to take me to the hospital, and tell him I've got money for medicine."

Father carried me to the hospital the next morning. Dash Babu met me there and took me in to see the doctor, a short forty-year-old with styled hair and a long, smiling face. He wore trousers and full shoes. After looking at the wound, the doctor said, "I've got to cut into it."

I was scared, so I said to Dash Babu, "If I can be cured without an operation, please get that done."

The doctor cleaned the wound, and gave me an injection and a tablet. Father carried me home on his shoulders—about a half a mile. For several days the doctor came to my house to give me injections and change the bandage. The wound was healing.

I wondered why the doctor took the time to visit me, a Bauri boy. One day, when we were alone in the house, I found out. Doctor Babu asked, "Can you tell me why Dash Babu likes you so much?"

I said, "I'm a stone cutter in his quarry. I help him a little. That's why he likes me."

He said, "No, no, there's something else. I know it; if you tell me first, then I'll tell you what I heard."

I said, "No you must tell me what you heard."

He said he had heard that I supply Dash Babu with girls; then he said, "I hope you'll arrange something for me."

I said, "You are my life-keeper; you have helped maintain my life. If I wouldn't arrange for you, for whom would I arrange?"

After that, the doctor kept coming to the house. One evening, I had already taken medicine paid for by Dash Babu, when Doctor Babu arrived. He brought some more medicine and told me he had paid for it out of his own pocket. He gave me some oranges and apples. We never eat these expensive items unless we are ill. Most of the time we cannot afford them even then.

I said, "I am indebted to you. My body is sick. Nobody can bring you to their house to treat them, but you come to my house regularly, and spend money on me. I don't understand why you have such sympathy for me. We are poor. We don't qualify to stay with you. We are people in want, 'people of a large family, so we are great sinners' [if a family is large, there are too many people and no food, thus they turn to cheating, begging, and debts]. But you show so much kindness to me that I can never repay it."

He said, "Who is giving, who is taking? Nobody is giving, nobody is taking. Everything is interchanged. What more do you need?"

He handed me two rupees. In gratitude, I touched my forehead to the ground and said, "What can I say about these things? I am just a poor Bauri boy. You are a qualified, highly educated man. You know everything." He pulled me up, saying, "What is this? You paid everything. What have I paid you?" Then he left. He was definitely on my chain.

Grandfather entered our house and saw the orange peel in the courtyard. "Who came to our house with an orange?" he asked Mother. "Nobody here bought it."

I replied, "Doctor Babu came to visit me. I gave him money to buy it for me, so he did."

Grandfather grumbled, "Has he become your orderly?" He praised the doctor for helping me, but then scolded me for making the doctor serve me. Then he sat down for dinner.

35. Bauri woman grinds spices for the evening meal.

Mother said, "Please eat slowly; your son brought some fish. I'm cooking it and will give it to you when it's ready."

We all ate.

The next day, while I was sitting on the veranda, I overheard the preparations made by Kalandi to bring back Batua's daughter Koki from her new husband's house. It was not proper for the father to go, so his ward leader went as his representative. Mother called me to eat: "Muli, watered rice."

I said, "No, I'll not eat watered rice."

She called, "The rice pot is on the stove. I'm going down to the village tank. Watch the stove from time to time. Put fuel on it. If I don't get back early enough, get someone to take care of it. I'm going to collect something for curry."

I crawled inside and sat by the stove. The rice boiled. It was time to pour the water off. I called Santi, my sister, to do it, but when she lifted the clay pot, it bumped one of the projections of the stove and shattered. I wasn't paying attention. When I looked, the rice and water had fallen into the stove. I shouted, "What have you done? What's happened?"

"I lifted it to carry it over there," she said. "I don't know what happened, the rice and water have fallen out of the bottom of the pot."

I shouted, "Bring another pot. We'll collect the rice."

We collected most of it from the stove, and also some from the broken pot. We couldn't get it all, and we didn't have another pot to put it in. I watched over it so that the cats didn't get to it.

When Mother returned and saw the broken pot, she was very unhappy and angry. She muttered to herself, "Why did I leave this pot of rice? Why did I go to collect curry? Where will we get another pot? How much rice did we lose?"

Around mid-afternoon, Father returned from the quarries in an angry mood. He called Mother; she was asleep and did not hear him. Father kicked her with the sole of his foot; she stirred, but didn't awaken. He kicked her again and again, harder and harder. She awoke with a start, began to cry, and then screamed, "Traveling, traveling, returning from who knows where, kicking me, causing me to digest faster, like a snake swallowing a whole animal, not bringing any money, why don't you prepare your own food this afternoon? What do you want from me? Why are you waking me up? After giving everyone food, I was resting. Don't you understand anything? Just going on beating me, making me digest!" She used the disrespectful personal pronoun "tu" [you] while addressing him. He became so enraged that he smashed her in the face with his fists many times.

I couldn't stand watching this, so I called out, "Don't beat her more! Why are you beating her?" Instead of replying, he just turned around and stomped out of the house.

Just before evening, Father returned with some money. Handing it to Gurei, my small sister, he said, "Send it to Mother."

Mother waved it away, "Give it back," she said.

Father took it, went out, and bought rice. He then lit the stove and cooked the rice. Mother lay half asleep, pouting. She did not move to help him, or to help the small children. They cried. She turned a deaf ear. Father called her several times. She turned her head away. Then she said angrily, "Why did you beat me for no reason?"

That night Father gave the children their meal. Then he ate. Since we had no water to wash the dishes, Father fetched some, the task of women and children.

We heard the creaking sounds of a bullock cart. Then we heard Koki wailing and crying loudly, as a new bride is expected to do when returning home and remembering with affection her father's house. I limped out to see. Some women threw a cloth over Koki's head to shield her from the gaze of others, and as she stooped over, they led her into her father's house. Kalandi, the ward leader, moved the cart to one side of the road and carried inside the things Koki had brought from her father-in-law's house.

I awoke at midnight. Mother was asleep near me. I remembered that she had not eaten. To wake her up, I called, "I want to go out, I want to go out."

She asked me what I wanted, and I said "I want to eat something." I wasn't hungry; I planned to give it to Mother when she brought it to me.

She got up slowly, scraping the utensils. The room was dark. As she groped about for a lamp, I grabbed her sari.

"Why are you holding me?"

"No need for light, just feed me."

She fed me a bite or two. Then I turned my head away, "I'll not eat any more. You eat it."

She said, "No, I'm not going to."

I said, "Why are you so angry? If you are angry at Father, why do you refuse food? Are you angry at the food too?"

I forced her to take a bite. She resisted, finally took a bite, and ate the rest. She cleaned the dishes and returned to sleep.

But the next morning, Mother behaved the same way. She lay there, without talking to anyone, didn't cook, didn't even look after the children. I told my eldest sister, Santi, "Don't go to collect firewood in the forest today; stay at home."

Santi took over the household chores. But she cooked only curry, since Father had gone to the quarry without leaving money to buy fresh rice. That morning, Sister and the children ate watered rice. Grandfather was in another village visiting a relative.

Mother asked me, "Father didn't leave any money for food, so all we've got is watered rice; it is sour and you are ill, so you shouldn't have any. What will you eat?"

I said, "If nobody else eats, why should I?"

She said, "You are ill; you shouldn't starve. Think about what you can eat."

I said, "First make some tea; then we'll think about other food."

She asked, "Where is the money to buy tea?"

I gave my small sister Gurei one anna to buy tea and sugar, and I gave one anna to my Mother to buy some puffed rice. They bought these things and we ate it. Then Mother said to me, "What will we have for lunch? Why don't you arrange something?"

I replied, "What can I do?" We had no money in the house and no food. We all thought we would not be eating again until Father brought home some money.

At that moment Doctor Babu arrived. He asked me how I was. I said I was okay. He asked me if there was any other news. I replied, "What other news? Unhappy and happy, mostly unhappy. Today we are all starving. We've only had tea today, nothing else."

Doctor Babu inquired anxiously, "What! Is nobody cooking?"

I replied, "What will they cook? Perhaps my Father didn't earn anything yesterday, so he didn't buy any food or come home. Where will we get money to buy food? Grandfather went to visit a relative in another village. My father's wage brings us one meal a day. The other meals come from the earnings of others."

He gave my mother two rupees and said, "Prepare some fish curry."

I said, "Who is going to catch the fish? We never buy fish. Where would we get the money for that? You gave us money for rice, so we'll buy rice. Otherwise we couldn't have bought anything, and we would have starved, as we do often. We prefer to starve than beg."

He gave Mother another rupee for curry, and departed. I sent a boy in our ward to buy fish, potatoes, limes, ginger, and white onions. Mother and Sister Santi fried the fish and cooked a vegetable curry with these items. We ate. When Father returned, he walked all over the house. I called Santi and said, "Bring food to Father. He is

36. Bauri woman lights a cigar from the fire at an earthen hearth. The pot on the hearth contains newly harvested paddy, which is being boiled.

angry, so he won't ask for food. He might not know there's anything. He left early without leaving us any money. If he asks where we got the fish, tell him Doctor Babu sent it."

Santi called Father to eat. He said angrily, "I'll not eat."

Santi said, "I cooked it. Why won't you eat it?"

He shouted, "If you ask more and more, I'll beat you!"

Santi backed off, afraid. I limped over to him, and he agreed to eat. When he saw the fish curry, his eyes widened with suspicion. He said harshly, "I'll not eat this! Where did this curry come from?"

I said, "Doctor Babu sent the fish to me. We made the vegetable curry here."

Father was enraged, his pride was hurt. He shouted, "How does Doctor Babu know we have no curry?"

I said, "He didn't send it to our family, but to me because I am ill. We had no curry, so I shared it with everybody. I could have eaten it all alone."

He stood up angrily. I called to him, "Wait, why are you so angry? We didn't beg outside on the road. He sent it, we took it." My words did not soften his attitude. Due to the grace of God, Doctor Babu had helped us, but Father simply walked off angrily and sat by himself in another room.

Later on we found out why Father had no money and had been so angry for several days. The spot in the quarry where he was working was so soft that the stones broke, and he had earned no money from all his work.

A couple of days later, I supplied Doctor Babu with the girl he wanted: Koki. That first time, I watched them at work, out in the taro field in the evening. I hid behind a hedge where they didn't see me. Afterward, Koki went home, while Doctor Babu washed himself, using a water pot he had with him. Then he changed his clothes, borrowing one of my shouldercloths. When I saw why, I laughed. His own shoulder cloth was wet. He threw it in my face playfully and said, "It was very nice, thank you."

When I saw him the next morning, I turned my face away. He asked, "Why aren't you talking to me? Are you angry with me?"

I replied, "I'm not angry. I am shy to see your face. When you came today, a laugh came to my mouth."

He asked, "Why? What happened? You are not a woman hiding from a man. Speak up."

I said, "You are a man. I am also a man. I saw everything of your work last night, a doctor, out in the taro field. You put on my cloth, the cloth of a Bauri boy. You acted according to my directions, creeping into the field, and so I can't help laughing."

He said, "You may be laughing, but anyway, I must give you an injection and change the bandage on your foot."

I thought to myself, how funny it was that our positions had reversed. Respected Doctor Babu was pressing to treat me.

12. Dash Babu's "Hot Disease," 1949

When Dash Babu, the Brahman contractor, is afflicted with a venereal disease, he calls upon Muli to take care of him. As in previous incidents, a man of status becomes a pitiful object of ridicule, depending on Muli the Bauri to rescue him. Muli delights in playing up the contrasts: a man of ritual purity becomes the polluted carrier of putrid, loathsome pus; a haughty Brahman becomes a whimpering patient; a shy Bauri boy talks disrespectfully to a Brahman.

Nevertheless, Dash Babu ultimately gains the upper hand. To hide his shame from his caste and family, he persuades Muli, an untouchable, to do the degrading work of caring for him. Muli complies, for in a sense the Brahman is in his power. But Muli recognizes that he is still being treated like an untouchable; he expresses his resentment of this by resorting to passive resistance, asserting, for example, that he can neither bring the Brahman water nor wash the Brahman's dishes because he is a polluting untouchable.

One morning, as I was strolling down the road of my ward, Dasia came up to me and said, "Dash Babu wants you to meet him at the construction site."

I walked to the construction site. He was outside the shed.

I asked, "Why did you call me?" He wouldn't speak until we had entered the shed.

He said, "I feel very bad. I can't tell you, I have to show you."

He lay down, took off his dhoti and pointed to his prick. It was covered with boils. He put his dhoti back on.

"How can I be cured of this?" he asked. "It is a disease which is embarrassing to talk about or show to anybody. I called you because you will treat me; then I can become cured."

I said, "I know nothing about this disease. What can I do? Doctor Babu is your friend. You should call him, not me."

153

He said, "I cannot call him and let him know. I'd be ashamed to tell him directly. If you'll tell him, it would be better."

He gave me a rupee for tiffin and told me to find Doctor Babu. I said, "That's not enough! I'm very hungry; I haven't eaten since last night."

He dug around until he found four annas, which he handed to me. I walked to the hospital. Doctor Babu, who was inside treating patients, told me to wait outside.

The hospital consisted of one large stone room divided into partitions, and a thatch, tile, and mud hut some distance away for cholera patients. At the lunch break Doctor Babu called me to his house. I told him, "Dash Babu is ill on the bed, unable to move. He's calling you. Come quickly; otherwise he will die!"

Doctor Babu rushed to his bicycle. I hopped on too. On the way, Natia and Ghania of my ward saw me on the bicycle and called, "Where are you going?"

I called back, "To the station!" They stared at us as we sped down the road. It was rare to see a Bauri on a bicycle.

Doctor Babu rushed inside and saw Dash Babu asleep. He called to him, and Dash Babu replied promptly. Doctor Babu turned to me and laughed, "You said he was dying! Look how well he replies! Dash Babu, this man Muli took me away from my lunch saying you were dying. What a wicked man he is!"

I tore off Dash Babu's cloth. He tried to hide in shame, but it hurt to move, so he remained exposed. Doctor Babu looked at him, then said, "Oh, where did you get it? Why didn't you tell me you had it?" He was worried that he too might get it, because he had enjoyed Koki right after Dash Babu had. "Did you put on the cloth of somebody else who has this disease, or did you get it from someone?"

I did not understand what he meant. I knew nothing about those diseases at that time. Dash Babu was silent. Doctor Babu said, "You shouldn't neglect your treatment. Don't walk, don't ride your bicycle; just rest. Then the pus won't touch other parts of your body." He gave Dash Babu some tablets and an injection. Then the doctor called to me, "Muli, let's go."

Dash Babu called out, "Oh, Muli, if you stay with me and take care of me, you can earn some money without working hard. I can use you. I won't go home, but will remain here, so I can be cured faster."

I agreed, but told him I had to return for rehearsal every day. He told me to call his mother. I went to his family house in a nearby village and waited on the veranda until someone came by who could go in and call the mother. When she came to the door, I told her that her son was ill and remaining at the construction shed. I told her he couldn't move, so she'd have to see him there.

She changed to a longer sari and rushed to his side. "What happened to you?" she asked.

He replied, "It's inflammation of my lymph glands around my crotch. I went to a rural area, and that's where it occurred. All my muscles are stiff. I have fever. The doctor told me to lie still."

His mother said, "I'll bring a rickshaw and take you home. Who will treat you here? I can't treat you here and care for your two children."

Dash Babu quickly replied, "I will stay here for two or three days. Muli will look after me. Around here I can defecate and bathe easily; how can I do that at home? I'd rather stay here; send some food."

His mother said angrily, "You are very disobedient! What do you think you are doing! You never accept our advice. If you think that you'll stay here, well okay, let it be, we'll bring food." She left.

Turning to me, Dash Babu said, "My recovery is in your hands; you are my only hope for recovery. I depend on you."

I replied, "If I stay here all the time, how can the people in my house eat? My father and grandfather are removing soil from a new quarry site. I have been supporting the family during this time, since they don't receive wages until they begin quarrying the stones. Also, I must return for rehearsals."

Dash Babu assured me, "I'll see to it that you have no troubles, but you should not leave me for a moment. After I recover, if you have some difficulties, I'll help you."

Dash Babu's father walked in carrying a plate of food. I waited outside and listened. He asked his son, "What happened to you?"

Dash Babu said, "Due to too much cycling, the seat rubbed against my crotch; it bled and became infected. I have kept Muli here to help me. Doctor has also seen me and says that I'll be cured within three days. Also, bring food for Muli."

Dash Babu's father said, "I brought food for both of you." He wanted to give me food, but there was no plate or pot. He would not let me use their bell-metal plates because my use would pollute them. I could have used brass plates because they are used in temples and can be purified, but Dash Babu's father had brought only bell-metal. Dash Babu's father told me to bring a plantain leaf from a nearby Bauri ward.

I refused to go, saying, "I can't go; the leaves aren't available there."

He replied, "Then how will you eat? Will you eat off the ground?"

I said, "Yes, I can do that. The ground is fine. Let Dash Babu eat; then I'll find a place to eat."

Dash Babu ate. His father gave him water, and he cleaned his hands. Dash Babu told his father to bring back some clothes for his bed, a blanket, a water pot, a glass, and a brass pot for me. The old man stood up and left.

Then I cleaned off a section of the wooden cot, washed my shouldercloth, put it down like a leaf, and asked Dash Babu to put the food on it. After he did this, I ate. Then I said to him, "Tell your father not to bring me any more food. I am not going to eat like this again. I'd rather starve."

Dash Babu said, "I already told Father to bring you a brass pot; why are you so upset?"

I said, "Well, how am I supposed to sleep here? I have nothing with me but my shouldercloth."

He said, "After eating you may go to my house and tell my father to bring an old dhoti; you may sleep on that."

I said, "Why should I do that? This evening I'll go to my own house."

He cried, "Don't do that! If you go, I'll die! Why are you so angry at me? I'll arrange everything so that nobody will be angry if you stay here."

Then Dash Babu told me to clean the pots.

"But they are bell-metal," I said. "I'll pollute them."

"So what?" he replied.

I shrugged and took the pots to the small tank in the compound, and washed them. I brought back a bucket of water, one used by the cement maker, and washed the spot where I ate. Then we both chewed betel.

Dash Babu said, "You are unhappy because you took food on the shouldercloth. If my father had not been here, you could have eaten on our bell-metal."

I said, "No, I don't want that. If I eat with you I'll get sin." I was truly afraid that something bad would happen to me if I ate off those plates.

Dash Babu then said, "This wooden cot hurts me; what should I do?"

I said, "Use my shouldercloth."

He put it under him and slept. Later he woke me up and told me to massage his body. While I massaged him, his cloth tore away from the dried pus on his prick. He screamed, "Stop it! Stop it! The cloth is stuck. Separate it carefully."

I pulled it away gently. Then he said, "My costly dhoti will be ruined with bad stains if I use it here. I need instead a small cloth like a shouldercloth."

I made him stand up, gave him my shouldercloth, and put his dhoti on the cot as a sheet and cover. After I massaged him, he fell asleep. I walked out to the road, hoping to see someone from my ward to tell them I wouldn't go home tonight. I saw nobody. Dash Babu awoke late in the afternoon and asked for water. I told him to tell his father to bring a large clay pot full of water. Dash Babu became impatient. "I am willing to use the water you bring."

I replied, "How can I bring you water? You are a Brahman. I am a Bauri. If I bring the water for you, sin will come to me."

Dash Babu replied, "You talk like this, but you should remember the proverb, 'At a bad [difficult] time, God had held the feet of an ass; I am surely the lowest man.' You know the story from the *mahaa-bhaarata*. Krishna went to kill the demon Jarasandha, who was protected by an ass who could tell if a person were a friend or an enemy. If the person was an enemy, the ass would make a great noise, warning Jarasandha. When Krishna came to him, the ass made a loud sound. Krishna dropped down and touched its feet, saying, 'Please allow us to pass by this one time.' So God himself touched the feet of an ass. How could the ass deny this request? He let him in. Thus our Oriya proverb. If God can touch the feet of an ass when he's in difficulty, surely I can do the same when my bad time comes. Certainly this is my bad time. Who looks at caste differences at a time like this? Bring the water; you'll not get sin for that."

I said, "Okay," and brought him some water. He washed his face and rinsed his mouth; then he went outside to urinate. But his prick expanded and the skin burst. It hurt him a lot.

He called me, "Look what happened. The urine does not come out freely." I looked. The foreskin had stuck with pus, so the urine splattered on the boils, and he screamed in pain, "It's like being burned! Hold me, I can't stand the pain! I've never had pain like this! Give me poison! I can't stand it anymore. Better to die!"

I helped him back inside. I fanned the air near his prick with my shouldercloth. The cool air helped a bit. He wanted to sleep, but I told him not to, or he wouldn't be able to sleep that night. So he continued sitting as I fanned his prick.

I heard a sound at the gate. A stone quarry worker named Bira was waiting, along with two or three other men. I let them in, and Bira said to Dash Babu that he needed money for marketing.

Dash Babu said, "It's good that you came, but it's bad that I've got no money. I am ill. Manage today without me and I'll pay you a large amount on the next market day." Other men came to the gate, asking for money. Dash Babu turned them all away without money. A couple of the workers were from my ward, and Dash Babu told them that because I would stay to take care of him, I wouldn't be going home that evening.

Just before evening, as the great god Sun went red, I went to Dash Babu's house and brought a lantern. I massaged him again. He had severe pain in his groin, and he cried. He sent me to bring Doctor Babu.

Doctor Babu was at home. He said to me, "That kind of disease will give lots of pain. This disease usually comes from bad women or from using the cloth of a diseased person. If it's not cured now it will get worse later. I'll go to Dash Babu later."

I returned to the shed. Dash Babu was talking to someone. I crept up softly and listened. My father was in the room, so I entered.

Father said to me, "If you stay here, how will our household survive? Your grandfather and I are cutting away the mud in the quarry. I asked you to take care of the house. Instead, you stay here. Thanks to you, all my children are going hungry."

Dash Babu said, "Oh Hata, you have your father, and you also usually take care of your household. Why should Muli do it? He's a small boy. It is not at all good for the father to depend on a small boy. Take this five rupees and let him remain here. Send his drama book and a blanket."

My father didn't want me there; he recalled the gossip and the scandals involving Dash Babu, Koki, and me. But he could not reply because Dash Babu employed people in our ward, and gave money to me. My father silently took the money and departed.

Later that night Doctor Babu came by to look at Dash Babu's boils. The doctor told me to heat some hot water to wash the boils. We had no stove, no matches, no place to cook. I went to the market and bought matches, cigarettes for the doctor, and a large tin. Back at the construction site I dug a hole in the ground which I ringed with three stones. That would be my stove. I heated the tin full of water and gave it to the doctor. He put some powder in the hot water, let it cool down, and sprinkled some of the warm water on Dash Babu's prick. Dash Babu screamed, "No, no, I am dying, I am dying!" The boils became soft. The doctor pulled out some cotton from his bag and told me to hold Dash Babu's prick while he washed it. Doctor cleaned the prick. Then he absorbed the water with the cotton and threw some powder on the boils.

Doctor Babu said, "Tell me how you got this. If it was from Koki, I would have it too, so it must have been from someone else."

Dash Babu said, "What will I tell? It was from that sort of thing. Five or six years ago I loved a girl named Gauri, who lived in a Bauri ward of Bhubaneswar. She was married four years ago. A couple of days ago I went to see her again. Right after working with her, my prick had a burning sensation. Two or three hours later boils formed on my 'gold' [penis]."

Doctor Babu said, "You shouldn't go to her any more. The germs are only on the outside. If they go inside your organs, they will spread. Be careful. Continue the treatment even after the boils go away or you will not be fully cured. And don't go to other women. Oh, Dash Babu instead of spending lots of money on women, why aren't you getting married again? If you bring a woman to your house, it will cost you less. You won't have to go outside like this any more. You may ask me why I go outside when I have a wife. I go outside when I get a chance, but not for the love of a particular girl. Also, the money I spend does not come from my regular public hospital salary but from the extra income of private patients. You should think of how you could be if you had a wife. You won't get any more pain like this, either. You are spending money, going outside, and earning this disease."

Dash Babu said, "I didn't know she had it. I went to her many times and never got it."

Doctor Babu said, "Whatever may be, you should become cured

first. Then I will tell you something which will make you happy and will strengthen our friendship."

Dash Babu said, "Why don't you tell me right now? If you don't, I'll just remain anxious, wondering about it."

Doctor Babu said, "That which I'm referring to requires a lot of money. In Cuttack district, I know of a girl who will marry this year. Her family requested me to arrange a groom. I'll contact them on your behalf, and you may send your people to look at the girl."

The people of Dash Babu's community considered him, a widower with two children, too old to marry a fourteen- or sixteen-year-old girl. His two children were a problem, because if he married again and had more children, his new wife might not treat the first wife's children well. If he had not had children and had been a little younger, he would have had no trouble finding a bride. But no family in his area would marry their girl to him. He wanted a wife, so he gladly accepted the doctor's offer.

While the doctor and Dash Babu were talking, Dash Babu's father arrived, and Dash Babu introduced them. Then he told his father about Doctor Babu's offer.

The old father said, "Oh, we are poor. How can I take care of a rich daughter-in-law who has desires we cannot satisfy or afford? If you can find a poor girl, that would be good. I don't require a dowry, just the girl, and I will marry her to my son, even if she is the poorest there is."

Doctor Babu said, "Yes, I know a possible bride who is so poor that she's unable to get food or cloth. Her mother and father work as cooks in different houses, while the girl takes care of her younger brothers and sisters. I don't know whether you would want to arrange a marriage with that family."

The old father jumped around excitedly, "I want her! I want her! A rich girl will want expensive food and clothes; if she's dissatisfied with our standard of living, she will leave us, and nobody else will give a daughter as a third wife to my son because they will think we don't have enough food or things to satisfy a new wife. If the poorest possible girl comes, she will be very happy to live with us. She'll do the housework, and we'll be able to control her. Forget rich girls; get us a poor one. If you do that, God will bless you and your service should improve." Then he quoted a proverb, "The pen should be victorious," which meant that the doctor should be promoted in his government service.

The old man blessed Doctor Babu and left. The doctor motioned to me, and we walked out to the gate, where he asked, "Aren't your father and mother angry about your staying here tonight?"

I shrugged, "What can I do? He called my father, gave him money for food, and told me to stay. I obeyed him because I like him. But when I cleaned and touched the boils, I hated it. When I am about to eat and I think of it, I cannot eat; it makes me sick. Don't tell this to Dash Babu. He would feel bad."

Doctor Babu said, "I won't tell him, but I'm telling you that whenever you clean or touch his prick, wash your hands immediately afterwards with hot water. Keep some ready to use. Be *very careful* or you'll get this disease too—it's very contagious. If you're not careful, it will get in you. Don't wear Dash Babu's cloth."

After Doctor Babu left, I locked the gate and went inside. Dash Babu said, "You should eat. I kept some food for you in a brass bowl."

I waved it away, "I'm not hungry. You go ahead and eat."

As Dash Babu ate, he asked, "Why are you sitting? My father brought some cloth. Make up my bed. Take my old dhoti for your bed."

I prepared his bed, I cleaned his dishes, and I ate outside. I felt like throwing up.

Dash Babu called out, "Why are you eating so slowly? This morning you ate off your shoulder cloth. Now you've got a brass dish. What's the problem?"

I answered, "I ate too much this afternoon. I'm not hungry now."

"Will you throw away the rice?" he asked.

I said, "No, no, no. People don't get enough to eat. How can I throw it away? I'll eat everything."

I ate slowly. After finishing, I washed the dishes. He asked for betel, and I gave him some. Then he said, "I'm feeling restless; please massage me."

So I had to massage him. While I was doing this, a bad smell arose from his boils. I couldn't tell him that, but I wanted to see why his boils were producing a bad smell. So I said to him, "Let's see the boils."

He showed me. The pus was coming out like a waterfall. I told him that.

Then he asked, "What medicine did the doctor give me? The pus keeps coming and running out! I want to see it."

I gathered up some pus in my left hand and showed it to him. I went to wash my hand, found we had no hot water, went outside to look for some sand, and rubbed my hand in the sand.

After giving him another betel, I started to make up a separate bed for myself. He asked, "Why are you making another bed? Come and sleep on this cot with me."

I refused; he persisted. I said, "No, you are a Brahman. If I sleep on the cot with you, and my leg touches your body, it will be a great sin." I didn't want to tell him I wanted to avoid his infection.

"Why do you always talk about sin, sin, sin?" he said. "Come over here and sleep."

In the end I was forced to sleep on the cot. He slept by the wall; I lay on the edge side. But as I lay down I remembered the warning of the doctor. What could I do? I fell asleep. I awoke at midnight to find that Dash Babu's legs had spread apart and his left thigh had fallen across my right thigh. I slowly moved off the cot. I lay on the ground, thinking, "Doctor Babu told me to be careful, but I'm mixing more and more. If I get the disease, I'll get pain. But Dash Babu has money to spend on me, and Doctor Babu will treat me." I fell asleep. Late at night, Dash Babu woke me up.

"Muli, Muli, where are you?" he called.

I replied, "Why are you calling me? I'm sleeping here."

"Why did you go there? You were sleeping with me."

I said, "When I slept there, I found that I threw my leg on your body. It's a great sin. I was afraid."

Then he said, "Come outside with me while I urinate."

I took the lantern and went with him. While urinating, his boils burst. He screamed, "Oh, my boils burn! Urine is getting on them! Get some cloth, put it on the boils, and the cloth will absorb the urine."

I asked, "Where will I get the cloth? Use your own dhoti."

He said, "That will ruin it. Get something else, like a shoulder-cloth." He did not have one, but he knew that I did. That's why he mentioned it this way.

I replied, "No, no. I'm using my shouldercloth for my bed. Use your own cloth."

He used his own dhoti. I stood some distance away. When a man urinates, he hides his prick from public view. So I stood some distance away from him.

We went back inside and fell asleep. The next morning I bought some soap and washed all the clothes we had—everything except what we were wearing.

After we ate some tiffin, I cleaned the dishes. I was over by the gate when I heard a horrible scream coming from the room, like that of a six-month-old infant. I rushed back. Dash Babu was moaning and turning and tossing back and forth on the cot. He screamed, "Give me poison, I'll die now, I don't want to survive! Call my father and mother!"

I said, "What happened, why are you shouting?"

He interrupted me and screamed, "First hold me, then I'll tell. I'm unable to bear this pain!"

I held him. He cried more and more. I opened his cloth and fanned his crotch with my shouldercloth. Gradually, as the cool air reached him, he quieted down. I continued. Then I became tired and stopped.

He shouted irritably, "Why did you stop? Go on."

I continued, but my hands became tired. I slowed down, and he cried, "Keep going!"

My hands were so tired that a corner of the shoulder cloth fell out of my fingers and hit his prick. He screamed and thrashed about. "What have you done! You did this on purpose! Don't do it again! I'll die if you do."

He told me to bring Doctor Babu, who hadn't come there that day. I went to the hospital.

When Doctor Babu arrived, Dash Babu was lying stark naked. When he heard the doctor, he tried to cover himself in shame. I uncovered him, and the doctor looked at him. Then Doctor Babu told me to heat some water.

I asked, "What will you do with that water?"

Doctor Babu said, "The boils should be washed."

"Who will wash them?" I asked.

"Why, you will, Muli."

I said, "Do you think I am your compounder [pharmacist-helper]?" I fetched the water and heated it.

Doctor Babu said to Dash Babu, "This Muli is a good boy, but his language is very strong."

Dash Babu said, "No, no, what he says is good, although it is hard to tolerate. Whatever may be, he helped me a lot. By his help I was able to live."

The doctor sprinkled the hot water on Dash Babu's boils, which had reduced greatly since the day before. Doctor Babu cleaned the boils with water and powder. Dash Babu moaned, so I passed a comment, "Pray to the goddess Gauri. Why are you getting pain? If Gauri Devi [goddess] comes, all pain will be cured."

Doctor Babu laughed, "Gauri Devi is present in his prick."

The doctor then told me to hold Dash Babu's scrotum; he swabbed it with cotton and sprinkled it with powder. We washed our hands in hot water. Doctor Babu gave me oil with an awful smell to rub on my hands.

Doctor Babu said, "Your boils are not as bad today. Always sleep on your back; stay naked." Then he left.

Later Dash Babu's father came with food. After we ate, I gathered the dirty serving plates to carry them to the tank. It was dark. I carried so many dishes that I couldn't carry a lantern. I climbed down the steps of the tank, unable to see where I was going. On the last step, I lurched forward and all the plates flew out of my hands and fell clattering to the stones. Hearing the noise, Dash Babu ran with the lantern, calling out, "What happened?"

I said, "I fell in the dark."

He said, "Why didn't you take the lantern?"

I answered irritably, "How could I? I was holding all the dishes with both hands."

I collected all the dishes—except two that had fallen in the tank. I washed them while Dash Babu waited by the lantern. Then we returned to the shed, and I massaged him before he fell asleep. I washed my hands in cold water and lay down to sleep.

Like this I took care of Dash Babu for several days while he suffered with the hot disease. One morning I asked him to let me leave. He had improved, so that he could walk around and take care of himself. He said, "No, wait until this afternoon." I waited until evening, but he said nothing more, so I finally said, "I'm going," and left without receiving his permission.

Part Three

The Reluctant Householder

13. Muli's Inauspicious Marriage, 1950–52

Grandfather Dharma arranges Muli's marriage with a fourteen-year-old girl named Kia. Although the horoscopes of the bride and groom do not match, Muli's grandfather and Kia's father insist on holding the ceremony because they are friends. Kia's father dies two days before the scheduled ceremony. Muli's grandfather is supposed to postpone the wedding for one year to give the dead man's spirit time to leave the house, but instead, he insists on holding the ceremony thirteen days after the burial, even though that day is inauspicious. Muli complains that his marriage has been doomed to be unhappy because of his grandfather's disregard of custom. Muli fails to acknowledge that his own irresponsibility might contribute to his marital woes.

The marriages both of Muli and his sister Santi illustrate the flexibility of the marriage selection process. Disregarding the rule of village exogamy as well as the objections of Muli's mother, Grandfather Dharma arranges Santi's marriage with Damodar, a man from her own village. Grandfather Dharma reasons that the prospective groom is a responsible man of good behavior who has a steady job as a skilled mason—characteristics that outweigh other criteria (see Mayer 1960:202–207 for a further discussion of the criteria of selection for marriage). Grandfather Dharma's assessment of the groom turns out to be excellent: Damodar is a good provider, a stable family man, and a dependable source of support when Grandfather's family encounters crises.

In Muli's narrative, Grandfather Dharma usually appears as a level-headed leader who bases his decisions on rational calculations. Although Muli never says so, Grandfather Dharma probably perceived qualities of dependability and stability in Muli's prospective bride and family that prompted him to disregard the ritual prohibitions that Muli considers so important.

When I was eighteen years old, Grandfather Dharma arranged the bethrothal of my sister Santi to Damodar, a man from another ward of our village. Mother objected to the match. "To marry within the village is not good," she said. "Everybody knows too much about a girl and her bad habits. Remember the proverb, 'A village bride has snot in her nose.' "

Mother also complained that Damodar was too old for Santi, and that he was dumping his first wife to marry my sister. Nevertheless, Grandfather Dharma insisted on negotiating the marriage with Damodar. "He's a good boy, young and hardworking. His behavior is *dosaraa* [set apart from others]. He's got a good job and income as a mason, and besides, he's good-looking. He's got lots of years left."

Grandfather Dharma hired a Brahman astrologer, who checked the horoscopes of Santi and Damodar and then announced that the match was a good one. Hearing this, Mother shrugged and recited a proverb, "If the chalk [diagrams of horoscopes] matches, Mother is satisfied." So our future in-laws came to our house for the ceremony of *bohuu dekhaa* [looking at the daughter-in-law for the first time] and settled the marriage of my sister.

One year later, Grandfather Dharma also arranged my marriage, despite the objections of everyone in my family. One day, Grandfather announced, "I saw a girl from Orakali. I think this year we'll marry Muli to her."

Father said, "We have no money; how can we do it? Last year we had a marriage. How can we do another one so soon?"

Grandfather said, "He should marry now. Do you think he should wait 'til he's an old man?"

Grandfather put the pressure on by talking. Then, without asking anyone, he went to the girl's house and brought back her father, Hadu Das, and the girl's horoscope.

Grandfather treated Hadu Das well. He went to Udayanath the astrologer, who compared the girl's horoscope with mine. They did not match; the marriage should not take place, or inauspicious things might happen. The men refused to accept this. Instead, they went to another astrologer, who inspected the two horoscopes and announced, "They do not match." Since Grandfather Dharma and Hadu Das had become good friends, they promised to hold the marriage anyway. To seal their agreement, they took an oath and then exchanged sacred food before a witness, the deity of Krishna in the village temple of Sakhigopal.

This is not really an alternative to having horoscopes match; the two men just thought it up. My marriage has been an unhappy one. Often my wife and I don't talk to each other; often we don't agree

—and it's all due to this bad thing, getting us married when our horoscopes did not match. Even my father did not want me to marry that girl, but he had to accept it because his father had promised me to that girl before Krishna.

The day that Hadu Das and Grandfather Dharma returned from Sakhigopal, Mala the wrestler came to our house and asked Grandfather if he would like to work with him jointly as a sharecropper. Mala said he could get seven or eight acres as a sharecropper, but needed help for that many acres. He said, "If you agree, we'll cultivate together and jointly share the share. But your grandson must work as my farm servant."

Grandfather didn't want me to work as Mala's servant because he feared that I didn't know enough about cultivation; but if he didn't offer me, Mala might not keep him as a joint sharecropper. So reluctantly he accepted Mala's request. Now he was pleased because a marriage would take place. And he decided that the marriage proposal had brought him this paddy, that his sudden new job as a joint sharecropper was a blessing from the deity of Sakhigopal.

From that day I worked with Mala as his servant. Since the land was not yet ready to be plowed, Mala sent me to work transporting stones by bullock cart from the quarries. I was paid a *gouṇii* [four kilos] of paddy per day.

Rain fell between the end of Magh [January-February] and the beginning of Phagun [February-March]. We have a proverb: "If rain falls at the end of Magh, thanks to that king, thanks to that country." And we have another proverb: "Water is not raining; gold is raining."

We believe that if rain falls at the end of Magh, the crop will be very good. I was in the quarry at the end of Magh and it rained. A couple of days later I started plowing the fields. Mala went with me to cut the weeds at the banks of the fields. I plowed; he cut the growths from the banks. I always feared in my heart; my heart thumped. If I make a mistake, Mala will give me a slap and I'll die! Nobody is here to save me. I greatly feared Mala, the strong man and great wrestler. When I first went with my father to the jointly held sharecropping fields, I wasn't afraid because Father was there. When I made a mistake, Father would correct and instruct me. Like that I continued my life there.

In the rainy season, during ceremonies like *khudurukuṇii* or *dutiiaa-*

osaa my family was supposed to send many things to my proposed wife's house. This was called the *dutiiaaosaa bhaara* [the shoulder bar that carries the gifts at the *dutiiaa* festival]. This ceremony is always very expensive. Since this was the first year of the relation between the two families and we were sending things for the first time, they had to be very good. For *dutiiaaosaa* we sent one good silk sari, some sacred food, cheese, twenty coconuts, a large bunch of plantain, two types of pumpkin, brinjal [eggplant], cucumber, taro, papaya, green plantain, lentils, and some cosmetics—red powder, red dye for painting one's feet, black eye-paste, coconut oil, toothbrush sticks, some scents, and some soap.

For the festival of the mother-goddess Khudurukuni, we sent fried pressed rice, *khai* [parched paddy, used as a sweet], coconut, sugar cane molasses, and rice powder.

But this season it would have been impossible to send all this to my future wife's house because we simply didn't have the money, so we took a loan on faith from Mala, who gave us the money because we were working with him. But at the time of *kumaara puurṇimaa*, at the end of the month of Aswin [September-October], it was hard for us to send the entire set of gifts because there was no work available for us, as is usually the case at this time of the year, and we had to borrow all the money.

This was a bad year. We were in great need; we couldn't earn, yet we had big expenses. I did not work at all during the October *dasaharaa* festival season, when nobody worked and employers didn't hire other workers.

At other times, I worked every day. I got very tired and looked terrible. I was weak and in ill health.

Four or five days after the month of Kartik [October-November] had started, I became ill. I did not take medicine for four or five days because I thought I would improve automatically. Instead, the disease got worse. I told Father to get some medicine from Doctor Babu. Father was afraid to go because he had no money, but I told him, "Just say you need medicine for Muli; Doctor Babu will give you some; he is a friend of mine." I didn't tell Father that Doctor Babu was a friend because I supplied him with Bauri girls. Father didn't ask, but brought me medicine.

After a few days I recovered a little. I heard that people were catching fish in the river and in the paddy fields. I couldn't stand it; I was inside the house while others were catching fish outside! So I went after them and stood in the water catching fish. I did this for a couple of days, but since I was not yet well, I became ill again.

Although Father brought some more medicine from Doctor Babu, I did not recover. For four months Doctor Babu treated me free of charge, but I made no improvement. [Muli may have had typhoid.] I could not move from the bed; I defecated and urinated on it, not even knowing when I did so. I could not eat, but only drink liquids. I became thin and weak. Father did not want to continue with treatments from Doctor Babu, so I stayed home another month without medicine.

Now it was harvest season. Many times I thought to myself that I had worked hard to plant the crop and make it grow, but someone else was cutting and getting the profit. I felt very bad about that.

About that time, a Mallia landowner saw me and told my father to consult an herbalist doctor named Sridhar, who used roots, fruits, skins, leaves of plants—only natural medicines for all diseases. We needed money for treatment. Father told Grandfather to borrow some money from Mala. As he had done throughout the year, Mala lent us some money, as well as the use of their bullock cart to carry me. People carried me to the cart, and accompanied me along with my father and grandfather. I don't remember anything about it. I felt I was being carried, but I didn't know by whom. I could not even think, where am I going, what am I doing? All I knew was that someone was sitting near my head. Once I looked up and asked, "Where are we going?"

Whoever sat next to me replied, "We're not going anywhere, just around the Old Town."

Under this herbalist doctor's treatment I recovered a little, but not much. Now I could recognize people. I understood that my parents were giving me food: *saagu* [sago] and barley.

When I tried to talk, many people gathered to hear me because my speech was strange.

After a while I could sit up and talk well. To defecate, I would go to the courtyard, helped by people in the house. Once in a while I would see my future father-in-law; I could not recognize him, but others told me who he was. He brought me sago and barley. So I tried to greet him by lying on the ground. He told me not to. "There is enough time to do that later." Then he fed me sweet water.

Mother said, "He comes almost every day. He wants to stay with you. He likes you a lot. He has supplied you most of the food and drink you are taking."

I remained like this in the house, neither completely cured nor completely ill. Finally, Grandfather took me to Jagamara village, near the Khandagiri hills. The leader of that village, a rich and famous herbalist curer, gave me medicine, and I gradually became cured.

It was the end of March, the time of harvesting *muga* lentils [green-gram, a variety of lentil]. My father-in-law came often. When he saw that I had recovered, he said to Grandfather, "Let's hold the marriage as soon as possible."

Nobody in my house wanted to get me married that year because of money problems and my bad health. But nobody could deny Hadu Das's request because he had helped me so much. Grandfather would say, "Yes," every time Hadu Das asked, but Grandfather never said just exactly when he'd do it.

At the time of the Lingaraj chariot festival [March-April] (see Freeman 1977b), Hadu Das tried to get us to settle the marriage day. Grandfather said, "See, friend, Muli is no longer my grandson, but rather he's your son now. You gave him life; so we have no claim on him. Don't worry; the marriage will definitely be held this year. But you see that we are poor now. We have not yet received our paddy —it hasn't been separated from the straw—so how can we hold a ceremony? Where will we get money for ornaments? Please wait 'til we can buy some."*

*Muli described changes in harvesting dates. "In the old days, we didn't finish separating straw and paddy until April or May, while these days we finish by February. In the old days, before 1964, we cultivated a lot of *muga* and *biri* lentils immediately after the rice harvest; so we delayed separating rice and straw. But in 1964 India was infested with a large locust called *pangapaaḷa*. They had never been seen before and came in great numbers. They ate up all the green plants. To kill them, the government supplied a huge amount of insecticide. When those locusts traveled, it was like a cloud.

"Our crops were destroyed completely. The next year, a kind of larva, a cater-pillar, ate the plants. For three or four years in a row we lost everything; even the seeds were eaten. So people grow *muga* lentils only on very good lands now, figuring that if all goes well, they can get a high yield. They don't bother working with inferior lands where the yield is less. Now we have more free time, and separate straw from paddy earlier now. Also: the monsoon has changed. In the old days it used to rain in the middle of Magh [January-February] month, but now this

Father-in-law agreed to wait until the month of Jyesta [May-June], and we agreed also to hold the ceremony then. Hadu Das said, "Why should I bother about the ornaments? If you prepare thousands of rupees' worth of ornaments for my daughter, I'll not get a single paise from it. You may give her ornaments or not. Any ornaments you make will come to your own house. If we are friends, and one knows the difficulties of others, what good will ornaments do?"

But Father thought, "How can I celebrate my first son's marriage without ornaments, without decorations, without showing high status?"

Then Father heard that Uncle Ghania's son-in-law had sold some dry land for a lot of money. Father went to him to get some help. Ghania's son-in-law agreed to give half the cost of some ornaments. He asked what my father planned to give.

Father said, "Wide, round bracelets made of silver." Silver was rare for our people; only Kalandi's son's wife had received silver ornaments among the people of our ward. We were trying to match our gifts with those of Kalandi. Usually we simply gave gifts of bell-metal. Father said he wanted a shark ornament made of silver, a silver armband, a silver bracelet, and a silver ring. We paid about fifty or sixty rupees for them. Only later did we find out that the Goldsmith had overcharged us: the cost of making the ornaments should have been one-fourth of the cost of the silver.

Father also wanted to buy cloth at the market, but none was available except in the government-controlled market, where you could buy only one cloth at a time.* To get a bale of cloth, Father went to my uncle's house and requested him to get some cloth with the permission of the village leader. Father said he had received a permit from the village leader, but we had to go to Badagad village, two miles away, to get the cloth.

To meet the rice expenses of the marriage ceremony, Grandfather Dharma borrowed paddy from Mala. The sharecropped paddy was not yet ready, not yet separated from the straw. Mala gave some paddy in advance.

After all these arrangements, our marriage ceremony started. For

---

is rare. People don't plow in February as they used to, since the land isn't softened by rain."

*At one time the government also controlled the sale of cloth, kerosene, matches, and sugar, because these things were in short supply.

the negotiation ceremony Damodar, my new brother-in-law, came by. When Father asked him for help, he gave fifteen rupees plus the other usual friendly gifts. The custom at marriages is that friends give gifts. Father bought spices and oil with that money.

We sent an invitation plus a gift of betel nuts to all our friends; the girl's house did the same. During this time, I also worked separating paddy from straw in Mala's crop when it was ready, and then I separated the paddy crops of other people.

It was summer, dry and hot. Yet two days before my marriage, it rained heavily. My father-in-law went to catch fish at a pond, got cold and wet, and became quite ill. My father and grandfather brought him two or three rupees' worth of food, along with some clarified butter. My father-in-law did not look so bad. But the next day, suddenly, we heard the news: Father-in-law had died. His stomach had bloated up with air. No stool or urine passed. No air passed through his rectum. His neighbors put him on a cart and rushed him to the hospital, but he died on the road near the high school. His neighbors stopped the cart, and one of them informed us. We went to see him and cried. His neighbors took Hadu Das back to his house for burial. My grandfather went along.

Grandfather saw that nobody was directing the funeral. Someone must call the ward leader and the Bauri priest and do other required tasks, such as get new cloth. Hadu Das had left behind a daughter [whom Muli married] and a small son. My future wife's maternal uncle refused to help with the burial because it would cost him money. So the people of Hadu's ward requested my grandfather to cover the expenses. Grandfather Dharma said to the priest, "Do the work; I'll pay the entire cost." The priest supplied the cloth and did the ceremony.

The people said to Grandfather, "Take the girl to your home at the end of the twelfth day of the funeral. There is no reason for her to stay here any longer."

Grandfather said, "Who will give her away in marriage?"

Her uncle said, "I'll do it."

We postponed the marriage until the thirteenth day after the death of Hadu Das. We sent invitations to our relatives. It is the custom that if there is a death in the family of high people such as father, mother, grandfather, grandmother, then no other ceremony should be held for one full year because the spirit of the dead stays at the house until the first anniversary of the death. The spirit of the dead, who stays in the bodies of all the family members for a full year, will do bad things, so people should avoid performing ceremonies during that first year.

Since we did not want to wait a year, my bride's maternal uncle adopted her, changing her *gotra* [lineage]. Thus the spirit of the dead left her.

However, the day we selected for marriage was not considered auspicious by the astrology book. The people in her village said, "If you don't take the daughter soon, she will be unhappy here."

Grandfather told us his problem. "What can I do? I promised before the deity Krishna that I would marry this girl to my grandson. I must keep my promise. If I don't, it will be a sin for me, for my grandson, and for seven generations to come. I must keep my word. We must prepare for the marriage on the thirteenth day because it's the first day after the twelve-day mourning period."

My father agreed unhappily, and we went ahead with the preparations.

The relatives criticized our highly unusual behavior: "Why are you performing this marriage on a bad day? Do you think if you wait a couple more days your son will be too old to get girls to marry him?"

My new brother-in-law then added, "Not only is the day inauspicious, their horoscopes don't match!"

Although everybody laughed at us mockingly, and our relatives disapproved, we went ahead with the marriage.

The hereditary priest of my caste conducted the ceremony [see Appendix B]. Three nights later, he performed the ceremony of the "modesty sacred fire" that nobody should see, the ceremony for the two people sleeping together. The ceremony began when my maternal uncle and my bride's maternal uncle each gave the priest one anna. The deputy leader's wife covered me and my bride with a big cloth. The priest began a sacred fire ceremony. Following his instructions, we placed our right hands in a bowl of turmeric water. The priest warned us, "Don't take your hands away from the pot." Inda, the deputy leader's wife, gave us the bowl and placed our hands in it. The priest continued the ritual. When finished, he called two more people to bring a new cloth, with which they would cover

37. The photo is of high-caste persons, but the actions shown resemble those Muli described. The groom sits next to the bride, who is covered completely with a cloth because she is considered both pure and vulnerable to evil spirits. Among high castes, the Barber and the Barber's wife attend to the groom and bride. Among the Bauris, the roles of the Barber and his wife are taken by the hereditary ward leader and his wife.

the sacred pot or pitcher while holding their fists with thumbs up. The cloth rested on their thumbs. While they held the cloth, the priest wrapped a piece of yarn around their thumbs fifteen or twenty times, then sang a song from the epic of the *raamaayaṇa*. The priest said to the two boys holding the cloth, "If you don't give me a donation, I'll not let you go." Father gave a donation for them.

During all this, from the starting of the sacred fire until the opening of the sacred pot or pitcher—taking the cover away from the pitcher—my bride and I had to remain under our cloth. It took more than an hour. During that time, we played jokes with each other. We call this "pinching back and forth." People frequently do this beneath the covering cloth.

Our right hands were together in the turmeric pot. First, I squeezed her fingers, but I got no reply. I did this several times. Finally, I placed my finger in her palm, with my thumb on the back of her hand. Then I squeezed very hard. Then she pressed her fingers on my palm. I stopped for a while. Then she caught hold of my index finger with her fingers and wouldn't let go. I was in pain, so with my left hand I pinched her waist. She jumped. The deputy leader's wife called, "Oh, priest, you should finish your song quickly. Our children are getting pain by sitting so long. You should be more civil by stopping the song here."

We stopped our pinching for a while. Suddenly I found that she was looking at me out of the corner of her eyes. But when I looked at her, she quickly looked away. I put my left hand on her left upper arm. She replied by placing her left hand on my right thigh. I pinched her hand. She grabbed my fingers as she had done before. It hurt! I tried to tickle her waist, but she moved away so that I couldn't do it, so I thrust my left hand into her crotch. She started suddenly and the cloth fell off us! The priest said, "Oh, children, sit quietly and carefully. Wicked children! My song is going to end. Wait a bit."

Inda covered us again and said to the priest, "Why don't you finish quickly?"

There we were again under the cloth. This time she tried to make me jump because I had tried to make her jump. She tried to poke me in the side, but this left her breasts exposed, so I quickly grasped one. She straightened up and forgot about poking me in the side. Then she suddenly jabbed my side again. It went on like this for an hour. Suddenly the song ended; the priest turned to my father and said, "Who will see [recognize] the bride and groom. Come."

Father brought Grandfather to the altar. The priest said, "Do you want to take your bride and groom?"

Grandfather Dharma said, "Yes."

Inda placed a wooden seat for Grandfather. The priest said, "If you want to take your bride and groom, it will cost you money."

Grandfather Dharma said, "Yes, I'll give."

The priest said, "Tell me the names of the seven generations of your ancestors."

Grandfather mentioned as many ancestors as he could remember, his father, grandfather, and great-grandfather. The priest filled in the remaining generations with the names of deities.

"What is your *gotra*?" asked the priest.

"*Mahaanachuaan* [the great untouchable]," said Grandfather.

"Who is that groom? How is he related to you?"

"He is my grandson."

"Who is your son?"

"Hata is my son."

"Why did you come?"

"I have come to take my son [groom] and *bohuu* [daughter-in-law]."

"Give me my money—fifteen rupees."

Grandfather gave him two rupees.*

The priest refused to take it. Grandfather gave him a little more money. [Bargaining is part of the ritual.] Then the priest said to Inda, "Take off the covers."

The deputy leader's wife said, "Why should I? Who will give me my gift? You got your things; who will get things for me? Until you do, they stay here."

Grandfather said, "What is your gift?"

"My gift is a sari."

Grandfather gave her two rupees. "What will I do with two rupees?" she asked. "If you give me two rupees, I won't be able to keep it. My son or daughter will take it. I'll take a sari, and with that will be able to remember you always."

Grandfather Dharma gave her a sari. She first patted my bride to warn her; then she removed the cloth.

The priest asked, "Did you get your bride and groom?"

Grandfather said, "Yes."

The priest then called out, "If anybody wants to do the ritual lamp waving, come. Is there any relative from the bride's side? They should come first." My wife's uncle stepped forward and offered me a silver ring. The priest gave him some unparboiled rice and *duba* grass to throw on our bodies, and while he threw them the priest recited incantations. Then my relatives did the waving of light, and Inda did it. The priest blessed us, throwing rice and grass on our bodies, and that ended the light waving rituals.

*The amount is unlikely (too high)—this was a joking donation. The entire donation for all the rituals probably was not over two rupees.

Inda now took us to the kitchen. Two leaves were there, just as in the morning. The leaves contained cake, *biri* lentils [black gram], and rice, but no fish. Then, as in the morning, we gave offerings to the sacred northeast corner, the *isaana* or *aisaana*. We offered food to the ancestors and the gods. I gave offerings seven times, my wife five times. Then we both offered water together. I ate and then left. My bride ate from my leaf and her own.

Inda arranged our bed. While doing this, she called me and said, "How many rupees have you kept to offer to your bride today?"

I replied, "I have nothing. Where will I get something to give?"

She said, "If you don't give today, how will she like you? Today you should pay something to her so that she will like you best."

I said to Inda, "Oh, 'elder brother's wife,' you should tell me something for tonight. I don't know what to do, how to do it. You should teach me." [Her teaching role is customary.]

She replied, "If you have no money, take my eight annas. I'll get it back from your father." I accepted the money. She continued, "I know how you have behaved from the very beginning of your marriage. She is wearing ornaments; don't break them. Don't think that she's sugar cane molasses and that you'll swallow her. What you do in the night, do slowly, so that no sound comes from the room. Many relatives will be in the adjoining rooms. Be careful to prevent noise, but don't try to sleep tonight! Enjoy her until the last of your strength!"

Then she pointed and said, "Stay there, I'll bring her." I looked at the bed. It was made up from the mat from the altar, on top of which rested a simple cloth and two pillows. I sat down and waited.

Several women dragged my bride into the room. She resisted. They pushed, dragged, and pulled her. Then they closed the door and locked it from the outside.

She stood by the door. I had no courage to call her to the bed. I waited for some time. Then I went over to her to pull her to the bed. She resisted. I dragged her against her will. I tried to talk with her, but she averted her face and covered it with a cloth. Forcibly I kissed her and tore away the cloth from her face. I called her with a soft voice. She did not reply. I told her many things. No reply. By this time we were facing each other, but she kept her eyes closed. I forcibly attempted to do "work" with her. After the first work she relaxed a little and replied to my questions. Then I gave her two rupees and eight annas. We talked some more, then "worked" again three or four more times that night.

Near the end of the night, Inda came and called her: "Oh, Daughter-in-law, oh Daughter-in-law." She was calling her to accompany her to the bath. Inda also called my mother. At this time my wife left.

Inda came to me and said, "Bathe at the deity's tank [Kapileswar tank]. Then greet the deity by lying down and touching your forehead to the ground. Take some money for sacred food. Give it to any Mallia priest, and he'll bring you sacred food and sacred flowers." She handed me some money given to her by my mother.

Inda and my bride—aged fourteen—went to the Gangua River to bathe. Inda took with her all of our cloths and mats used the night before, and she washed them.

When I returned from the temple tank, the *kuniaa* people [the relatives of my bride] were just awakening. My father gave them oil and toothbrush sticks and later brought them snacks. The priest took snacks first, then the bride's relatives, then me. The priest then asked for his "end of ceremony payment." Grandfather gave him rice, lentils, vegetables, cloth, and some money. The priest asked for more money. Grandfather said, "Take this money now. Bless my children. If they are happy, they'll pay you more later."

The priest and the bride's relatives left. I went to the hall to rest; I was tired from last night. Teacher saw me and said, teasingly, "Why does your face look narrow and long? Why aren't you cheerful? Why aren't you laughing? What happened to you?"

I said, "Don't you know what happened to me last night? Nothing happened. Why do you ask?"

"If nothing happened to you," he said, "let's ask other men their opinion—whether you have reduced your health or not."*

"Don't argue with me," I replied, "I want to get some sleep. I didn't get any last night." I turned toward the wall and fell asleep.

*He assumed that the loss of semen led to weakening, loss of health and fitness. This is a widespread belief among Hindus (see Carstairs 1967:83–88).

14. Traveling with Lakhi the Prostitute, 1953

Shortly after Muli's wedding, a woman named Lakhi seduces him and goes to work as his prostitute. Meanwhile, his new bride remains in her parental house, several miles away. A building contractor hires Muli and Lakhi as unskilled laborers, and also propositions Lakhi. Although Lakhi acquiesces, the incident highlights the plight of Bauri women who must work as unskilled laborers, earning low wages and subjected to sexual exploitation.

A few days after my wedding, I went to the stone quarry with my father. I worked for an hour. I was lifting a stone from the ground, when suddenly the end of my father's pickaxe broke. Father told me to get it repaired at a nearby village. I cut across the field and passed near the shrine of the untouchable Sweepers. Someone had drawn a single word in big black letters on the whitewashed wall of the shrine; the word was *mailaa* [dirty].

When I reached the village, I saw Lakshmi or Lakhi the flat-chested, waiting at the Blacksmith's shop. She spoke to me. "Oh, brother, why have you come to this place?"

I said, "My tool broke; I'm getting it repaired. Why did you come?"

She said, "The blade of my small sickle is dull and needs sharpening. What will you do with your axe now? It's afternoon—do you think you'll go back and work now?" Before waiting for my answer she continued, "Don't go now. Come to my house; take some watered rice. We'll cut some grass together, then you can go back."

I accepted her offer; we went to her house, where I left the axe. Then we went out to the field and cut the grass. After a while she asked me to take a betel. I went over to her. She sat on the bank of the field, but in such a way that she showed her *yoni* [vagina].

I said, "What's this, Lakshmi? What are you showing me?"

She replied, looking around, "What, what, where, where?" She looked about her body in such a way as to expose her body further. Then I placed my finger in her vagina—to show her.

"See, see, what is this!" I said.

She asked, "Oh, what are we doing? I address you as brother. Why are you putting a peg in my vagina? You call me sister. It is not a good thing to do that. If I'll pull your peg [prick], what will be the relation between us? It would be improper."

I said, "Who is doing anything improper? How can you believe that wax near a fire won't melt? If a young girl shows her vagina or her breast to a young man, how will he suppress his heat when he's alone with her?"

I pressed her breast. She moved toward me and fell on me as if she was shocked. Then I pulled her and without saying a word "worked" with her.

At the end of my work she said, "You are not a good man. I called you for your benefit. But you behaved badly."

I replied, "I am not a bad man; you are not a bad woman. I know why this thing happened."

"Why?"

"What can I say? If I'll tell you, you will want me always to remain with you. I have lots of gentleman friends. If you'll ever meet them, you'll never forget them. Now sell this bundle of grass and buy snacks for me. In the meantime, I'll cut another bundle. When you return, I'll tell you all about my abilities."

She sold the grass and brought back puffed rice and a fried sweet. She said, "Now, tell me about your abilities."

We saw on the bank. I ate the puffed rice, then told her about all the babus I had known—Dash Babu, Bihari Babu, Doctor Babu—and then I said, "If you go with me, you'll not work. You'll simply sleep on the bed a couple of times, and you'll get your daily wage plus good food, "snow" [a cosmetic white face cream], powder, and scented oil. You'll forget your grass cutting work."

She said, "Yes? Do you have friends like this? If you'll take me to meet them, I'll be very happy. What we'll earn, we'll both share. Let's start tomorrow. Tell me where I can meet you."

I said, "I'll meet you early in the morning at the Fisherman's bazaar."

When I reached home in the evening, Mother scolded me, "Your father is searching for you! He went to the Blacksmith and to your sister's house, but where were you? Oh, you'll be beaten by your father now!"

I said, "Give me some food first. Then I'll tell you where I was."

She pushed food in front of me and said, "Eat and get out of here fast before your father comes!"

I said, "When I returned to the stone quarry, Father had already left. On the way home, I saw some herdsmen boys playing around a banyan tree. I sat there for a while and dozed. I've just returned from that place."

It was a lame lie, and she knew it. She said, "Well, leave quickly nonetheless. At night, your father will be less angry. Come back then."

I left. Later that night, I told Father the same story. He scolded me and told me, "If anybody had taken our axe while you dozed, how would we have earned any money?"

The next morning, I told Mother, "I'm not going to the quarry today, but to some work outside the village."

I met Lakhi at the Fisherman's bazaar. But where should I go? I hadn't told anyone I would be coming, although all of them had requested that I bring them a new girl. I thought about Doctor Babu. No, he would be busy at the hospital. Dash Babu would be working in the quarry. So I took her to Bihari Babu at the railway station rest-house. He was absent. We waited. He returned, and I told him I had a new girl for him. He was busy, so he gave me the key to one of the rooms, and Lakhi and I waited for him inside.

I said to Lakhi, "This babu is a very rich man. You should talk to him respectfully. You should not give your body easily. Protect it first, so that he will not think you are a corrupted girl."

I went out and sat on the veranda. Bihari Babu came by and asked "How did you get this girl here on a day which was not arranged?"

I thought up a quick answer. "Just when I went to defecate, I saw her. She comes from a different ward. When I asked her to go to work, she agreed. Then I dragged her here. She doesn't know what the work is."

He ordered snacks for Lakhi and me. Then he entered the room. I went outside and waited for two hours. Finally he came out and called me. "Where did you get this person? She's good to work with.

She has great stamina to bear the pressure. I think she's had practice in this work. Otherwise, she would have been in pain today because I 'drank' too much. I climbed her for over an hour. She never was unhappy, never had pain. Rather she was pleased. She is very expert, with a great deal of stamina. For work she's good. But she's not very pretty. Her skin is not good—it's dark."

I said, "If she is good for work, what will you do with the color?"

"No, I don't care about the color," he said. "What will you do now, go or stay longer? If you stay, I think I'll try to 'fight' one more time. It is good to do. If you want to stay, I'll order a meal for you."

I said, "If you want us to stay, how can we go? Arrange some food for us and we'll stay."

His servant brought us two vegetarian meals and two pieces of fish. We ate in that room. I asked her, "How do you like these things, snacks, meals, satisfaction?"

She said, "It's good."

I went outside, telling her to wait for Bihari. While he "drank" again, I slept under a mango tree. In the late afternoon, I returned to Bihari's office. He handed me three rupees and said, "See, today I don't have much money; I'm in a hurry and don't have time to talk, so go home now."

The next morning, we again started aimlessly. She said, "Let's go—going, going, we'll get a good customer, no doubt."

We took the airport road. Near the railroad crossing, a contractor met us and asked us, "Do you want to go to work?"

I said, "Yes, where?"

He said, "Unit three." That's near the legislative assembly building in the new capital.

We agreed. Nowadays many large stores stand near the place where he sent us, but at that time only one metal shed stood there.

The contractor, whose name was Chakradhar, went ahead on his bicycle while we walked leisurely. It was a big contract job, with lots of people working, so we relaxed along with everybody else and did as little as possible. That day, the contractor didn't pay us. "We don't pay daily," he said. "Just once a week. If you return tomorrow, you'll be paid." That's what he said.

The next day we went back, and worked well into the afternoon before receiving an hour's break for snacks. Since we were new on the job and had no money, how could we buy tiffin? We just sat alone at the work site with nothing to eat. All the others had gone. The contractor saw us and invited us to go to the canteen. "I'll get snacks for you on credit," he said.

He led us inside the only place near there to get food, a Punjabi eating place. We sat on a bench, with Lakhi between us. The contractor ordered cream of wheat; a dish of onions, lentils, peppers, and peas; and a dish of another kind of peas. A boy set spoons before us. These foods were new for us. Since we saw everybody eating with spoons, we tried it too, but food kept spilling on our laps. We had never done this before. Somehow I managed, picking up the food that fell. But Lakhi was unable to eat. She couldn't get the spoon to her mouth—it kept hitting her face and the food fell off. She sat there puzzled, spoon in hand.

The contractor, after finishing his meal, noticed her difficulties. "Use the spoon this way," he said. He put the spoon to her mouth and fed her a couple of bites. She would open her mouth; he would put the spoon in. When there were only a couple of bites left on the plate, Chakradhar took a spoonful and lifted it. She opened her mouth again, but suddenly he spilled the spoonful on her lap. I couldn't see what he did next, but I heard about it later. He took back the spoon and with his left hand wiped the food off her lap, rubbing his hand across her thighs and pressing his fingers into the area around her vagina. He did this a couple of times. Suddenly she stood up. We left and went back to work.

Later the contractor gave me a betel and called to Lakhi to take some betel. She did not reply. He called out, "Oh, take the betel." No answer. So he called again, *"ki lo, paana neunu* [dear, why are you not taking the betel]?" The word *ki lo* is an intimate word used by a man when he calls his wife or his wife's younger sister. Also, he used the intimate form of the word for "you."

At first Lakhi did not reply. Finally she called out, "I'll not accept betel from you! I want to talk to you after work is finished this evening!"

Later, Lakhi told me everything that had happened, from the spoon incident to the betel affair. Work ended. I was working apart from Lakhi. She saw the contractor and asked angrily, "Why did you spill that spoon of food on me intentionally, and push your fingers to a place of prestige? And when you offered me betel, you called me 'ki lo'—don't you know for whom you use that word? Am I your wife or sister-in-law?"

I reached her side at that moment and overheard her saying these things. She angrily repeated the questions again. Then she asked, "Is this the proper behavior of a contractor toward a laborer? Have you no mother, no sister?"

Chakradhar replied, "We contractors do a lot more than that. During work, our hands go to many parts of the bodies of the women—as a joke. If you can't stand this, you needn't come to work tomorrow."

Lakhi shouted, "Yes, we will not return tomorrow. Give us our wage now!"

He said, "I have no money now. Come to work tomorrow. You'll get three days' wages in the evening."

We walked home; the contractor rode his cycle. We saw him at a crossroads in the new capital at a tea stall. He called me over to take tea. I refused because we had quarreled with him before. He insisted. "This is not the work site. As a friendly gesture, I'm offering you tea. Why don't you take it with me?"

I accepted. Then he asked, "Why don't you ask her to take some tea?"

I called her over. He bought us good sweets, fried lentils, and tea. He asked me, "Why are you angry with me? I wanted to be friends with you. What is your name? What is her name? What is the relation between you two?"

I replied, "We are from different families, but she calls me brother; I call her sister."

Then he said, "I want to tell you one thing, but I am afraid to."

I said, "Why are you afraid? If you want to ask, ask. For asking, no one is taking another's property. I won't mind." I figured he wanted Lakhi.

"I want to mix with her," he said.

"Why should she mix with you?"

"I will give you some money; not every day, only once a week—but then I'll pay her ten rupees above her regular wage. For that I'll have her all week. If you don't help me, I won't be able to get her. I'll pay you free snacks."

I said, "Let me ask her."

I called her over. She had been taking tea separately. I asked, "Do you agree to go with him? He wants it."

She agreed. I said to Chakradhar Babu, "She agrees, but you should give both of us free food." He agreed, pulled out two rupees, and gave it to me.

The three of us walked near the railway line, to a shaded place with plants. I waited while they went into the weeds and did their work.

One of the workers at the construction site was a wicked woman from my ward named Hadi, who was born in the contractor's village. Although she was not really a relative, as a mark of respect we called her Auntie [father's brother's wife]. Hadi always chased after men. One evening, when Lakhi and I planned to stay at the site, Hadi said she wanted to go back to her father's house with the contractor. She hoped to seduce him. That night, they went off together; Lakhi and I returned to our villages.

The next day, Hadi was back on the work site, and from that day she watched us all the time, looking to see how we acted with the contractor. She returned each night to her father's house. Her husband knew what she was doing, so after three or four days he went to her village and dragged her back. Because she was unhappy about this, she declared in our ward, "Muli is going with Lakhi to that work site, but they always stay with the contractor when the work is over. What the contractor does with Lakhi, who knows?"

When my parents heard this, they scolded me, and Father beat me. "You are a married person! Why are you traveling with a mature unmarried young girl? Why is Hadi talking like this? Why would anyone say such things? Because they are true! You can no longer work at that site! You cannot leave the house today!"

That day Lakhi waited for me, and when I did not turn up she returned to her village. That evening when I went outside to defecate, I walked over the fields until I reached the village and Lakhi's house, where I told her what had happened. She replied, "We should change our work."

Once again we traveled about, looking to collect good consumers. We continued like this for two or three months.

Where was the time to think of my wife? I went to work with Lakhi, in the evening I rehearsed at the drama hall, and at night I slept.

15. Kia Possessed, 1953–56

Fourteen-year-old Kia, fatherless and abandoned for nine months by her new husband Muli, becomes possessed by a malevolent spirit. Kia probably was calling attention to her plight, as suggested by the words that the spirit within her is said to have uttered: ". . . I came from that hill. Why aren't people worshiping me? That's why I am traveling back and forth without finding any shelter." Demonic possession often occurs among young Indian women confronted with personal conflicts that they are afraid to discuss openly or directly (see Opler 1958:553–566; and the Freeds 1964[1967]; 295–320).

The exorcist curing ritual of a possessed person consists of removing polluting substances and spirits from the body, thus cleansing and purifying it. Exorcist curers throughout South Asia use items symbolizing purity and pollution in their rituals (see, for example, Yalman 1964:115–150). To cure Kia, the magician draws a picture of a house in which he places polluting items on the upper half and pure ones on the lower half. By beating her repeatedly with a cane and pushing her face into hot burning peppers, he weakens the spirit in her, gains control over her, and ultimately draws out the spirit.

Successful exorcist-magicians usually are skilled at uncovering the social tensions and personal problems that have contributed to possession attacks. Once Muli had brought his wife back to his home, she suffered no further attacks.

My wife Kia remained in her deceased father's house for many months. I was supposed to request her return, but I neglected to do so. I was busy with Lakhi and her prostitute business.

One morning a man from the village of Balakati came to our ward and informed my father that Chandi [a form of the mother-goddess] had entered my wife's body while she was collecting dried leaves from a mango grove. She had been visiting her uncle's house in Balakati.

Then I remembered that I had a wife who belonged to me. She was fourteen years old. My mind was moved toward her; I wanted to meet her. She had been away from me for nearly nine months. I became restless, thinking about how she was, what she was doing, how much suffering she was enduring. Grandfather Dharma said to my father, "They have informed us. Who will go to see our son's wife? I cannot go; you should go."

Father replied, "If I go, who will go to the stone quarry? I have stones half-cut there, and today we get paid."

I said, "I'll go."

Grandfather said, "No, it is improper. They should invite you and show you respect. Then you may go. What happened to your wife is not serious. She will recover within two or three days. Why should you worry or go there?"

I said, "Then who will go? If Father goes, we get no money. You don't want to go. I am free, doing nothing. If I go we'll have no financial difficulty."

Grandfather finally gave me permission, but then said, "You shouldn't go empty-handed. We have no money. So mortgage that water pot for five rupees. If a magician has been hired to remove the goddess from your wife's body, pay for it."

My mother took the water pot to a high-caste ward and mortgaged it. Men don't like to mortgage articles; they feel ashamed because their prestige declines. They send the women to do it instead.

As I started off, Grandfather called, "Don't spend money on yourself, but on the exorcist-magician. Go to the house of Uchaba Das, your wife's maternal uncle. He helped your wife as much as he could. So help him; give him the five rupees."

I said "Yes," but promptly forgot my grandfather's warning. On the way I bought some betel and some village cigarettes. When I asked for directions, an old woman led me to the house of Uchaba Das. Upon entering, I greeted my wife's uncle with respect by giving a *muṇḍiaa* greeting, lying down and touching my forehead to the ground. I sat on a mat and waited. After a long while my wife's uncle saw his son and ordered him to fetch some water for cleaning my legs and hands.

I was insulted that no one had shown me respect. I said, "I don't want that. I've already washed in the river."

Uncle Uchaba said, "Why are you pouting? When you arrived, all of the people here were *maanya* [respected persons] to you. It would be a sin for you to take water from them, so I called your younger brother-in-law to give it to you because he is not a respected person for you. This caused the delay."

The young boy pulled my hand. "Oh, how much pouting you do. Come, I'll wash your feet."

After washing and taking some betel, I asked, "What's the news? We received a message that something is wrong with your daughter." I would not refer to my wife as "wife" in front of respected persons.

Uncle Uchaba said, "Some days ago, many girls went to collect firewood from the mango grove. Under a thorny screwpine bush nearby they heard a sound, 'khas! khas!' She was alone there; the others were a distance away. She became afraid and ran over the fields, shouting, 'Oh Father, oh father, who is coming out from that place?' Suddenly she fell down. Her friends took her home. After that she became very taciturn. In the evening she suddenly started laughing in a strange way and was unable to stop. She jerked her shoulders, bared her teeth, and spoke in a strange way, saying strange things: 'I am the mother of Chandi. I came from that hill. Why aren't people worshiping me? That's why I am traveling back and forth without finding any shelter.'

"I got the help of a high-caste magician. While our daughter [Muli's wife] sat nearby, the magician drew a picture of a house. On the upper half he drew an image of a person. He placed next to it a human bone, a bowl of wine, and a bowl containing a fish. On the lower half of the house he placed sacred food, sacred sweet water, a scissors to cut the magical spell, and red China roses. The magician lit a smokepot full of hot peppers under her nose. She sneezed; he beat her hard with a cane. Over twenty times the cane landed on her legs, back, hands, and chest. She feared, and the spirit in her called out, 'I am the spirit; I will go back.' The magician offered flowers, swept her body with a broom, uttered magical incantations, beat her, and pushed her face in the burning peppers until the spirit left her body. As proof that the spirit was leaving, the magician ordered it to carry a big bell-metal jar of water with her teeth. Grasping a jar with her teeth, our daughter carried it out of the house and down the road until she fell senseless. At that spot, the magician pounded an iron nail into the ground. From that day she has improved slightly. Chandi was swept out of her body, but she became very weak. Since that night when she was cured, our daughter has ceased talking like Chandi."

I asked, "How much did the magician cost?"

Uncle Uchaba said, "He is my friend, so he took no fee, just two rupees' worth of betel. But she is very weak; she needs good food. If you can contribute, she can recover faster. Give me the cost of medicine for her."

I said, "We've got financial difficulties at home, so I can't give much." I handed him two rupees. Then I told him,"I want to meet your daughter."

He said, "Yes, why not? I'm calling your 'aunt.' " Out of respect, he referred to his wife as "aunt."

His wife was inside my wife's room. He called his wife, referring to me as his son. "Oh, Aunt, come from that room; our son will go to that room."

I went inside, sat beside my wife, and asked, "How are you?"

She replied slowly, "A little better."

I touched her forehead; she had a fever. I asked her, "What would you like to eat?"

She replied, "I don't want anything."

I said, "Tell me what your tongue needs. After a couple of days someone will bring it."

"No, I don't want any food."

I looked out. Many women of the ward had gathered in the courtyard to see me. They were gossiping, passing remarks: "How did the new bridegroom, the son-in-law, come and visit the wife without an invitation! Is there no one at his house to come here except him? Has that house no leader? Who sent him? Why did he come? Did the guardians die? It is not nice on his part to go to his father-in-law's house without an invitation."

I heard all this *cup-caap tup-taap* [gossip] noise and didn't like it. I wanted to leave, so I said to my wife, "I've got to leave. Tell me quickly if you want anything."

She said nothing. I gave her the remaining two rupees and stepped out of the room. I told Uncle Uchaba that I wished to leave. He asked me to stay. I would have, except for that gossip I heard. So I insisted on leaving.

Uchaba's son said to his father, "Why do you request him to stay? If he does, it will cost us money—betel, gifts of cloth, and a feast, since he is a respected person on his first visit."

Uncle Uchaba replied, "Why shouldn't we do it? We'll have to someday anyway. Why not now?"

I said, "I've no time to stay. There's time later in my life."

I touched my forehead to the ground in a *muṇḍiaa* greeting and started out of the ward. Uncle Uchaba and his wife accompanied me to the end of the street; his son went with me to the river near the village.

A few days later, my grandfather brought my wife back to our house.

My wife isn't the only person who has been attacked by dead spirits. We fear these spirits because they enter the bodies of people, mostly women, and cause them harm. This has happened many times, not only to our women, but also to high-caste women.

Now we returned to work. I didn't want to, but I had to do some plowing for different people. Also, I had to sow some seeds during the month of Jyesta [May-June]. With a little difficulty we managed during these days.

In the next month, Asadha [June-July], we couldn't get any work. It started to rain. No agricultural work was available. We went to Lingapur and Nathapur villages for weeding a rainy-season rice crop. We worked there fifteen days, returning to our village each night.

Once, we met a gentleman from the capital city. He hired thirty people from my ward to do construction work in the capital. After we had worked for him for a month, the gentleman showed bad behavior to our women. In our village, weeding had begun, so the people of the ward stopped construction work. Sometimes we got two weeding jobs in one day. Working from early morning 'til 10 A.M., we earned one-fourth of a daily wage. From 10:00 to 4:00 we earned a full day's wage. So we did not need construction work in the city during those days.

My son was born that year in the rainy season—the month of Bhadra [August-September]. We held a seven-day *uṭhiari* ceremony, burning firewood to keep the mother and infant warm. We used a special wood, *kocilaa* [nux vomica], which is especially strong. On the seventh day, we carried the wood away.

For that ceremony, I invited my mother's uncles, my wife's uncle, and my own sisters and their husbands. We celebrated that according to our own custom [Appendix B]. Some guests stayed two days, others three, then all of them went home. Although my newly married sister wanted to go back with her husband, I asked them to stay longer because my wife couldn't work. They remained four more months.

16. Grandfather Dharma, 1956–57

Several crises beset Muli's family members, particularly Grandfather Dharma. He fights with his high-caste landlord, and as a consequence receives no further payment for his season's work. When Muli's aunt, a notorious thief, hides out in Muli's house, the police arrest her and all the men of Muli's household. After they are released, Grandfather Dharma becomes ill, seeks magical cures, accuses the drama teacher of causing his illness, and fires the teacher. Grandfather Dharma possibly wished to dismiss the teacher because of his scandals with Muli but did not want to mention this.

Four Bauri families, including Muli's, become embroiled in an expensive court case over the assault of a man caught sleeping with another man's wife. High-caste lawyers drag out the court hearings for eighteen months, charging the Bauris exorbitant fees, then force them to settle out of court so that neither side wins anything. Court cases in India often last years and cost thousands of rupees. Poor families drawn into such cases are ruined financially (for examples of expensive cases in Muli's village, see Freeman 1977a:133–34).

The final crisis is Grandfather Dharma's sudden death.

When Bira Pradhan, a Cultivator-caste man and stone quarry contractor, married a girl from a village about seven miles away, my paternal Grandfather Dharma and I walked in the procession. Mala the wrestler, a high-caste leader, organized the procession of about a hundred people and hired Bauris to hold torches, flowers, and other decorations. The Sunderpada Muslims and the Kapileswar Bauris and Mallias went along for gymnastics exhibitions. I carried a decorated flower wreath.

My grandfather and I had been working with Mala as joint sharecroppers. Up to the time of the marriage of Bira Pradhan in May, we had received only 200 kilos of paddy of our share of the harvest from Mala. Usually we separated our shares in April, after completing *biri* and *muga* lentil cultivation, and doing other necessary farm tasks such as fixing the cart and selling and buying bullocks for the new agricultural season. The rains came in June; we began our plowing. Still, Mala had not paid us for our previous year's work.

A few days later, Grandfather Dharma went to Mala's house to receive his share of the payment for walking in Bira's marriage procession. Mala said, "I haven't received any money yet from Bira; wait until he gives it to me."

Grandfather returned home. He talked to some Mallias, who told him they had already received their pay. Grandfather became angry.

The next day Mala called me to work. When Mala, Grandfather, and I went to the middle of the paddy fields, Grandfather asked Mala, "Why haven't you given me my procession money? You have paid everybody else; why not me?"

Mala replied angrily, "I don't know anything about your money. Who took you to the party? I didn't."

Right there the two started shouting and insulting each other. Suddenly Grandfather leaped onto Mala's chest. Taken by surprise, Mala tripped and fell backward to the ground. Grandfather fell on him and held him down. A lot of cultivators gathered and said to Grandfather, "Keep him there; if you leave him now, he'll kill you! By chance Mala must have tripped; otherwise he would have already killed you. Why are you fighting with him?"

Suddenly Mala stood up and showered blows on my grandfather, beating him badly. Grandfather lay in bed for a week, unable to move. He and Father became afraid to ask Mala for our share of paddy and straw; we never received it. We had worked an entire year for nothing except what we had received before the wedding: 200 kilos of paddy, some money to send gifts on the shoulder-carrier to my wife's house, and some money to help me recover from my disease. As joint sharecroppers with Mala, we had cultivated seven acres. Mala and ourselves together should have received and shared half the yield. My family should have received the yield from about two acres of paddy, or about 800 kilos.

One February night about eight months later, my maternal aunt suddenly arrived at our house carrying four brass pots which she had stolen from a village near Khurda, about fifteen miles away. Auntie, who had married a man from Mancheswar village, had become a fearless thief once she had borne many children whom she was unable to feed. Father refused to let his sister stay. He was suspicious: "Where could she have gotten four metal pots? She does not need them." So he said to her, "No, no, you can't stay here. If you do, we'll be arrested. So go."

My aunt touched his feet and begged him to let her stay just for a few hours. He let her remain.

That night, my aunt got us to dig four holes in the mud floor of our room. She placed the pots in these holes and covered them up. She slept in that room, saying, "Don't let anyone else in this room. I cannot leave here tonight. Tomorrow evening I'll leave. Don't awaken me until evening. I'll sleep through the day. I don't need any food or anything else."

We did as she said because we did not want anyone to know she was there.

At midday we asked her if she wanted to eat. She replied, "Don't talk to me. I'll wake up in the evening. Then I'll go."

Two *ghadi* [one and a half hours by a lunar time reckoning] into the evening, she awakened, asked us for a twig to brush her teeth, ate some fruit, and gave us five rupees to buy sweets for ourselves. Then she had us dig up the pots. Placing one on each shoulder and two on her head, she walked off toward the Gangua River.

A few days later she appeared again, this time with a huge bed roll and a suitcase which she had lifted from the railroad station. Father became angry. "Why did you come to my house again? I told you just a few days ago not to come here when you are fleeing with stolen goods."

She did not listen to his scolding, but lay at his feet and implored him to take her in. Again he relented.

This time the police had followed her to our house. Suspecting that all of us were thieves, they took Auntie, Father, and me to the police station jail in the Old Town for two days.

When my maternal uncle heard that we had been jailed, he paid bail, and Father and I were released. But Auntie was taken to the district jail in the town of Puri.

The case went into court at Khurda, the subdivisional headquarters of the district. We attended two or three times but were not cross-examined. On the fifth day of the trial, the magistrate asked us about the theft. We all told the truth, including Auntie, who explained why a woman like herself had turned to stealing.

She said, "From my childhood I used to give ritual worship to Thakurani, the mother-goddess, whom I used to serve. In my mother-in-law's house I bore many children, but I found that I was unable to feed them. I prayed to my mother-goddess, 'What can I do? What can I do?' Once, I was starving, so I went out to steal some rice, praying to the deity all the time, 'Oh, save me, save me.' Since I didn't get caught, I thought to myself, 'Well, the deity helped me.' I took a half a bag of rice. I found that I gained enormous strength, and easily carried off the rice. The rice was sufficient to feed my children for several days.

"The next day I went to the deity and worshiped her. That night I had a dream in which the mother-goddess told me, 'I'll help you. Go ahead with stealing from the rich people and feed your poor children.' From that day, whenever I started out to steal, I first worshiped the mother-goddess at my house. When I returned, even if it was late at night, I worshiped her again. Even when I wasn't at home, I hired a priest to worship the deity. Like this, I passed my days.

"Since my present situation was one of great need, I worked a lot during the last month. I stole more often."

When the magistrate heard her statement, he ordered her to be released, but he made her promise not to steal any more. She took an oath that she would not steal.

Her sons brought her back to Mancheswar. They said to her, "You admitted that you fed us by stealing, and we grew on stolen property. Now we are all grown up. You need not do this any more; we can earn enough. You should promise by touching our heads, swearing an oath on our lives, that you'll never steal again."

She touched their heads and promised, "I'll not steal again."

My father and I were released along with Auntie. Like this, we had been given a punishment, jailed for two days, and forced to attend the court. But we had done nothing wrong.

The people of our village and street passed snide remarks when they saw us. "Oh, you are a family of thieves!"

From that day, feeling shame, we could not look people in the face. Most of the time we sat at home, ashamed to go out.

Not long after Auntie was released from court, our drama teacher asked the people of our ward for an advance of 200 rupees so that he could buy a bullock. This was an enormous amount of money;

we told him we did not have that much money. My grandfather Dharma, the informal leader of the ward, refused to give him anything. He asked me to ask my grandfather for money; I also refused.

A few days later, Teacher asked permission to leave for his home for eight days. Grandfather Dharma refused to grant permission.

A couple of days later, Teacher slipped something into Grandfather Dharma's food that caused him to get a severe stomach disease. Anything he ate came back up without being digested. His stool was full of blood. We took him to many herbalist doctors, the hospital doctor, and others, but all of their efforts failed. We heard that there was a famous magician at Banki village who could cure such diseases, and we took Grandfather Dharma to him.

The magician told Grandfather Dharma to collect special water which can determine whether a person's ailment is caused by disease or by magic. Early the next morning, even before washing his face, Grandfather collected water from a tank where nobody bathes. He had to do this without looking at anyone. He placed this water before the magician. Stirring a straw in the water, the magician recited incantations. Dharma then drank the water.

We stayed overnight, waiting for the results. The next afternoon, Grandfather vomited huge quantities. Up came rice and lentils, but in the middle of it we saw a cowrie shell and a piece of root.

The magician announced, "His illness is due to magic."

We did not know who had caused this until later.

The magician gave Grandfather several different roots and a seed, and told him to make a paste from each kind of root and eat it early each morning. The magician placed some medicine in a tiny copper cylinder and handed it to my grandfather. Grandfather tied it on his upper right arm, and we left for home. Soon after, Grandfather was cured, at least for a while.

About a month later, the disease returned. Again we went to Banki and asked the magician, "Who has done this to our Dharma?"

He replied, "How can I tell? He must be a magician or a person who has hired a magician. You can find out by carefully watching your food, drink, and clothes. If you are drinking water that someone else hands you, he might put something in it; then you come under his control. The same with food. So don't take food or water from anyone else. Don't wear anybody else's cloth, or you may come under their power. Be very careful when drying your cloth. Do it inside your yard. Otherwise someone might cut out a piece of that cloth, recite incantations on it, and hurt you."

He gave Grandfather some very powerful medicine, which cured him. Like this we went to the magician of Banki three or four times. Each time, he said, "You were cured! Then your enemy recited incantations and made you ill again."

We tried to find out who our enemy could be. We thought we had no enemy. The magician told us to go to the village of Charchika, near Banki, and consult a *sarbajaana* [all-knowing seer]. We went to him; my grandfather threw himself at his feet and prayed to him. Seeing this, we also threw ourselves at his feet and prayed.

The seer remained silent for a moment, then asked Grandfather, "Why are you lying there?" A seer is supposed to be able to read people's thoughts.

Grandfather answered, "Very often I am attacked by magic. I don't know who is doing it."

The all-knower thought for a moment and said, "Your drama teacher is doing this to you. Why are you making him unhappy and causing him trouble?"

Then Grandfather told the all-knower why Teacher was unhappy with him. The all-knower said, "You should be careful about that teacher."

Grandfather determined to drive Teacher out of our ward. At the end of the month, Teacher asked for his pay. Grandfather said to him, "You cannot get anything from us. Instead, you should return the money you took in advance."

Teacher was displeased, and so were the people of our ward. If a man is not paid, how can he feed his family? The people felt sympathy for Teacher and felt he should be paid something. But because Grandfather was our leader, they wouldn't tell him this to his face. They waited until he left; then they complained that he was wrong to deduct a man's entire pay. When Teacher came to know that the people supported him except for my grandfather, he went to Grandfather many times, asking to be paid. Grandfather refused.

Finally, Teacher charged him. "Why aren't you paying me? How can I run my life?"

Grandfather answered angrily, "I don't know, but we gave you an advance, so we've got to deduct your pay. We can't pay you more."

Grandfather didn't tell him the real reason because he feared that the people of the ward wouldn't believe him.

Teacher angrily replied, "From today, I'll not stay here!"

That evening, Teacher called a meeting. He said, "I'll no longer work for you; I received no monthly pay."

The people of the ward said, "If you are quitting, then give us back the money we advanced you."

Teacher said, "How? I spent the money. If you pay me a monthly wage and deduct five rupees a month, then I'll remain."

Dharma said, "No, we'll deduct the entire amount each month, and if you don't like it, then leave!"

From that day, Teacher no longer worked for us. He remained friendly with the other people of the ward, but not with my family. Grandfather Dharma returned to the magician at Banki and told him that he had driven out the teacher, and that we needed a new one for our drama troupe. The magician recommended a friend of his from Banki, a Militia-caste man named Prafulla, who was tall, bulky, hairy, and very black. Grandfather hired him without consulting the other people of the ward.

After one month, Prafulla asked to be paid, and wanted an advance. The people of the ward refused to pay him, either from the ward treasury or from their own pockets. Someone called out insultingly, "Whoever brought that teacher here should pay him. No money will come from us; we didn't hire him." A quarrel developed; Grandfather became angry that the people did not support his decision. The next day he sent Prafulla home after promising to pay his salary.

After that, our drama rehearsals stopped; our ward broke into two enemy groups: my family and two others versus the other families of the ward.

Each night a cousin of mine named Annam used to sleep outside on a veranda in our ward. He was the grandson of Grandfather's brother. Annam was having an affair with the wife of Kubera, Kalandi's son. The household of Kalandi was enemy to us. One night, Kubera left his house. Seeing an opportunity to visit his lover, Annam slipped inside Kalandi's house, passing through the first room, the courtyard, and finally to the room where his lover slept. As he opened her door, someone saw him, but he didn't realize this. He entered the room and started his "work." Kubera's two brothers and a brother-in-law, now fully awakened, locked all the outside entrances and then waited for Annam. When he opened the door of his lover's room, they caught hold of him, bound him with a rope, and beat him with heavy sticks. Annam cried, "I am dead! I am dead!" His cries awakened the entire ward. We ran out to the road. Kubera's brothers and brother-in-law shouted, "Who is there to save him? If there is anybody, let him come forward. We are going to kill Annam!"

They went inside and beat Annam. He screamed in fright and pain. We stood outside wondering what to do. Annam was from one of our three families, but we were greatly outnumbered and we feared to attempt a rescue.

We looked for Annam's father, Ghania, but could not find him. We thought he had gone to commit suicide because his son was being killed. But he had run to the Old Town and brought back several policemen and an important Congress party leader named Ramahari. The policemen pushed their way into Kubera's house and brought out Annam. He was still alive. They scolded the three relatives: "Why did you beat this man so much? If he did something wrong, you should tell us; we would take care of it."

The police suggested that we get a doctor's certificate testifying to the wounds Annam had received. Then we could file an assault case against Kubera's three relatives. With Ramahari's help, Ghania filed a case. We three families bore the expenses of this case. When the accused received their summons to court, they held a meeting and decided to file a case of their own. They filed a defamation suit and also accused Annam of seducing a woman of their household, causing that household to lose prestige.

So each side was defendant and accuser in a case. Every month, both sides had to spend huge amounts of money for the cases. We had to go to Khurda town, fifteen miles away, where the court was located at that time. Ramahari and his friend Shiva arranged to have the case presented in court. They gave us a contract which stated that at the end of the court case they would each take 150 rupees.

Every time we met in court, we had to hire two people, the pleader and the scribe, who writes documents on official stamped paper. We also hired Ramahari and Shiva as *maamalatkaara* helpers [court touts], to help see the case through. We were simple Bauri people. What did we know about how things should be done? They gave us advice. A court tout is not officially a part of the court, he simply listens in court and gives advice. Most people think it's better to hire a court tout because they have had a lot of experience in court cases and know how to make their way around the court, how to contact people, and whom to bribe. Our main helper was Ramahari. He was short, stout, and bald, with legs and testicles greatly swollen with elephantiasis. He always wore homespun dhotis and overhanging *punjaabi* shirts, plus full leather shoes—not sandals—and a gold wristwatch. He was a good speaker.

The case ran for one and a half years. We starved most of the time to meet the expenses. We would collect the money a week before the scheduled sessions.

After six months, we learned that Kubera's family was paying all the expenses of their case; their allies did not help cover their costs. Unknown to us, they secretly went to our court touts and paid them to convince us to settle the case out of court. But our court touts did nothing until the case had run for one and a half years. Then Ramahari told us to compromise. We refused. He said, "Why don't you settle? It is not good. If you win the case, they will bear a grudge; if they win, you will bear a grudge. So compromise."

Why didn't he tell us this a year and a half before, when he per-suaded us to file the case? We feared that if we refused to take his advice, he might become angry and help our rivals: then we'd lose everything, so we agreed to settle out of court.

Ramahari called a meeting of high-caste and Bauri leaders from our village and the Old Town, including *thaana baḍu baabu* [big policeman gentleman]. The leaders decided that both sides were at fault. A leader named Kedar spoke: "A young man should not enter another's house to seduce women, so he was guilty. Kubera's wife was also guilty: a married woman should not sleep with a young man other than her husband because it disturbs the young man; he spends money on the woman and not on his own household. This is bad, and it is the woman's fault. She was more guilty than he was because she was married and he wasn't. A young man needs love; he may chase after women. But a married woman does not need two men; she's got one at home, her husband. So she is not justified in looking for other men to love. If the total guilt is sixteen annas [one rupee], the woman bears ten annas of guilt, the man six annas. The person who is ten annas' guilty will pay ten rupees. The six annas' guilty person will pay six rupees."

Both sides deposited their fines. Eight rupees of the sixteen were given to the village deity, four rupees to the big policeman, and the remaining money to the other policemen at the station. We signed a statement of compromise; the case ended.

But what a cost for us! Every time we went to court, the pleader took five rupees, the pleader's clerk two rupees, the court messenger one-fourth rupee to call out our names, and the magistrate's clerk one rupee; he arranges the date of the session, and if we are nice to him, he arranges a date that's convenient for us. In addition, travel and food expenses were about twenty rupees; so each time we went, we spent twenty-five to thirty rupees.

We paid forty-five rupees to file the case. Then, each time we went, we gave our court touts our money; they spent whatever they needed and returned what was left. If the expenses were more than we had given them, they asked us for more money.

All this cost each family ten rupees per month. We did not have so much money. In order to get it, we would starve, eating nothing one week out of four. At market time, we might have five rupees. We used one rupee for food and saved four rupees for the court touts. We gave them the money long in advance so we wouldn't have to worry about money at the time of the sessions.

After the case was compromised and withdrawn from court, Ramahari and Shiva presented us with their bill for services: 300 rupees, payable immediately. We didn't know where to get so much money immediately, and we told Ramahari.

He replied, "Do you think we are your *bethi* [forced free labor]? Did we work for you two years for nothing? We worked for you and became enemy to your enemy. If you don't give us our money, we'll file a court case against you. We have sufficient proof of what you owe us. See here: you signed this official government-stamped paper. It says you borrowed 150 rupees from each of us, and now you owe it to us, 300 rupees in all."

We had signed many papers when the case began. We did not know what we were signing. When we heard this, we became quite afraid. We threw ourselves at his feet and cried, "Where will we get such money?" We had agreed verbally to pay him, but we did not realize that we had signed a statement, too. "You may kill us or beat us, or do whatever you want; we still cannot pay!"

Ramahari's partner Shiva said, "I'm cutting stone from my own quarry to build a house. You can pay me by working for me. I'll deduct part of your wages."

We agreed to work for him this way, and we paid back Ramahari the same way. For one year we worked two or three days each month without being paid. In that way we worked off our debts.

One day, Grandfather Dharma suddenly got a pain in his stomach, like someone cutting it open, he said. He vomited blood. My father and some neighbors put him on a bullock cart and rushed him to the Old Town hospital, where he received some medicine. He couldn't walk, and his leg, swollen with elephantiasis, hurt him. An hour after he returned home, he vomited blood again and died right on the spot.

I was visiting my mother's uncle's house six miles away in Panchagang village, where mother's aunt had just died. I went with some shoulder-carrier gifts for their funeral ceremony. I ate fish that day, unaware that at that moment my grandfather was dying at home.

I walked home. When Mother saw me she started crying. I wondered, What happened? I went inside and asked my wife why Mother was crying.

My wife said, "Grandfather died."

I asked, "How did he die?"

She told me, and then said, "He shocked us twice, and the second time he was dead—at the second vomiting. I was alarmed, I feared, and he died."

My pregnant wife had received a shock and was trembling. I went to the gates of the village temple and got some sacred flowers of the deity from a Mallia temple servant. I gave this to her; but it did no good, because we were in a polluted state due to the death of my grandfather. The child aborted. After that my wife was very weak. She bled from her body; for two months, each day there was some blood.

In the hour before Grandfather died, the people of the house asked him, "What wrongs have you done in your life?"

He answered, "Once I ate in a Washerman's house."

Because of this, the people of the ward refused to help bury Dharma. If anybody had helped in the burial, he would have remained impure for forty-five days, along with the immediate family who had buried him. Any Bauri who eats in a Washerman's house is considered polluted and is automatically outcasted, often for a period of thirty to forty-five days, three half-moon phases. So no one helped us with the burial or with the funeral arrangements. Some people in the ward carried lights and sticks to the burial ground, but would not touch the body. Nobody came to our house or touched us for three half-moons: the three families of our lineage lived separately because all had touched Grandfather.

We required purification. When the third half-moon period began, my father asked the ward leader, who no longer belonged to a rival faction, to invite the leaders of the *daasadesa* [ten countries] and the *baaradesa* [twelve countries] to a purification ceremony. He gave money for the distribution of betel nuts and sacred food as invitation items. The leaders met at the deity of Chungudei, under the banyan tree in the Fisherman's bazaar.

Our caste priest purified my family at the Gangua River. We returned to the meeting place, and Father distributed his sin by giving *khai* sweets and pressed rice to everybody. Another man gave betel and water. People now had taken food from the hands of Father; whatever sin he had all of them had, because they had shared food with him. He became a good man, not a man of sin.

Back in our ward, we gave the visitors some sacred food, *khai*, and a sour dish. The leaders ate and left.

The next day, we began our twelve-days' funeral ritual for Grandfather, one and a half months after his death.

17. The White Bullocks, 1957

In this and other chapters, Muli displays characteristic behaviors that invariably lead him into unanticipated difficulties. He spends more than he can afford on a gift for a high-caste friend whom he wishes to impress. Pretending to be wealthy, he buys two white bullocks from his friend's brother. The terms are immediate cash payment in full, but since Muli has no cash, he tricks his friend into putting up the money for the bullocks, and thus destroys their friendship.

This chapter also provides further examples of everyday discrimination against untouchables, information about the nature of oath-friendships—formalized friendships sealed with religious vows—and some idea of the relationship between Muli and his wife.

I thought my bad fate had changed when a labor recruiter from the city hired me to work on a two-month house construction project. I had not worked for twenty days, and our rice was running low; I thought we would starve again. I am a small-caste man with no skills. During the rains I work in my master's paddy fields. When the harvest is over I sit on the veranda of my house waiting for the recruiter, hoping for a lucky day when I have work and can eat.

At the construction site I carried pails of water and sand for a high-caste skilled mason named Bhima, a short, muscular man of thirty. Unlike most people of his caste, he was very dark, even darker than I.

One evening after work we walked together to the market. As we talked about the good and bad fortunes of our lives, I told him that I had one son who was a few months old.

He replied unhappily, "My two children have died. Now a new one is on the way." He shrugged hopelessly, "Perhaps I am living under a bad star. What will happen to this one?"

I suddenly saw a way to make him come to my door. High-caste men don't mix with small-caste men unless they want something. If they itch to sleep with one of our girls, I supply them. This gentleman's needs were different, but I could satisfy him too.

I said, "Offer this unborn child to a small-caste man. Then fate will view the child as small-caste, even though his caste is unchanged. If your fate stays bad, it won't transfer to the child; he won't die."

Bhima knew of this custom; as I expected, he asked me to become the child's *dharma-baapaa* [godfather]. I made a show of refusing. He begged me; I did not give in until we reached the market.

To seal our agreement, I suggested that we become *saangataa* [oath-friends] by pledging a sacred oath of everlasting friendship. To my surprise, he agreed. Oath-friends must make their pledges inside a temple and share a meal of the deity's sacred rice. An oath-friendship can never break; you must always meet the demands of your oath-friend, no matter how difficult. Even if you later hate your oath-friend, you must do what he asks because you made an oath before God.*

Because I am a small-caste man, high-caste people never let me into their temples. So standing on the road, facing the ancient gray stone temple of the Lord Shiva next to the market, Bhima and I swore our oath, "In front of Lord Shiva, our witness, we will be oath-friends forever." Even though we had not shared Shiva's meal, we believed that our oath was binding.†

My spirits soared. What lucky planets I had! How many of my people ever became oath-friends with high-caste gentlemen? Who would have believed it possible? Since I wanted to impress my new friend, I bought more eggplants, potatoes, and lentils than I needed, hoping that Bhima would think, "Muli isn't like the others of his caste; he's rich."

At home, my wife saw my bulging shopping bag and frowned. "Did you get those vegetables free?"

I replied, "No, I became oath-friends with a high-caste gentleman,

*Muli interprets literally an unrealistic ideal; in practice, oath-friends distrust those who make unreasonable demands or fail to give gifts that are equal in value to those they receive. Oath-friendships often terminate among those who are unequal in wealth.

†Muli mistakenly thought that he had a binding friendship. Bhima humored him to maintain the godfather relationship. Oath-friendships frequently cut across caste lines but rarely involve both high castes and untouchables.

and I decided to buy just as much as he did. He wants to offer his child-in-the-womb to me. Five days after the child is born, he will invite us to the ceremony of removing the fire that warms the baby. So we have to prepare a gift."

My wife asked, "How much will it cost?" Her face looked dark; she always ridicules my new schemes.

I talked fast and lied a little to smooth things over, "It will cost us a lot, but what can I do? I did not ask for this friendship. A higher-caste man asked me. When I suggested that he protect the child by offering him to a small-caste man, he selected me in front of Lord Shiva."

Her eyes looked angry as I continued, "I found a good new friend, and we shall surely benefit from it, but right now trouble comes to my mind. The oath of friendship can never be broken. The ceremony is next month. What shall we give? Their eyes may not be pleased with our gift if it is cheap."

My wife shouted, "Don't try to oil me! Don't tell *me* so openly that we'll have to make a gift larger than usual because they are of higher caste. Don't tell *me* about it. *You* decide what to do. Don't bother me about that gift." She was angry: only a few days ago we had faced starvation; now I was talking of spending more on outsiders than I did on my own family.

I replied, "I don't care. My construction work will continue until planting season. I can save one rupee a day from my wage. I'll pay for the gift that way."

The following day my new friend told me that he wanted to see my house. Outwardly I smiled at him, but inwardly I worried, "Maybe he is having second thoughts about our friendship. He probably wants to see if I am rich. What can I do?" My house is a compound with three mud and thatch huts and a cowshed, each no larger than three steps by four steps. Ten of us—my father and mother, brothers and sisters, and my wife and son—plus our two bullocks, live there all crowded together.

That evening after work my friend and I walked to my village. When he saw my miserable house, his face became long. I knew I had to impress him fast, so I left him sitting on our outside veranda while I hurried to the house of a Confectioner-caste woman who lived on a high-caste street.

"What do you want?" she asked harshly, using the familiar address. She was about forty years old, short, fat, and irritable.

I folded my hands humbly and said, "Please bring some snacks and a pot of water. I have a friend who is of high status, like a master. He won't touch water from my house because of my caste, but he will take food and water from you. If you refuse me, my prestige will go down."

She shook her head and turned away, but I begged her. Reluctantly she brought some molasses-rice and one glass of water to my house. I knew she would overcharge me, but this time I overlooked it. Like this I treated him. As my friend left, he promised to return soon.

Several days passed without my seeing Bhima. We were working at different sites on the construction project. Suddenly one evening he appeared unannounced at our door. He told us we had missed the fifth-day ceremony of his newborn daughter; he had been working and hadn't had time to inform us. He invited us to his daughter's twenty-first-day ceremony, saying, however, "I am not wealthy; I cannot give a gift to everyone. I'll offer only one cloth, either to you or your wife, plus a gift for your son."

I replied graciously, like a rich man, "Do what you can according to your wealth. Don't worry about showing respect to all of us. We'll be happy, even if you give us nothing."

I invited him for a snack: "You must not leave without pouring water" [eating or drinking].

This time the Confectioner woman refused to carry a plate of food to my house. So I led my friend to her house and told him, "Please go inside. These people are lovely friends of ours, just like you."

Since he was of high caste, Bhima could enter the outer room of the Confectioner woman's house; I stood outside in the doorway. Bhima protested politely that he didn't want to eat. Good host that I was, I told the Confectioner woman, "Force him to eat." He took a few bites, then left for home.

For days I searched for a nice gift. I didn't know the caste customs of my friend, so I didn't know what to bring him. Finally I asked Dhruba Prusty, a Goldsmith of my village, and he said, "Take a gold ring, and for the *satyanaaraayana puuja* bring some plantain, sugar, and milk. If you weren't an untouchable, you could bring cooked food." The *satyanaaraayana puuja* is a ceremony for a child's twenty-first day and first birthday; it ensures the child's health and good fortune.

The Goldsmith's idea sounded good; giving him an advance of ten rupees, I ordered him to fashion a gold ring. By evening he had finished it at a cost of fourteen rupees. I paid him two more rupees and promised the rest later.

On the afternoon of the ceremony, I walked alone to my new friend's house, three miles away. My wife refused to go; she was still angry about the cost of the ring.

Bhima had told me he was poor, but his house was that of a rich master and landlord—a large compound shaded by coconut trees, with many paddy fields that were cultivated by his younger brother, and even a small pond stocked with fish.

My friend gave me an empty aluminum pot and a rope, and he pointed to an open well in the backyard. Because of my caste, his family refused to draw water for me. After I had washed my legs and face, a child gave me a sitting mat made of coconut leaves. I sat in the backyard, ten to fifteen feet from where men lit cooking fires in earthen stoves specially built for the feast.

My friend and his wife came over. We talked for a while about the ceremony and the feast that would follow: fine rice, lentils with potatoes, sour chutney, and the sacred food of the *satyanaaraayana* ceremony, a dish of green plantain, sweetened rice, milk, and flour.

I told my friend, "It is all very nice." I handed him my gift, and he and his wife left. I watched men cut potatoes and plantain, while others placed huge metal pots full of rice onto blazing fires.

I went to the front of the house to watch the *satyanaaraayana* ceremony. A chanting priest sat on the veranda balancing Bhima's infant daughter on his lap, holding in his right hand a palm-leaf manuscript containing sacred verses. In front of him the flame of a butter-soaked wick flickered in a clay lamp resting on a high wooden holder. On his left a bower of branches arched over a raised clay altar smeared with sacred cow dung and strewn with offerings of red and white flowers.

The gifts were on display near the Brahman priest. Some guests had brought rings, others chains or money. The guests compared and admired the gifts; among the rings mine stood first! I smiled

38. The *satyanaaraayaṇa puuja*.

inside and said, "Thank you, Dhruba Prusty." I could hardly afford a ring like that for myself, but to make my friend think I was wealthy, I bought that ring for his daughter.

Bhima came over to me smiling. He said, "Have you heard the news?"

I pretended to know nothing. "Why, did any news come from my house?"

"No, from my house," he replied. "Your ornament stood first in craftsmanship."

I protested, "No, no, I am a poor man. Where would I get such a fine gift? Please excuse me for giving you such a poor gift."

Four *paalaa* [recitation] singers appeared, dressed in court cos-

39. High-caste feast, at which Bauris sit separated from other guests.

tumes of long blue and white robes with wide, flowing trousers. For hours they entertained us, singing comic songs and dancing while beating drums, cymbals, and rhythm sticks with bells.

At the feast I ate apart from the high-caste guests. Afterward, Bhima told me to sleep on a cot in the cowshed. I settled down right next to two fine white bullocks. I thought, "Oh, how proud I would be if I could own animals like that instead of those sorry stumbling beasts my father and I use for plowing our master's lands!"

The next day Bhima supplied me with oil, a twig toothbrush, and tobacco paste for cleaning my teeth. Tobacco paste is a rare luxury for the people of my caste. I bathed in the village pond, then took a meal. Bhima gave me an infant's shirt and pants for my son, but nothing else, even though he had promised a cloth for me or my wife. I had given him a good gift, an expensive gift, and look what he gave me!

Just as I was leaving, my friend's brother pointed to the pair of white bullocks that I had admired the night before. He said, "My bullocks are old and cannot work well any more. I shall sell them and buy a pair of water buffalo."

He thought that I had money, so he talked to me as if I were a babu [man of importance]. I was flattered; how could I tell him that I was penniless? I replied like a wealthy man, "If you will sell those bullocks, I'll buy them. We've got to buy a pair."

At home I told my father about the white bullocks. Last year he had bought an old bullock which was poorly matched to our other one. Now we had an opportunity to sell our old bullocks and buy better ones. He agreed to look at them.

A few days later Father and I returned to Bhima's house. Bhima was absent, as was his brother. At the cowshed Father and I inspected the bullocks. Their legs were straight and strong, not bowed or lame. Their hooves were just the right size, neither too large, which would make them bump against stones, nor too small, which would prevent them from walking properly. Their hides were white. We prefer this because white bullocks can stay in the sun longer and work harder. They had no skin diseases or sores on their humps.

Next we examined the bullocks for bad signs and holy marks; we won't buy such animals. If a bullock eats the urine of other bullocks, we consider it weak. This is a bad sign. If it has white snakelike marks on the black tip of its nose, it is always angry, and will cause the death of other bullocks, as well as misfortunes in the owner's family. A bullock whose hide has an extra fold near the hump brings bad luck: Lakshmi, the goddess of wealth, will leave the bullock's owner and take his wealth with her. We consider a bullock holy if its tongue constantly moves outside its mouth, for this is the sign of the *hulahuli*, the holy [ululating] sound that women make at festivals. Animals with holy signs must never work; and we won't buy them. We believe a calf to be the sacred animal of the god Shiva if it has extra horns, extra muscles around its neck, or a fifth leg growing out of the hump area. No one will use such an animal for work; we don't castrate it, but leave it a bull.

Since we found no bad signs or holy marks, Father agreed to buy the bullocks. We waited until Bhima's brother returned. He had been directing coolie laborers in his paddy fields. After he bathed he came to see us. I greeted him respectfully, with palms together, and he greeted my father the same way.

Bhima's brother asked, "Why have you come?" Of course he knew why.

I replied, "To take your two bullocks. But first you should finish your lunch; then we'll talk."

He invited us to eat at his house; but Bhima's wife, who lived next door, had seen us arrive and had prepared a meal for us. She served us on the outer veranda of her house while Bhima's brother ate lunch inside his own house.We finished first and waited.

When he returned, he asked, "Have you seen the bullocks?"

I said, "Yes, Father and I have seen them. Now, about the price, it should be fixed. Then I'll take them."

He said, "You fix the price."

I protested, "No, it's your bullock. How can I name the price? You tell us."

"I cannot say."

Father said, "We are all friends, so nobody will offer a price, or bargain. We should call a mediator, an outsider who can fix the price. Call someone from your village."

Bhima's brother came back with several gentlemen. He said to them, "The man buying the bullocks is a friend, so I don't want to quote a price. You should fix the approximate rate."

After carefully inspecting the bullocks, the gentlemen announced, "150 rupees for the pair."

We did not reply. My tongue became stuck. How could impartial mediators charge us so much? And how could we pay them? We had barely twenty rupees.

Then one of the gentlemen asked my father, "Oh friend, what do you think? Will you take the bullocks?"

Father replied bravely, "Yes, I want them, but the price is too high."

"High? We think it is fair. Why do you think it's too high?"

Bhima's brother interrupted, "If you think it high, why don't you mention the price you consider right?"

My father said, "It would be nice if it were seventy rupees."

The gentleman shook his head vigorously, "No, no, that cannot be."

"Well, how about seventy-five?"

"No, impossible."

"Well, eighty-five."

"Not at all."

"Ninety."

"Look, if you want to bargain, why did you call us here?" Father was rude to bargain in the presence of a mediator. But he thought they wanted too much. What could I do? I saw my prestige melting away as Father bargained, but respect for my father forced me to remain silent.

Father said, "Since you won't bargain, I'll pay one hundred rupees."

Bhima's brother said, "Let it be."

The gentlemen left. We returned to the house of Bhima's brother. I gave him twenty rupees, saying, "I'll pay the rest of the money tomorrow, or the day after that."

Bhima's brother said, "No, no. Why should I allow credit on the selling of fur? It is not nice." We believe that bullocks and cows are Lakshmi ["wealth," or the goddess of wealth]. If you divide payments for the goddess you insult her.

I replied, "I'll give some money now. If possible, I'll pay the rest tomorrow. Don't worry, the money will automatically come to your feet."

His face looked unhappy. I said, "Go to your brother and ask him. He can give the money for me. Or wait, I'll ask him."

I went to Bhima's wife and said "I want to buy your brother-in-law's bullocks. We've already fixed the price, but I cannot pay all of it now due to temporary difficulties. If you fail to help, we'll lose our *jidi* [strength of obstinacy]. People will laugh at me, coming to buy a bullock with no money. I can never show my face in this village again. I can pay you the day after tomorrow. You should be my guarantor. If you don't, who is to help me? I came here depending on you. Go and say something to your brother-in-law. Say that you will be responsible for the payment."

She said, "I see your trouble, but will you really pay the day after tomorrow?"

"Definitely. I'll give it tomorrow, why the day after tomorrow?" At this point I was willing to promise anything.

Because of my expensive gift to her daughter, Bhima's wife thought that I was rich and no risk. She went with me to her brother-in-law and told him a false tale: "Don't worry about the money; you can get it from my house. Muli gave some money to your brother, so you may give Muli the bullocks."

He agreed; we led the bullocks home.

Later that day I met Bhima and told him how my father and I had bought the bullocks. He said angrily, "Why did you do like this without asking me? Well, since you have taken the bullocks away, be sure that you pay tomorrow."

I said quickly, "Sure! I'll pay tomorrow, or the day after."

I went home and told Father that we had to find eighty rupees by the following day to pay for the bullocks.

He said, "Tomorrow Gafur the Muslim cattle merchant will come. We'll sell our old bullocks to him. That will give us a little money. But where will we get the rest?"

I shrugged, "I don't know. Find a way."

Father replied, "How can I? You show me how to get some money."

The next morning Gafur bought our pair of bullocks for twenty rupees. As Gafur led them away, I muttered, "Who knows what will happen to them?" Father shrugged. We pretended not to know that Gafur would butcher them and sell the meat.

Father handed me the twenty rupees. I said, "What will I do with this? I need eighty rupees, and I need it badly. Bring another sixty rupees from somewhere."

Father complained, "From where? What a lot of trouble! I should never have bought a pair of bullocks at such a cost."

He went off; after some time he returned with ten rupees. "I can't get any more money than that," he sighed. "You'd better return the bullocks."

But how could we? Gafur had already taken our old pair. I decided to send the thirty rupees. I was so ashamed that I didn't want to go myself. Pretending to be a rich man, I had brought my family nothing but disgrace. How could I keep my word before my new friend? I went to my small-caste friends and asked them to run the errand; they wouldn't. I went to my brother-in-law Damodar and asked him. He refused irritably, saying, "I cannot go on this errand. I don't know your friend. Your father just came to me and borrowed ten rupees."

Damodar was annoyed at my father's improper and shameful behavior. A father-in-law, a respected person, must never borrow even a betel from his son-in-law. I left Damodar and walked slowly toward the place where my friend Bhima was working, all the while thinking, "How can I get the money? How can I show my face to him?" Suddenly I thought, "Maybe I should go to my other brother-in-law, Bisia, and borrow some money." I turned toward his house.

Bisia wasn't at home; I waited until he returned, late at night. I told him the whole story. He listened, frowning, and then asked, "Why are you acting like this with a new friend? It is not good. Even so, I would help you, but I have no money."

I went home. I couldn't face my friend. I didn't tell my wife; she would have scolded me.

That night I thought, "Tomorrow I'll go to my friend and give him the thirty rupees. I'll beg him to take my apology. For now, out of his own pocket, he should give his brother the remaining money I owe."

I went to Bhima the next day. When he heard my proposal, he shook his head disapprovingly. "I don't know about that. You bought bullocks from my brother; you should pay him. Why are you always dragging me into this mess, first the other day, and now today? My brother sold you the bullocks to have the money to buy a pair of buffalo. If you give him ten rupees a week, how can he buy them? I cannot take this thirty rupees to him, and I cannot be your guarantor."

I lied desperately, "What can I do? I'm in a lot of trouble, but it's my brother-in-law's fault. He promised to buy the bullocks I took from your brother, but when he saw them he refused. So we quarreled."

I touched his feet and said, "Oh friend, protect me in my moment of danger. Save me! I can surely repay you within one and a half months, but gradually. You are my oath-friend. If you won't help me now, when would you help me? What I did was wrong. Please forgive me!"

He accepted the money silently. As I went home, I thought, "How can I give back the money?" Borrowing a pickaxe from my father, I went to work in the stone quarries.

After one week I had saved ten rupees. I gave it to my friend. The next week I didn't work as much; I only paid him five rupees. I hate stone quarrying; it is too exhausting, and I always hurt myself. After two weeks of quarrying I became ill. My wages stopped. So did my payments.

A month later I handed him another five rupees. Avoiding his eyes, I apologized, "What could I do? I had a lot of trouble; I couldn't work and haven't worked for a week."

I could see from my friend's silent face that he was irritated with me.

After four months I repaid all the money. But my bad fame was in that house to stay. I no longer wanted to show my face there. I never returned. [Muli nevertheless remains Bhima's child's godfather.]

Why do my friendships with high-caste people always end up like this? It must be my bad fate.

18. Starvation and Family Quarrels, 1957–58

Before the harvest in November, prices rise because rice is scarce. Muli's family is without food and is unable to find work. They starve, eating one meal every other day. Muli's six-month-old son develops boils, which soon spread to Muli and his wife. They are in such pain that they cannot work and thus have no money to buy food. Muli's mother refuses to give them food because they are contributing nothing to the household income. After Muli's wife and mother quarrel over food, Muli moves himself, his wife, and his son out of his father's house. Although Muli mentions only food, his wife and mother probably quarreled over their competition for Muli's allegiance and Muli's scandals with women, which by now had become public knowledge.

Before the harvest came in November, rice became very scarce, prices rose, and no one would lend us rice. We could not find any work, so we had no money to buy food. In order to survive, we dug up roots and stole yams from the fields of wealthy landowners. Even then, we were hungry. We ate one meal a day, or none. Sometimes we ate one meal every other day.

Right at harvest time, my infant son developed boils. They soon spread to my body, all over except my face. It was severe and painful. I could not walk because of the pain, so I could not harvest paddy, at the one time we could expect to have steady work. My wife also developed boils and could not work. My father, mother, and brother went to cut paddy.

Mother resented that my wife and I were earning nothing, and she refused to give us any food. But my sister stole food from the kitchen and fed us. We sat at home, in agony, covered with boils. Whenever my mother found us eating, she scolded us and told us to leave. "Two people will sit in the house and eat," she said, "and there is their son, who requires two to three coins' worth of sugar each day! So we feed three people every day from our earnings.

Why aren't you looking after your own stomachs? We cannot feed you any more!"

Each night my wife cried under my feet. And we both prayed to God to cure us.

One morning I hobbled to the hospital, hoping to get some help from the doctor whom I used to supply with prostitutes. But he had been transferred; another doctor was there whom I did not know. I was a man of small caste, an untouchable, so I despaired. How could I talk to an important man like that? I turned away and returned home.

I was such a lucky man that my boils, instead of going away, got bigger day by day, and so did those of my wife. Meanwhile, my mother scolded us more and more.

My wife could no longer stand the scolding. One morning she borrowed some berries from a neighbor and sold them in the village.* Even though she was in terrible pain, she worked; I couldn't do that. So I stayed home and took care of our infant son. I borrowed some sugar on credit from a high-caste shopkeeper. I mixed the sugar with water and fed it to my son two to three times that day. When my wife returned she nursed him. With the money she earned I went to the market and bought rice, sulphur, and coconut oil. It was very painful for me to walk. My wife boiled the sulphur and oil together and spread the hot paste on our boils; soon they burst, and pus drained out. Throughout the day, up to that time late at night, we had not eaten anything. Now we ate. That night, for the first time in weeks, we were able to sleep without horrible pain and with our bellies full.

But the boils returned. We survived like this for one month, with my wife working while I took care of our child, feeding him sugar-water until his mother returned late at night and nursed him. Sometimes during that month we were able to eat even twice a day. My mother saw this and was jealous. She picked quarrels with my wife, screaming, "Who took my fuel, my rice, my vegetables? You did!"

Finally, my wife could stand this no longer, and answered harshly, "Who is taking your property? Whose pubic hair cares for your property?" This was a grave insult to give to one's respected superior, so my mother hit her, and they fought, screaming curses at each

*By selling berries, Muli's wife was begging indirectly. Buyers exchanged rice for berries, knowing that the seller was poor and probably starving.

40. Bauri woman gestures during an argument.

other, "You daughter of a whore! You cholera-eaten corpse! Leprosy will eat away your fingers!"

The women of the ward ran in and pulled them apart.

My mother had beaten my wife a great deal, and my wife was hurt. When I came home, I found everyone in the house angry. I also became angry when I saw my wife's injuries. I complained to the elders of my ward, the hereditary leader, the assistant leader, and my father's brothers.

I said, "When my wife, my son and I became ill, my parents separated from us and wouldn't feed us. When we became well, they quarreled with us over food, and today my mother beat my wife. They eat well; we eat only once a day. Still, my mother is unhappy. Why? You should give me justice. What can I do? How can I run my life?"

They asked my father, "Why is Muli dissatisfied with you and your wife? He is your son, as you are the son of your father. Your father helped you earn until his death. Why aren't you looking after your son like that?"

41. Bauri children collecting twigs for kindling, plus snails and wild plants for food.

My father replied, "I can't say anything about this, or about these women's quarrels and dissatisfactions. You should ask my wife."

They asked my mother, "Why is Muli unhappy? Why don't you give him food from your kitchen? Why are you cooking separately?"

My mother replied, "Where will I get food to give him and his wife? Because we gave them food, we used up all the crops we earned at the harvest. Only two persons earn wages, my husband and my son-in-law. Suddenly my son's wife finds a way to sell berries. Why not before? Each year they always wait for the chance to eat while sitting idly. They should do their own work and make their own meals. They are not small children. They can feed themselves."*

*Muli's mother, supportive, nurturing, and indulgent during Muli's youth, now throws him out of the house. She changed her attitude toward Muli for four reasons: 1) she was competing for his affection with his wife, and saw her own hold on him slipping away; 2) extreme conditions of scarcity provoked her to quarrel over food; 3) Muli was a poor earner; 4) his scandals had been uncovered, and his father had been publicly criticized and fined (see Chapter 2).

The men replied, "Why are you so angry? You should cook jointly, and eat jointly, and your son's wife should give you what she earns. Today your son is ill. Tomorrow he will be well and will give you his earnings."

Mother remained silent. The elders assumed that she had accepted their decision, so they said to my wife, "Go and cook in the kitchen." They said to my mother, "Supply her with the food and fuel. Don't quarrel any more. Don't act so that others can laugh at you." To my father they said, "You, Hata, are a responsible man, so you should pay attention to your prestige and prevent quarreling."

I told my wife to start cooking for everyone. I said to Mother, "Why don't you help her? You are keeping every jealous thought in your mind. How will you go?"

She sat without moving. I asked my sister, "Go and help her." She went inside and cooked with my wife. Everybody ate except my mother. She sat silently, and went to sleep without a word.

When I awoke the next morning, my mother was still sitting. The rest of us ate watered rice. Mother stood up and walked out of the house. Later I heard that she ate at the house of my sister, who lived in another ward.

That evening I asked the leaders of our ward what I should do. I told them, "You made a decision, but my mother refuses to follow it. She is not eating at our house."

They said, "You go ahead with your cooking and eating. Don't ask her to eat. She is very wicked. Wait and see how many days she will do this."

That night nobody ate. My father, younger brother, and mother sat silently. My wife and I did not care about that. They went to my sister's house to eat and probably gave their day's earnings to my sister's family.

This continued for about fifteen days. No one asked anything or spoke. Suddenly one day just before cooking time, they burst into the kitchen and threw our clay pots into the courtyard, shattering them. Then they put their own new pots on the stove and started cooking.

I complained to the gentlemen of the ward. They called my father, and we all sat in the courtyard.

I said to the gentlemen, "I called you fifteen days ago. You made a decision and I obeyed it. But these others refused to stay with me. The first day after your decision, Mother refused to eat. On the second

42. Bauri grandmother collecting scraps of iron and glass, which she sells in the city.

day, the others would not eat. Today, they threw our pots out of the kitchen. Where will I cook? Where will I get food to cook?"

The gentlemen asked my father, "Oh, Hata, why has this happened?"

He replied, "What can I do? The opinion of mother and son do not match. Nobody likes anybody else. So what can I do?"

The leader of the ward asked: "Muli right now is unable to earn, so your wife is displeased. But when he brought in a good income, and gave it to your wife, did she like him or not? Why does she dislike him now?"

Father replied, "Of course my wife is wrong. But what can I do? I have no power to change her. Muli is doing his own cooking. I don't like to mix these two together, for they will simply quarrel more and more. I am becoming old. I may depend on Muli, but he cannot

43. Bauris begging at a religious festival.

expect to depend on me. To prevent more quarrels, I would be happy
if he would leave us."

When my wife heard this, she whispered to me, "You should tell
the leader that we are ready to separate, but that they should not
blame us, or think that after marriage a son separated from his parents because of his attraction to his wife."

I agreed with my wife. I spoke out, "Oh, gentlemen, my parents
wish me to leave. Although times are bad for me and my wife, I agree
to separate. But my parents should not blame me. It was their choice,
not mine, to separate."

The leaders said, "Why would anyone blame you? If both sides
agree to separate, it is good."

From that day, we separated. We remained in my father's compound but cooked in separate pots. My wife sold berries and nuts
and palm fruit. I took care of my son. When I felt hungry during the
daytime, waiting for our one meal at night, I recalled the past days

when I had spent a lot of money for treating everyone in the joint family with snacks, giving them as much or more than I took. When they were in need, I had disregarded all the obstacles they had put in my way. I had spent all of my daily earnings on them and saved nothing for my own son! Remembering this, I would catch hold of my son, cry, and pray to God. I decided to look for work.

My large boils healed; except for scars, they were gone. Nevertheless, I wore a dirty old bandage on my leg, not to cure the boils, but to protect me from Kanduri and Kubera, two bad people in my ward who have *aakhi garuaa* [heavy eyes].These persons can poison or destroy anything by looking at it. I feared that they would use incantations to make my boils grow again, or that my boils would grow again if the two men looked upon them.

Kanduri is my wife's maternal uncle. Once he visited us while my wife was preparing rice cakes. She was mixing powder and water on our floor. While roasting a fish in our earthen stove, Kanduri looked at that floor. Because of this, the cakes would not cook. Although my wife boiled them for hours, they never softened, but remained raw. If only one or two cakes hadn't cooked, there might have been some other reason, but when none of the cakes cooked, we knew that Uncle Kanduri caused it.

Yesterday, Uncle Kanduri came to our door. Even though he is a relative to whom my wife must give respect, she scolded him and wouldn't let him in the house. "Please wait; don't go in the house. I'll go outside to you." She will see him outside, but inside his heavy eyes cause trouble. It is not Uncle Kanduri's fault; he was born that way and cannot help it. Whenever he is around, things go wrong.

After talking with my wife, Kanduri visited Diga's house; the women were boiling *jaau*, a dish made of sugar cane molasses and rice flour. The molasses was boiling, and the pot of rice flour was near the stove ready to be poured into the molasses. The women poured the flour. It should have taken half an hour to boil. The women boiled the mixture for four hours, but the flour did not cook, and nothing mixed together. The next morning the men and women of Diga's house went to Kanduri's house and scolded him angrily. Kanduri listened but said nothing. They did not beat him because they knew he couldn't help what happened; but they told him never to barge in while they were preparing food. Nowadays he asks before entering houses because he knows he has heavy eyes.

19. Brother Anadi, 1959–60

Muli's mother flatters Kia, Muli's wife, to persuade her to contribute money and help for the wedding of Muli's brother Anadi. After the wedding, Muli's mother and wife again quarrel and separate. Muli considers himself victimized by his quarrelsome mother, and also by his ineffectual father, who makes no effort to prevent the separation. Muli thus reverses the conventional belief in India that wives, seeking greater independence, often instigate the breakup of joint households. Although Muli often quarrels with his wife, he always depicts her as blameless and victimized by his parents—a characterization that may well be idealized.

In one of the rare occasions in which Muli discusses his son, he mentions how he sent his son to school. Significantly, the incident involves both high-caste people who discriminate against Bauris and a rare high-caste person who exhibits no prejudice against them.

Gradually during the rainy season our income improved. My wife saved some money, although I did not know this. When harvest season came, I found she was not selling paddy for other necessities, such as oil and lentils, but was spending money she had saved. That year we also saved a lot of paddy because we didn't sell any at all.

After the harvest, my father settled the betrothal of my brother Anadi to a girl from Ekchalia village, fifteen miles away. Father asked me to contribute money and paddy to pay for the wedding. I said, "Why ask me? Ask your daughter-in-law [Muli's wife]."

My father asked her. She replied, "Where can we get money and paddy?"

My father said, "If you won't help, how can we pay for this marriage? If you don't help your brother-in-law, how will you get his help later when you need it?"

I didn't reply. I said nothing. But that night I talked with my wife. She said, "Why do you forget the trouble they gave us last year? They never helped us when we were diseased and starving. Indirectly they wanted our death. We owe them nothing."

I replied, "I remember everything. But what should I do? A

younger brother is like a son. Sometimes your son defecates and urinates on your body. Do you forgive him or do you kill him? Forget the past, for the happiness of your younger brother—our son. Can property take a man to heaven?"

While we were talking, Father entered the room. He said, "Why are you pulling against one another? Your brother's marriage cannot be held. Isn't this shameful to you? If the marriage is held, but lacks things, so that people laugh at us, won't that cause a loss of prestige for you? Forget the past. Join with us and help us to celebrate the marriage. Remember the proverb, 'At the time of fighting, the flat horns of the buffalo become round'; during a crisis, the flat horns which are bad for fighting become round solid horns good for fighting; so, too, during a crisis, a disunited family unites. Oh, *dhana* [wealth], forget the past. Help with the wedding."

Father turned to my wife and said, "Oh, daughter, don't refuse my request. If you were my daughter, could you refuse my request? Forget past quarrels. Think of it as your own son's marriage."

I had agreed before, but I feared what my wife would say to me if I helped in the marriage.

While Father was there, my wife remained silent because the husband should appear to make the decisions, but after Father left, she told me she would cooperate.

The next day, my mother came and called to my wife, "Oh, daughter, why are you pouting? Forget my faults. You should not cook separately. Cook with us. If guests come for negotiations, what will they think, seeing father and son separated? Come, we'll cook and eat together."

My wife replied, "If I mix with you, I'll not give my savings, paddy, and rice to you for six months, but I'll give my daily wage to you for food expenses."

Mother said, "Oh, oooh why are you talking like this? For the death of your uncle?" This was a gentle, joking, scolding kind of reprimand. It has no meaning; it's just what we say.

My wife laughed. I thought my wife had been won over by my mother. She had been flattered into being happy and friendly. She was so happy at the attention being paid her that, without asking my permission, she immediately fetched one and a half bags of paddy and gave it to my mother. I sat there watching this, overjoyed at our reconciliation. This was eight days before the wedding was scheduled.

That day my wife stayed at home. She boiled the rice she had given to mother. We cooked together and became one family again.

The day before the marriage, three or four of my neighbors went to bring Anadi's new bride. I asked Father, "What ornaments have you bought for your new bride?"

Mother overheard and replied, "If we had bought ornaments, how could you not have known? Where will we get money to buy ornaments? Your wife has ornaments. Can't we give those? Is the elder daughter to have ornaments while the younger daughter wears nothing?"

Hearing this, my wife promptly offered her ornaments, thereby showing merit. So for my brother's wedding my parents had plenty of paddy, rice, and ornaments; we supplied everything. The wedding occured as planned; the guests returned home the day after. For the fourth-night ceremony my parents ran out of rice, although they had lots of vegetables. My wife gave them unparboiled rice. We still had some unboiled paddy. I didn't want to stop our aid for the marriage because the new bride was in the house. If I had stopped and people had gone hungry that day, it would have looked very bad.

I said to my wife, "We'll stop our help after my brother's wife goes back home. She'll go back after the seventh day."

My wife said, "Yes, they like us. Forget about past quarrels. Let's give them what they need."

She did this for *baahaadurii* [glory, merit], so that she might overhear the gossip in the ward: "Oh, did you know, Muli's wife gave rice and even her own ornaments for the marriage of Muli's brother. What a good woman she is!" She wanted to bask in the praise of the women. Often after a woman does a good deed she will listen to the idle gossip, in the hope that she will hear herself praised. If she doesn't, she may volunteer the information: "Did you know, for that new bride in our house I gave two bags of rice." Then others will praise her, "Oh, you are very good to do that."

On the tenth day after the marriage, my brother's new wife returned to her father's house. In our custom, a woman may go back on the seventh, tenth, or twenty-first day; the twenty-first is often used with younger brothers' wives.

Ten days after she left, she returned to our house. While she was absent, we did not stop aid to our family. Once you start giving help, it is hard to stop. We did not stop when she returned.

Gradually, all that we had saved was consumed. At the Bhubaneswar chariot festival, we spent ten or fifteen rupees on pressed rice which we gave to the family. We had happiness in our family, so we did not care for our property. We worked. We ate. When we had no work, we gave from our savings. Until the rains came, we had some rice saved. But by the month of Aswin [September-October], we had nothing left. We went hungry. Most of the time we starved. My father went to the stone quarry during these days. He liked that work, did it expertly, and made more money at it than others did. Since I did not like stone quarry work, I never went there to help my father. Sometimes Anadi went with him, but not every day.

My mother became angry at both Anadi and me. "Go and separate from us. Look after your job. Where will you get food otherwise? One man is earning; ten people are eating. That's why we aren't getting any food. We reared you, we fed you, we married you. Are we still supposed to feed you?"

We separated. Before separation, I talked it over with Anadi. "Our mother is very quarrelsome. Her promises disappear according to her own needs. If we break into three families, everybody will laugh. Everybody knows the character of our mother. If we separate from Mother, nobody will blame us. But we should stay together, if your wife agrees."

His family agreed, and so our family broke into two parts: the family of my parents and the family of we two brothers. In an atmosphere of enmity we lived in that house.

Four years we lived like this until, because of a great quarrel, Anadi's family and mine also separated.

When four years had crossed [passed], and my child had reached the fifth year of life, I decided to send him to school. I went to a caaṭasaaḷaa [informal school] teacher who lived in a high-caste Mallia ward. I said, "Would you teach my son?"

He accepted my son for instruction. He taught children preliminary things before they went to regular school. His pupils learned the letters of the Oriya language. The teacher, himself educated in an informal school, instructed his pupils in the house of a Brahman. For initial payment I gave him one coconut. He told me to bring a cloth, turmeric, coconut, slate, chalk, some sacred dry food, and religious donation money. But when I sent my child I gave him one rupee for everything plus one coconut.

That day, when my son returned from school, he had turmeric

smeared in a line from the bridge of his nose up to his hairline. That was for the ritual that started him as a student.

Monthly fees were a half a rupee. My son, Gopala, liked to go to school. Since the school was in a Brahman's house, Gopala sat outside on the veranda and listened, while the other students sat inside. After five months the teacher went somewhere else for a job, and the school ceased.

Later in the rainy season, we heard from one of the people of our caste about a good private school in Santrapur village, much better than Kapileswar's public school, where the teachers beat Bauri children and often yelled at them. The students in Santrapur were learning a lot, we heard. I wanted to put my son in the Santrapur school. But how could he go there alone, a half-mile from our village? I asked Father to send my youngest brother Sarala to that school. He was one and a half years older than my son but not yet in school. Father agreed. I went to the schoolteacher, a man of the Scribe caste, and he said, "Yes, any number of students may come; I'll be happy to enroll them."

I told my father and neighbors the good news, and also what good behavior the rich, high-caste teacher in Santrapur had shown me. Diga and a couple of other men offered to send their sons to the Santrapur school. One day, we took our sons to the school and enrolled them.

While my son was studying in Santrapur, my wife and Anadi's wife quarreled about who was working harder. My wife told me, "Actually, that's not the real cause of the quarrel. She's quarreling because my son is going to school; she cooks for my son, and is jealous because we are three people; they are two people and sharing is unequal."

A few days later, the women quarreled again, then again and again. Anadi became angry at his wife. "If you are quarreling like this, you should go back to your father's house," he said. He took her to her father's house. He did not return home.

20. Kia's Illness, 1960

Kia, Muli's wife, becomes seriously ill; but Muli, lacking money, cannot pay for daily medical treatment. For over a year Kia suffers through intermittent unsuccessful modern medical treatments and home remedies until a midwife finally cures her. Kia's greatest concern during her illness is what will happen to her son if she dies. In a moving scene, she wails as she imagines that he will be neglected.

During Kia's illness, the wife of brother Anadi steals the ornaments of Kia and of Muli's sister. Eventually Anadi's wife is forced to return the ornaments, but the bitterness between Muli's family and her remains for a long time. Muli narrated many incidents involving quarrels with Anadi's family; I omitted all except the story of the stolen ornaments, which I shortened.

That year, during the rainy season, my wife's belly became diseased. It was her spleen. I hired an herbalist doctor who lived in the village; his treatment did not help. Although the pain was reduced, my wife could not work. I asked brother Anadi to bring his wife to my house to look after my wife. He agreed and brought his wife. Anadi and I went out to work.

Since I couldn't earn enough to pay for my wife's treatment, her recovery was very slow. Once a month I would go to the herbalist doctor to buy medicine. When this did no good, I took her to the town hospital. Her treatment from the doctors there lasted two or three months but also failed. I despaired.

I would buy medicine for five days or so. She would use it up. Then, because we had no money, we let her treatment go for the rest of the month. Then I'd buy more medicine, which would run out in a couple of days. Every time she got much worse, I dragged her to the hospital, with no improvement. I only bought medicine occasionally. This lasted for one year.

One day, my maternal uncle and aunt from Nuagaon village came to pay their last respects to my wife. They had heard that she might not live. My uncle liked my wife very much because she always showed him more respect than she did my father. When Uncle saw her, he told me he'd take my wife to see a famous high-caste herbalist doctor whom he knew. He said that, while the doctor would not come to my village, he would visit Kia if we moved her to Nuagaon. I agreed to move her, but how? It was the rainy season; rickshaws sank in the mud. I joined together two shoulder-carrying baskets and placed Kia in them, and Anadi and I carried her on our shoulders to Nuagaon. As we walked, the basket bumped the ground; my wife screamed, "Stop! If you keep dropping me like this, I will die!" Later she cried, "Why didn't you bring my son? I will die and he'll never see me again; I'll never see him again. Who will care for him and feed him? Nobody cares for him now except me. What will happen to him after I die?"

I said, "Why are you so worried? I'll stay with my son; I'll take care of him. I'll tell *saana bohuu* [younger brother's wife] to go to work. And I'll stay home and cook and care for my child. Why are you worried?"

We reached Uncle's house and put her down. Anadi went home. I stayed overnight but the next morning left for work. That evening I returned to Nuagaon, and I did this every day during her treatment.

The herbalist doctor gave my wife *moduka*—huge lumps of medicine made of dried leaves, roots, seeds, hashish, sugar, and salt. I fed her the medicine each morning, and Uncle gave her food during the day. After several days the pain was less, but the disease did not go away.

My sister and her husband from Orakali village visited my wife and afterward went to my village and stayed with me. They earned more money weeding fields around my village than they would have in their own village.

But my sister's husband didn't want to remain because it was his father-in-law's house. My sister gave me her silver ornaments to keep in my suitcase while she stayed in my house. She didn't want to wear ornaments while working in the fields; they interfered with working.

My brother's wife saw me put my sister's ornaments in the suitcase. At the time I did not realize that she had seen this. I returned that evening to Uncle's house. Kia asked, "Where is my son? I want to see him. Why didn't you bring him? I want him, I want him!"

I said, "If I bring your son, it will cost your uncle more money. They will hate us. I'll bring your son, but only for a brief time."

She said, "How cruel you are! How can I live without seeing my son's face!"

I said, "I'll bring him for a *while*. Then he can go back in the morning. He's attending school."

My wife said, "You think about Uncle's expenses, but you never consider his other troubles. They need men for weeding. Don't bring your son. Stay here and make Uncle and Aunt happy. We owe them for their help. Work for them while they need labor. Then they'll look after me cheerfully."

I worked at Uncle's. Another sister of mine, who lives in the town, visited us that night. I slept outside on the veranda, while the two women slept inside.

That night, my wife had a bad dream. She shouted "Oh, Gopala, oh, Gopala!" and awakened me.

I rushed inside. "What happened?"

She said, "You see, I saw a shadow while I slept, my son returning from school hungry, going here and there, nobody paying any attention to him, nobody feeding him, so he goes out to the river calling 'Mother! Father!' "

When I heard all this, I got a little nervous. I tried to calm her down. "Dreams are not always true, don't worry about it. My younger brother and his wife are not like this; they wouldn't neglect him. Nobody would. Could you neglect even your enemy's child if your enemy's household were in trouble? Don't feel bad."

She said, "Why are you trying to convince me? I don't want to hear anything from your mouth. I want to see my son! Go and bring him." She started crying.

I said, "It's night. How could anyone go there now? I'll go tomorrow morning."

She cried more and more. By now Uncle and Aunt had awakened. My uncle asked, "What happened? What happened? Why is *bohuu* [daughter-in-law] crying?"

I said, "Uncle, she had a bad dream that her son is being neglected in our village."

Uncle said, "If she had a bad dream, why don't you bring your son back to her? Go tomorrow morning. You can return to work here later. It's her only son."

I said, "Yes, I'll do that. Tell your daughter-in-law not to cry."

Uncle said, "Daughter-in-law, don't cry more. Pray to God. Depend on your fate and fortune. Nobody can alter your fate. You are getting your past sins, the fruits of your past existence. Your unhappiness will disappear soon. You have had too much punishment. Why are you unhappy about your son? Everybody will look after your property. God is there to help your son. If Muli doesn't bring him back tomorrow, I'll do it. Don't worry about his schoolwork. Studying doesn't take a man to heaven."

We all remained silent. I thought I should take my wife home. Due to medicine and good food she was improved, but her disease had not gone away. I remembered a doctor in the town; I decided to take her there as a last resort.

Early the next morning, I went to the town and talked to my brother-in-law Biswanath [Bisia]. He said, "If her situation is as you describe, then she may not live. Why throw her after death [on the funeral pyre] in a distant place? Why not bring her home to die?"

I had no power to decide anything then. I told Bisia that we'd bring her back in a shoulder basket. He said, "No need; I'll carry her on my back."

Bisia was large, young, and strong, but not strong enough to carry my wife all the way home. On the way he put her down. Then I carried her on my back for a while. We took turns until we reached the Gangua River. At that place I said, "Bisia, you must carry her the rest of the way. If my villagers see me carrying my wife, I'd feel ashamed."

He carried her into the village. At home, my wife called, "Where is my son? Show me." When he arrived, she threw her arms around him and sobbed.

From that day we stayed home. I looked for work; none was available. I couldn't save a single coin for medicine because I could find no work.

One afternoon, my neighbor Raji met an old woman of our caste who worked as a midwife in the Old Town hospital. Raji asked her to examine my wife. The old woman pressed different parts of my wife's belly and said, "It is a very harmful disease. A big gland has formed inside the womb [Muli uses the word womb but means stomach]. She is lucky she hasn't died."

She pushed her hand inside my wife's vagina. She felt something there. "It is a very old disease. It will be hard to cure. Why didn't you ask me to look at this before? You must bring two kinds of roots from the medical store. Boil them with black pepper. Give this to her three times a day for three days. Then if she drinks warm water her gland-colic lumps will soften; then I'll rub them with oil, making them go back to their original place."

I said, "We don't know the roots you mentioned. Could you buy them for us?"

She said, "Yes, I'll bring them tomorrow."

We gave her half a rupee for medicine and she left. Two days later she returned with the roots and black pepper. She gave this to my wife along with hot water. She heated mustard oil and rubbed it on my wife's stomach and chest, praying to a deity while she did this. She placed a one-anna coin on the place where my wife's lumps were. My wife was in great pain through this. The old woman paid no attention, but just went ahead with her work. Then the old woman told me to bring hot water and a rolled-up plantain leaf. She put the leaf on my wife's stomach, dropped a cloth in the hot water, and placed the cloth on the leaf. She did this several times.

The old woman stayed with us for several nights, giving treatments once a night and once in the morning before going to the hospital. After eight days my wife was cured. The old woman told me to feed my wife good food like papayas, green plantain, meat, and clarified butter, but most of the time I couldn't; we had no money.

During the time of my wife's illness, the bracelets and anklets of Anadi's wife were stolen; nobody knew who stole them. Who took them? Many people had come to see my sick wife. It could have been almost anybody. Since we did not know even whom to suspect, or what day the theft occurred, I did not accuse anyone. It was hopeless; I did not even try to get them back.

A few days later, the father of Anadi's wife came to our house for a day. I heard that he had told many people that I had been needy when my wife was ill, so I probably had taken the ornaments, and that's why I hadn't taken any interest in discovering the thief and getting the ornaments back.

Those who heard this believed the old man because it was believable. I was indeed desperate for money at that time. I told Anadi and his wife, Tanu, "If you believe I took your ornaments, make me take whatever oath you want; take me to any deity you want for a test, or you may report it to the police."

They replied, "Who told you these things? We never said anything like that."

I felt sad that people had accused me unjustly of being a thief. I told this to all the people of my ward. They listened. Then they disliked Anadi's father-in-law for making false accusations. They believed me, not him.

The next morning, that man went home while I was at the market. The morning after, I went to put the money I had earned the day before into my metal suitcase. I found it wide open. I asked my wife, "Who opened the box?"

She replied, "How should I know? You've got the key. Did you open it yesterday to deposit our savings?"

"No, I'm putting our money in now." I looked for our ornaments wrapped in cloth. They were gone! My mouth dropped. I tried to call my wife, but the only sounds that came out were, "Ah! ah ah!" My head swam; everything's gone!

"What happened, what happened?" She looked into the empty box; not only were our own ornaments gone, but also those of my sister from Orakali. My wife sank to the ground and wailed, crying out while remembering the past, "Oh where have my ornaments gone? Someone has taken them! Why has fortune treated us like this? It is the savings of many days. Where will we get more ornaments? Oh, who took them? What can we do?"

I also wailed. After a while I invited my maternal uncle at Nuagaon and all my sisters' husbands to meet me. I sent messengers. The relatives came the following day and asked me why I had called them.

I told them that my brother's wife's ornaments had been stolen, that my brother's father-in-law had insulted me by accusing me of stealing them to pay for my wife's medical costs, and that someone had also stolen all of my ornaments and those of my sister. I then cried, "What can I do? Who took them? I don't know. Throughout my life I'll never be able to earn money for such ornaments. When my wife was ill, I starved for many days rather than sell my ornaments. Many times, my maternal uncle offered to give me food during those days; I told him I had already eaten, but in fact I hadn't. With all my troubles, I never mortgaged a single thing; I starved first. So you should determine how I can get back my ornaments and those of my sister. That's why I called you."

My maternal uncle asked, "Whom do you suspect? Anybody of this house?"

I replied, "How can I suspect an outsider? When my wife was ill, many people came here, but since she has become well, nobody has come. I suspect my brother's wife."

Bisia, my brother-in-law from Bhubaneswar, asked my brother's wife, "Have you taken those ornaments?"

"No," she said, and then added quickly, "I vow that he who took those ornaments should lose all hope of living, and all of his hopes should die."

My Uncle Satyabadi said, "Why are you taking an oath? You should tell the truth. You take an oath that all your hopes will die. Your hope is your husband. You are hoping that he should die. Where is the gain from that? He is our son. It is our loss too, not only yours. So tell the truth, making an oath by touching me and saying that you haven't taken it."

By touching someone and making an oath, a person wagers the life of the person he touches: if my sister-in-law were guilty and she touched Satyabadi, then Satyabadi would die, and the sin of murder would rest on her. Therefore, people are reluctant to make oaths.

She immediately stepped forward and touched Uncle Satyabadi's hand, saying, "I did not take any ornaments."

Uncle Satyabadi said, "You should not ask her any more questions; I am sure she did not take the ornaments. When she touches my body like this—leave her, she is not guilty."

Bisia said, "I am sure she did not take the ornaments. She touched your body and swore she's not guilty."

Bisia asked everyone present, from father to younger son, but everyone denied they had taken the ornaments. He said, "Everybody denies that they took the ornaments. But in the village of Kantaunia there is a magician who knows how to discover the thief. He'll give some salt and some root to everybody suspected of taking them. The root has magic. The mixture will not react on those who are innocent, but only in the body of the thief: his stomach will swell; he'll get blood dysentery and blood vomiting, and anyone else who is involved in the crime also will suffer like this."

Uncle Satyabadi said, "How can we get the magician here?"

Bisia said, "Don't worry; I'll go with Muli and bring him. Let him come here, and we'll *see* how the thief escapes! Not only will he be uncovered, but he will also come down with a horrible disease; as the proverb says, 'What has been taken will be returned.' And not only will the ornaments be recovered, but the guilty one will have to spend money to cure himself of the disease. Come, Muli, what are we waiting for? Get some money for the magician, and we'll be on our way! No one should blame us later for not warning him. Whoever took the things will get severely sick and may die but cannot blame, curse, or scold us for our actions, since we warned him. That magician is very wicked and strong. No one caught in his test can get away."

We started on our way. We went as far as Santrapur, about one mile, and then Bisia stopped. "You know, Muli, I don't know any magician. I was simply bluffing to frighten the guilty into confessing." We proceeded to Balakati and then to other villages, visiting friends, and in the evening we returned to my village. There we heard that the *saana bohuu* [younger brother's wife], Anadi's wife, had left the house.

"When did she leave?" I asked.

Someone said, "Just after you two left, she went to the Gangua River to take a bath. A group of women went to the river, which was high after flooding, to catch snails. Near the Mallia dam they saw that *saana bou* [contraction of *bohuu*] had crossed the river. They called to her, 'Where are you going?' But she did not look back or respond. The women returned and reported this. The people of our street then gossiped, 'Younger brother's wife has stolen things! If she hadn't, what was she doing crossing the river at flood time and running away?' So we know for sure that she took the ornaments."

Although we knew who had them, we had to quarrel with her family many times before we forced her to return them. She begged forgiveness, and we let her return to her husband Anadi.

21. Marrying and Divorcing a Tree Trunk, 1961

Muli's family helps his sister Gurei to run away from her husband, who has been beating her. They then arrange her remarriage to a man named Krushna [a variant of Krishna] who claims he has never been married. The Bauris believe that an unmarried man must not marry a divorced woman; he must also be divorced. Consequently, Krushna, the new groom, goes through a ceremony in which he marries a tree trunk, divorces it, and then marries Muli's sister.

The tree trunk, wrapped with five pieces of cloth to resemble arms, legs, and head, is symbolically not only the first bride but also the elder sister of the second bride. A ward leader, holding the tree trunk, acts the role of the tree-bride throughout all the ceremonies. The tree-bride and groom are considered married for four days. But at that time the groom refuses to consummate the marriage, saying that when he touched the tree-bride, she scolded him with a terrible curse: "Die from cholera! Die from the goddess Chandi!" He demands and receives a divorce after paying her family compensation. The tree-bride's symbolic father then substitutes his younger daughter, saying that he would like to maintain his relationship with the groom's family. Bauri men sometimes marry the wife's younger sister, usually if the elder sister dies or is barren.

The wedding of the groom with the second bride occurs immediately after divorce from the tree-bride. Significantly, many elements of this second ceremony of two divorcees are reversals of the first ceremony: both bride and groom sit on a bundle of straw rather than on a sacred marriage mat; they face west instead of toward the sacred east; and the family priest joins their left palms instead of the auspicious and pure right palms.

The tree-bride ceremony illustrates the flexibility of Bauri marriage systems, and the propensity of Bauris to adapt rituals to their social needs. Muli observes that marriages among Bauris frequently end in divorce: sister Gurei, the subject of this chapter, has been married four times.

Until the harvest season began, I worked at a house construction site. During the harvest, all four of us, my wife and I, Anadi and his wife, harvested and saved a lot of paddy. After the harvest, we traveled about for work, one day sitting, one day working. After early March, we worked in *muga*-lentil cultivation.

At that time we heard from some people who lived in Orakali village that my sister Gurei's mother-in-law and husband were always beating her. My sister tried to come back to our house; her mother-in-law and husband dragged her back and beat her more and more. They refused to let her go. Often she would run off and pout, coming to our house. Her in-laws would come and get her. When we heard she was being beaten, we decided to bring her back ourselves. But how could we do this? We wanted to keep her with us forever.*

We devised a plan. We wouldn't go to her house now; we would wait for some days after the quarrel ended. Then several women of the ward, along with my mother and wife, would go to Orakali for *muga*-lentil cultivation.

Every day there they met my sister when going out to work; sometimes they would work together. Eventually my mother said to her, "We want to take you to your father's house. What do you say?"

Gurei replied, "They always beat me at my husband's house. I would be happy to leave forever."

"Get all your ornaments together at night," said Mother. "Tomorrow early in the morning, before dawn, I'll come. I'll call you to accompany me for lentil harvest work. You carry a basket in which you will keep your ornaments. We'll go home, not to work."

They did this, heading straight over the paddy fields toward our village. We met them halfway to see if they were all right.

My sister did not want to stay with Mother, but with us. Nobody opposed that, so she lived on our side of the compound. Mother brought her back; she ate my head [Muli fed her]. She stayed hidden in the house for a few days.

Several days later, while returning from work in the capital, I saw my sister Radhi, who is married to Bisia. She said, "A young man from Niali village in Cuttack district [twenty-four miles away], black-skinned but young, strong, and very handsome, is staying with us. Your brother-in-law [Bisia] brought him into our house. I would like to marry our sister Gurei with him. If you'll agree, it would be better."

"Was he ever married?" I asked.

"No."

*Possibly Gurei was being beaten because she was chasing after her old Watchman-caste lover.

"How is this possible! Our sister was married once and divorced. Do you think he'll accept that?"

She said, "He's here; why don't you ask him?"

Bisia overheard us and called the young man: "Oh, Krushna, tell us the truth: are you married or not? If you are unmarried, I can find you a bride here and build a house for you."

"I'm telling the truth," he said. "I've never been married."

"Well, then, I'll arrange a marriage for you."

The next morning I told my father about Krushna, and he said we should meet Krushna's family. We told Krushna, who wrote a letter to his father. On the arranged day, my father, our ward leader, and I visited Krushna's ancestral village. The people there said that Krushna had never married. He had a stepmother who did not like him, so he didn't stay in his house.

My father agreed to marry his daughter to Krushna. After consulting the astrological book and the family priest, we set a marriage date. My house made all the arrangements; the groom's side gave nothing.

Since Krushna was a bachelor and his future wife had been married once, Krushna first had to marry a *kaaṇḍa* [long, straight reed cane or tree trunk]: it is not good for a previously unmarried man to marry a previously married woman, so the man first must marry and divorce. Krushna went through a full marriage at the altar, where he married a tree trunk and divorced it, saying, as the priest had instructed him to do, that the tree trunk had cursed him.

The days passed, some happily, some not. One day Gurei walked into our village accompanied by Batia, a man of Krushna's village of Niali. She had left Krushna for good.*

I was at my house when they came to the door. I gave Batia water to wash his feet, placed a mat for him on the veranda, and gave him betel. Sister Gurei went into a room, crying. My mother, wife, and younger brother's wife went into the room; Gurei held them and sobbed.

Batia said, "You are sitting in your house after giving your sister in marriage, never thinking about her. You don't even remember whether your sister has died or gone. Krushna told you he had never been married, but that was not true. He drove his first wife out of the

---

*The probable reason for the breakup was that she had continued to see her old lover.

house, beating her frequently. She left after a terrible beating, when she had not been given food for several days and had tried to kill herself by drowning in the village well. Her father and mother saw her drowning, saved her, and took her back to their house.

"Without inquiring about the family of Krushna, you gave the daughter of your house to them.* Well, now accept her back. Don't let her go back; if she ever returns, they'll beat her so badly that she'll die. Yesterday at midnight I took your daughter to another village. Early in the morning we caught a bus from there. Several friends and relatives accompanied us to the bus to protect us from Krushna's family."

I was very unhappy when I heard this. I asked Gurei about it; she said the same thing. She added, "Batia adopted me; he is my *dharma baapaa* [godfather]."

We kept Batia at the house and treated him well, giving him *majyedaa* [respect by offering cloth]. We had good vegetables, and we cooked them for him that night. The next morning, we took him on a tour of the capital market, the Old Town bazaar, the new buildings of the capital, and the airfield, where we saw a plane going up and down.† He stayed with us for eight days before returning home.

Since that time, my sister Gurei has married two more times. She's now enjoying her fourth husband. What's four husbands like my sister had? My next-door neighbor has had six wives, and he's now looking for a seventh.

*Krushna's neighbors may have lied to Muli's family in order to protect the prestige of Krushna's family and ward. Batia may have brought Gurei to her father's house in order to avoid further scandals involving Gurei and her lover.
†In those days one flight a week arrived from Calcutta and one from Madras.

Part Four
Bad Times

22. A Successful
Business Venture, 1962

A high-caste customer of Muli's prostitutes helps him to start a betel selling business (betel is for chewing) and secures for him a permanent spot in the city market. Muli becomes the first and only untouchable of his village to hold a permanent spot in the market. His earnings improve. Gone are the days of starvation, of toiling in the stone quarries, of desperately seeking work where none is available. Muli has a steady income, and he buys sweets and clothes for himself, his wife, and his son.

Muli presents a revealing account of the ways in which his negative self-image as a Bauri inhibits his seizing new business opportunities. He fears that high-caste people will refuse to buy from him, and that he knows neither how to start nor run a business. A high-caste businessman prods him, gives him his start, and instructs him in business practices. Even so, Muli's wife warns him not to try business. "We are sons of laborers," she says, "that is better for us." Throughout Muli's life history she consistently prefers a lower, steady-income job to a new venture with an unpredictable outcome.

After the harvest, I did women's work, collecting grass which my wife and I sold in the market area near the Old Town. People bought the grass for their cows. Each afternoon, after returning from work, I would sit at Marua's shop. Marua, a light-skinned, balding, clean-shaven, round-faced man of twenty-six, was the first high-caste person to open a shop in a Bauri ward. One day Marua asked me, "Why are you sitting idly?"

I replied, "What can I do? I'm not going to the quarry, and have no other work. The quarry contractor doesn't like me because I work poorly. If I had other work, I'd do it."

Marua said, "You should start a business, Muli."

I replied, "What business do I know that I could start?"

Marua said, "Whatever business you start, the market is open." He used to talk to me like this every day, telling me of opportunities in business. Sometimes he sent me to his house or to the bazaar on errands.

A Cultivator-caste man from a nearby ward used to sit on the veranda of Marua's shop, which was located near Koki's house. Koki had left her husband and lived again in our village. Whenever she walked by, the Cultivator would pass indirect remarks about her. She overheard and made remarks about him. A man and woman who are not relatives must not speak openly to each other. By joking and teasing indirectly, they showed that they liked each other. Marua and I listened to them.

One day Marua said, "See how these two are doing." I figured he also wanted to meet Koki, and hoped that I would arrange it for him. I had another babu on my chain.

In January, several days before the Khandagiri Jatra, a fair held at the Khandagiri hill, Marua told me that I should put together a betel vendor's box and sell betel at the fair.

I asked, "Where will I get money to start such a business?"

He said, "I'll give you everything you need."

He sent me to a merchant in the Old Town, who gave me an old wooden crate. Marua hired a carpenter to construct the vendor's box out of the crate.

So I agreed to become a businessman.

Marua said, "Muli, I'll give you all the items, but you must do the selling."

I said, "Yes, I'll do it."

Marua gave me betel nut, spices, leaves, village cigarettes, and regular cigarettes, and I put all of that in the box.

I said, "I'll take it, but I don't know if people will buy from me, a small-caste man."

He replied, "Oh, fool, who will recognize you in the big crowd? Who will know that you are a Bauri? Only our own villagers won't buy from you. But they don't buy from anybody—they carry their own. Other villagers and people from the capital city will buy from you."

Then he counted the cost of the items. It came to forty-eight rupees.

That night I told my wife about my new business. She didn't like it. "We are poor people. Business is not useful for us. We are sons of laborers. That is better for us. But if you want to do it, go ahead."

I went to the fair. On the first two days the crowd was quite small, and I sold nothing. On the third day the crowd increased, and I

44. Vendor like Muli sits near the palanquins of village deities. that have been brought to a mela, or fair.

45. Betel and cigarette seller with vendor's box.

began to sell betel. That evening a relative of my wife saw me at the fair. He lived in a village about one mile away. He was very happy to see me and invited me to stay overnight at his house. I did not want to refuse him, so I went there.

I took some cookies and berries with me. The night was cold and the journey to his house difficult. My wife's relative wanted me to stay at his house every night. I returned the following night. Then I decided to stay away and eat in a hotel [restaurant] which cost me less than taking berries and cookies to my hosts each night. The only advantage of going to their house was that I could sleep in peace. On the third night I slept on the steps of the pilgrim rest-house.

On the fifth night, I put the box behind my head and fell asleep. A transvestite slept behind me. Since we were friends, I didn't worry about him. But the next morning I found that some money, betel nut, spices, and cigarettes were missing from my box, even though it was locked and the key was at my waist. I knew who had done it. In the middle of the night that man had unlocked the box, stolen the things, and relocked the box. I was quite unhappy. The next night I slept in the sweet shop of a Confectioner.

On the sixth day, two days before the close of the fair, my sales were high. On the seventh day, almost all my neighbors and relatives from the village turned up. That day, I gave away about ten rupees' worth of betel, almost as much as I sold. Many children from our street stood by me, and I gave them four annas, or two annas, or a paise.

On the *puurṇṇimaa*, the last day of the lunar month, which was also the last day of the fair, I sold so much betel that I had no time to go off for lunch. I ate fried snacks at my box.

That night, although the fair had ended, villagers still came to buy agricultural instruments, large baskets, bamboo manure baskets, plows, carts, household articles, wood for window frames, and other items. Since people came to the fairgrounds for another five days, I stayed and sold betel, taking in five to seven rupees a day. Each day, the crowds thinned and the sales declined until I was making less than the two and a half rupees I could have made at other work. One afternoon, I walked home.

As I passed the food shop, Marua saw me and passed the remark, "Oh look, a businessman is going, a businessman is going! How did you do at Khandagiri?"

I said, "I don't know yet, I must count my money and check out my goods. Then I'll tell you."

At home, my wife gave me some watered rice. After eating, I returned to Marua's shop to sit, as usual. I did not take any money for Marua. He asked me again, "How was business? Good?"

I said, "How can I say? I have no experience with this. It's my first year. I only know that I didn't buy anything at Khandagiri. What you gave me lasted thoughout the fair."

Marua asked, "Do you want to pay what you owe me now?"

I said, "Yes, why not? I can give it now, or tomorrow."

He said, "Why not now?"

I went home and counted the change. The rupees and large coins in one tin added up to 35 rupees. The small coins in another tin amounted to nearly 20 rupees. The materials left were worth about 10 rupees. I realized that from the initial investment of 48 rupees, I had brought in about 90 rupees. I had spent 25 rupees in those eleven days, and had given away 10. So my expenses had been about 35 rupees. I had earned a profit of 55 rupees—more than 50 percent!*

Since I had made a lot of money, I decided to continue in business. But why return all the money right now? I kept the tin of small change in my house and brought Marua the tin of large change. He counted it, frowned, and looked up, saying, "It's only 35 rupees! Why so little?"

I replied quickly, "What could I do? With that money plus the 10 rupees' worth of materials in my box, I have just a little less than the initial investment. I realize that I made big profits, but I stayed there eleven days, spent money for food, gave my relatives at the fair small change and betel. I did not keep track of how much I sold or how much profit I got. I brought no other money to my house from the fair. So you decide how much money I will take, and how much

---

*Muli failed to take into account that he had sold 38 rupees' worth of goods which either had to be paid for or replenished before he could start figuring his profit. He also ignored the money the transvestite stole from his box, the 10 rupees plus goods that he had given to friends and relatives at the fair, and the 2 rupees' worth of berries that he had given to the relatives at whose house he had stayed. If Muli had been capable of making the simplest possible accounting of his profit and loss, he could have realized that the 55 rupees in cash on hand when added to the 10 rupees' worth of unsold stock (total 65 rupees) left him with a profit in hand of 17 rupees, plus whatever he had spent or given away.

46. Children peer into a kaleidoscope at a village fair.

47. Shopkeeper at a temporary food stall at a fair gives a donation to a mendicant leper.

you will take. Don't worry. Next month I'll return what I owe you by selling at the festival of Shiva's birthday."*

He gave me 5 rupees. I gladly took it and put it in the tin with my other money.

One day before the Festival of Shiva, I bought 15 rupees' worth of goods at the bazaar. These items were much cheaper yet better than Marua's things. I mixed all the materials together. Now I had goods worth 25 rupees.

For two days I sold betel at the festival of Shiva's birthday. After paying my peddler's temple tax and giving 3 or 4 rupees to my wife, I brought back 50 rupees and still had goods worth 7.

I went to Marua and said, "See, brother Marua, I made a big profit. I don't want to leave this business. If you could get a place for me in the market, you would help me a lot. You dragged me in this direction. If you don't help me in the middle of the river, I'll drown. If you take back your money, I'll not be able to continue. Let me keep it to start a business."

He replied, "You need not return it now. I'll arrange a place for you at the capital market. The market is new, and the opportunities there are very good."

Marua talked to the manager of the capital market and arranged to have a place made there for me. From that day, I sold betel in the market.

At that time, 1962, the market was open three days a week. I used to carry my box up there each day, a three-mile walk. In those days, venders had no line or place number, but took whatever place they could find. To get a good spot, I had to go early in the morning. No matter how early I arrived, other betel venders who lived in the city had already come and taken the best places.

For six months I sat near the men who sold pots, coconuts, and brooms. No one questioned what I was doing there. Each day a man would come, take the rent, and go.

One day the manager of the market saw me sitting there and asked, "What is your name? What is your village? Who gave you a permit to sit here?"

I said, "My house is in the same village as that of Marua, the businessman who sent me to this place. I used to work for him."

*Jagaara jaatraa or sivaraatri, the festival of Shiva's birthday, is one of Bhubaneswar's most important religious festivals. Muli describes it briefly in Chapter 26.

48. The Bhubaneswar Chariot festival at which Muli sold betel and cigarettes.

The manager said, "You cannot stay here. You should sit with the betel sellers."

The manager sent me there with an assistant of his. I sat at the front of the line of betel sellers, a top placement right next to a front entrance. I earned more in that spot than I had previously, so my wife liked me. Between market days I used to sit idle at home. Although she never depended on me for her food or household expenses, she was pleased that I no longer had to depend on her.

Some of the young high-caste people of my village bought betel from my box, but not the old ones. The Cultivator and Service-caste people also bought betel from me. That year I also sold betel at the Chariot Festival of Lord Lingaraj, and earned 20 rupees in one day!

Now that I had money, I bought a sari for my wife and gave her money which she spent on bracelets and at religious festivals. We were very happy in those days. Although our profit was not great, we never starved unless there was a flood and I couldn't work. But we never saved anything. What I earned I spent.

Who cares for savings? We ate well and wore good clothes. I did not realize that one day my business would end and we would return to our earlier condition of hunger.

23. Muli's Other Wife, 1962

At the market, Muli spends money freely on his friends and relatives. A transvestite named Bana befriends him, invites him to his village, and introduces him to his sister Tafulla. Bana's family flatters and entertains Muli, who remains overnight. Soon Muli and Tafulla are sleeping together, while Kia remains alone in Muli's village. Muli lives with Tafulla for over a year. When she becomes pregnant, the caste elders of her ward demand that Muli marry her. Muli's parents refuse to attend the ceremony; his first wife attends, but remains secluded in a nearby hut, wailing.

Muli blames his difficulties, not on himself, but on Tafulla and her relatives, whom he says put a magic love spell on him. He views himself as utterly dependent, first on Tafulla and later on his first wife to rescue him from his predicament.

This chapter contains a number of fascinating colloquial expressions and proverbs, as well as Tafulla's devastating rebuttal to the men in her ward who demand that she reveal the name of the man who made her pregnant.

Although I did not know it at the time, my bad fortune began the day I met Bana, a transvestite who lived in a village two miles from my house. I was earning a lot of money at the market and spending it freely on my friends and relatives. I offered Bana some betel; he invited me to his house. His uncle and mother liked me and treated me well and with respect. They invited me to their house many times, so I jokingly called Bana my brother-in-law, Bana's mother my mother-in-law, and Bana's uncle my uncle-in-law, and I called their household father-in-law's house.

One day, while I was at my usual spot in the market, Bana's uncle, a man named Shiva, came over to talk to me. He looked grave as he said, "Your mother-in-law is quite ill. She wants to see you and your wife."

The following day, my son, Gopala, my wife, and I walked to Bana's village. Because she was ill, I bought Bana's mother a very expensive present to help cure her—a whole rupee's worth of oranges—and I also brought her some large sugar blocks.

I was surprised when I saw her. She did not look ill to me. She is a short, stocky woman, with great strength from carrying large loads of firewood. She was talking and laughing loudly, chewing betel, and when she saw me she invited me with a quick wave to come to her side.

"What's wrong with your body?" I asked.

She answered, "My body was bad for eight days, but in the last two days I've felt better."

Nothing was wrong with her. She gave us water to wash the dust of the road from our legs. I gave mother-in-law the fruit and sugar.

She asked, "Why did you bring these? I've already recovered."

I sat there for an hour. Then I told the old woman that I wanted to leave.

She said, "Why? Sit. Wait. Your uncle-in-law will arive soon, and so will my daughter Tafulla. She just went to the village food shop."

Bana arrived; we talked for a few minutes, and then I stood up to leave. My wife stepped onto the road.

Bana grabbed my hand, "Wait, I'm making tea for you."

I said that I had no time, but he insisted, so my wife and I drank some tea. He handed us some puffed rice, and I threw some of it into my mouth. My wife refused it. Again I stood up to leave.

Bana said, "No, no, you can't go. Today you must stay here. To-morrow is market day. You can go to the market from our village. Why go back to your house for one night? Stay here. We'll play cards and have fun."

My wife's face became angry. "Bana, I'm going. Your brother-in-law may stay." She was referring to me.

Without looking back to see if I followed, she walked out, drag-ging our son. Bana ran after her calling, "Wait! Wait!" She never even slowed her pace. She was anxious to return to our village so that she could find work. My wife is a hard worker, and certainly much stronger than I am. She usually earns more than I do. She cuts paddy faster and better than most men, and hardly anyone can keep up with her when she works in road construction gangs. She doesn't like eating unless she has earned a wage. She becomes impatient when she has to spend time idly.

When I tried to follow her, Tafulla stood in the doorway. She said, "Stay the night. We'll kill a chicken and have a nice dinner. Stay! Tomorrow you can go."

I shook my head, but she grabbed my waist and wouldn't let go. My body went cold; my heart bore new feelings, like a plant putting forth new leaves. I was unable to leave; that night I stayed in her uncle's house. My wife did not return.

Bana's uncle grabbed a chicken, and while the bird flapped and squawked, he wrung its neck. After he had plucked the feathers, his wife made chicken curry.

When Bana appeared several hours later, dinner was ready. I asked him, "What is your sister's opinion about my staying here?" I was referring to my wife; she and Bana called themselves brother and sister.

He replied, "At first she was very angry with you. I walked with her all the way to your village trying to change her mind. She thought that you would follow her. Every time someone appeared behind us she looked back and asked, 'Is that your brother-in-law, Bana? . . . Who is that? . . . Surely that is he . . . Can you see . . . Who is that? . . . This time it must be your brother-in-law.' Like this she spoke all the way to your village. When you did not appear she became quite angry. I told her that I'd take you back tonight after our feast. So she calmed down."

We ate dinner. I found a straw in the water that they gave me. Was someone putting a magic spell on me? I didn't want to drink it, but what could I do? I was in Father-in-law's house [Bana's father].* If I had refused the water, the family would have been insulted. So without complaining I drank the water.

Uncle-in-law Shiva and I went inside a room to talk. Tafulla and her mother now sat down and ate out of our plates [wives eat from husbands' plates]. Bana gave us betel.

While we were talking I began to feel lazy, so very tired, as if someone were pricking the soles of my feet with a needle. I turned to Uncle-in-law. "What's happening to me? . . . my feet, I'm so tired."

His voice seemed far away. "Go and sleep in that cot there. You'll be all right after resting for a while."

I fell onto the cot. I awakened at midnight. Someone was sleeping with me.

I murmured, "Who are you?"

---

*Bana's father was deceased, but since he had been the eldest brother, Muli referred to him still as father-in-law, the head of the household. Shiva, the deceased man's younger brother and the uncle of Bana and Tafulla, was the actual guardian of the house.

"I'm Tafulla."

"Why did you come here?"

"Your body's in pain. I came to massage it."

"How do you know I'm in pain?"

"Uncle Shiva sent me to massage you. He said your leg hurts."

"Are you telling the truth?"

"Yes, he sent me."

I was quite surprised. In the past, whenever I had tried to joke or play with her, she had always become angry, like a snake. How was it that now she came alone to me in the night, slept with me, and said that her uncle had sent her? I fell asleep. I awakened to the touch of her hands as she massaged my legs. When she moved up my thighs my mind changed toward her. Why had she come here, for good or bad?

After massaging my thighs, she lay down beside me. I was suspicious. Was she playing tricks with me? Was she the one that had put the straw in my water? Her youth, her beauty, attracted me. She was short like her mother, but her body was firm, her skin smooth to the touch. I became blind; suspicion faded, desire increased. I threw my legs and hands on her body. She did not resist. We played, touching each other in different places. Lastly we did our "work." She did not complain. She stayed beside me until night ended. I enjoyed her twice that night. Before dawn she slipped away.

That morning I feared to face her mother and uncle. What if her uncle hadn't sent her to me? What would happen if they found out? My relationship with her would be destroyed. I fell asleep again.

Everyone else was up. Sister-in-law [Tafulla] entered the room and said, "It's eight o'clock, wake up!" She gave me water to wash my face. Then she asked, "Do you want to bathe?"

I said, "Yes."

She brought me coconut oil full of foam. I asked, "Why are there bubbles in this oil?"

She replied, "I threw some scented powder in the oil and shook it. So the foam formed."

I said nothing more due to my love and affection for her. I failed to remember until much later that my wife's brother had died from a magic spell, the *kimiaa mantra*. People use the *kimiaa mantra* to tie a chain around someone's neck—to pull him toward you and make him love only you.

I daubed the oil on my body and went to the village pond. I didn't take any extra clothes, only my dhoti and towel. As is my custom, I bathed wearing my dhoti, and then walked from the pond, wearing the wet cloth, which dried in the wind.

Bana saw me and called out, "Oh, who is this guest? Where have you come from?" He laughed.

"You can't recognize me?"

"How can I? First I have to be introduced."

"Come here; then I'll *show* you who I am!" I raised a fist.

Joking like this, we returned to Tafulla's house. She placed watered rice before both of us, and we ate. Then I threw some betel in my mouth and started off toward the city market.

Tafulla called out, "You must return here."

I called back, "I may, I may not."

She ran in front of me and blocked the way. "If you don't promise to return, I'll not let you go."

"I'll return, surely; I'll positively come. Don't be unhappy."

Instead of going back, I returned to my village. My wife was furious at me and wouldn't lie on our bed; she moved a mat to the other side of the room. She said, "I came back yesterday. Why did you stay there?"

"To keep their friendship. They requested us to stay, but you left angrily. Had I left, they might have been angry."

She pouted in the corner. That night she slept on the floor. The following night she was less angry and returned to our bed.

Although I stayed at home for ten days, I couldn't forget Tafulla. I desired her, more and more each day. One day, after the market closed, I accompanied Bana to Tafulla's house, where I stayed for a week.

Suddenly my wife appeared and ordered me home. I returned with her.

A few days later my desire for Tafulla returned. I tried to forget her; I tried to suppress my desire. My wife and I quarreled over some minor matters. At the height of the argument, I stormed out of the house and went straight to Tafulla. I did not return to my village.

Whatever I earned at the market I gave to Sister-in-law Tafulla, who gladly accepted it. Sometimes she ordered me to buy her cosmetics. I bought them or gave her the money to buy what she wanted. She lived with me just like a wife. Nobody opposed this or even seemed to notice. She slept in my bed, cooked meals for me, washed my clothes, everything.

I stayed there for one year. We were happy. But after some time my sister-in-law became pregnant.

The people of the ward suspected that Tafulla was pregnant. When I would walk along the road, people would pass remarks about me, loud enough so that I could hear: "This man, he stayed here like a son-in-law, a married man; he's caused Tafulla's pregnancy. But he's already married, with a wife and child living in another village." Nobody asked Tafulla who was responsible. Since they had no direct proof that I was the man, they didn't confront me directly. Instead, they made these indirect remarks. I couldn't reply because they weren't talking directly to me.

One day, some Bauri people from my village came to me in the market and said, "What is this news? Your wife stays in your father's house, caring for your child, while you stay elsewhere. Why? Your wife is in trouble. Why don't you go to see her?"

I replied, "I'd rather stay where I am. My wife is not in trouble. If she needs help later, I'll give it."

They left shaking their heads.

A few days later, the people on Tafulla's street began to discuss her pregnancy openly. Some of my friends in that ward asked me for the facts. I didn't reply. I didn't care. I had no power to judge good or bad; I was under the spell of the incantations placed on me.

Now that everyone was discussing the pregnancy, the men of the ward held a big meeting at the clubhouse. They did not invite me. I sat two doors away, on my uncle-in-law's veranda, listening to the loud voices of the ward leaders.

They summoned Shiva, Tafulla's uncle. The leader of the ward, a powerfully built man named Rama, asked him, "Do you know why we have called this meeting?"

Shiva replied cautiously, "How can I know until I'm told?"

"You may not know, but we have heard from public talk that your unmarried girl is pregnant by your son-in-law. Don't you know this?"

"What! Who told you? I know nothing about it!"

"We know definitely that the daughter in your house has become pregnant.* But we want to be sure by *whom*."

*Because Tafulla's uncle is her guardian, the leaders refer to her as his daughter.

"You should not talk like this. She is my unmarried girl. She has a future. How dare you speak like this?"

I heard Uncle-in-law shout, "No! No! No! No one can speak like this!"

I silently tiptoed inside Uncle-in-law's house. Tafulla was there. I whispered, "Go and listen."

She crept close to the doorway of the meeting house and listened to the shouting. I stayed behind at Uncle-in-law's, peering out of the doorway. The voices became louder and louder. I shivered with fear. Sister-in-law returned.

She said, "Why are you sitting there? Come to our room!"

I replied, "Wait, you go ahead. I'll be there in a moment." My trembling voice betrayed my fear.

Tafulla hissed, "Why do they hold such a meeting and quarrel? Nobody has earned sin, neither me nor you. Brother-in-law to sister-in-law, what happened there? It is not a sin. Why do these cholera-eaten corpses hold a meeting? What can they do? Who cares for them? They are 'as useless as hair.' When it burns, it produces neither charcoal nor powder. Come to our room. Why are you sitting there? Are you afraid they'll do something to my uncle? If anyone touches him or scolds him in a bad way, I'll eat him up while standing!"

My ears were not attracted by her words, which were those of a coarse woman. I thought, "I've got to run away and hide!" I didn't answer her. I became more grave, and sat without moving. She stood next to me.

Someone said to my uncle-in-law Shiva, "If you say that your daughter did not conceive, then bring her here! We'll call an old woman who can easily determine the truth! Women know well about women's matters."

Uncle-in-law protested, "How do you know my daughter is pregnant? When I tell you that she's not, why do you force me to say she is?"

The leader, Rama, said, "We *know* your daughter has conceived. Let her come. From her we'll find out by whom she became pregnant. 'For a mother knows the father like a mind knows sin!' "

Without Uncle-in-law's permission, the leaders of the ward sent for Tafulla. Uncle-in-law shouted, "Why do you call my daughter here when I tell you that she's not pregnant? 'If one person correctly says he sees a goat, and three say they see a dog, does that make it a dog?' All right, if everyone says so, a goat is a dog! Though she's not pregnant, if you say so, she's pregnant. What can be done?" He threw up his hands in defeat.

Rama pressed him further, "If she is pregnant, from which caste is the father? Where will she go now? To our caste? To the Muslims? To the Sweepers who are lower than us? How can we know the caste of the child? If you know something, tell us now."

Uncle-in-law replied, "I don't know anything. How can I tell you anything?"

Rama pointed at him and shouted, "If you refuse to tell us, and we find no proof of the child's caste, do you think we will bear the bad name and infamy of this in our caste? If you want to mix with Sweepers and Pathans [Muslims], do you think that we will go with you? You should leave our ward today! If you know that one of our men made your daughter pregnant, then we'll consider her case and find some way out of this problem."

Uncle-in-law tried to placate the angry leader, "What you suspect, well, that is not so. My daughter never goes out. If the matter of pregnancy is true, I think that it might be because of her brother-in-law. She might have played with him and conceived by him."

Rama smiled and said, "If so, that is nice! Our prestige is preserved! Now, call your daughter here. She should tell us who did it."

"Why call her? What's the need?"

"What's so bad if she comes here? She's a girl of our own ward. Everybody knows her. She's not an outsider, not a daughter-in-law; she's our own daughter."

Uncle-in-law protested, still trying to preserve the prestige of his family. "Why should a young girl face all you men? If she's your daughter, one of you, or perhaps three or four of you, should go to her and ask her whatever you want."

Rama nodded. He arose, along with two other men. They walked slowly out of the meeting hall. I was sitting outside. They passed by me without even looking in my direction. Tafulla was inside the house, perhaps in the kitchen. The men stood at the outside doorway and called, "Tafulla, Tafulla . . ."

I called out, "*Who* are you?"

Rama turned to me and shouted, "Who are *you* to answer? We're calling Tafulla. Have you become her master?"

I became silent. They pushed their way into the house. I followed them. They found her sitting in a room.

Rama asked softly, "Who made you pregnant?"

She looked him straight in the eye and said, "What's it to you?"

Rama said, "How is it nothing to us? Aren't you from our ward and our village?"

Tafulla shouted, "Then what's it to you? Do you think I travel all over, from five or twenty-five places, like your mother and sister, earning money as whores, and picking up sin-pregnancy—by who knows whom?* If I am pregnant, it's not my fault, it's *your* fault! Now suddenly you run to my house to ask me who made me pregnant. Did you ever think that I remained in my house as an unmarried girl after I became mature? Did you ever try to find me a groom, or hold a marriage ceremony for me, seeing that you are my own people, of my ward and village? What do you do about our girls who have hundreds and hundreds of abortions? Haven't you ever heard about them or seen them? No, but you come over to *me*. We are always going out [of the village], always mixing with and screwing other men, like your mothers and sisters.† How will we bear our ripened youth and desires? When we see a beautiful young boy, will we only want and wonder about the chance to get him? You have no power to keep your own wives and sisters at home. If you don't get your young daughters married immediately, these things happen, and after it happens, you'll sit there and say, 'We are the people of the ward, we are the brotherly lineage people, we have society, we have caste, we have prestige.' Go back to your house. I never went outside, like your women. I became pregnant from among my own people. You have nothing to say about it. Do you know who is staying in my house? Look who is standing there. My pregnancy did not happen on the city road, or at the market, or just out in any field. He has stayed in my house for nearly one and a half years. Can you show me a brother-in-law and a sister-in-law in our ward who don't have their

---

*"Five or twenty-five" is a conventional expression that means "many."

†Tafulla refers to herself as "we." She ridicules the men by saying sarcastically that she has affairs outside the village, just as their women do. But the men know that Tafulla, unlike their women, does not work outside of the village, where there is less control over women's activities.

illicit secrets? Everybody's house has that! The seed may stay or be destroyed. In whom it stays, she may destroy the child. But I don't want to destroy it! I don't think it's a sin!"

Rama, the leader of the ward, stood with his mouth open. The other two men just stared at the wall. Finally, Rama stammered, "We just came to get the explanation of this matter. We got it. We're going." They marched out without saying another word.

Tafulla turned to me, "Why are you standing there, showing a pale face? What's happened to you? Why are you afraid? Do you think someone's going to kill you or eat you? If your mind and my mind are in agreement, nobody will do anything to us. Even if a thousand people like those come to us, I'll *see* to them!* Why are you sitting here? Go to the meeting and listen!"

I went out and sat on the veranda. I heard Rama say, "Tafulla . . . the brother-in-law."

Another man said, "If Tafulla became pregnant from him, she should catch hold of his head."

A third man said, "You should be sure if it was he or someone else. He's there; you should call him."

Rama said, "Good idea."

I hurried inside Tafulla's house. I cried, "Tafulla, they're going to call me to their meeting!"

She replied, "Why are you always afraid? You tell them straight and true, just as I did. When they asked me, 'Who made you pregnant?' I told them it was you, and you should tell them the same. Don't fear them, they're not tigers."

Two men entered the room, pointed to me and said, "Come with us."

My feet wouldn't move.

Tafulla said, "Why are you standing? Go ahead. I'll *see* how they'll castrate you!"

I shuffled my feet slowly, slowly.

At the meeting hall, Rama asked, "Did you do this thing with Tafulla?"

"Yes."

"Do you know that she is an unmarried girl?"

"Yes."

*The phrase "I'll *see* to them!" is a serious threat and insult that means, "They have no power; if they dare to act, I'll really hurt them!"

"Since your child is in her womb, she will catch hold of your head now. She has no other way. You should prepare to marry her as soon as possible. Then the prestige of our caste, country [ward], and leaders will remain."

"I did everything, true, but I can't say about marriage. I'm not the guardian who gives permission; my father is. I have my father, mother, my married wife, my son. Without their consent I cannot marry Tafulla."

"Did you ask your father, mother, and child when you did this thing?"

I replied, "Can anyone ever tell another he's doing these things?"

"If you think it shouldn't be known to others, you should agree to this marriage without anybody's knowledge. You *must* marry her. Wherever you go, we'll drag you back. We'll *see* what you can do! You admitted that you did it. She says so too. But when the marriage question comes, you plead that you have a mother and father. You think you are the only intelligent boy? We'll *see* how you can play with us! 'The blind think there is no sun or moon'; they miss the truth of the world. Leave those foolish excuses about your father and mother. Tell us now, on which day the marriage will occur."

I was afraid of their threats! I agreed to marry her.

The men left the meeting hall. I sat alone, head in hands, saying to myself, "What appetite dragged me to this hell?"

Uncle-in-law came to the door. "Why are you sitting," he called. "Come to the house."

The next day, I went to the city market. I had no interest in my business. I sat thinking, "What can I do, what can I do?" Finally, I wrote a letter to my wife: "I am in a very dangerous position. 'The head of the elephant may fall on this side or that side.' I am in such danger that you cannot imagine it, and you are equally in danger. I have lost all my intelligence, so danger has come to me. You should get up from sitting and come to me at once. Don't talk with anyone. Bring your son."

I handed the letter to Gobinda, a Confectioner-caste man of my home village, and told him, "Give this letter to my wife and warn her that she should not let anyone see it except her son, who should read it to her secretly."

Gobinda left for my village; I closed up my betel business and returned to Tafulla's village with some vegetables. I ate and slept, but I was unhappy. Always one thought kept running, running. "What can I do, what can I do?"

The next morning, after bathing, I waited for my wife and child to arrive. Several hours passed. I thought that they might not have received the letter until morning. I waited without eating lunch.

About noon, my wife arrived at Bana's house with her son. Perhaps she asked Bana's wife and heard the news from her. I heard her crying. I wanted to go to her, but I didn't have the courage. She continued to cry in such a way that I couldn't face her. I knew that I'd have to meet her later. I hid in a room until evening, when I hoped to see her alone.

People from the ward came to meet her. The more they talked to her, the more she cried. I hid.

In the evening, I went to my wife. When she saw me, she cried louder and louder. What could I tell her? I stood by her like a lifeless statue. She fell on the floor, weeping, unable to speak. I sat next to her and stroked her hair. Tears welled up in my eyes; I cried with her.

After some time, Bana came into our room and stuffed cloth into our mouths. When we stopped crying, Bana left.

I said to her, "Listen, what could I do? It was written in my fortune and also in yours. Why was such a fortune written for a wife like you? I have no way to get out of this. But listen and believe me. I cannot forget you, or my own son!" I cried as I told her this. I continued, "This news must be painful to you, like a menstrual pain. I know how much pain you are getting. But you can't understand the condition of my mind. I understand yours. I'm giving my oath to you: you and I will have no disunity for any reason. After Tafulla delivers her baby, our things will be ours, hers will be hers."

She paid no attention to me.

Finally, I told her, "I'm taking an oath that I'll never stay away from my word! You think that by staying here I forget all of you. That's not so, but rather that my fortune has been faulty from birth. Sasthi, the creator, who gives us birth, has written that I am suffering. You are also suffering like that. You can do one thing, if you believe in me."

She neither replied nor even looked at me.

I continued. "When I came here to see the sick mother-in-law, someone put a *kimiaa mantra* on me. It's been on me ever since. I knew it from that first day, but due to misfortune, I couldn't tell you. You could call it good fortune that I didn't die from the *kimiaa mantra*. What a great blow has come to me! Look! You are my real wife. I never forget this, or that you are trying for my happiness. I touch your feet! If you'll not have patience during my dangerous condition, I'll not escape from this. I'll take poison! If you like me, spend some money. Try to help me escape from this bad luck. Without you I have nobody to rescue me, to give me life from this danger. Father, mother, what will they care? They will say, 'For a poor family, two brides is good. One will earn, one will stay home.' But what peace is there? You may tell me, 'Many people have two wives.' You may talk like this. But two wives will always argue. She is also an outsider's daughter, not your sister, born from your mother's womb. Marrying Taffula is not like marrying you and your younger sister. So I know that this is very bad for our family. Don't think I've forgotten my family peace. Since I am touching your feet and palms, you must help me. You saved me from danger. If you'll give me your word that you'll save me, I'll survive. If you won't allow this marriage, if Tafulla's people throw her out of the house onto the footpath, I'll commit suicide. Do one thing: until the *kimiaa mantra* goes out of my body, I cannot leave them, although I do not like them. So try to take the *kimiaa mantra* out of my body."

When I talked so much like this, she stopped crying. But she wouldn't talk to me or turn toward me.

Suddenly she began to wail, crying while speaking of the past. "Was it in your mind to show me this behavior of yours? It was also my bad fortune to live to see these things. The son watches the marriage of his father! What a man you are!"

I tried to calm her down, "Don't think like that. I wish to see your happiness forever. I promise before you that I'll not move toward anybody else; only you and your son. Just after Tafulla's delivery, I'll forget her forever. Then we'll start our house again. Forget everything. Have mercy on me. Be kind to me. Try to remove the *kimiaa mantra* from my body. What can I do? What's to be gained from thinking about what has passed? As the proverb says, 'the palm molasses has run down the elbow, so how can it be eaten?' I have given my oath to you. My life depends on it. Believe in me! You should allow this marriage."

She averted her head and said nothing. Bana's wife was sitting in the room with us. My wife turned to her and recited a proverb, " 'To the earlier wife, slap! slap! To the later wife, fondling, patting.' " She continued, bitterly, "Who likes the first wife? Everybody says things like *he* does before the marriage. But after the new one comes to the house, she'll be the one whom he likes, isn't that so? Tell that fellow to do what he wants."

I said, "Why do you talk to her, not me?"

My wife said, "If my mother and father were alive today, would your marriage be possible? I could have immediately dragged you from her house and pulled you from your purpose. What will I ever get from you? What is there in my fortune, and my son's fortune? Who knows?"

Then she wailed, "Oh my son! O, my property!"

I said, "Don't cry, don't cry." But she didn't stop. Many women gathered around her. No eye was without tears.

Tafulla entered the room. She said to me, "Come and eat." When my wife saw pregnant Tafulla calling me to eat, she fell on the ground and sobbed more and more. Suddenly she lay still; she had fainted.

People threw water on her face and blew in her ear; she regained consciousness. She started crying again. Bana's wife put a cloth in her mouth, and she sobbed into the cloth.

I said, "Don't cry any more. I've explained everything to you. Believe me, I'll do good for you, forever. You should do just this one thing for me, help me to escape from the *kimiaa* disease."

She relaxed a little and gradually stopped crying.

Tafulla said sarcastically, "For which matter do you cry so much? Oh, what a serious thing has happened to us! Is that why you are crying? If anything worse than this had happened, how could you keep alive?"

Hearing these pinching words, my wife burst out crying. I tried to catch her and put her on my lap, but she wrenched herself from my grasp and crawled away rapidly.

The women made crude remarks about me. "What a bad man he is! How can he forget his wife and son like this and stay here for what sexual work! His mother conceived him from the pricks of how many men! Must have been from many! So how could good [decent] ideas come from his mind?"

Tears came to my eyes. I was unable to stand the comments plus my wife's crying. I cried with her.

Bana's wife pushed Tafulla out of the room, saying, "Why are you standing here? Why don't you do some chores? Do you think it's your right to talk with this son-in-law here? This is not the right time to call him to eat."

Bana led me to the clubhouse. I was crying, and I didn't want to leave my wife. Bana fell asleep, but I lay awake thinking, "How can I go to my wife? Look what I've done! My golden family is turned into powder. This unhappiness is more than death!"

Dawn came; I was still awake. I arose and walked to the pond to bathe. On the way back I remembered Gopala, my son. He was eight years old, a small, quiet boy. I looked for him and found him on the road in front of Uncle-in-law's house. I led him inside and we ate our morning meal together. I invited him to go to the market with me. He refused. I said, "I'll buy sweets for you if you come along."

He replied, "Let me ask my mother first."

He ran to his mother while I waited. He walked back and said, "My mother won't let me go."

I replied, "Go and tell your mother to put a shirt on you, and then you'll come with me. We'll return in the afternoon."

He went again to his mother and returned with a shirt.

"Mother said no."

I said, "Come with me; your mother won't be angry."

He didn't answer. But as he walked along with me he looked furtively from side to side to see if his mother was watching.

At the market, I fed him puffed rice. He seemed happy, so I didn't take him back at noon. I tried to sway him to me. "If you stay with me, I'll take you to the market every day and feed you sweets."

We stayed until evening. Suddenly my son burst out crying. "I want to go to my mother! I want to go to my mother!"

I said, "All right, wait a little bit. Why are you so worried? We'll go after I close the business."

Every time he asked to go, I fed him a sweet. He would calm down for a few minutes. In this way I kept him satisfied.

I kept Gopala there until business ended and the market closed. I carried him home on my shoulders. When we reached the door where his mother slept, I gave him two and a half rupees to give her.

He opened the door and called softly, "Mother, Mother."

She awakened, came over to me, touched my feet, and began to cry. After a few moments she said, "Don't marry that girl!"

I replied, "Don't worry, I'll punish them as much as they have punished me. Just after she delivers her child, I'll prepare my way to leave this place. I'll *see* who'll try to do anything to me! You should help me escape from the *kimiaa mantra*."

I dabbed her tears with my cloth. I took her in my arms and said, "Don't think any more about this; go and sleep beside your son."

My wife stayed in Bana's house, while I remained in Uncle-in-law's house. I gave Bana money and vegetables for my wife. I brought my son to eat and sleep with me, but my wife never stepped into Uncle-in-law's courtyard.

Nobody at Uncle-in-law's criticized me for feeding my child in their house. I didn't want to talk to anyone in that family. Every day I would spend some time with my wife, talking to her, trying to win her over. Bana also helped.

Gradually she began to soften, so one day I asked Bana, "How can I meet my wife at night? I want to sleep with her."

Bana told her, then returned with her message: "She refuses."

For three days I ordered Bana to ask her. Each day she refused. On the fourth day Bana returned and said, "She's willing, one night only."

That night I went to her. We talked freely. I stayed for four nights.

In the meanwhile, Uncle-in-law was making arrangements for my marriage. Two days before the marriage, he went to my village to invite my father. He returned the same day and told me what had happened. "We went to your father and invited him. He replied, 'I'm happy to hear the news of my son's marriage, but I cannot participate. Since he's done the work alone of arranging the marriage, what's it to us? He asked neither me nor the people of my ward, nor the people of my brotherly lineage. Why should I go there?' Then I told him why you had to get married.

"Your father replied, 'I did not know all this. If you want me to participate in this marriage after all this trouble, well, then, you should pay all expenses.'

"I returned without your father; he won't come unless I pay for his feasts as well as mine.* But I cannot afford that. You may be unhappy, but we don't have the money to pay for everything. We hope that your father's blessing will be good for you. If not, let it be."

The day of my wedding arrived. At dawn I was up, thinking, thinking, crying, "Oh, my past life, when I was young and enthusiastic, and looked forward to my first marriage, but this one!" I cried.

When visitors came to see the groom, I tried to stop my tears, but I couldn't. The morning went like this. I called Bana, "How is she? I'm worried about her. As the proverb says, 'Salt eats the pot; thought eats the body.' "

Bana said, "She's beating her breast, over and over and over, silently. Seeing that, your son began crying, and his eyes swelled. My wife saw this and took him away from her."

At evening the ceremony began. One of the men of Tafulla's ward sat on the marriage platform, substituting for my father, who had refused to attend.

Finally it was over.

---

*Muli's father made the conditions of his participation so outrageously expensive that Tafulla's uncle would refuse to accept them.

24. Living with Two Wives, 1962–63

A few days after the wedding of Tafulla and Muli, Tafulla's parents tell Muli that they are retiring, now that they have a new son-in-law to support them. To feed four adults, Muli draws on the funds from his business, which fails. He loses his place in the market and returns to working as an unskilled laborer.

Tafulla gives birth to an infant who dies within three days. Muli, seeking an excuse to leave her, accuses her of seducing him with a magic spell. Muli's first wife, Kia, and Muli's brothers-in-law drag Muli back to his village; Tafulla runs after them. That night, Muli sleeps uncomfortably between his two wives. When Tafulla realizes that she has lost him, she returns to her own village and never comes back.

As in the previous chapter, Muli depicts himself as without a will of his own. His brothers-in-law take him to a magical curer to break the spell that Tafulla is said to have put on him. While narrating this strange tale, Muli insisted that his downfall was caused by the magic spell, and not by any fault on his part.

Whatever the causes, Muli's downfall in this chapter is a crucial turning point in his life. Rarely do untouchables receive an opportunity to break out of the cycle of poverty, hunger, and unskilled labor; Muli was given such a chance but destroyed it.

My wife Kia and my son remained in Tafulla's village. For seven days after the ceremony, my first wife and I did not talk. She hid in her room. In the mornings, I took my son to the market, where I bought him sweets. Each day I gave him money to give to his mother. Sometimes I saw her, but I was unable to talk. At other times I called out to her, but she would only answer "Yes" or "No," or she would simply nod, nothing else.

The days passed. My wife and son lived in Bana's house. After one month, my new father-in-law came to me and said, "I have a son-in-law now, so I'm retiring from work. I'm turning the responsibility of our house over to you."

He was my father-in-law, so I was unable to refuse. Now I had six mouths to feed: father-in-law, mother-in-law, Tafulla, and myself in one house, and my wife and son in Bana's house. Father-in-law and Mother-in-law worked each day, but they often supplied nothing for household expenses; they expected me to supply their food. They used the money they earned for who knows what? It was very hard on me to maintain their house on my small income. I couldn't feed my wife, but I never neglected my son. Each day I gave him sweets and money, and he was always happy to take them. Father-in-law and Mother-in-law trained their daughter Tafulla to order me to buy her scented oil, glycerine soap, and good ribbons. She would tell me, "Buy these cosmetics."

But I often neglected her orders. Then she became angry at me and shouted loudly. My wife Kia heard her; other people told me that she felt very sad when she heard Tafulla yelling at me. I lived in trouble.

One day, my wife Kia said to me, "I want to go to your father's house; I don't want to remain here any longer."

I pleaded, "Don't go, stay here."

She replied, "It is not good to stay in someone else's house for a long time. The child's schooling has been interrupted. You cannot support me because you are feeding those other people, always quarreling with them because you don't have enough money. You have only trouble here. In the future all you'll have is more and more trouble. I can't stand seeing you so miserable, so I'm leaving. You live here happily if you can. I'm starting on my way."

I said, "No, wait, I'll support you."

She smiled bitterly, "You are a man who is not even able to separate two pieces of straw in a single day, you are unable to earn enough to buy even a single paise worth of kerosene at the food shop, you cannot even fill a tiny clay lamp with a fraction of a paise worth of kerosene. Yet now you are maintaining a house. When she scolds you in my presence, I can't stand it! So let me go!"

I said, "When you go, we'll all go. Don't leave me alone. Wait a few more days, until the new marriage has become old."

She stayed.

But I delayed going. She asked me time after time to go. I still delayed. During the ninth month of Tafulla's pregnancy my wife Kia came to me and said, "I'll not sit idle in Bana's house and be fed.

That will lower my prestige. You stay here happily. Why think more about our house? I'm going. Why should you go to your father's house any more? What's there that's yours? You stay here; we'll stay there, depending on our own fate and luck. Nobody lives there for us now but God."

She burst into tears. Bana gave her some rice, lentils, betel nuts, oil, turmeric, and other spices. I offered her a sari, rice, vegetables, lentils—about ten days' worth of food. I had no cash other than that in my vendor's box. I gave her three rupees and my son two rupees. She took Bana's gifts and then, crying, turned to me and said, "I don't want yours." She threw my gifts on the ground. She cried so much that I couldn't stand it, so I fled.

Bana and a young boy accompanied my wife to my father's house. I cried as they left. I went back to my bed and lay face downward. I couldn't sleep. I arose and walked out of the village toward the railroad station. I returned late at night.

Four days later, I walked to my father's house carrying three rupees' worth of rice, two rupees' worth of vegetables, and some sweets.

My wife refused to talk to me; she fled at my presence. I stood for some time on the inside veranda. When my wife saw me there she turned and ran out of the house. I put my bag in our room, went outside, and sat on the veranda.

My mother and brother appeared; they passed into the house without even looking in my direction. I sat. They went back and forth without a word or a glance.

Some of my friends from the ward saw me sitting. They came over to me and made jokes criticizing me. "Oh, how's your second wife? . . . How's your new piece? . . . How did you come from her place to our village? You didn't invite us to the wedding, so how about inviting us for the ceremony of the seventh day after the wedding? . . . How's your coming child?"

The leaders of the ward criticized me in other ways. "Why didn't you avoid marrying her? Here's a wife, there's a wife. This woman here cries all the time. This is not humane . . . You didn't ask your father or mother. How could you become so blind? All right, why are you sitting out here? Go inside your house."

After the leaders had finished with me, the children started in, "Hey, hey, come and see—look who is sitting there . . . He married another one elsewhere, and he's got another one here . . . Look, he's sitting on the veranda. Nobody's calling him. Look at him!" They pointed at me and laughed.

But the cruelest remarks were the curses made by the older women. "That dead body who died of cholera, who was eaten by a demon and buried, why did he develop these attitudes? He gave such bad treatment to a woman that he killed her."

My wife appeared at the doorway and said, "Why are you sitting outside, causing noise? Have you no room?"

I replied angrily, "What noise? I'm sitting on my own veranda. What's that to anybody else?"

My wife said, "Are you a small child? Don't you understand what noise is? Come in the house; then you'll understand."

Pulling my hand, she led me inside. She said, "It's not nice to sit on the road."

She gave me water. I washed the dust off my legs. I was so angry that I cried. I remembered the past, how my father and mother had liked me, how my friends and neighbors of the ward had respected me. I became restless, agitated. Nobody cared about me, nobody asked me why I was sitting outside, not going inside. I think that if my wife had not called me I would have had so much pain in my heart that I could not have borne it. Now, inside my house, my heart changed. I threw my arms around my son and reached for some sweets from my bag. I looked into the bag; she had taken nothing from it.

We ate food that my wife had bought and cooked. My son went off to sleep beside his grandmother. My wife lay down beside me, but with her back toward me. I lay awake waiting; she didn't move. I put my hand on her; she cried. I talked a lot, but she didn't understand at all.

I said, "I promise that as long as the moon and sun remain, your marriage and mine will remain true. You are mine. I am yours. Our marriage will have no defect at all."

Finally she changed her mind, talked a little, and slept with her face toward me.

The next day after lunch I went to the market. I heard later that soon after my departure my father-in-law, Tafulla's uncle, had come to my house.

My mother asked him, "Why have you come?"

He replied, "My son came to your house. He was supposed to return to mine. I came to see him."

"Whose son?"

"Your son came here yesterday. He told only our daughter, not us. If he must come to your house, he should tell us. Why did he come on his own decision? He should think of the big and the small, the elder and the younger."

My mother replied, sarcastically, "When you are his father, his father-in-law, and his guardian, all at once, how is it that he did not ask you before leaving? He has made a great fault! Is it really true that he left without asking you? How brave he is! He stayed in my house without asking your permission; what a big thing he did!"

Father-in-law replied angrily, "I'm not saying it for that reason. He must show some courtesy, yes?"

My mother replied, "Oooh, not enough courtesy? What a courteous man you are! He ought to ask one such as you for permission to come to his own house! Well, whatever may be, come inside, why should we talk on the road? But Gopala's mother has already gone to collect grass, and the door is locked. Well, all right, sit on the outside veranda, she'll come back soon." It was a terrible insult to invite the guest in, say that the house is locked, and make him sit on the outside veranda.

Then my mother shouted, "O, Gopala, Gopala, bring some water, your *grandfather* has come!"

This remark was too much for Tafulla's uncle. He stood up saying, "No, no. No need for water. I can't stay any longer. I've got no time. I'm going."

My mother said loudly, "Is it a good thing? You came to your friend's house. Now you leave without pouring water on your legs, without eating or sitting. This is not very good. Does this strike your mind as a good thing? The friend comes to the friend's house. He sits and talks; at least he talks about the sad and happy events. Then after this he may go back. Have you ever heard of someone returning from the road, like you want to do?"

"What can I do? This is a very bad time for me. I've got to go fast. If you want to treat me, give me a betel."

Mother wouldn't quit her sarcasm, "Why should we give you a betel? We are inviting you to our house, to wash your legs, eat, and sit. And you have refused everything. If you do not eat in my house, do you think that we'll go to your house to eat? Without going to the house of a friend like you, do you think that we can maintain our friendship?"

Tafulla's uncle shouted, "I've not invited you to my house. I also did not come to see you. I came to this place because my child is here. Otherwise, who are you, or who am I? We're strangers."

My mother replied, "How is this? Did your wife deliver this son you claim? Did she suffer birth pains for him? Then how indeed could he not be your child? You are truly his father, and also his father-in-law."

Suddenly she screamed at him, "I gave birth to him. He is *my* son; you cannot enjoy his fruit, the results of his life. If he wants to come back to my house forever, what are you going to do about it?"

Tafulla's uncle said, "He may return to my house if he wishes. If he doesn't I don't care. I already did what I had to do, marry him to my daughter. If you are strong enough to keep your son with you, then keep him. Nobody can say to my daughter that she's a whore. Everyone will say that her child came from your son. And my daughter has a claim on your son. No one can deny it: she married him at the altar."

He left the village, searched me out in the market, and told me the whole story. I said nothing.

That night I went to Tafulla's village. Her uncle had told her about the quarrel. She said to me, "Look how your mother insulted my uncle."

I replied, impatiently, "Why did your uncle go there? Did you think I would stay there? Was that what worried him?"

She replied, "He's a man like that, always impatient."

We quarreled that night.

I remained in Tafulla's village, supporting her household. Father-in-law [Tafulla's uncle] and Mother-in-law [Tafulla's mother] now worked only rarely, and when they did, they kept the money for themselves. To keep the household running, I had to dip into the capital of my betel business. I didn't keep accounts; I had no idea how much I used up. I borrowed market goods for my business. All of the money I earned went to pay for food in Tafulla's household.

One day I found that I owed a shopkeeper thirty rupees. That man asked me for the money. I felt ashamed: how could I pay it back? I went to my father-in-law for some money.

I said, "If you give me the money, I'll be able to continue my market business. Otherwise, it will cease. I fear to go to the market. I owe one man a lot of money."

Father-in-law said, "Where will we get money? We don't have any."

I said, "If you cannot help me, then you should take care of your own family expenses. After working for a few days for myself, I'll be able to pay back what I owe. Right now I cannot show my face in the market."

I searched for work but found nothing. I went to the market with a small amount of betel. I had no money for anything else. I felt so ashamed, yet I went there with a shameless face. My spices were not good, my sales were poor, and my earnings declined; I had no money to pay the rent on my market spot. In the meantime, the shopkeeper demanded his money every day. I found it unbearable, so I stopped my business. Another merchant rented my spot in the market. I had lost my place.

I sat in Tafulla's village, unable to find work. I thought of my bad fortune; I was back to being a laborer again. No, worse than that, a laborer without any work.

One month passed. Tafulla gave birth to a daughter. After three days, the daughter died.

We sent the news to my father's house, informing them that they were under death pollution for eleven days and should eat no fish, meat, clarified butter, or eggs.

The people of my father's household were furious. We had told them of the child's death, but not of her birth.

We heard that in my father's house the people followed the custom, changing all of their clay pots, shaving, getting holy water, and washing all their clothes. They complained that we sent them no oil, turmeric for bathing, holy water, or payment for the expenses of the hereditary leader and deputy leader who perform the rituals of purification. We should have met those expenses, but we were starving. How could we send them money?

A few days later my father-in-law said, "I have some paddy lands for sharecropping that are so good that they can be double-cropped.

If you want to, we'll sharecrop those lands. But we'll have to buy a bullock. We'll borrow money for that. For the first plowing, we should rent a plow and bullock and get started. If we wait, the landlord may hire someone else."

I agreed to do the work. Since we had run out of money and food, and no one else in the household was working, I plowed without eating anything. While plowing I remembered my first wife's behavior and talk, and I saw my son's face; I couldn't forget them that day. I felt depressed. That night, although there was food, I could not eat.

Day by day I became thinner and thinner, working hard but unable to eat. Some days I would work our sharecropper lands; on others I worked as a day laborer. With those earnings the household members ate.

After the harvest, we had sufficient food again. One day I said to Tafulla, "I want to go to my house. Prepare some rice for me to take."

She boiled the paddy, dried it, and milled it with a husking pedal. I took the rice and sold some of it for two rupees. I took the rest to my wife Kia and gave the money to my son.

My wife Kia treated me well, not as she had in past days. I ate, and later that night we talked. She asked, "Why did you send news of the death, but not of the birth of your daughter?"

I said, "I sent you the news. You may not have received it." Actually I had not sent any news.

She asked, "Any other news?"

I replied, "Unhappy news, all of it. Six or seven months ago, my business failed. Since then, every day, I have been dying, working so hard. We cultivated some paddy lands which gave us a good crop, but we eat only once and go hungry the rest of the day. That's why my body is so thin."

She cried unhappily, "What love did you get there? Why am I not dying, listening to these things! Why isn't Jama, the god of death, taking me away!"

I said, "Don't be unhappy. It depends on fortune. My fate took me to the path of unhappiness. You shouldn't worry. The day will come that God will bless me; I'll come back to my own place."

She wasn't persuaded. She wailed, remembering the past. "My king, how I kept him! And how is he now? Like a beggar! I never gave pain to my king. I fed him just like a child. My babu went to the market to earn money and to spend it luxuriously. No one could say that my babu was a day laborer. My babu was a real babu! A businessman! Who brought my property to such depths?"

I could not stop her. I cried with her. I tried to console her, "I told you that what happens depends on fate. Wait until good times come again."

She stopped crying. We fell asleep in each other's arms. She had no courage to ask me to stay with her.

The next day, I said to her, "I'm leaving."

She made no reply.

I repeated, "What do you say? I'm going."

With a catch in her throat she replied, "Why should you stay here? What is here? Everything you have is there—property, jewels, and name—all are there. Why stay here? Who is here?"

I said, "By working too much I am too tired. I have no wish to return there. I want to stay here for four to eight days, for relaxation, promenading, and enjoyment."

She said, "Who drove you out? Who has the power to make you stay? Your magnet is there. If you can forget the life of that place for four to eight days, I have no objection. Can you stay here?"

I said nothing else. I changed back into my lungi and sat on the veranda.

By the time I had changed clothes, my wife had put some watered rice before me and left for the fields to cut grass.

I wanted to stay with her, but I had no courage to tell her. And she had no courage to ask me. Although I said I wanted to go, I didn't. Neither of us would say what we really wanted.

I stayed that day. I started cooking in the afternoon. When my wife returned the meal was ready. While she ate I tied up the grass she had brought. Then we went to the bazaar, she to sell the grass, I to tour about. She handed me four annas. "Pocket money."

I said, "No, no. I've got some."

She said, "Show me, show me!"

I had nothing, so I accepted the four annas. I bought sweets for my son and betel for myself. That night at home we ate leftover watered rice. Afterwards, as my wife and I lay together in our bed, I said to her, "You've got to find a way to bring me back from Tafulla's village. Otherwise I'll die there, working, working."

She said, "I don't know what I can do. Everything will be done according to God's plan."

I stayed ten days, and during that time I asked her again and again to find a way to save me. Then I returned to Tafulla's village to help with cultivation. I worked hard in the fields. One day I noticed that the paddy we had stored from the harvest was gradually becoming smaller and smaller. Since we were not using this paddy, but storing it for the future, I asked Father-in-law where the paddy had gone.

He said, "I borrowed money during the rainy season to buy food. I'm paying back the loan with the paddy."

I asked, "Why? I paid for daily expenses. What were your expenses?"

He said, "Well, your wedding ceremony, and my own use."

I said, "During those days of cultivation, we starved, we went hungry. You never borrowed for me. You took much more paddy than you needed simply for food loans."

I was displeased. I had worked hard, and someone else had enjoyed the profits. I didn't quarrel because the man was my father-in-law. While we worked in the fields, we consumed all our paddy; we went hungry again.

One day my wife Kia and my brothers-in-law Damodar and Bisia came to take me home. Kia entered my father-in-law's house and said, "I've come to take back your son-in-law. We've got a lot of financial trouble at home and we need him." To me she said, "Father is sick. You should come quickly to see him."

Father-in-law replied, "I sent your mother-in-law away when she came; what will she think if your husband goes with you when he didn't go with her? Send your mother-in-law again, and I'll send your husband back with her."

Kia said, "I don't know who is mother-in-law, father-in-law, or who is what. He goes with me now! I'm in a hurry."

Father-in-law replied, "We have eight more days of harvest work. I don't want him to go until we finish that work."

Kia said, "We've also got work. I need him. I'm taking him back today! I'll not wait for your order. If you don't give him permission to leave, I'll drag him! We'll *see* how you stop it!"

He said, "If you want you, take him, but return him after four days."

My wife Kia made no reply. So I found myself going back to my home village. I did not know whether I was more willing or less willing to return home. They forced me to return. I remember that I didn't feel very happy about returning to my home. I did not talk to anyone on the way back. I was so afraid of my relatives that I said nothing.

Tafulla and her mother followed us to the edge of their village. What my Tafulla thought, I do not know, but she cried and begged, "Take me with you!"

Bisia said, "No, no, nobody there will like you."

She held my cloth and wouldn't let go. The others walked a few steps ahead. She still held me. Damodar turned to her and said, "There's not enough room in Muli's house. You don't know anyone there. Nobody will like you. It's better that you don't go."

She bawled like a child, so Damodar said, "Okay, come along if you want. I don't know how they'll accept you."

She trailed along, wearing her dirty, torn sari. Bisia told Tafulla's mother to bring a good sari for her. We waited while her mother brought one; then Tafulla's mother returned home.

Near my village, my wife Kia told Tafulla to change into her good sari. When we reached our ward, I felt faint. I know I became pale. My brothers-in-law were talking to me but I understood nothing they said. They took me to the house, sat me down on the inside veranda, and gave me some watered rice.

After eating, my brothers-in-law took me to the railway station. The women remained at home. We boarded a train. I didn't know where we were going. We got off at Jatni. I asked, "Why are we here?" They didn't reply except to say, "Come along."

They led me to a village and told me to sit near a man. They told him about me. Bisia said, "This man we brought always remains silent. He never talks to anyone. He will not remain in one house; he doesn't know the difference between good and bad. He's forgotten everything in his life. He is taciturn. He doesn't want to return home. He's staying in another place. Who did this to him?"

The old man asked some question. Bisia replied. I did not understand what they were saying.

The old man, a magician, brought a pot of water, pulled out a long strand of straw, cut it into eight pieces, and threw it into the pot. He uttered some incantations. Then he took a pair of scissors and "cut" the water; he recited more incantations while cutting. By doing this, he cut the magic of the *kimiaa mantra* that Tafulla's family had placed on me. The magician led me outside and ordered me to drink the water from the pot. After I drank some, he took a few drops and sprinkled them on my head. Then he asked for *daaksiṇa* [donation].

My brother-in-law Bisia gave him four annas. The magician kept one anna and returned the rest.

The old magician then said, "Go back to your house." He said to Bisia, "Don't let him eat anything on the way back home. Take the water in this pot. The silent one should drink it tomorrow morning."

We reached home late that night. Damodar went home; Bisia remained on the veranda of my house that night. From that day, I stayed at home. The *kimiaa mantra* had been destroyed.

That night, what a great crowd we had in my room—three people in one bed! I wondered where to sleep, how to sleep. If I slept next to the wall, or on the outer edge of the bed, it would not be good. I thought, it's better to keep my wives separated. So I slept between them. Both of them turned their backs toward me. To whom should I request to sleep facing me? A great problem. I decided to sleep face down, and threw one arm and leg over each wife.

I was very tired that night, but I could not sleep. At dawn my wives awakened. I remained on the bed pretending to sleep, hoping to hear what they would say to each other. Kia led Tafulla to the river to bathe. When they returned, they hung their wet saris outside to dry. Kia invited Tafulla to eat some watered rice. She refused. Kia was displeased; she ate some watered rice and went to cut grass. I lay on the bed. Since nobody tried to awaken me, I remained there. After a while Tanu, the wife of my younger brother Anadi, called Tafulla to eat watered rice. She refused; she went to my room and stood by the door. My son also refused to eat. He wouldn't even enter the house.

Anadi's wife Tanu talked aloud. "What can we do? The child doesn't want to eat or enter the house. How can he eat? I'll take some rice and curry to someone else's house to feed him."

Anadi's wife finally dragged Tafulla over to the food. She ate. Then Tanu said to her, "Awaken your husband."

Tafulla said, "No, I'll not awaken him."

Tanu said, "Who will wake him up? It's going to be afternoon. When will he awaken?"

Tafulla went outside and sent a small boy from the road to awaken me. He shook me roughly. I arose and took a bath.

When I returned, Tanu avoided me because a younger brother's wife should avoid the elder brother. Tafulla also refused to show her face before me because she was a new wife in the household. Each one tried to get the other to serve me food. In the presence of another, proud Tafulla would not serve me. Finally Tanu brought the bell-metal dishes full of food. Hiding her face, she put them down quickly and hurried away. According to custom, she would not clean the dishes, or even eat out of them until someone else had cleaned them. Tafulla took the dishes away after I had finished. While she washed the dishes, I went back to sleep.

Kia returned, awakened me, and asked, "Where is Bisia?"

I replied, "I don't know. I awakened late. After eating I went back to sleep."

She asked Tafulla, "Oh, Tafulla, do you know where Bisia is?"

Tafulla said, "No, I haven't seen him."

Kia was quite unhappy that Bisia had left without eating. She scolded us. "Everyone who lives here is an animal. There are no humans here. A guest has left this house without eating."

I replied, "I didn't see him. He might have left early. He's not a man to pout or be angry. I'll see him later today and make it up to him."

For ten days or so, I sat around the house doing nothing. One worker, my wife, could not feed all of us, so I took a job as a truck coolie, loading and unloading things. My wife didn't want me to take that job because it was low-paying and hard work, and I'd be traveling about. I worked for three or four months on the truck, earning two and a quarter rupees a day and receiving free snacks besides.

Then I heard that Tafulla's grandmother had died. Tafulla's uncle sent us a betel nut, an invitation to the funeral feast. Then he visited us and informed me that he wanted Tafulla back for a few days.

I said, "No, she cannot go."

He said, "We've got to prepare for the funeral ceremony, smearing the house with mud and washing old cloths. If Tafulla cannot go home, who will do my work? Everywhere in the world, a mother depends on her daughters for heavy household work. Do you think my wife and sisters are different from others in the world?"

I insulted him, hoping to start an argument. "Oh, you are quite a gentlemen! You know nothing of courtesy. You invite one wife; who will invite the other one? The other wife may or may not agree to go to your house, but you should invite her anyway. You have no sense. Go home; no one from here can go to your house today. We will go on the funeral ceremony day."

He left without uttering another word.

I decided to go to the ceremony, but only to insult him. Kia refused to go, and my son screamed, "No, I'll not go to that house!"

I took Tafulla back to her house. Because I was a relative, I received a gift of cloth. It was neither good nor bad. I made a face and asked, "Is this cloth for us?"

The assistant leader who was conducting the ritual said, "Others are wearing it; why can't you?"

I threw it down and said, "Take back your cloth! I don't need a cheap thing like this. I've got lots of cloth!" I turned my back on him and walked out. I couldn't get a quarrel going. No one would pay any attention. I refused to eat anything at the feast, saying it wasn't good enough. Finally, I told Father-in-law it was time to take Tafulla back with me. He objected. When we quarreled over that, I stomped out of the village. Tafulla remained behind.

Tafulla never returned to my village. I didn't care. I was tired of her. Actually, I now wonder what I ever saw in her, other than that she was a fresh girl. She was not pretty. Actually, she was ugly; her face wasn't nice. She had black skin, a flat, wide nose, short and stringy hair, a short, stocky body, and flat feet. She was much younger than I was. I had never thought I would marry her; I played with her for fun. I wanted to try her once or twice because she was a fresh one. But my misfortune was that she trapped me with the *kimiaa mantra*. I was unable to forget her. You can't imagine how bad it was when she came to my village. She didn't like to work. She just sat around. Many people disliked her. Everybody in the ward laughed at me.

25. "We Sit Under People's Feet," 1965–69

Muli gives a prospective landowning employer gifts of food, fish caught in the river, free labor, and profuse flattery, hoping that the landowner will make him his sharecropper. The landowner hires him but cheats him at harvest time.

Muli's description vividly portrays the desperate situation of landless farm laborers, as well as the paternalistic setting in which they work. Muli tries to befriend his employer, which enables his employer to exploit him all the more by taking loans that he never repays.

One day, I went to a Goldsmith named Dhruba and ordered him to repair some old ornaments and make two new silver ornaments for my maternal uncle's house. He promised to have the work done by a particular day, but he delayed it. I went to his house many days and found he had done nothing, despite his promises.

While I was sitting on the Goldsmith's veranda, a Cultivator-caste man quarreled with the Goldsmith. The Cultivator had rented the Goldsmith's land for a year. The Goldsmith claimed, "The land was to be rented only for the paddy crop; you owe me a share of the dry season lentil crop. That's the custom."

The Cultivator said, "I rented that land for the whole year. Why should I give you lentil crops?" He refused to give a share to the Goldsmith. Their voices became louder and louder. Finally the Cultivator left.

Dhruba turned to me and said, "I'll not give him land again this year!"

When I heard this, I wanted to get that land for cultivation. I increased my visits to Dhruba's house, hoping to get the land. I went with him the day he went to the Cultivator's house and announced, "You'll not cultivate my land any more!"

As we were returning from the Cultivator's village, I told Dhruba that I wanted to cultivate his land.

He said, "My word has no value. You should tell my wife, who owns that land."

I went to his house many times to get the land, but his wife was absent. I used to wait around their house day after day, without cause. Sometimes the Goldsmith made tea on the charcoal fire that he used for fashioning ornaments, and sometimes he offered me some.

I said, "I'll not take any tea. If I do, I'll break our caste rules and be outcasted. It will cost me too much to return to my caste."

The Goldsmith asked, "If you will lose your caste [be outcasted] for taking tea here, how many Bauri people would eat in my house?"

I replied, "No one should; it's prohibited. But, if you don't tell anyone else, I'll take tea here because I'm greedy for your field. Otherwise I wouldn't accept." Although Goldsmith-caste are people higher than we, our caste rules prohibit our taking food or water from them. We have a belief that Goldsmiths are so greedy that they wash excrement to dig out gold. Although higher in caste, they are therefore more polluting than we are. We also don't take food from other higher castes who do polluting things: Washermen, who work with dirty clothes, and Oilpressers, who crush and kill seeds to make oil.

I took tea at the Goldsmith's many times, and each time I told him how much I wanted to cultivate that land. Once, when the Goldsmith's wife was present, she said, "You are always coming here and sitting, but not bringing any leaves for curry."

I said, "I'll bring you leaves for curry; I'll bring you red soil for painting your house; I'll do all sorts of things for you if you accept my one request."

"What?"

"What I need I've already told to the man who is supposed to grant the request. But he leaves the decision to you because it's your land. To whom do you wish to give that disputed land for cultivation?"

She said, "That Cultivator who worked the land has left our service. We have to find a new person."

I said, "You don't need to look any more. That person is sitting before you. Give me the land. I'll obey your orders."

I had been on their doorstep for many days, pleading for the land. Their hearts softened. She said, "You may cultivate the land."

This is the way we find work, or receive other benefits. We sit under people's feet until they soften and give us the job or grant our request for money or help.

To keep them happy, I sometimes gave them fish that I caught in the river, vegetables, coins for their children. Except on market days, I was at their house all day long. On market days I bought the Goldsmith tiffin, betel, and vegetables. Even on nonmarket days, we went to the bazaar, where I bought him tiffin and tea. Like this, I satisfied both the Goldsmith and his wife and in turn got the land for cultivation. They gave me *hetaa* land [land that a farm servant is allowed to cultivate and harvest for his own use] in the *baaunsa bandha* [Bamboo Dam] area.

On the religious day of *doḷa puurṇṇimaa*, the full-moon day of the month of Phalgun [February-March], my master invited me to eat a meal. This was my official appointment day. *Doḷa puurṇṇimaa* is the day when new employment is begun and old ones are stopped. An employer should not terminate your appointment before *doḷa puurṇṇimaa*, which is considered the end of the agricultural season, when both paddy and lentil crops usually have been harvested.

Dhruba also had some land on which, for the previous two years, a sharecropper had cultivated sugar cane. When this sharecropper died, Dhruba decided to return to paddy cultivation. That gave me the opportunity; I asked for it, and Dhruba gave me the land to cultivate.

That first year was very expensive and difficult. First you must dig up the land, pulling out the sugar cane roots. Only then can you plow. That year I cultivated the land. Our friendship increased day by day. I always paid for his tea and tiffin in the tea stalls.

Each year in Aswin month [September-October] and Kartik [October-November], Goldsmiths become needy. For the *dasaharaa* celebration [see Chapter 5] they need money to perform a ritual to their tools. Most people don't have spare money at that time, so they don't hire Goldsmiths. That first year, Dhruba asked me for some money to tide him over during those lean months. "I will pay you back," he said. "You can take it out of the paddy you cultivate."*

I gave him money, sometimes three rupees, sometimes five, ac-

*A landowner rarely asks for loans from his employees. Muli's description fits his stereotype of Goldsmiths as misers who are so shameless that they even ask untouchables for loans.

cording to what he needed. That first year I gave him twenty rupees.

When the harvest was over and the paddy was in the Goldsmith's barn, I asked him to return the loan. "I gave you money," I said. "I'll not charge you interest, since you are my friend. Just give me the value of the loan in paddy."

But the land belonged to Dhruba's wife. She came to the barn and said, "Give me my share. If he borrowed money from you, I don't know about that. He'll pay you back; I'm not responsible; I never saw any of that money. If you don't give me my total share, then what will my child eat during the coming year? I don't care about his debt."

What was I to do? I divided the paddy fifty-fifty. I got no repayment of the loan.

The next year, I got another two plots of land to cultivate from this family. All the plots together were about one and an eighth acres. This year my friend Dhruba again borrowed for his *dasaharaa* celebration. He wanted a new cloth to place under the tools during the ceremony. I told him, "I have no money; I cannot borrow from anyone."

I had a cheap shouldercloth, which I had thrown over my shoulders only once—at the time a relative had given it to me as a gift. I asked Dhruba whether he could accept that used cloth for a sacred ceremony.

He said, "Oh, yes, when we purchase cloth from the market, we eat tiffin while holding it. Nobody cares. Give it to me."

I thought that Dhruba might return the cloth to me after finishing the holy work, but he never did.

The ritual usually begins after the seventh lunar day of the month and finishes on the tenth day of *dasaharaa*. On the last day, Dhruba needed some sacred food and some cakes fried in clarified butter. So he came to me and sat down, looking very unhappy, holding his head in his hands. He moaned sorrowfully, "Oh what will we do this year; we cannot do our traditional ceremony because I have no money, not even a quarter of a rupee for dry sacred food like *khai*. Forget the butter-fried sacred food, I cannot even afford *khai*. What to do? I have no money." He did not ask me directly, but just moaned on my veranda.

I said, "Why will you stop your traditional ritual? You should do it."

Dhruba replied, "What can I do? When the children of other houses have cake, what will I say to mine? When they see others eating cake and ask me for some, what can I say, what can I do? I am in need."

I thought I would teach him a lesson. I said, "We made a friendship, and that means I should help my friend in need, as he should help me when I'm in need. Then we'll be friends forever. Since I am now running my life happily, I should help you. But you are not following the truth of friendship. You borrowed money from me last year, promising to give me payment from your wife's paddy, and then had no courage to ask her for it and pay me back. I don't like this. You have no claim on the paddy since your wife is the landlord. I have forgotten about that loan—I assume that it is lost. I gave money to you, borrowing from others, and I paid back others for you. I did not worry about that because I considered your time of need to be mine also. But if you want to keep our relationship forever, you should consider that one of us should always help the other when he needs it. Now let's go and buy materials for making cakes. I have no money, so I'll borrow for it."

At a village shop I borrowed on credit some molasses, clarified butter, coconut, spices, and one and a half kilos of flour, which I gave to Dhruba. He took it happily and did his ceremony.

In the next month, Kartik, Dhruba again asked me for ten rupees to be repaid by paddy. "Not from my wife's near lands," he said, "but from some of my wife's land near Diapur. It is far away and my wife won't know about it. On the way back from collecting the harvest, I will give you the extra amount. So please give me ten rupees."

I gave him five rupees that I borrowed from someone else, and two weeks later I gave him another three rupees. The following month, Margasira [November-December], he asked me to give him some white paddy so that he could worship Lakshmi, the goddess of wealth. Each Thursday of this month, and again in the month of Magh [January-February] most households worship four kilos of white paddy, which represents Lakshmi, and offer another four kilos of white rice cakes to her. I borrowed from others to give Dhruba eight kilos of paddy. Each year that I worked for him I did this; and in this way he always took from me, but in return never helped me in any way.

That year, I had a bad season on the land I cultivated. Very little paddy survived. The only paddy in Dhruba's house belonged to his wife, and she refused to give him any. "Go and earn," she said to him, "otherwise you won't eat. If you earn some wages, our paddy will last a month. If you can't find work as a Goldsmith, work as a day wage laborer. My father did not give me land to feed an idle man."

The Goldsmith had never worked as an unskilled laborer. He tried it for a while, and found it very difficult and exhausting. And he still lacked money to feed his family. He asked me in despair, "What should I do? If I work as a day laborer, I'll die! It is too difficult!"

I also sat idle, worrying what to do. A few days later, the wife of one of my maternal uncles from Nuagaon village brought some old broken silver ornaments and asked me to go with her to a Goldsmith.

I took her to Dhruba, and she ordered new ornaments made from her old ones. Dhruba said, "I need more silver to make such ornaments."

Auntie replied, "You get the silver; we'll pay you for that."

I told him, "See, she is my auntie, so don't cheat her. You'll get whatever money you need, but don't cheat her."

He said, "Of course."

A few days later, the Goldsmith called me, "Oh friend, let's go to your uncle's house. We'll not only take the ornaments ordered, but another five or seven [an idiom meaning "a few"] ornaments. People may buy them."

That day I was sitting, doing nothing, so I went with him. He carried a hairpin, toe rings, hair flowers, bracelets, and my aunt's ornaments—a silver anklet set. He sold some things and received money from my aunt, and he took some orders for ornaments. He was very pleased with the day's results: he had earned something.

Dhruba's wife was very happy with the help I had given her husband, so she suggested that I help him with his business, and I agreed to do so. We began a business. Dhruba mortgaged some of his land to pay for ornaments. One day we went to Cuttack city to buy ornaments. I selected ornaments which Bauri people like. Dhruba paid all the travel expenses.

I took him to different Bauri wards in different villages. I spent a month selling ornaments with him. The people bought new ornaments from him and gave him repair work, thanks to me. But he never gave me anything for my help, not a single paise.

One day, I was in great need and I asked him for ten rupees. "Where will I get money?" he replied. "What I earn one day, I spend that day. What can I do?"

I said nothing. He offered two rupees; I refused. I left and went to the bazaar. I found out later that he went to my house and gave my wife the two rupees. Two or three days later, Dhruba asked me for money. I decided I didn't need him as a friend. The next time he called me to go with him to sell ornaments, I said, "Who can spend his days walking about without earning anything? I won't go."

From that day our friendship ended. Dhruba's wife transferred the land from me; I'm no longer the sharecropper. She didn't like me. Since that time Dhruba has not tried to borrow money from me, and I wouldn't lend him anything anyway.

That was how a friend gave help and was cheated in return. I gave up hope of ever getting back all the money and ornaments I lost through that fellow. If I had quarreled with him, people would have laughed, "Before they were friends; now they are fighting."

26. Transvestites and Prostitutes, 1969–72

Muli befriends several transvestites of various castes who work as male prostitutes. These men also work with Muli on house construction projects. They joke with Muli and with each other, using women's expressions and feminine forms of address. They dress and behave like women who follow purdah and kinship avoidance restrictions. Muli befriends one of their customers, a man named Madhusudana, who sleeps with both males and females. At the great festival of Shiva, Muli supplies Madhusudana with his prostitutes. For a while Madhusudana depends on Muli for prostitutes, but ultimately Muli becomes psychologically and economically dependent on Madhusudana, who leaves him.

Muli provides a rare account of an unusual life-style in India that has received little attention. While transvestites are tolerated, they are a subject of ridicule and are associated with pollution and the breaking of caste rules and boundaries (see Carstairs 1967: 59–62). Ironically, the transvestites are the only people who accept Muli as he is; his own caste and family downgrade him because he is lazy and does women's work, and high-caste men simply exploit him for his prostitutes.

One evening I ran into three transvestite friends in the Old Town market: Kula, the cousin of Lakhi the prostitute; Nisa, the Weaver-caste man; and Karuna, a Bauri man like Kula and me. Although they wore men's shouldercloths and long lungi loincloths, they draped them to look like women's saris, and they wore women's undergarments. Their clothes were brightly colored like those of women, not white like those of men. They wore lipstick like the women of the capital city, as well as black paste under their eyes and vermilion marks on their foreheads. They wore shoulder-length hair. From a distance they passed as women.

I called to them, "Oh, where are you working these days? Why haven't you called me? I've been sitting at home unable to find any work."

Kula replied, with women's expressions and intonations, "Are you speaking truthfully, or lying? Where is work not available for you?"* Kula was thirty years old, short, stocky, and black, with a long face and a long nose.

I replied, "Truly, I'm sitting idle at home."

Kula said, "Why don't you work with us in the capital city? We are digging holes for flower trees in a king's [wealthy man's] house. We'll finish that in two days and then dig holes for a foundation wall. Come, work with us. Are you telling the truth that you want to go with us, or are your words pretense?"

I said, "No, no, brother, I really want to go."

Kula said, "Why don't you start tomorrow?"

I asked him what the wages were. He replied, "Only two and a half rupees a day, but the contractor pays us twice a week."

I agreed to work with them. The following morning I waited for them at the Fisherman's square. When they arrived, Kula asked, "When did you get here?"

"I got here a long time ago, " I replied. "By looking and looking for you, the water of my eyes dried."

Nisa said, "Where will you get water? Why not use the sap of the *siju* plant on him!" He laughed. *Siju* sap blinds people.

I replied, "You always think of my welfare." Joking like this we went to the work site.

A few days later, an exhibition of tribal arts and crafts came to the capital city. Each day we passed the tribal exhibition grounds, to and from work.

One day, after work, we heard that a drama would be held at the exhibition field. We went to see it. Karuna wanted to remain without eating. I said that we should walk to our villages three miles away, eat something, and then return to the exhibition grounds. The others agreed with me, and we all went home.†

When we returned three hours later, the field was so crowded that

---

*"*Satare kahucha* naa *michaare* baa? *aa kukuaaḍe kaama aaparuga?*" Words in roman type indicate female and transvestite expressions. Females and transvestites use "naa" and "baa" as interrogatives; "aaparuga" [available] is an archaic word. Kula delighted in using peculiar and distinctive expressions that called attention to himself.

†Dramatic performances frequently start around midnight and do not end until dawn. Muli and his friends thus had plenty of time to walk six miles to grab a bite to eat.

we could not sit together. We stood, stretching our necks to catch a glimpse of the drama. We pushed through the crowd and stood in front of a bulky man, blocking his view. He pushed us aside and stood in front of us.

Kula spoke loudly, "Hoie! Didn't you see us here? Why did you push in front of us? You moved your hands in such a way that your fingers went across our arms and touched our chests. Do you think this is gentlemanly? Have you no shame? Why do you walk between us, just like a bull? Why didn't you ask us, if you wanted to go in front of us? We could have stepped aside and you could have easily stepped in front."

The fat man grabbed Kula's chin in his fingers and said, "Oh, my gold, why are you so angry?" He moved his hand over Kula's head, slid his hands over Kula's body, and gently touched his cheeks and face. Then he continued, "If anything bad has happened to you, please excuse me. For every fault, will you excuse me, or will you cut off my head? Anyway, we'll manage with each other." Again catching hold of Kula's chin, he inquired, "What do you say? Can we get along, or not?"

Kula replied, "Hey, look. Who is he? Who are we? We've never seen or heard each other, not even for a day or part of a day. Yet look at how many ways he's touching my body! What kind of a man is this?"

The fat babu replied, "What's the need to have met before? This is our meeting. From today we'll look at each other and hear each other. Get it?" He ended his statement with the upper intonation used by females, and he gently chucked Kula under the chin.

We left them sitting together but watched with amusement as they entertained each other and began their courtship. From a distance I saw them look at each other, touch, and talk for a moment. Suddenly they both jumped up and slipped away from the crowd.

I said, "Just a while ago, Kula quarreled with him. Now they are friends. Let's follow them." We trailed them without their knowing it. The fat babu walked ahead; Kula followed a few feet behind. We stayed well behind them, too far, in fact—suddenly they disappeared. They must have turned down a small lane. We searched but couldn't pick up their trail. We returned to the drama and separated. After a while, Kula and the fat man returned and sat where they had been before. I sat a few feet behind them.

49. Workman eating lunch in the New Capital.

Later, Kula came over to me. I asked, "Where's your friend?"

He replied, "How do I know?"

I said, "You quarreled with him. Then you became friends. Since you did not stay with us, we thought you might drop us and start up with him."

Kula said, "Oh, he pushed us and we quarreled. Why shouldn't we reply to him? Is he related to us, of our blood?"

I said, "How do we know if he's of our blood or not? We saw you joking with him, and you went away with him for hours. Tell the truth, where did you go?"

Kula smiled, "Why should I lie? He's a very juicy man. Can you imagine that? You saw him with me earlier, touching my lips and chin, running his hands over me. He called me, and he gave me some food at a tea stall. He took me into a lane, and there he gave me trouble for one hour, right at the back door of someone's house. I refused, but he wouldn't leave me alone. Finally I did it with him. You can't imagine. It took him an hour! Such a man he is, very nice!"

The next day I told Karuna and Nisa that Kula had enjoyed the babu from the capital. Karuna and Nisa always scolded Kula in a teasing way, taking the roles of women. "Where is your husband, Kula?" they would ask. Karuna was the eldest, and so his two friends called him *naanii* [elder sister]. Nisa, the next in age, was *majia naanii* [middle sister]; Kula, the youngest, was *saana bhaunii* [youngest sister]. Kula called the other two *naanii*.

Karuna and Nisa teased Kula: "When your husband comes, Kula, how can we show our face to him? We must respect him, and he must respect us. We must hide when he appears. What a great thing you did. We who are the eldest sisters are unmarried. You, the younger, are married. How can we mix with him? First we should be married. Then you should marry." They were parodying rules of avoidance between relatives.

I said, "Yes, yes, Karuna should marry first, because she's the first sister. Then her husband can mix freely with you all since you are the younger sisters-in-law. It is very bad, Kula. From today, you should give your husband to your big sister, and you'll become his sister-in-law. Then everyone can enjoy the first sister's husband. No problem!"

We used to talk like this. One day, I said, "Let's go to the capital city market. If we meet that babu, we'll tell him to exchange his position from younger sister's husband to elder sister's husband."

We looked all over for him. After an hour, we stopped at a tobacco shop. Suddenly Kula shouted, "Hey, our son-in-law is coming, our son-in-law is coming!" Out of respect the younger sister or younger brother call their elder sister's husband son-in-law, rather than by his formal title of *bhinoi* [sister's husband]. A father and mother will say to their young child, "Go and call *juain* [son-in-law]." So the child runs off and calls, "Son-in-law, where are you?" To show respect in the presence of her mother, father, or elder brothers, a wife refers to her own husband as "son-in-law." If she used her husband's name, or titles like "husband" or "brother-in-law" she would be disrespectful.

When the fat man came up to us he asked, "Did you see the exhibition that night? I met you there, I think."

Nisa said, "Why do you say we met you at the exhibition?"

The fat man gathered courage, "Yes, I did. I'm sure I met you there."

I asked, "Why do you ask?"

He replied, "Why? One of you quarreled with me that day, and later became friendly with me."

I said, "If you tell us the truth, I'll tell you the truth. These people went to the exhibition. Tell us what really happened that night. Who quarreled with you and made friends? Tell truly."

He said, "What will you get from that?"

I said, "If you are shy to talk here, come outside. Please bring betel for us."*

The babu said, "If you want to hear about it, you bring the betel."

The babu left with my friends while I ordered betel. The betel seller spread lime over the soft green leaves, sprinkled chopped betel nuts, spices, and tobacco on them, and folded them into little green cones. I paid him, popped a betel into my mouth, and started chewing as I searched for my friends. I found them under a tree, sitting and laughing. They stopped laughing when they saw me.

Kula said, "All our plans have changed. I have become the eldest sister and wife of that babu. Karuna has become my younger sister, and Nisa remains my elder sister. But we don't know how you are related to us. You are friends with us all."

They all laughed. Nisa, taking the role of elder sister in the presence of younger sister's husband, pulled his orange shouldercloth over his head and averted his face.

The babu brought us tea and snacks. Everybody talked as women do, even the babu, using the interrogatives *naa* and *baa* and frequently ending words with *-lo*. We called to each other *hai lo*, "hey," as men call to their wives or wives to their female friends. We addressed each other as *ki lo*, an intimate term which husbands use for wives and wives sometimes use with their husbands.

Finally we started home. The babu accompanied us as far as the railway line before he suddenly remembered that he had forgotten to buy vegetables.

I asked him if I could go to his house. He said, "No, this is not the right time. If the people in my compound see us, it will be bad. I'll take you there some other day." We parted.

I often wandered through the capital market with Kula and his friends. One evening, a Brahman of the Old Town saw us standing

*Muli brashly ordered the babu to buy betel because he knew that the babu, who was attracted to the transvestites, would not be offended.

50. Transvestite dancer (second from the left) at the *durgaa puuja* celebration.

51. A transvestite *kaaḷasi*-shaman at a firewalking ceremony.

outside the market and called to us jokingly, *"Hai lo,* mother's sister, hey elder sister, come hear a little something."

I felt very bad. He had addressed us as women with whom he was intimate. I walked over to him and said angrily, "Hey brother, why do you call out like this? Don't you feel any shame?"

He replied, "Why is this so hard on you?" He looked at the others as he continued, "We usually talk this way. What's wrong with you? They are people from my village. Who are you, shouting like this? You'll get a beating!" He was angry at me because he disliked untouchables talking back to Brahmans.

I replied, "You live in the Old Town. My friends and I come from three different villages—none from the Old Town. So who is your villager? Tell me? Why do you make statements like this? You speak this way because of the way you are. If you talk like that to another man, do you know what he will do to you?"

He shouted, "You've become quite smart, haven't you! The people I called to haven't replied. Just you, again and again."

I said, "Oh, if you want to, go and talk with them. See them, talk with them." My friends were laughing. I called angrily to them. "Why are you waiting? Why aren't you going over and talking to this fine gentleman from the Old Town? No one should talk with me. On account of you fellows, other people get beaten. You were born *maaiaa* [feminine]; everything you do is *maaiaa!*"* I left angrily.

The next day I waited for the three of them at the Fisherman's square. When I saw them in the distance, I started down the road toward our work site. I stayed in front of them without talking. They called, "Wait, wait." I made no reply. They ran up to me.

Kula said, "Everybody is talking except one person because a frog is in his mouth! If there is no frog, then someone must have made him dumb by casting magic spells."

I replied, "No one should talk to you. Someone beat [scolded] me on account of you. But you laughed."

Nisa said, "Where there is Kula, there is unhappiness!"

Kula replied, "Oooh! Nisa is the only peaceful man. He doesn't know anything bad. And elder sister Karuna will always cry, 'Oh, Brother Muli; oh, Brother Muli!' But Brother Muli has a big pouting

---

*Muli used the term *maaiaa,* a colloquial variant of *maaiciaa* [feminine, effeminate: derived from *maai,* woman]. The term specifically refers to transvestite men who wear women's clothes and talk and gesture like women.

face. See! Your brother Muli, oh, how he likes you. Oh ho!" He caught hold of my chin and rocked it gently back and forth, as he said, "Oh, my beautiful face! Please don't divorce my sister! Every fault is mine. Everybody should forgive me. Oh, moonface, please laugh. Are we outsiders or insiders? I am not an outsider. I am your own. Don't be angry."

All my anger disappeared. How could one stay angry at Kula? I laughed and joked and played with them. I forgot everything.

Later, Karuna said, "Today is Sunday. We'll quit work a little early and go to the capital market to meet Kula's bridegroom. We'll spend our weekly wages there."

We laughed and agreed.

At Kula's request, the contractor gave us our wages a little early, and we walked to the market. Although we wandered all over, we could not find our new friend. We became tired, and the others went to fetch a bicycle rickshaw to take them home. I stayed behind to buy some betel. I thought to myself, "Who has money for a rickshaw? It's only a three-mile walk to my village. Anyway, I might hitch a ride with cart drivers from my village." So I deliberately delayed and walked away from my friends.

Then I saw the fat babu bargaining with my uncle Satyabadi for a coconut-branch broom. I walked over and looked straight at the babu. He said, "It seems to me that I've seen you somewhere before. Do you recognize me?"

"Yes, surely," I replied.

"From where do you know me?" he asked.

I replied, "We'll talk about that later. Finish buying whatever you're going to get."

He said, "I've finished everything. I'm just bargaining for this broom."

"Oh, you need a broom?"

"Yes."

I said to my uncle, "Give it to him."

The babu offered money. I said, "Don't. It's free for you. Uncle, don't accept money. I'll take it."

The fat gentleman asked, "Why are you doing this?"

I replied, "The seller is my uncle. You don't need to pay him."

"Why? He's in business. At least I should pay the cost."

I said, "Not necessary. He won't accept it from you." We talked like this as we left the market.

He asked me, "What is your name?"

I replied, "My name is Muli."

He told me that his name was Madhusudana, and then he asked, "Who is Kula? Is he your relative? Why isn't he with you now?"

I said, "What can I say about him here? Let's go to an isolated place."

"All right, but first, get some betel for us both." He handed me ten paise and I bought two betel.

Then I asked, "Why are you involved with a homosexual? What gain do you get out of that?"

He replied, "What can be done? For a hungry man sour mango is sweet. Whatever food I get, I eat. I have no reserve at home."

I asked, "Are you married?"

He replied, "Yes, but my family lives in my home village. My brother and his family stay in my government quarters here in the city."

We passed a football field and then arrived at his house. He left his market bag in the house and we walked to the bus station, where he bought many magazines and newspapers. He hires a man to sell these magazines door to door. I realized by the way he talked that this babu liked any kind of sexual work he could get, with women too.

Again I asked him, "What do you get out of going with homosexuals?"

He replied, "When I was in school, and we learned about sex, we wanted girls. But where could we get them? It was impossible. Instead, we found out which boy in the class was like a female and enjoyed him instead. When I found that I had no wife with me, or no women, I went after the homosexual for my pleasure. Also, nowadays, hiring women costs a lot of money, five or seven rupees (U.S. $.60 to $1.00). But a feminine man like Kula is satisfied with half a rupee. They are a lot of fun to talk with. Although they are men, they have no shyness. They will talk about sex freely. On the contrary, talking with a woman is hard because they are very shy. Usually when I have no woman I hire a man. Since my wife is not here, I went with Kula. I take whatever is available."

We reached his house, and he went to the door, asking, "Do you want to go home?"

I said, "Yes, I'm hungry."

He said, "Why don't you stay here? You can go home tomorrow."

I told him, "No, I've not eaten since morning, except for a small snack. I'm hungry."

He said, "Oh, without eating, what will you do? You're very concerned about food. Today we met for the first time. Let's stay together for a while."

I agreed, and we walked back toward the bus stand. He asked, "Do you know where Kula is? How can I find him?"

I said, "I'm not traveling with them now. They laughed at me when I quarreled with a man from the Old Town who called them *ki lo* and *hai lo*—like his own wife—right on the main road in front of the capital market. I realized then that Kula and his friends were bad people, so I now avoid them. They have made obstructions like this for me two or three times. Don't keep your relationship with Kula. He goes to different places, different people. Who knows what diseases he carries from them? He goes all over, five or twenty-five places, he doesn't care."

The fat babu said, "Is that so? I shouldn't go to him again. He is a very dangerous man."

I said, "You don't know him. Today he's on good terms with you. If he finds someone else tomorrow, he'll leave you."

The babu said, "Let's forget him. I'll not have anything more to do with him."

We reached the bus station. Madhusudana Babu brought me snacks. Then he went inside the bus station and collected more newspapers while I waited outside.

When he returned, he said, "Let's go somewhere. We'll make friends with others."

We went to a Barber's wooden stall located a few feet in front of a house. The fat babu said to the Barber, "Oh, *saangataa* [oath friend], we came here just for a moment."

The Barber asked, "What have you been doing for the past five or six days? I haven't seen you. Why haven't you come? Go into the house, go into the house."

The babu told me to sit on the veranda while he went inside.

I sat on a cot. I listened to the gossip between the babu and the woman inside. Then the sound of enjoyment came, "hu-hu," the panting like a dog. The hairs on my arms stood up when I heard them.

After some time, Madhusudana called to me to enter. I didn't know what he wanted; I feared to enter. Instead, I asked, "Why are you calling me?"

He said, "The people here would like to see you."

I replied, "What's there to see? I'm dirty; so are my clothes. I've just come from construction work."

He asked, "Why are you afraid? I am requesting you to come in and sit beside me."

I went inside. He put me on one side of that woman, and he sat on her other side. He introduced us. She sat for a moment; she asked me where I lived, and about my family. I replied. Then her husband came in from the Barber's stall and said to the babu, "I've got no food, no money, and your oath-friend's wife has no oil or soap. You haven't been here for many days, and we've been waiting and waiting."

Madhusudana Babu replied, "Yes, I had difficulties, so I couldn't come."

The Barber asked his wife, "Did you give them water to wash their legs?"

She said, "No, we were talking, but I'll get it now."

The Barber said, "I'm going to bring some tea and snacks from the market." Then he turned to me and said, "Oh, friend, come with me. Take tea at the tea stall. I'll bring a cup of tea for the babu."

I said, "No, I've already had some."

The babu said, "Why don't you go along with him and have some tea?"

So I went with the Barber. At the tea stall he ordered two cups of tea and four snacks made of fried lentils. Then he said, "After you've finished, please come to my shop."

I ate, then I went to his stall and sat on a wooden bench. After some time, the babu called me to enter the Barber's house. He said to the Barber's wife, "He is my own friend. Treat him as you treat me." He walked out. She started to play with my body. I pulled away. I had not eaten a full dinner, and I was tired from working all day. I said, "I'll come back and be friendly some other day. It can't be done today."

Madhusudana Babu took me with him to the Barber's many

times. I usually sat on the veranda while he performed inside. Once or twice, though, I went inside.

Afterward, we would return to his house. On the way, he would complain, "This woman is very expensive. The moment I arrive, they tell me how much they need. She charges a lot. Although I have many women like this, I cannot always go to them and satisfy my desire because they cost too much."

One day, I said to him, "When we first met you gave me something, a woman to enjoy. You should come to my house one day. I also have people like this. Please give me the opportunity to offer them to you."

He asked, "Is it so? If I go to your house, can you arrange one?"

I said, "Why not? Do you think that you are the only one who has this, and we don't? Any day you come, I'll give you one."

He said, "Why should I say when? You should invite me on the day you select."

I replied, "Come on the evening of the festival of Shivaratri, the birthday of Lord Shiva."

Madhusudana Babu used to visit the great temple of Lingaraj [Shiva] in the Old Town many times, and the priests would perform a ceremony for him. I often met him afterward at the lion's gate entrance to the temple.

A few days before the festival of Shiva's birthday, I lined up two girls for him named Gauri and Supa. I then went to the babu and asked where we should meet that night.

He said, "My wife and children are coming from the village to visit Lord Shiva on his birthday. I'll leave them near the temple and then meet you at the lion's gate."

On the evening of the festival, I waited for him at the lion's gate. Thousands of people had gathered to see the lamplighter climb the 175-foot tower and place a torch he had carried on the top of the temple. Pilgrims were streaming into the temple to catch a glimpse of the deity. The streets around the temple were so crowded that I could hardly turn around. Finally, I saw my babu. I pushed my way over to him. He said, "Make your arrangements. I have settled my family so that they have a good view of the lighting ceremony."

I told him to wait for me at the lion's gate. I went home and brought my wife and mother to the Old Town market next to the temple. They selected a spot that gave them a good view of the Lamplighter's climb. I searched for the women. Gauri and Supa were walking with Lakhi, Kula's cousin, so I said to all three of them, "Please sit here, I've got a customer for you." I led Madhusudana Babu to the three women and told him to choose the one he wanted.

He selected Supa. I could see why. The others were older. Lakhi's body was all used up. Callouses had formed on the hole in her lap. Her tits were all dried up. I led Supa and the babu behind the hospital on the far side of the temple. The babu had her there, during the middle of the festival.

Supa came out alone. The babu remained hidden until she had left. Then he accompanied me back toward the temple. On the way, we met ten or twelve transvestites, including Kula, Nisa, and Karuna. When they called to us, the babu replied, "Oh, you are all here. I've been wandering about, looking for you, but I couldn't find you."

Nisa said, "What you said is enough. You should bring some sweets for us. Otherwise we'll not leave you alone."

The babu said, "Yes, come with me, I'll feed you sweets."

The transvestites demanded sweets from a particular shop. Madhusudana Babu bought and distributed some cookies and hard candies. Of course, Kula and his friends complained loudly. They would have been dissatisfied no matter what he gave them.

The babu walked away, and I went with him. He gave me five rupees for Supa and one rupee each for Lakhi and Gauri, since they had reserved themselves for him.

After Madhusudana Babu had returned to his family, I gave four rupees to Supa and kept the other three rupees. I went to my wife and said, "Let's wander through the market. You can buy whatever you want."

My wife said sternly, "I'll not move from this spot, nor disturb the lamp I am burning until the Lamplighter carries the great lamp to the top of the temple."

I sat beside her. The Lamplighter delayed a long time. I stood up and said, "You wait here for me."

I wandered about, looking for different customers. I found three more, and I sent them to the three girls. While they were out with the girls, the Lamplighter climbed to the top of the temple. When the crowd below saw him, men shouted the name of the god, while women made sounds of the *huḷahuḷi* [ululations] because it was an auspicious, holy moment. I got some money, and so did the girls. It was a profitable evening.

One evening a few days later, Madhusudana Babu and I were walking from his house to the capital city bus station when he stopped to urinate near a dark footpath. While I held his bicycle, he urinated standing up, instead of squatting as we usually do, holding his prick in his left hand. He rested his right hand on my shoulder.

I disliked this, so I said, "How much urine you pass, like a cow!"

He replied, "What a bad man you are! Are you looking at my urine?" Saying this, he slapped me on the back and laughed.

I didn't appreciate this, so I pushed over his bicycle.

"Why did you knock over my bike?" he asked angrily. "What did the bike do to you? I slapped you on the back for fun. Do you mind that? Actually, by throwing my bike down, you were doing the same as hitting me."

I said with a pout, "Well, if you think so, it might be."

He said, "Pick up the bicycle; otherwise I'll be unhappy."

I said angrily, "Oh, you are a rich man; that's why your argument will always win; I'm poor, my argument will always be false. Oh *sukha* [happiness, joy: used as a nickname], you urinated with one hand on your 'gold' and one on my body. What do you think I am, a male or a female? I disliked this, so in criticism I said that you urinated like a cow. You slapped me in fun. I took it as fun. I threw the bike in fun. Why, then, do you feel bad? Because you are a rich man, you have power, prestige, and noble character.* But we are poor; we have no power or prestige. Okay, now that I recognize your behavior, I'm leaving."

I walked quickly; he hurried after me, calling, "Oh, *sukha, sukha.*" He caught my arm and said, "Why are you so angry, acting like a bullock flicking flies away? If you are like this, how can our friendship run?" He told me to sit on the back of the bicycle. I was unable to reply because he was really more respected and richer than I. He

*Muli used the words *maana* [weight, power]; *sammaana* [respect or prestige: for a position]; and *ijjat* [noble character]. A man of noble character has *ijjat*; a man of *maana* has power, or "weight"; so people fear to talk to them directly or criticize them directly. The man with *sammaana* is respected for his position—like a school-teacher. People do not fear to talk to the teacher, who may not have power, but they respect him.

held my hand and requested me, so how could I refuse? It was my fault that we had argued; I had pouted.

I laughed aloud when I thought of this. A rich and respected man was holding my hand and begging me because I had pouted over a trivial matter.* Madhusudana stopped the bike and we both got off. At first I didn't know why he had stopped. I felt shy, so I looked down, trying to keep from laughing. He couldn't see my face in the dark.

Madhusudana called, "Muli, Muli." Then he shook my arm.†

I said in a low pouting voice, "What?"

He replied, "Why are you crying over such a minor thing? How can we be friends until we die?"

He left the cycle standing and clasped me to his chest. Lifting my chin, he said, "I ask you to forgive me. I'm keeping your prestige. Why are you so angry?"

I kept my eyes closed, and said, "I'm not crying; in fact I'm happy."

He said, "No, no, you are not at all happy. You feel bad. Okay, so let's walk and talk until you feel better." He steered the cycle with his right hand and put his left on my arm, and we proceeded down the road. Then he continued, "Oh, friend, listen. We both know why we became friends, because I like chasing after women, various women. Did you ever read the *gopaa liilaa* of our deity Krishna? It tells how Lord Krishna enjoyed each and every *gopii* [milkmaid], but neither Krishna nor his various girls betrayed their relationship or talked about it to others."

I replied, "I never read it. I am unable to read. But I heard that there was a Krishna who enjoyed many girls; I heard it from people like you." In fact I could read a little, but I never told that to these babus; instead, I flattered them by making them think that they knew a lot and were teaching me something.

Madhusudana said, "Whatever may be, I like you a lot. I choose you among all people as my best friend. Why? Because I like you."

I said, "Some people prefer family responsibilities; others prefer to make friends with various people; others prefer women; some like

*Madhusudana's caste was low except to an untouchable Bauri. His job as a peon or messenger was the lowest position in the civil service.
†Muli was acting like a shy girl being wooed by her man, and Madhusudana like a man trying to change his lover's pouting into a better mood.

animals. Anyway, you like me and I like you for only one reason. That's why you say all these things and I reply."

"Yes," he said, "And I've heard from someone that you go to a certain woman's house in another village. Is that true or not?"

I said, "I visit many people."

We were on the road. Madhusudana bought some peanuts in a paper cone and handed some to me. Since he couldn't eat peanuts while steering the bike, I shelled them for him until we reached the bus stand. He bought a cocola [Coca-Cola], took a swig of it, handed it to me, and then bought another one for himself. He bought a magazine and showed me the picture of a beautiful woman. He exclaimed, "Oh, if we could get a girl like this, wouldn't it be good?"

I replied, "It's good for you, not for me. I don't like this picture."

He said, "Oh, what a beautiful woman you must be enjoying if this one doesn't appeal to you!"

I spoke loudly, "I'm not saying that. Rather, why be so tempted by a photograph? What can you do with it? Who knows where the girl is? What can you gain by looking at the photo? It's better to have someone bodily."

Madhusudana replied, "Don't shout; don't shout! I was joking. You are speaking loudly. People might hear!"

We walked to the market. At the gate, Madhusudana said, "Why are you carrying an empty bag? Won't you do marketing?"

I said, "Yes, I want to, but I have no money."

"If you have no money, why did you carry a bag?" he asked.

I said, pouting, "I brought it; I'll take it. What's it to you?"

He replied, "Oh, you are a pouting man! Are you going inside the market or do I have to do the marketing for you?"

I replied, "Do you think I'll answer that?"

He said, "Yes, I'll do your marketing for you. What do you want?"

"Must I tell you what's needed? You shop for your family. Don't you know?"

He exclaimed, "Oh, he's a prick man!" He slapped his bag against his leg and continued, "I never saw such a man who refuses to tell his market needs!"

Madhusudana went into the market irritated. I waited, laughing. He returned with potatoes, eggplant, onion, ginger, betel nut and spices, and turnips. He asked, "Do you need anything else?"

I replied, in irritation, "Show me a man like you who will supply me with tobacco paste every morning so that I'll get my teeth cleaned every day."

He didn't like my sarcasm and muttered, "This *saḷaa* [wife's brother] accuses from all sides." He returned for tobacco paste, and I called out, "Salt, we have no salt; get some." He brought the items. I sat on his bicycle, and he drove me to the edge of my village.

The next evening, I was walking down the road to my village when suddenly Madhusudana Babu appeared. He said, "I want to go to that woman's house; I don't have much time; I've got to be back home by 8:00."

I said, "Okay, let's go." I led him to the edge of the Bauri ward in that woman's village, stopped, and said, "Wait here, I'm going ahead." I led him to an isolated house just outside the ward. He sat on the veranda, unaware that he was sitting in view of everybody at the door of the woman he wanted to see.

I went further into the Bauri ward. I saw her sitting on her father's veranda. Lakshmi [Lakhi] was a tall, healthy girl with a medium complexion and a big, round face, styled and waved hair, and a sharp nose. She was a bit short-tempered in nature. Her feet, the ugly portion of her body, were big, larger than those of a man. She was taller than most men and very flat-chested, I suppose because she'd had so many men that they had pressed her tits flat. Her arms and thighs were thick, though, and men considered that beautiful. She wore colorful saris, but never any undergarment or blouse. Because she chewed a lot of betel, her teeth were reddish-black.

When Lakhi saw me, she called to her younger cousin, "Oh, Kula, oh, Kula, look who has come!"

Kula the transvestite minced out of the house, looked at me, and said to his cousin, "This one man? Haven't we seen him [before]? Is this the reason you make so much noise?" Turning to me, Kula said, "Okay, okay, come, to which place have you come?"* He used

*Eei *goṭie maṇisa? eeku ame dekhinu? eeeṭhi paain, eḍe paatire dekucu? hou, hou, aaasa saanga* aaa*sa kuaṟe aailu baa?* Words in roman indicate the transvestite's intonations, which included the lengthening of many initial and final vowels. He also altered consonants, saying *caaura* instead of *caauḷa* [rice], and *sikita* instead of *siksita* [educated].

the familiar form [of the personal pronoun] used by parents to children or masters to servants, or between lovers.

I said, "I have a friend with me."

Kula exclaimed, with an upward feminine intonation, "Where is he; who is he; what's his name?"*

I replied, "That capital city man came with me."

"Oooh! Where is he?"

I said, joking, "He's sitting at the veranda of your cousin. I came to *you!*"

Kula said, "Has he not brought anything? I should go to see him first." He ran toward the capital babu.

I turned to Lakhi and said, "Oh elder sister, I brought a man for you. He's sitting on your veranda."

She asked, "How does Kula know him? Has Kula ever been with him?"†

I said, "Yes, he knows him and has experienced him a couple of times."

Lakhi shook her head irritably. "Then what do you want from me?"

"Don't you understand why I came to you? A gentleman is waiting for you. I came here because he wants you."

"Is he diseased?" she asked.

I said, "I never mix with diseased men. Do you think I'd bring one to you? Don't you trust me? Why ask all these questions? If you want him, I'll arrange it for you. Otherwise I'll leave."

She said, "Yes, I want him. Get Kula out of there. How can I talk to a gentleman with my cousin present—it's shameful."

As I stood up, I said, "He's very rich. Remember that I sent him to you. If you forget me, I'll stop him from coming to you."

I went to Kula and said, "Why are you sitting here? Have you no work? Go somewhere else."

Kula replied, "Why, are you jealous, dying for me too?"

Madhusudana Babu said, "Let him sit."

I said, "What work does he have here? He must move."

Kula replied with a woman's curse, "Why are you not tolerating my presence, you cremated cholera corpse!"

---

se keunti, kie basee ta naam ka-aṇaa?

†Muli's easy access to women—talking like this—suggests he is also a transvestite, as does the roles he takes with Madhusudana Babu.

I replied, "Don't you know why we came to this place and why I'm telling you to leave? Do you think we came here for other work?"

He replied with another curse, all in jest: "This burned cholera body is my enemy!"* He spoke as he always did, using not ordinary language, but Bauri women's dialect.

I replied, "Don't be unhappy; go to the house of Dasa; when we return, we'll call you and satisfy you."

Kula left. I said to Madhusudana Babu, "Kula knew we will not call him again, but he left to avoid embarrassing his cousin."

I called Lakhi, and she led Madhusudana Babu inside her hut. I sat waiting. Those two took a very long time. I wondered what was happening. Finally Lakhi came out looking satisfied. But I wondered about the gentleman. Lakhi was old, not as beautiful as other younger girls.

When he came out, I asked him, "How are you? How did you like the merry-making?"

He replied, "Yes, she's beautiful. Everything is nice with her. But she is a little black and a little old."

"Tell me, were you satisfied with her?"

"It was good."

I wondered, "Was he really satisfied? She [her vagina] is like a breeze. One can easily pass through the breeze. How could he be satisfied? Well, why should I worry about it if he says she is okay?"

I replied, "Why worry about her skin if she is beautiful and well behaved? What will you do with the dark complexion?"

Madhusudana Babu replied, "She's not totally black, but not entirely white. Not bad at all."

On the way back to my village, we heard the sound of many womanlike voices. We were passing by the house of Dasa, the lame transvestite. Because he was a leper, his house was well outside the village.

Lakhi also lived in a house outside her ward, because she had been outcasted for working as a prostitute. She had married my wife's brother, but had left him and returned to her father's house, where she practiced prostitution. Her husband refused to take her back. Her father's neighbors threatened to outcaste him as well as his daughter unless he threw her out of the house. So she herself paid to build a house outside the ward.

*e baaḍi poḍaa mara sataaru.

Anyway, inside the house of Dasa, the people were singing loudly and playing jokes. I said to Madhusudana, "Look at all those transvestites in there, and listen to the noise they make! Kula is there."

Madhusudana asked, "Who are the others?"

I replied, "Lokanath the Farmer-caste man, Hadu the Confectioner, and Manu the temple priest."

Madhusudana said, "Let's go to them. We told Kula we would meet him."

I said, "Don't go there. They will play sexual jokes on us, pulling off our clothes, forcing us to enjoy them. They'll try to touch your prick or grab it. It's late and I'm tired; let's go."

He came along with me reluctantly. He rode me on his bicycle —up to Tuan's tea stall, where he ordered a potato chop and some sweet cake and tea. I refused to eat anything, saying that my stomach hurt. After eating some of his tiffin, he handed the plate to me and said, "Take a little of mine." He patted the bench. I was sitting outside on the road.

I whispered to him, "No, no, don't talk like that. We're in my village area. Many high-caste masters come here. I can't do that around here."

Madhusudana silently ate his tiffin. Then we both took some betel and went off to the bazaar.

My relationship with Madhusudana Babu was friendly for about three years, from 1969 to 1971. But in the past year, he no longer likes me so much, and I don't know why. I'm not supplying him with girls now.

To bind my fat capital babu to me, I decided to do some magic. I thought all the time, "Where can I find magic; how can I bind him?"

One day I met a *guṇiaa* [magician] in the capital city. He had come to remove magic from a woman who was possessed by a demon. I asked him how I could keep a person in my hands forever.

He said, "I can do that. If you bring the necessary things, no one can break the power of your relationship, not even with magic. You need to sacrifice a pregnant black cat, a cock, and a hen egg."

I replied, "We eat the cock and the egg, so I'm not afraid to sacrifice them. But I fear to sacrifice a pregnant black cat—that's too sinful. It might give me a bad fruit [result] later in my life."

I left that magician. I looked for others, but I haven't found any.

Madhusudana Babu does not like me nowadays because I am unable to satisfy his desires. He is old, but he always wants a new piece. How can I get an old man like that a new young piece each time? I'm not young; I cannot mix with the young ones so easily now.

27. Kia's Attempted Suicide, 1971–72

Kia criticizes Muli for being incompetent, lazy, and selfish, and for spending money on himself while she works and supports the family by cutting grass for cattle. When she insults him by asking what kind of man would allow his wife to support him, Muli strikes her hard. She becomes sullen and sits in a corner all night. When Muli awakens in the morning, he finds that his wife has left without taking her grass-cutting knife or other work implements. Muli fears that she might try to commit suicide. In the afternoon, two men report that she threw herself under a train. Muli cries out; then sits numb with grief. In the evening he hears that his wife is alive and unhurt: some men pulled her off the tracks and took her to her sister-in-law's house. Eventually she returns to Muli, but the reconciliation is slow.

Unlike his affair with Tafulla, Muli takes the blame for causing Kia's attempted suicide, and he conveys a genuine, overwhelming grief when he believes that she has died. He also wryly describes the wailing of his mother for the daughter-in-law whom she had thrown out of her house, "Where did you go, my lovely daughter-in-law, what happened to you, how were you cut?"

In another incident included in this chapter, a wealthy Oilpresser uses his power to threaten the Bauris when they accuse him of having impregnated a Bauri widow. Here Muli highlights the double standard of Bauri men, who intimidate the widow and meekly submit to the Oilpresser.

One night my son asked me for money for his school examination fee, which he needed the following morning. I had spent the day traveling about the bazaar, had returned home late at night for dinner, and was now sitting outside on our front veranda. I told my son to get the money from my wife. He said that she had sent him to me.

I went inside. My wife had finished eating and gone to sleep; she would awaken before dawn the next day and leave for work while I still slept. I shook her awake and said, "Our son needs money for his school examination."

She said angrily, "You are a big earner. What are you doing with all your money? I run our household and buy the food with the money I earn. What do you do with yours? You even refuse to give it to your son."

I said, "I ate snacks, I spent it in the bazaar, on my wishes and happiness." I left the house. I figured my wife would give the money to my son.

I spent the next day at the bazaar. When I returned at night, my wife was cooking. She scolded me, "This is the male of our house, who feeds nobody. What is our man doing with his money?"

I replied, "Why? Do you think I work every day? I work three or four days a week. Those days I work, I earn, and I spend it. When I don't work, do you give me anything to spend?"

She replied, "Are you supposed to feed me, or am I supposed to feed you? In the world, people marry and look after their families. You never do. I take the responsibility for everything. From now on, starting tomorrow, *you* take charge. You feed your wife and son."

I replied, "I don't know of any wife or son. I earn. I'll do whatever I wish. I can't give money to anyone."

She shouted, "You can't give? Why did you become a man? How will you support your family?"

I said, "I can't support any family. If you wish to stay with me, stay. If you wish to go, then go."

"Why did you marry? Why did you make a household? Why do you sleep beside me? Why was a child born? After the birth of the child, you say you can't support a household. Who will do it? You must do it! Do you think you are the only clever man?"

When she asked why I slept with her and got her a child, I became enraged and beat her badly. She put out the stove, put aside the half-cooked food, and went to sleep in a corner. She gave us no food and took none herself; we went to bed hungry that night. She wouldn't even sleep with me.

She left the house early the next morning, long before I awakened. I thought she had gone to the fields to defecate. She didn't return. The sun rose higher. When I found her grass-cutting knife, her binding rope, and her betel, I knew she hadn't gone to work. My brain reeled. Where had she gone? I asked several people if she had gone to sleep in any of their houses the night before. No one had seen her.

Later that afternoon, Kubera, a neighbor, ran into our ward, shouting, "Muli's wife is dead! She threw herself in front of a train!"

I sat on my veranda, unable to move or speak. My mother wailed,

"Where did you go, my lovely daughter-in-law, what happened to you, how were you cut?" My son wept loudly, and my sisters-in-law wailed.

Some of the women of the ward saw me sitting, and they rebuked me for quarreling with my wife. I became restless and thought, "Why haven't I died?" My heart and mind hurt, but I did not cry in public. I felt shy. I just sat and listened as my neighbors criticized me. I couldn't bear their words, but what could I do? A person like my wife died. It was a great loss to me. Everyone who passed by me scolded me and blamed me.

After a while a gentleman named Ananta Babu, whom I regularly supplied with women, drove up to our ward on a motorbike. He asked, "Oh, Muli, did you quarrel with your wife yesterday?"

I said, "Yes, but I can't believe she would commit suicide. Others might, but she would never do 'the big thing.' "

He said, "Well, if you think that, then hop on my motorbike. We'll go to the railway line, and you can identify whether the body is that of your wife."

I refused. "No, no, I'll not go. If you can, send someone else to my sister's house. My wife might have gone there. I'm sure she wouldn't kill herself."

Ananta Babu left for my sister's house. I sat on the veranda. Everybody left. I thought of my wife and cried. When my son heard me crying, he came out of the house and cried even more, so I tried to hold back my tears.

After an hour, Ananta Babu returned smiling, "I've come from your sister's house. Your wife is there: she's alive and well! What you heard were rumors. She went to a remote place on the railway line, but a workman saw what she was doing there. She told him she had come to throw herself under the train, and she told him of her quarrel with you. By this time, many people had gathered around her. They took her to a forest gate nearby and stayed with her until she settled down. Later, she asked to be taken to the house of your sister. And that's where she is right now."

The following morning my wife's younger sister arrived at my house; she had heard that her sister had died. When she found out that her sister was alive, she went to visit her. The following day, my sister Radhi, her husband Bisia, and my wife's sister brought my wife home in a rickshaw, accompanied by Ananta Babu. He said to me,

"It's better if we can get you two back together again; the longer you remain separated, the more difficult it will be to reunite."

Then he said to my wife, "You should not get angry at your husband. Instead, you should pout. By pouting, a woman can make a curve straight. Go back to your house. At first you'll feel awkward mixing with your husband. So keep your sister with you for some days, until you settle down. Then you should go back to your husband and run your lives happily."

So that day my wife's sister cooked our meals, and my brother-in-law Bisia did the chores, buying vegetables, collecting fuel, and supplying water. I ate, but my wife refused to. She slept inside the house; I remained on the outside veranda. That night, while I was out on the veranda, I felt lonely. I pounded loudly on the wooden door. My sister-in-law opened it slowly. I said, "I'll not stay outside. I want to sleep inside, between you two."

They did not say no, so I slept between them. I talked to my wife. She said nothing. Her sister said, "Why aren't you replying? Until the end of your life you are his wife, he is your husband. How many days do you think I can stay here? If you talk to him, I can go home."

Then she replied to my questions, but only in monosyllables, "Yes," "No." After a while she started to talk more. I said, "Don't look into what I earn. You must promise that. I promise you that when I get some extra money, I'll give it to you."

She replied, "Well, I promise I'll not ask about your money."

We were back together again, although it was a long time before we talked freely with each other.

[Hari asked Muli, "Why didn't your wife beat you when you struck her? Why did she try to commit suicide instead?"]

Even if I'd beaten her to death, my wife wouldn't have fought back. She was not that sort of woman. Generally women should not beat men, even if they are stronger than their husbands, as my wife is.

My middle brother Anadi's wife is the strongest person in the family.* Once he and my wife were quarreling in the house, beating each other. His wife separated them, shoving them aside, one arm on each. Anadi was thrown to the ground. My wife picked up a stick to beat Anadi while he was on the ground. When Anadi's wife saw this,

---

*Although Hari and I questioned his claim, Muli repeated that Anadi's wife was stronger than any male in the household.

she picked up her husband and carried him in her arms into their room.

From that we learned about her strength. Several times Anadi beat her. She could have beaten him, but she never raised a hand to her husband.

Sarala, my youngest brother, also beats his wife a lot. Once Anadi wanted to go to Bharata's sister's house. Bharata's sister's husband had a sister, and both Bharata and Sarala had short for her [The English word "short" means "were affectionate with, were sleeping with."] Most of the women of the ward knew this, although how I don't know. Even Sarala's wife knew it. When she found out he was going to that woman, she was very unhappy. She grabbed hold of his trousers in the front and said, "I'll not let you go. Where are you going?"

He said, "To Bharata's village for touring about."

She said, "No, what work do you have at Bharata's house?"

"Nothing, I'm just traveling."

"You can't go there. I'll not let you go today. I know where you are going. You may go some other time. Today I'll not let you go."

"If you know, tell me where I'm going."

She said, "You are going to another woman to make her a wife."

When he heard this, he struck his wife again and again. She let him go. He left the house. Then she scolded him out loud, cursing him, "That cholera cat! Going to another woman! When I tell him that, he beats me. With a man like this, it's better to die!"

The next day, when Sarala returned, Anadi's wife told him, "After your departure your wife scolded you badly, calling you a cholera cat."

Sarala's wife had gone to a distant village to work. She returned, took some watered rice, and roasted one or two small fish.

While she was eating, Sarala arrived and asked her, "Did you scold me after my departure yesterday?"

"No."

"Tell me truthfully."

"No, I didn't."

Then Sarala asked my wife, "Is it true that yesterday after my departure my wife scolded me?"

My wife replied, "I don't know; I didn't hear anything."

Sarala returned to his wife. "Tell me truly by touching my head [in an oath]. Did you scold me or not?"

She did not reply.

Sarala exploded in anger, beating her again and again. My wife stepped in between them. Sarala angrily walked through the outdoor passage to the street, pretending to leave the house; but in fact, he stepped back into the outside room, hid, and listened.

Again Sarala's wife scolded, "Whoever told him, which made him beat me today, she should become a widow! He who beat me should die! I'll become a widow, and she who told him should become a widow!"

Sarala burst into the room and struck her with a wooden stick. Since I could not tolerate this, I stepped between them and pushed Sarala's wife, and she fell down. Although it is not our custom to touch the younger brother's wife, I had to in order to save her.

Then my wife went outside and screamed, "Who told him, causing that woman to be beaten so badly!"

Anadi's wife replied, "I did," and they were in another quarrel. Sarala's wife did not fight back, even though her husband beat her savagely with a stick.

A few days after Kia's attempted suicide, the women of the ward began to gossip about the illicit, sinful pregnancy of Babua's daughter-in-law, Passeri. Although a widow for the past twelve years, Passeri had remained in her father-in-law's house, "looking into the faces of her children" [a stock expression]. She worked every day at the house of Sankar, a wealthy Oilpresser-caste man. For three months, however, she had never bathed alone, as she should during her menstrual period. So the women gossiped.

One day the men of the ward gathered on Babua's veranda. They asked Passeri, "Who did it to you? Where was this thing done?"

She said, "Nothing happened, why are you gathering here?"

They said, "Yes, it happened; why are you lying? Tell the truth! If you won't tell, we'll take you to the hospital for examination."

Under pressure, she fell silent. The men said, "Why don't you tell us? We are sitting and waiting."

She named two Mallia priests, saying, "Sometimes they stop here on the way to go fishing. It was both of them."

The men asked, "Who else?"

She replied, "Nobody else."

The men of the ward called a policeman off the street and told him what had happened. He asked her, "Who did it?"

This time she mentioned the two Mallias, two Fisherman-caste men, and her father-in-law. Babua, the father-in-law, said, "Before the deity, I swear that I am not the father!" He broke down and cried. So the people of the ward were unable to tell who was really the father.

The men angrily scolded her, "If you don't tell us the truth, we'll take you inside and kill you!"

She did not become frightened; saying nothing, she went into her room. The men were tired of waiting. A young man named Purna entered her room and said, "Tell me secretly, tell me the true name. If you do, I'll keep you, making you my wife. I am your husband's younger cousin. Only I will know the name. For the public, you announce my name. Only the two of us will know who it really was."

She said, "Sankar the Oilpresser. All the other names were false. I mentioned their names because Sankar told me to. He said that I should never mention his name, and that if I obeyed him, he'd maintain me forever."

Purna went outside and told the assembled men, "It was Sankar the Oilpresser. She said he was the only one."

The next day, the men of the ward went in a group to Sankar the Oilpresser, a wealthy businessman who often boasted that he had begun as an itinerant vendor. They said to him, "You are the father of this woman's child. Who will care for this woman?"

Sankar the Oilpresser was furious, "Who uttered my name? Why would I bother with a woman like that? I have money. If I would spend money, a high-class girl would come to me. Why would I look at a *chaara bauraanii* [a very low Bauri woman]? Who dares to mention my name? A couple of days ago she came and sat on my veranda. Well, if anyone opposes me, he should do it openly. But I'm telling you, if anyone does, I'll *see* to him! Look at the property I've got now. It was not my father's; I earned it all by myself. If you people go against me, if all of you do, I'll spend all of my wealth to crush you, or anyone else who dares to oppose me! I'll *see* how far you can run!"

The men of the ward left meekly. At home in their own ward, they talked softly, visibly shaken by Sankar the Oilpresser's threat. "Who can oppose Sankar the Oilpresser? Who would start a litigation against him? Let somebody be outcasted. Let it be Babua if he doesn't throw out his daughter-in-law."

So our great leaders, trembling from fear of Sankar, threw Babua's daughter-in-law out of the village.

28. "The Taker of Discarded Rinds," 1970–71

*Despite his wife's objections, Muli takes a job as farm servant of Jadu, a wealthy Brah-
man miser who is renowned for cheating his employees. Men work for Jadu only if
they can find no other work or if they need something special from him. Muli hopes
that the miser, because of his high social status, will resolve Muli's longstanding quarrel with his father and mother. The miser never attempts to settle Muli's family dispute,
but instead continually cheats him. Muli gives a devastating caricature of the miser,
but a moving portrayal of the miser's long-suffering wife, who tries to be generous to
Muli, the employee.*

*Throughout the narrative, Muli provides a wealth of detail and character devel-
opment that brings his story to life: plowing with reluctant bullocks, receiving a betel
from a man who meets him in the field, watching Jadu the miser bargain and cheat in
the market, and listening to Jadu's wife complain about her husband's stinginess.*

In 1970, during the middle of the farming season, my father became too ill to work the two acres that he sharecropped. He hired me
to finish the work as a laborer for three rupees a day.

The next year, in April, at the time for the first plowing, my father
called me to his house and said, "I'm still too ill and weak to work.
You, son, must do it. I'll not sell my bullock if you agree to do my
sharecropping work for me. I'll help you by paying half the expenses of cultivating. And from our 50 percent of the share, you'll
take half and I'll take half."

The old man continued, "It is very difficult to get permission to
sharecrop someone's land. Too many people like us have no land.
We have to beg the owners to let us work for them. Don't let go of
this sharecropped land. Do the work; use my bullock."

I agreed to do it. Because of earlier quarrels, I didn't live in Father's house. I went back to the house I rented and told my wife of my
father's offer. She did not want to take it. She reminded me that, for

three or four years I had worked as a sharecropper, my crops were destroyed by floods—and that I still have not repaid all the money I had to borrow. "You are a laborer," she said, "so work as a laborer. Feed us with a wage. Tell your father that he should be the share-cropper and we'll be his laborers."

Although my wife objected, I thought my opinion was better than hers. I told Father I'd do the sharecropping.

Father said, "Your middle brother is working as a farm servant, while your youngest brother is an automobile mechanic in the city. They are well set up, but you are not. That's why I gave you this sharecropper work. We have only one bullock, so you should bor-row the bullock of Jadu the Brahman when you need a pair for plowing. Since he also has only one bullock, he'll borrow ours when he needs it. Jadu and I have exchanged bullocks like this for four years."

The following day I took Jadu's bullock. Several days later, Jadu said, "You should cultivate my land for a wage. My old farm ser-vant quarreled with me." Jadu is a tall, thin, dour and dark man re-nowned as a *krupaṇa* [miser].

I asked, "Why did he quarrel with you?"

He replied, "I'll tell you this evening. First, do the work."

I plowed his fields that day. In the evening I asked for my wage, three rupees.

Instead of paying me, Jadu said, "Diga, my farm servant, a man from your street, needed some money fast; his son is appearing in court for beating up a man to whom he owed money. I refused to give Diga money for this. He got angry and quit working for me. So you Muli, should become my farm servant instead. Why be a day laborer who doesn't find work every day? If you help me now, later in the year I can give you rice when you need it."

I said, "Yes, I'll work for you, but first I want my day's wages."

Jadu said, "Today I have no money. Work tomorrow, and I'll pay you for both days."

The next day I plowed for Jadu. When I asked for my wages, Jadu said, "First sit and take a betel." He ordered his wife to make tea. Since they were Brahmans, I couldn't use their pots. They handed me a coconut shell and poured tea into it. Jadu said, "I know your father and brothers threw you out of the house. How much rent do you pay each month?"

"Five rupees per month."

"How long have you been there?"

"Three years."

"Three years! You pay sixty rupees a year! You have paid almost 200 rupees to your landlord. If you saved this much money you could build your own house! I am a great man. I settle family disputes at many meetings. I'll settle your dispute, don't worry, and you can move back home."

I said, "Yes, I'll be very grateful if you do that."

Jadu said, "You are my farm servant—you'll cultivate for me all year and work around my house. I'll pay you the standard farm servant wage of two rupees a day plus a sixth of the crop you cultivate. In addition, instead of giving you *hetaa* land of one-fifth acre to cultivate for yourself, I'll give you twenty *gouṇii* of paddy and 300 bundles of straw.* For the past four years harvests have been poor. Twenty *gouṇii* which is certain is better than a *hetaa* crop which is uncertain."

I replied, "Usually farm servants get *hetaa* land for their own crop. I will lose one rupee out of three working as your farm servant rather than as your daily laborer, where I get three rupees a day. Twenty *gouṇii* of paddy does not make up the loss. I don't accept your offer. If you want, I'll ask my wife whether she wants me to take the job." I said this to avoid a direct denial.

I asked him for my wage for the last two days. He offered me four rupees, the wage of a farm servant.

I said, "Why four rupees when my wage is six?"

"I'm giving you farm servant wage now."

I replied, "You should give me six rupees. You can pay servant's wages once I start working as a farm servant. Up 'til now, I've worked as a day laborer."

"No. Take four rupees today. If your wife refuses to let you become my farm servant, I'll give you the remaining two rupees."

"I'll not take only four rupees. You should keep it until tomorrow. If you'll give me six rupees, I'll take it."

The miser shook his head in denial. I left without getting paid. That night I asked my wife what she thought of Jadu's offer.

My wife said, "He's a good cheater. Why won't he give *hetaa* land

*Twenty *gouṇii* is about eighty kilos of paddy; with one-fifth acre, Muli could earn 100 to 120 kilos of paddy or more.

like everybody else? Every year he changes his farm servant, and then gives his new farm servant a hard time with payment."

I replied, "On the day Jadu takes our bullock, I'll be useless. I'll have to seek work elsewhere. If I find no work, I'll be idle and will lose many days of work. I think it's better to be Jadu's farm servant—that way I'll be earning every day."

My wife replied, "No, don't work for him. Collect grass with me. I'll sell it in the market, and we will get a definite earning. Do this instead of farm servant work. Then you'll never lose a day's work."*

I didn't tell my wife that the reason I wanted to work for Jadu was that he had offered to mediate the dispute with my father. If I took the job and he didn't settle the dispute, my wife would never let me hear the end of it. Instead I said to her, "If he gives me the piece of land, then I think I'll accept the work."

She shrugged, "If you can get the land and want to do that work, then do it."

I went to Diga, the miser's previous farm servant, and asked him if he objected to my working for Jadu. Diga said, "Don't you know what kind of man he is? He'll cheat you. I'll never work for him again. You may if you wish."

I told Jadu, "I'm working with my father, but I'll also work for you if you give me *hetaa* land. I don't want twenty *gounii* of paddy."

The miser said, "From which place will you take the *hetaa* land?"

I replied, "It depends on what land you'll give."

He said, "You may take the land called *baaunsa bandha* [Bamboo Dam: each cultivated land has its own name] field, which my previous farm servants used."

This land was acceptable, so I agreed to become his farm servant.

After a few days, Jadu told me to plow and seed some low-lying land two miles away which was dry only one month a year. The previous farm servant had already plowed the field twice. I plowed the third time. Since it was a large plot, I took three or four days to finish it. Then Jadu said, "Finish the planting today. It might be too late tomorrow; it might rain. Start before dawn, and work in the field

*Collecting grass is women's work. Muli's wife knows he is incompetent and will be cheated; she prefers the lower but certain income to Muli's speculative schemes. Muli, however, wants the farm servant work also because it is more prestigious than day wage labor.

all day. Don't return to the village for lunch; I'll bring food for you and grass for the bullocks."

I said, "Don't forget to bring betel for me; otherwise I'll go for it myself."

Jadu said, "Don't worry, I'll bring everything for you."

The next morning I left before anyone else was up and worked there steadily until after 12:00. All the other cultivators had returned to the village for their meals. The bullocks were exhausted.

I waited, exhausted, under a banyan tree on a road about 200 yards from the field. The miser did not appear. I took the bullocks to a pond on the opposite side of the road, where they and I drank some water. I returned to the tree. The bullocks grazed nearby. Every once in a while I would climb the tree to see if anybody was coming this way.

After a long time, a man walked by and rested under the tree. He looked up, and to his surprise he saw me climbing down. "What are you doing there?" he asked. "Who are you looking for?"

I replied, "I am waiting for my master, who will bring me food and betel."

The man closed his umbrella, which had shaded him from the sun. He said, "I want to find a place to sit down."

I pointed to a huge banyan root that looked like a sleeping body, and said, "That's a good seat."

After sitting down, he asked, "Who is your master?"

I replied, "You wouldn't know him. We are from a far-away village."

As I spoke he beat the dust off his feet with his shouldercloth. Without hearing my reply, he said, "What a hot sun! A man will die in this sun! Why are you plowing in this hot sun, while your master sleeps inside his room? Who is your master? Where do you come from?"

I told him, "My village is Kapileswar; my master's name is Jadu. He told me to finish plowing and seeding this land in one day, and that he would bring food out to the field for me. I worked until noon. I am still waiting for my master."

"Oh, do you think I don't know Jadu the Miser! I know many people from your village; they own land around here." He mentioned them.

I asked, "How do you know them?"

The old man replied, "Each year I spend three or four days in your village collecting revenue. That's how I know most of the landowners of your village."

Opening his bag, the man pulled out a smaller bag that contained five small tins, for betel leaves, lime, nuts, spices, and tobacco. After preparing some betel, he offered me one. I refused, saying I had some, although I didn't have any. The man said, "While I am taking betel, and a betel eater is sitting nearby, and I offer it to him, he must accept it."

I accepted it. Then I said, "You don't know me; yet you offer me a betel. Why?"

He replied, "When a man who takes betel sees betel preparation, his tongue will dance. When a man who smokes *biḍi* sees another man smoking, he will salivate for village cigarettes. And if they don't satisfy his craving, he will be very unhappy. Let me tell you a story that happened to me about twenty years ago, when I was young. At that time, while unemployed, I was wandering here and there seeking a government job. Once I went for an interview where I had to stay until evening. I soon used up the betel I took from my house, and I couldn't get any more. An old man in that office had a bag like the one I now carry. He prepared five or six betel, which he placed in a small box, in front of me. Seeing that, I became more thirsty for betel. I went up to him three times to ask for a betel, but since I did not know him personally, I feared to speak out. He was a clerk in the office, a man of importance. All three times I returned to my seat without asking him for a betel. I became very anxious. Lacking money, I couldn't buy any betel. What could I do? I vowed from that day that, to stop my craving, I would never again take betel.

"Since many applicants were in front of me, my turn for the interview did not come that day. I returned the next day observing my vow, without a betel. A few days later, the office informed me that I got the job. After some months, I found that my craving for betel had not gone away. I resumed betel chewing, and I always carry a bag with betel materials, so that when I see a betel eater, I can give him one."

I thought, "I have really learned a lesson in courtesy from this old man."

The old man was delivering a special letter to a government office in the town. Standing up, he opened his umbrella. I placed my palms together in farewell, and he did the same. I did not take my betel, but put it around my waist and waited for the miser to bring food. When I looked down the road, the old man had reached the next village; but I still saw no sign of anybody else. I thought that the miser would not come. I went to drink more water to lessen my hunger. I was very tired, so I slept under a tree.

When I woke up, the bullocks were gone. Where were they? If I didn't find them, the miser would force me to hunt the bullocks, pestering me, "Where is my bullock, where is it?" I climbed up the tree and looked around; the bullocks were marching home. I ran after them. They had nearly reached the next village before I caught them. After running, in the hot sun, I was exhausted. I took them back to the field and yoked them, but I didn't want to work. Every time someone passed by I looked to see if it was Jadu. Becoming irritable, I beat the bullocks to hurry them through their plowing, not caring whether I did a good or bad job. I became very thirsty. Remembering the betel the old man had given me, I popped it into my mouth. I praised that man for his generosity, thinking, "This betel is more than my food; God should bless that man."

Jadu appeared an hour later without any food. I did not see him approach because he had cut across the paddy fields. Although it was about 5:00, I had eaten nothing since before dawn. I thought, "I should beat him like a bullock. But I cannot do that; he's my master. If my father had treated me like that I would have beaten him. If my wife had done something like this to me I would have killed her! But I fear to beat my master, who's a Brahman."

I said nothing to him as he approached, and he said nothing to me. The first thing he did was to walk around the field and inspect it. Then he said, "What, the work isn't finished yet?"*

I replied, "What do you know? And what can I do if you don't know? In midday, when the sun was too hot for anyone to work, I went to the pond to give water to the bullocks and myself. After sleeping for a while, I returned to work. Then I rested again. So the work is not done. I have been plowing here three or four days. And

---

*At seeding time, cultivators use a wide plow that makes a wide, shallow furrow instead of a narrow, deep one. Since wide-furrow plowing takes one-third the time of normal plowing, Jadu had expected Muli to finish the work in one day; but Muli, slow and incompetent, had not finished.

you say I must complete the seeding in one day. Do you think it's not difficult?"

Jadu said, "Won't it be finished today?"

I replied, "I *must* finish it. Otherwise, do you think we will return home? I may die here, but I'll finish it." Then I thought, "What a bad man he is. He promised to bring food. Bringing nothing, he first asks about the work. If a man is alive he can work; if he is dead, he can't."

Jadu walked around the boundaries of the field. He said, "Stop work for a moment. Go and take two or four paise of tiffin and tea. Then you'll start again."

I thought to myself, "I haven't eaten all day. Then this man wants me to walk back to the village to buy a snack worth two or four paise, referring to the coins as if they were the old valuable coins, not the new ones. These days, tea and snacks cost twenty paise."

I angrily replied, "I don't want to eat!"

Jadu said, "If you won't go, let me bring tea for you, since the tea stall owner won't give the glass if he sees you."

I thought, "That's the miser's way of getting out of bringing me a meal." I did not like his way of talking. I did not reply. I angrily hit the bullocks to get them to run and finish the work quickly.

Jadu said, "I'm going to the village to get some pressed rice."

What a generous man! After I work in his fields all day, he offers me a light snack. I talked aloud to myself, "Who will eat pressed rice now? Without soaking it, it's hard to eat."

The miser replied sharply, "You don't like anything! If you don't like it, then don't eat it."

Jadu said no more about food. I worked until sunset. While returning home, we saw a huge rain cloud moving toward us from the Khandagiri hills. Jadu said, "See, Muli, if it rains today all your work will be destroyed."

I did not reply, but angrily beat the bullocks to hurry them, and inwardly prayed, "If there is a god, it should rain today; so much that all the seeds rot in the water! Oh, God, make it rain!"

Saying this, I hit the bullocks. The miser's bullock was weak because he never fed it, but simply let it scrounge for itself. His bullock stumbled and couldn't go fast. My bullock dragged the other on the yoke. Leaving the miser far behind, I reached the village of Sundarpada, near my home. He called me to wait. The bullocks turned and tangled themselves in the rope. I freed them. As the miser caught up to me, I thought, "What, still only clouds and no rain? I have put down ten *gouṇii* [eighty kilos] of seeds costing forty rupees. If it rains, it all will be destroyed. Oh, why isn't the rain coming!" While passing through the village of Sundarpada, I felt a couple of drops of rain. Just at the place where the Muslims kill and butcher goats to sell for meat, the downpour started.

My bullock, unable to stand it, bucked, threw off the rope, and streaked toward our village, all four hoofs hitting at once. I couldn't catch him. I carried his yoke as I went toward the miser's house, shivering in the cold rain.

The miser wailed, "We'll get nothing, everything will be gone!" He repeated this all the way to the village.

When we reached his house, his wife said to me, "Your bullock came here long ago. Come up on the veranda and dry your body!"

When the miser arrived, he said to his wife, "Muli's making our veranda muddy. He'll just have to get wet again when he leaves, so let him take his bullock home!"

The miser brought my bullock. His wife said to me, "Take a betel."

I said, "Don't give me a betel; if you have *guṇḍi* [strong chewing tobacco] give me that." But they had none.

I went to my father's house. Father asked, "Why are you so late in returning our bullock?"

I told him what had happened. Father scolded the miser; then said to me, "If you continue to work like this you'll die soon."

I left him while he was still scolding me. I was tired and hungry. My wife, quite worried, was waiting, wondering what had happened to me. When she saw me she said, "Does anybody else work like this, from before dawn to evening night!"

After drying me off, she gave me another dry cloth. I threw my wet cloth on the veranda, sat near the earthen stove, and warmed up.

My wife asked, "What will you eat?"

I told her to make some tea. After frying a half kilogram of rice, she made a bowl of tea and put the fried rice in the tea to soften it. I ate about half of it, and gave the rest to my son.* Then my wife put the rice pot on the earthen stove for the evening meal.

I asked her, "What do we need to buy for tonight's dinner?"

She said, "Just a little oil, nothing else."

---

*Muli gave the food to his son, not to his wife, according to his custom.

I placed a palm-leaf basket over my head to keep off the rain and took our little oil bottles to a shop in a high-caste ward. Leaving the bottles at the shop, I went to the miser's house for my money. It was still drizzling; the road was a slimy mess. The miser told me to sit on his veranda while he ordered tea. I entered his front room.

After an hour, his daughter appeared and said, "We have no sugar for tea." I said, "I don't want any tea; my wife prepared a lot. I came to take money for buying spices and oil."

The miser offered me a betel without tobacco powder or betel nut. He gave his second son the key to open a box in his shrine room next door. The box contained whole betel nuts for offerings in family priest rituals.

The child lifted the box and said, "Look Father, the box is unlocked."

The miser said, "Your elder brother Indra might have taken something." He went to look. I followed him to the door of the shrine room; as I stepped on the high doorsill of the room, he cried, "Oh, why are you coming inside! Don't come in, don't come in! This is our goddess Lakshmi's house, our property; you've polluted her room! Now I'll purify it!"

I looked inside the room. It had many rat holes and piles of rat dirt; pitchers and pots were half covered with dirt moved by the rats. People would fear to enter such a room, thinking that snakes live there. I never saw a room like this. Maybe he buries his gold in that room and keeps it that way to frighten thieves. I returned to the entrance room.

The miser checked the materials and money in the box. He looked up and shouted angrily, "Ten rupees are missing; who came into this room?"

For ten minutes the miser muttered to himself, complained, and scolded about the money. Seeing this, I didn't want to ask for money. He came to the front room, used as a cowshed and a waiting room for outsiders, and said "It's raining too much today; tomorrow you cannot plow. Come here tomorrow and we'll prepare manure."

I said, "I'll come, but give me some money now."

He pulled out a couple of coins—fifty paise. I thought, "What can I do with this 50 paise? I should give it back." Then I thought, "Someone stole his money, so I don't want to ask for more money."

I took the coins, bought some oil at the shop, and took it home.

When I went to my master's house the next morning, he was not there. I asked his wife, "What work do you have at the threshing floor behind the house?"

She said, "Wait until he returns. I don't know."

When he returned, he set me to work cutting a tree and leveling the ground. I scattered some straw and spread manure over it to dry. While I was doing this, the miser called to his fourteen-year-old daughter, "Oh Bidu, Bidu, prepare some tea."

An hour and a half later I was still working when Jadu said, "What's happened to the tea, Bidu, did you prepare it?"

She replied, "We have no sugar and no tea leaves. How can I prepare tea?"

Jadu gave ten paise to his youngest son, who was seven years old, and told him to bring some tea and sugar. Tea is sold in small, five-paise packets, but hardly anyone orders only five paise worth of sugar —one teaspoonful.

After some time the miser called to me, "Oh Muli, would you like some tea?"

I replied, "Oh no, no. I have already eaten; I'll not take tea."

Jadu brought some tea to the threshing floor. "Take some tea; it's only water, take a small quantity." When people give a great amount, they say it is small, but the amount this miser gave really was small!

I replied, "I don't want a small quantity. Whenever we eat tea, we must have half a kilogram of fried rice and a full bowl of tea. We eat some of the fried rice and throw some in the tea and eat it, then we drink the tea. But you will give me simply a small amount of tea in a coconut cup, as you did yesterday. Well, yesterday I threw it away. And I would today, too." A master is supposed to treat his farm servant well. A farm servant values his job because he gets not only security during the year, but also meals, tea nowadays, betel, a dhoti, and sometimes a blanket for winter. But Jadu, that miser, did the reverse: he offered things in such a way as to make people refuse to take them.

Jadu said, "Oh, you take that much puffed rice and tea? Who would give you anything like that? We have only a small amount. If it won't satisfy you, why should you take it? Then take a betel."

I thought, "He's offering tea—I refused. He's offering betel. If I refuse that too, he'll be angry. So okay, I'll take it." But what he offered wasn't a betel; it was a fourth of a betel. I thought, "I ought to throw it away, but not in front of my master." Instead I took his betel, pulled out another piece from my own cloth, and popped both in my mouth.

Jadu, watching this, asked, "How much betel do you take? I gave one, you are taking another."

"You gave me a very small piece of betel; that is not sufficient for my mouth."

He pointed and said, "Then take another one."

"I don't require more."

I had finished all the work except drying cow dung. Each day we throw cow dung into a large pit. Once a year we dig up the pit and spread out the manure to dry. Then we beat it into powder with a big stick, for use as fertilizer in the fields. I returned to drying the dung. When my work was half done, Jadu turned over some straw that was drying. At lunch time, I told my master I wanted to go home to eat.

He said, "What? How many times a day do you eat? You came from your house after eating once. Now you'll eat again? We have not even started our cooking yet in this house. The water for rice was just put on the stoves."

I replied, "You people sit in your house and don't do any work, so you can stay without eating much. But we work. Our bodies consume everything we eat. We are always hungry."

"If you're like this," he said, "I think that you'll eat everything in the world. That's why you people are always in need. You should spend less than what you earn."

I replied, "How could I spend less?"

"You stick with me. I'll teach you how to save money."

I said, "Yes, I'll learn from you, I can see that. What we earn we always spend. Well, okay, now let me go. After bathing, eating, and resting, I'll return in the afternoon."

Jadu replied, "What, you will take your bath? I am a Brahman, but I haven't bathed yet. I must do many ritual duties after bathing. You don't have to do anything after your bath except eat and sleep. Daytime sleeping is not good for your health. You have all night to sleep! If you want to go to eat, just wait. My Bidu will prepare a good curry today."

I said, "You just put your water pot for rice on the stove. After boiling the rice, you'll cook the curry. Then you will give it to me. That is not today's meal; it's tomorrow's. I'm hungry; I'm going."

He called out, "Wait half an hour. My daughter will finish the curry by then. Such a fool you are! What will you eat at your house? Watered rice and salt! What's wrong with eating curry? Wait; do some work while you are waiting. Then you'll have less work to do later."

There was no "less work"—we had two days' work, which he wanted me to finish in one day. That's why he wanted me to stay. Nevertheless, I stayed. What could I do? That miser was out there doing a small amount of work, moving straw around, so what could I do, how could I leave?

An hour went by. No one called me to eat. At 1:00 I told my master, "I'm going home to eat."

He called out, "Wait, wait. Both of us will bathe. The curry is not done yet. But when we return I'll give you curry."

As I passed through Jadu's courtyard on the way to the entrance, I saw his children eating curry. Jadu was with me.

I said, "Oh, I see your curry is not done yet. How are your children eating, then?"

Jadu's face contorted in anger, "Oh, wicked children! Not waiting for curry; taking simple rice! As if you hadn't eaten for seven days."

But I had seen that those children were eating curry.

Jadu turned to me and said, "Really, Muli, our curry is not finished yet. Those children are simply taking rice with salt. Such children! I have never seen such children in other houses!"

I left, bathed in a small pond near my house, went home to lunch of watered rice, salt, onion, and ginger, and then took a nap.

That afternoon, I returned to that miser's house. He was sleeping inside the front room. I went into the courtyard and asked his wife, "What more work is there for me to do? *Nanaa* [brother or father] is sleeping now. I don't want to wake him and ask him."

She asked, "Have you finished the manure work of this morning?"

"No."

"Then do that work."

I worked in the cow dung pit. When I was half finished, Jadu woke up, saw me, and asked, "When did you come back?"

"I came back a long time ago. You were asleep; you don't know when I came. But see how much work I have done!"

He replied, "You shouldn't wait for me. You should work like this all the time. Once you know what to do, you just go ahead, and ask for money when you finish the work."

I finished the work about evening. Without asking permission, I went to the bazaar. I did not return home until 9:00 that night. My wife had cooked rice and lentils.

She asked me, "What have you been doing for such a long time at your master's house?" She always referred to that miser as *saa-aanta* [more than master]. As far as I was concerned he was no master, so I called him brother.

I didn't reply. So she asked again, "Where did you go? Didn't you finish work until now? It's late at night!"

I said, "I went to the bazaar, just to look around."

She raised her voice, "What did you get in the bazaar? Oh, you got some sweet tiffin there!" She was accusing me again of spending money foolishly. "You must have gotten money from your master. That's why you remember your previous good times, traveling to the bazaar. That's why you went."

I said, "Why are you always talking like this? I don't always want to sit in the ward. When I am here I find the people always talk about different women, how poor various people are, all sorts of jealous talk—who is starving, who is eating. I don't like this sort of thing. At the bazaar, I meet many outsiders, people from different places, with different sorts of behavior. I like to go there rather than stay here."

She replied, "While you roam in the bazaar, what happens to your family? Why do you forget what your wife is doing, or how your child will be fed? You should think about these first before going off to the bazaar, but you never do; you are always careless about your family. I always have trouble feeding your family." She put my food before me: rice and lentils and roasted dried fish.

The next morning before sunrise I threw water on my face and, without stopping to defecate or brush my teeth, I took my father's bullock to Jadu's house, joined Jadu's bullock with my father's, and led them with the plow back to my ward. I asked a small child to watch the bullocks so they would not wander off. I got some tobacco paste, betel, and a twig toothbrush. In the middle of the paddy fields near my ward a pool had formed from flooding. I defecated near there, cleaned myself with the water from that pool, brushed my teeth, and drank some of the water. Then I returned to the village and led the bullocks to the field called Merchant's-Broken-Dam.

The first of the three plots of land I was supposed to plow was so muddy that the plow could not even move. The second one was just as bad. The third was slightly drier, so I plowed it, although it was difficult and the going was slow. By the end of the morning I had finished only three-fourths of it. Other people working nearby went home for their meal. I wanted to finish the plowing, but when my bullocks saw other bullocks leaving, they became nervous and started to buck. They refused to follow orders. I had to let them stop until afternoon.

We had worked from six until ten in the morning. The sun was burning hot now. Neither man nor animal could work until about midafternoon; then we could continue for another three hours. I took the bullocks back to their houses. After bathing, eating a lunch of watered rice, and sleeping. I collected and hitched the two bullocks and set out for a nearby field of mine; Jadu's field was too far to reach and still have time to do any work.

That evening, when I returned Jadu's bullock, his wife said, "Who will tie the bullock? Your *nanaa* [father] is not present now." She was afraid to tie it because it might buck and hurt her.

I said, "I won't do it. If I tie the bullock in the stall, I'll be held responsible if it dies." A person guilty of the death of a cow or bullock must go through an expensive purification ritual, the *gobaadhiaa*, in which he drinks the *pancagabya* [the five sacred substances of the cow]: milk, clarified butter, curds, urine, and dung.*

She said, "If you will not tie the bullock, come inside."

I left the bullock in the front cowshed room and entered the inner courtyard. She said, "Take some *saaga* [spinach-like leaves] curry. We just cooked it."

I replied, "What will I do with the curry? I have no rice."

She said, "I'll give you a small amount of rice. Eat quickly before your *nanaa* gets back!"

I was hungry, and nodded in agreement. She looked around for a pot with which to serve me. She found a clay pot used for taking sacred food from temples. I knew it would be thrown away if I were to eat out of it.

I don't like to eat out of clay pots. At home we use bell-metal plates. I didn't expect Brahmans to give me a bell-metal pot, since they believed I would pollute it. But they had aluminum pots, and they have no restriction on my using those.

---

*Few villagers actually perform the *gobaadhiaa*, even if they are supposed to. For an example of a *gobaadhiaa* ceremony see Freeman 1977a:34–35.

So I said, "I may not eat, but I won't eat out of a clay pot."

She said, "Well, then, how will you eat?"

"I'm not allowed to use your brass dishes, but most people also have aluminum pots. You may give me food in one of those."

She replied, "We have only one aluminum pot, which we are using. If I give you rice in that, and the children tell their father, your *nanaa* will get angry with me."

"If you fear *nanaa*, don't give me rice, just curry; I'll eat it in my hands."

She said, "Sit. Why should you eat only curry? I'll give you some tiffin."

She brought a mixture of roasted rice in molasses and fried pressed rice. All four children came to the room, sat silently behind me, and watched my face as I ate. So I stopped. I don't like others to watch me while I eat.

While I sat there, Jadu's wife told me about her father's house and criticized her husband. "See, Muli, my father is a wealthy man, with forty acres of land, four or five farm servants, and many day laborers working for him. In my father's house the farm servants eat once a day. When I was young, like Bidu here, I served them. They were just like our family; we invited them to all of our ceremonies, and gave them our special foods for ritual occasions. Each day about ten or twelve workers ate at our house.

"But here I don't get enough food. My husband is such a *cothaa* [miser] that he won't even feed his own children. Whenever they eat, he barks like a dog. Whenever he is around my children never eat enough to be satisfied. He never orders cooking earlier than 1:00 P.M.* How can the children wait so long? So at night I cook more than we need without his knowing it. In the morning, I secretly feed my children the leftover food. They eat hiding from their father. They are children; they must eat well enough. But when my husband sees them eating, he scolds, 'How much they are eating! Just like a *raksasa* [cannibal demon]!' My sister, married in Cuttack district, is very happy because her husband's house is just like our father's. I don't know why Father gave me to this sort of house. It's my *bhaagya* [fortune]."

I listened attentively as she continued. "My husband doesn't know how to treat farm servants. No one stays a year. What can I do? I can't tolerate these things. I am suppressing my desire. I want

*In other houses the cooking of the first meal begins between 7:00 and 11:00 A.M.

to look after you fellows, but am unable to do so. Why do you work for him? Haven't you heard about this fellow's behavior? You are a man of this village. How could you forget his behavior?"

I replied, "What can I do? I team my bullock with his. My father has exchanged bullocks with him for the past three years. We're on friendly terms with him, so I agreed to work for him."

Right then the miser fellow arrived. "How did the work go?" he asked.

I told him that I couldn't finish plowing his field because it was too wet.

"What?" he exclaimed. "You haven't completed that small plot of land? What kind of work do you do? You should work for me as you would work for yourself. In the rainy season, when food is scarce, I'll give you food so that you won't starve. Think of the future and work accordingly."

He offered me a betel. I waved it away, saying, "If you look at it, you'll find betel nut, but no leaf; or a leaf without a nut; or a nut and leaf but no tobacco powder. I don't want your half-prepared betel. It has no value to me."

I got up to leave. The miser asked me, "Where will you work tomorrow?"

I said, "Where will you send me?"

"Go to my fields for plowing."

I agreed and said, "I must leave now."

Then I remembered I hadn't been paid. I said, "Give me my money. I have worked for four days and have received two rupees. I'd like the other six rupees."

The miser called his daughter, Bidu, who brought a small cloth bag. The miser pulled out a ten rupee note and some change. He gave me the change. "It's only two rupees," I said.

"I don't have anything else except this ten-rupee note. I could have given you more had I broken the bill. Tomorrow is market day. I'll pay you then."

I said, "Give me the ten-rupee note. I did six rupees' worth of work. By the day after tomorrow I'll have completed your ten rupees' worth."

He said, "What would you do with it today? You'll just spend it in some way. Then tomorrow you wouldn't have any for marketing. Take the two rupees."

I went home with two rupees. My wife had not yet returned from the bazaar. I collected wood for the stove. When she came, I said, "Wife, you are very late today, what happened?"

She said, "I sold my grass to buy firewood and food. We had no food. I had to purchase everything."

"What, have we nothing in the house?"

She replied, "Oh, you brought a lot with you? Why should I have purchased my small quantity? You came from the house of that great man, who gives you many things. Really, I'm very sorry I bought anything. Let me see what the head of the household bought!"

I replied angrily, "Why do you talk like this? You don't know how to behave toward your husband. I am a *maanyaloka* [person of respect] for you. I think you did not learn properly from your parents."

I went angrily to Father's house. As I massaged him, he asked me how the cultivation work was going. I told him. After feeding the bullock, I washed in the pond and went home. My wife gave me rice and taro curry. The curry did not have enough salt, so I complained sarcastically, "Why does this curry have so much salt? Do we have so much salt that we can't find other uses for it? You put more and more in the curry so that it would be used up, isn't that so?"

She said, "If there's too much salt, put some water in the curry. That will improve the taste."

"What, you're giving instruction? You learned this behavior at your father's house. Who do you think I am? You should learn how to behave to other people."

She laughed, "I don't know what 'behavior' means. I cooked. If anybody likes it, he may eat; if anybody doesn't like it, he may not eat."

I was furious, "What, did you bring any of this food from your father's house? How dare you tell me not to eat!"

I stood up, grabbed her head, and hit her on the back with my right fist two or three times. Then I went to Father's house and told Mother to give me something to eat.

She said, "Why, didn't you cook at your house?"

I told her what had happened. She was very unhappy that I had beaten my wife. She said, "Look, son, she works hard all day, then she comes home, cooks, and feeds you. You are a lazy boy. You earn very little—a lot less than she does. Why are you beating her? What will you do if she doesn't go to work tomorrow? You should praise her. If she irritates you by her speech, you should reply with your tongue. Why are you using your fists?"

I was angry at mother. "I asked for food. If you don't want to give it to me, just tell me and I'll go. Why are you talking about these other things?"

Mother put the food down, and I ate. While I was eating, my son Gopala came in from the band party rehearsal. He asked, "Oh, Father, why are you eating here?"

I replied, "They have some good curry; that's why."

He asked, "What curry do they have?"

I said, "Don't try to eat here. If you do, they won't have enough for themselves."

The boy went to massage his grandfather. The old man said, "Your father gave me a massage; I don't need more. Go take your meal."

Gopala left. After finishing dinner I went home. As I came near the door I heard Gopala inside saying, "Mother, why don't you eat? Come, eat with me."

She replied, "How can I eat? Your father didn't. He got angry with me." By custom, a wife waits until the husband eats.

Gopala replied. "He already ate at Grandfather's house."

When I went inside, they were eating. I lay down and slept. My wife and I did not talk to each other.

The next morning I got up while they were still asleep. I pulled out the two rupees that the miser had given me and placed it carefully on the bed. Then I tiptoed out silently.

By the time I finished plowing the miser's land, it was very late and I was exhausted. When I returned Jadu's bullock that evening, he asked, "Are you going to the market today? Won't you take money for the market?"

I replied, "If I don't take the money, how can I do the marketing?"

He said, "Then come with me. I'm going to the market."

At Bhikari's tea stall, the miser went inside, sat, sipped tea, chewed betel, and talked idly with all sorts of people. I stood outside, since I was not allowed in. When I eat at this shop, the owner brings tea or sweets to me outside. He keeps a couple of plates and glasses under the bench for Bauris.

52. The Old Town market with the Lingaraj temple in the background.

After about thirty minutes, the miser left the shop and continued toward the market. As we passed the post office, I asked him, "Oh, *nanaa* [brother], you took betel and tea. Why didn't you pay Bhikari for it?"

He replied, "Every *sankraanti* day [first day of the lunar month] I do his fire purification ceremony for his house. He owes me one rupee and one meal for this, but instead of a meal, I sometimes take tea and betel from his shop. So I don't pay for it."

Jadu went inside a cloth shop, sat, and talked there until well into the night, while I stood outside waiting. Finally I called to him, "Give me my money. I want to get to the market. It will close while you are sitting here. How can I buy anything?"

He came outside and said, "I haven't got any money. Kartik the lentil seller will give me some money. I'll give you your money at his spot in the market. Go there. I'll be along soon."

"No, no, no," I said. "You should get the money from Kartik, give it to me, and then return to this cloth shop if you have business here."

He went inside and sat down. I called to him again, "You went for a bag. Now you're sitting again."

"Oh, I forgot. I'm going."

He came out. He went to Ramesh's tea stall in the market, where he had another tea and borrowed a betel from a Brahman while I waited outside. Finally, Jadu said to me, "Go to Kartik's market spot. I'll be there soon."

I waited at Kartik's spot, which was only ten feet away. After a few minutes Jadu arrived and asked Kartik for some money for me. Jadu had lent Kartik some money at a high rate of interest—60 percent a year. On market days Jadu took the interest on that money.

Kartik offered me a rupee. I turned to Jadu and said, "What will I do with one rupee?"

Jadu then asked for five rupees, and upon receiving it said to me, "Come, we'll buy some things. I'll give you money there."

I said, "Why not give me those five rupees? You owe me six."

He replied, "What! You'll take five rupees for marketing? Such a foolish man! Come and learn marketing from me. Two rupees is all you need."

We went to the front section of the market near the main road, where most of the sellers from remote villages place their vegetables. It was so late that only two sellers remained. One, a fifteen-year-old youth, had only one and a half kilograms of okra, half rotten and half eaten by insects.

Jadu asked the boy, "What is the price of this?"

The boy replied, "I was selling these for 80 paise per kilo. But what's left here is not good, so if you want it, name your price."

Jadu said, "How can I tell you? It is your thing; you name the price."

"Give me half price, 40 paise."

Jadu's voice rose. "How much will you take? Tell me correctly! You're quoting an impossible price. Oh, Muli would you buy it?"

I said, "These are very bad okra. I wouldn't buy them. What would I do with rotten okra?"

Jadu replied, "You can eat it, today and tomorrow." Squatting near the okra, he picked through it, throwing aside the completely rotten ones. The boy, busily counting his money, took no notice of Jadu's activities.

Jadu said to him, "Oh, Babu [used as a term of respect for the boy], these are all rotten and fifteen days old. Nobody will buy them.

53. Vegetable sellers in the Old Town market.

Why do you quote such a high price? You have made a big profit. The rest of these ought to be thrown away. The market will close soon. Nobody else will buy this okra. Don't try to be greedy and get more profit from it. Give me a low price; then I'll buy them, and you'll earn somehing from it."

The boy said, "Let it be. I'll take 20 paise."

Jadu replied, "Again you are too greedy! How much profit will you take from these? If nobody takes them, you'll have to carry them home. Since they are all rotten, you'll throw them away. If I take them, I'll cook them all tonight. Take 15 paise; then you can buy a cup of tea instead of throwing the money away. First think: where will 15 paise come from? You have to work for it, here, but you can get this money free! You have to work for it, here, but you can get this money free! Why are you refusing? Accept the 15 paise."

The boy said, "I didn't ask you to buy it. If you want it, give me 30 paise. If you don't want it, go away."

Jadu threw up his hands, "Oh God! We are trying to help you better yourself, and you are behaving like this! [He refers to himself as "we," as people of status often do.] This age we live in is very bad. A man tries to help others, and those whom he tries to help become his enemies."

The young vegetable seller remained silent. Then Jadu continued, "I'm not trying to make you lose money. I am your elder [literally, big man]. So accept what I tell you. Take 15 paise for yourself. Don't throw the food away." While speaking, Jadu was scooping the okra into his bag.

The boy stopped him, "Why are you putting those in your bag? I don't want to sell them for 15 paise! When I refuse to sell, why do you take forcibly?"

Jadu asked, "I said 15 paise; do you think it's a bad price? If so, I'll give 2 or 3 paise more."

The boy laughed, indicating that he would not argue more. He was plainly irritated that this rich babu wouldn't agree to a reasonable price, of 20 or 25 paise. He let Jadu scoop up the vegetables.

Jadu turned to me and said, "Do you want to take half of it?"

I said, "I don't want to."

Jadu handed the boy 15 paise, not even 17 or 18. After counting, the boy angrily threw the coins on the ground, saying, "Keep my okra! Are you playing with me? Again you give me 15 paise?"

Jadu said nothing. He picked up the coins, added 3 paise, and gave them to the boy. Jadu stood up. Seeing the rotten okra that he had set aside behind him, he quickly bent down and scooped those into the bag.

I asked, "Those are bad. Why are you taking those too? Earlier you threw them away."

Jadu showed me an okra. "See, the two sides are rotten, but the middle isn't. We can cut the sides away and use it. It's edible."

He started to walk away. I followed. The boy called out loudly, "Such a man! He is very bad. Nobody can find a man like that anywhere else in the world! This man is a *copa chaḍaa loka* [taker of discarded rinds]!" To call a miser a taker of discarded rinds is so insulting that people very rarely say it.

I said to the child, "Why do you talk like this? You took money and you sold your things. Why do you pass remarks like this?"

Jadu said, "Leave it! Are you a fool? We got the things—we'll go and see others now."

I replied, "Then give me my money. I'll do my own shopping."

I pleaded, "Please cash the five-rupee bill. When can I do my marketing?"

Jadu said, "Let's go to buy potatoes. We can cash money there."

I went with him to the potato salesman. The price everywhere was 90 paise per kilo. We walked back and forth until the miser found a seller who had tiny potatoes, the size of small pebbles, which he was selling at 80 paise per kilo.

Jadu said to me, "What is to be done? Everywhere the price of potatoes is too high. We should not buy any potatoes today."

I said, "Then cash the money and give me some."

He replied, "Oh fool, nobody will change this money unless we buy from them."

I thought, "When will this man buy something, and when will I be able to buy some food? What good marketing I am doing today!"

Jadu saw a crowd at one spot. "Let's go and see what's happening there."

I was compelled to follow him. Someone was selling half-rotten potatoes for 60 paise per kilo.

Jadu asked, "Do you want to take some of these?"

I answered, "These potatoes are cold storage potatoes with no taste. They are like sweet potatoes, which costs 40 paise per kilo. Buy sweet potato, not this."

"Whatever may be, I'll take a half-kilo of these potatoes. The children will understand. If they are satisfied, that is good." The market meets twice a week. He was buying a half-kilo of potatoes to last six people for four days, but he made it sound as if he were bringing sweets for his children.

I said, "Take them if you wish; I don't want them."

Jadu gave the seller some potatoes to weigh. He took off his shouldercloth and held it outstretched to receive the potatoes. Looking back and forth quickly, to see that nobody was watching, he palmed a potato in each hand and slipped the stolen potatoes into his shouldercloth as he folded it.

Then he asked the seller, "Did you weigh it properly?"

The seller said, "Do you think there's a defect in the government-inspected balance?"

I figured that the miser asked this to escape trouble if the seller caught him stealing potatoes and asked to reweigh the lot. I wonder what the miser would have done if the seller had found him out?

The miser gave the seller five rupees and got the change. He gave me two rupees and kept two rupees seventy paise for himself.

I asked, "What will I do with these two rupees?"

He replied, "How much money do you need to do marketing?"

I said, "If I buy vegetables with small change, do you think I have no other expenses? Won't I buy rice? You gave me two rupees. You still owe me four."

He replied, "I've not brought money from my house. I got this five rupees from Kartik. Take two rupees for your marketing. If you want more money, I'll give you some tomorrow at my house."

I left him and did my marketing, thinking to myself, "That miser is a cheat, a 420 man" [420 is the number of an anticorruption act].

By the time I reached home, dinner had already been cooked and the family was waiting for me. My wife said, "What good marketing you have done today with that master of yours! Oh, we are waiting for your marketing because we will make curry from the things you brought!"

I told her why I was delayed. My wife and son both laughed. When I told my wife that I had brought some fish, she became angry. "All the people of the ward are asleep. And you bring fish now. When will we sleep?"

"Take it and clean it," I said.

She said, "I can't. The person who brought it should do it. Who will do this work now?"

I had to clean the fish. I lit the fire, but it went out. I blew on the wood to get it going, but the embers died out. My wife pushed me aside and started the fire. She said, "I already made curry. Eat it while I fry the fish."

I said, "Oh, it's not so late. Make curry out of the fish." She ground some spices and cooked the fish. I ate; then my son and wife ate some.

The next day, I went out to plow the fields before dawn. To keep me working there all day, the miser went out to the fields at about noon and watched me. When we returned late that evening, he offered me some tea, which I refused because I figured he would give it to me in a clay cup or a coconut shell. I also refused some fried rice, but he forced me to take some. Thinking I would receive a fairly good amount, I stretched out my shouldercloth to receive the fried rice.

54. A wealthy landlord prepares betel for himself.

55. Betel seller in his Old Town shop.

Jadu said, "Show your palm. Why do you stretch out your shouldercloth?"

I held out my hand. He dropped a few grains of fried rice into it.
So I thought, "Why did I let my name be written that I had taken this
stuff?" I thought of a proverb, "I left my caste [by eating forbidden
food] but my stomach was not filled." I ate the fried rice. Jadu told me
to take a betel. I refused. He pushed it on me, saying, "You threw
away your betel when you took the fried rice. Will you now sit without a betel? Take one." He handed me a skimpy half-betel. I took
it and said nothing.

The next morning, out at Merchant's-Broken-Dam Field, my bullock lay down and wouldn't move. I pulled his horns, pulled his tail,
and squeezed his nose, but he wouldn't budge. I was tired. Releasing
him from the yoke, I sat on the bank and let the bullocks rest.

Again I tried to make the bullocks work, but with no success. I
let them wander. They went to the dam and started to graze. I went
after mine. I found a thorny bush and broke off two branches. I put
his tail between the two branches and pressed hard. He had been
sitting. He stood up fast! I led both bullocks back to the yoke and
started to plow.

Since it was late and too hot, I quit without finishing. I thought,
"This greedy Brahman will scold me, saying it's my fault, not the
fault of the bullocks. I returned the miser's bullock. He was not
home. His wife offered me some spinach-leaf curry, but asked,
"How [in what container] will you take this curry?"

I said, "I don't know; I have nothing with me."

She said, "Shall I give it to you in a coconut cup?"

I said, "Okay, then I'll take it to my house."

She couldn't find a coconut cup, so she brought some castor-oil
leaves. The curry, containing too much water, dripped through my
hands. I thought, "These Brahmans will hate it if cooked food from
my hands falls on the ground in their house. I should cover the
ground with fresh cow dung to purify it. But if the water runs down
the courtyard, how far would I have to smear it with cow dung?" I
pressed my hands together, and most of the water ran out all in one
place. I smeared the spot with cow dung. Holding the curry so that it
wouldn't drip, I carried it home and put it down.

56. The deity's room in a high-caste house. The walls are painted for the festival of Lakshmi, the goddess of wealth.

Without closing the door I went to wash my hands and legs. When I returned, I saw a cat leaving the house. Suspecting that the cat had eaten my curry, I kicked at him, but missed, and my foot hit the wall. I shouted with pain. I rushed inside, limping. Half the curry was gone. I went to my mother's house and asked her for some curry; my wife was out collecting grass as usual. My mother gave me a curry made of taro, *simba* bean, dried fish, and some leaves. I ate some watered rice with it and slept.

The next morning, as I was getting Jadu's bullock, I saw his wife cutting vegetables for curry. She asked, "Did you go the market yesterday?"

"Yes."

"You must know what sort of vegetables came to my house."

"I didn't see what he bought, but I can guess!"

She showed them to me, "Look, eggplant half eaten by insects, another green vegetable too old and hard to eat, half-rotten pumpkin, and some damaged *khaḍaa* leaf [for curries]: a quarter of these are usable; I'll have to throw away the rest. He'll complain tomorrow that he brought a basket of vegetables and it didn't go far. He'll scold the children when the vegetables are gone. Just wait a little; I'm making some curry. You take some."

I replied, "I've no time."

I returned later in the day, after plowing. Jadu's wife said that he was at the Old Town market.

I asked, "Did he leave any money for me?"

"No. Meet him there and get some money."

I said, "He owes me ten and a half rupees. I am poor. He's not paying me. How can I feed my family? He's not concerned with my troubles."

She said, "Why ask me? I have no power. Meet him there."

I said, "If I ask him there, he'll say he hasn't brought any money. How can I ever get paid?" I went home, collected my oil and kerosene bottles, and went to the Old Town market.

I waited for several hours at Kartik's shop until Jadu arrived. I said to him, "Oh, you are a very good man! I've been waiting since early evening. Didn't you know it's market day? I need money for the market. You may not have work at home, but I do. You can travel about, but I can't.

He said, "What can I do? I just returned from settling a dispute between two cloth merchants and a merchant of our village."

"You got some profit from your work. What profit did I get waiting here? How much money did you make?"

"They gave me something."

"I don't want to listen about your business. Give me my money first."

Jadu told Kartik to give me two rupees. I refused to take it. "You owe me ten and a half rupees. Why should I take two? What can I buy with that?"

Jadu said, "Well, how much does a man need to buy food for a family like yours?"

I replied, "Why do you ask about my family and my food? You should pay me what you owe me. I need to buy rice."

Jadu said, "Kartik, give him five rupees."

I said, "Give me fifteen rupees. I'll buy ten rupees' worth of rice and five rupees' worth of vegetables. I want to buy some fish. Five rupees is not enough."

Jadu said, "Why are you lying? You never buy rice with your money. You spend it on luxuries. Your wife earns and buys rice for long periods. Why do you lie?"

He was trying to raise my prestige, to flatter me. If a man must buy rice every day, he has low prestige, for it means he has no rice at home. If he only buys rice once in a month, or six months, or never, if he has enough from his own fields, then he is considered to have higher prestige. Jadu was trying to say that I wasn't needy and didn't need to take the money.

I replied, "What's it to you? I may throw away the money without purchasing rice. You owe me, so pay me."

He said, "Do you think you are working for me for nothing? Why are you always asking for money?" He turned his head aside and mumbled aloud, as if he were talking to himself. "This man thinks I'll keep his money, that he's working for nothing. Why should I keep the money? I'll not become rich through his money."

He borrowed five rupees from a tobacco paste seller and, together with the five rupees he had taken from Kartik, threw it at me, saying, "Take your money! I'm not eating it."

I picked up the money and went home.

29. Harvest Tragedy, 1971–72

Muli discovers, for the first time, that Jadu has never owned the land he hired Muli to cultivate, but rather has sharecropped it for a Goldsmith, who has just sold it to an Oilpresser. When Muli claims and tries to harvest his share of the crop, the Oilpresser chases him off the land and calls the police to arrest him as a thief. Muli quarrels with the miser in front of a village tea stall, exchanging insults and curses. Although high-caste witnesses side with Muli, they do not force the miser to pay him for cultivating the crop.

Muli is the first untouchable of his village to dare to publicly challenge and insult a Brahman. His final debacle provides insights into the relationships between landowners, sharecroppers, permanent farm servants, and unskilled laborers; it also provides a glimpse of the procedures men use to resolve conflicts, as well as the circumstances in which these procedures fail.

Jadu's constant cheating, and the warnings of my wife, father, and friends, should have prepared me for the payment I was to receive for my year's cultivation of his fields. In August, as I was transplanting paddy shoots in my *hetaa* land, a fly landed on my face and wouldn't go away, a sign of bad fortune. Not long after, Sankar, the wealthy Oilpresser, ran out to the field and shouted, "Why are you transplanting this rice? This field is mine. I just bought it from Dhruba the Goldsmith. I'll decide when people will work on my land!"

My heart sank. I thought Jadu was the owner of my *hetaa* land! If he didn't own it, how could I be paid for my labors? I said to Sankar, "Jadu told me he was the owner, and he hired me as his farm servant, giving me this plot as *hetaa* land."

Sankar laughed, "Oh, no. It doesn't belong to him. I don't know what you are doing here. Get out!"

He was short and black, with a loud voice, and boasted of his success as a self-made businessman. Starting with nothing, he had become a wealthy rice mill owner with many powerful friends. I remembered how he had threatened to crush any Bauri who dared mention

Harvest Tragedy, 1971–72   355

his affair with Passeri, the pregnant Bauri widow. What could I do or say? Nothing. I went to Dhruba the Goldsmith's house.

Dhruba said, "I used to own that land. I hired Jadu as my share-cropper. He hired you as his farm servant. I've just sold the land to Sankar. He owns the *hetaa* land Jadu gave you."

Had I known all this when Jadu hired me as his farm servant, I wouldn't have taken the job. Without owning the land, he had no right to offer it to me as *hetaa* unless the owner also agreed. But Jadu had made no agreement either with Dhruba or Sankar. Without permission both from the owner and the sharecropper, I had no right to harvest my *hetaa* crop. Still, I would have cut the crop if Jadu had told me to because then he would have been responsible.

On large holdings of land a sharecropper often hires additional laborers, paying them cash wages [two rupees for farm servants; three for day laborers] during plowing, planting, transplanting, and weeding. After the harvest he pays them in grain out of his own share of fifty percent of the crop. He gives day laborers one-twelfth of the paddy they cut; he gives farm servants one-sixth or one-eighth of what they cut and, with the permission of the owner, also gives them *hetaa* land. Since the owner takes half of the crop from all of his lands, he also takes half of the *hetaa* crop, or its equivalent from another field. The sharecropper owes his farm servant an amount equal to the entire *hetaa* crop; he must make up the half that goes to the owner. He can do this by hiring day laborers to harvest land equal to half of the *hetaa* plot, paying the laborers a one-twelfth share from the plot they harvested, and giving the farm servant whatever is left of the harvested grain. Farm servants don't like this because they lose a share of their *hetaa* crop to day laborers. They prefer to receive the entire *hetaa* field to cultivate and have the sharecropper pay the half-share of the *hetaa* crop from the harvest in another field. But this requires permission of the owner.

If the *hetaa* field is too big to harvest alone, the farm servant can hire his son, wife, and parents and pay them wages: that way all the harvested grain remains within the family. In all these arrangements, the sharecropper must be reasonable in adjusting shares from different fields so that both the owner and the farm servant are satisfied. What a reasonable sharecropper I was working for!

In my case, since Jadu had not substituted other crops for the owner's share of the *hetaa*, Sankar, the new owner, had the right to claim half of all the crops, including half of my *hetaa* crop. As sharecropper of that *hetaa* land, Jadu then should have paid me back as much as the owner had taken from me. When Dhruba the Goldsmith had owned the land, he had never collected half of the *hetaa* crop because he was in debt to his sharecropper, Jadu. If Dhruba had pressed his *hetaa* claim, Jadu would have collected Dhruba's debt out of that *hetaa* crop. Jadu had no power like this over Sankar, the new owner, and I had no power to get Jadu to pay me back the owner's share of my *hetaa*. I couldn't even get him to pay my daily wages.*

From the month of Aswin [September-October], I became even more unhappy with Jadu. I asked him permission to throw the seeds of pulses [lentils] not only in my *hetaa* field, but also in his other fields. He said, "Every year people lose their lentil crop. Insects eat it, sometimes cows eat it. I haven't tried lentil crops for the past seven years. Since it is not profitable, forget it."

I replied, "Why isn't it profitable? You may not get much, but you'll get back more than you invest. If everybody's crop is eaten by insects, we will lose ours too, but nobody should worry about that."

He still refused to give permission. I was unhappy. Everybody who is a farm servant throws lentil seeds and gets a crop to eat. That's one of the benefits of being a farm servant. But I'd get no benefit.

In the month of Margasira [November-December], Jadu said to me, "What are you doing nowadays, Muli?"

I replied, "Mostly I've been ill, unable to walk because of infections from boils. Just now I am going to James's house."

He asked, "What do you do there?"

I replied, "Oh, we just sit and talk."

"Well," he asked, "have you ever gone to the fields to see if the paddy is ripe?"

I replied, "My small *hetaa* crop is ripe now. If you'll permit, I'll cut it now."

He said, "My neighbor, who is expanding his house, scattered building stones, bamboo, and wood all over my threshing floor. When he removes those materials, we'll prepare the threshing floor and cut the paddy."

I replied, "Ripe crops won't wait; we must cut them before they dry out."

*The four paragraphs above are rewritten from interviews with Muli in which his responses were elicited by my numerous direct questions.

He said, "Okay, cut, but put the paddy on Daitari's threshing floor." Daitari, a wealthy Confectioner-caste man, is a great miser just like my master.

During the next week, I saw Jadu many times, but he never again mentioned the subject of cutting my *hetaa* land. Time was passing. I was really unhappy with him. I thought of cutting the paddy without his knowledge. But ownership of the land was complicated; it did not belong to Jadu. I thought I'd better wait for his permission so that he'd be the one in trouble, not me.

One day Jadu came by and said, "Let's cut the paddy of the Bamboo-Dam Field. I've no more straw for my bullocks, and no rice for myself."

Bamboo-Dam Field was my *hetaa* land, but he made no reference to that. I did not reply to him; if I had, I would have said, "It's my *hetaa* land; why should you take the crop?" Then we would have quarreled. Since no witnesses were present, I kept quiet.

Instead I finally said, "If you want to cut it, go and cut it."

Jadu said nothing about that land, and neither did I. The paddy remained uncut.

Three days later Jadu came to my house and said, "Go and press down the paddy stalks with a bamboo pole today so that we can cut more easily."

I said, "Today I cannot do it. I'm going to my other work. Bring and place the bamboo pole in front of my house and I'll do it tomorrow."

He replied, "Why aren't you cutting the Bamboo-Dam Field? You see that my bullock is not getting food, but you don't care about that. Let's go tomorrow with two or three people to cut that land." He never mentioned it as my *hetaa* field.

I was silent again. His bullock was starving all right; he treated it as others treat dogs. Since he never fed the bullock at home, it foraged outside. It was weak and small, fell asleep at the yoke, could not keep up with my bullock, was always desperate for food, and wouldn't work.

Since my *hetaa* crop was good this year, this greedy Brahman neglected our agreement so that he could get the crop for himself. I thought I ought to call this matter to the attention of at least five people who could mediate the dispute. I figured that when I was alone with Jadu, I ought to say yes to everything he said. So I said, "Okay," and went to the river to bathe. Jadu left.

Two days later, Jadu's young son Prafula dragged a fifteen-foot bamboo pole to my house just as I was starting to your [author's] house. I told the boy, "You got the bamboo; it is good. But I can't do the work right now." I put the pole inside my house and went to your house for work. Prafula went with me. We are friends, even though I am on bad terms with Jadu. I gave a village cigarette to Prafula, who took it gladly and lit it.

I returned home about 5:00 P.M. and took the pole to Lime-Paste Field, near my house. Just as I was finishing, Jadu arrived. I ignored him as I rolled the stalks with the pole; he silently cut grass for feeding the bullock.

Suddenly he spoke aloud to himself. "This bullock is not getting food. Who cares for the bullock? People in my house are not getting food. The only things that get done are what I will do myself. Nobody else helps me or works for me. Up to now the threshing floor is not yet ready. That man put building stones on my threshing floor, but now he took them away. A young boy and a young woman, my wife, live in my house. If they both try, they can prepare the threshing floor. They can do the work for nothing, except for eating baskets of food at a meal. I told that first child of mine to cut the paddy himself, using a couple of other people, but he did not listen. I told that man who is supposed to be working for me to cut the paddy. He's not listening either. What a bad life I am maintaining. I should die quickly."

Then he turned to me and called, "Oh, Muli, do you know what happened at my house yesterday?"

"What?"

"I went to another village. When I returned, I found my trunk open and ten rupees gone. I asked my wife and daughter, but they said they didn't know. My five-year-old son said he saw his eldest brother take it. I waited until that wife's brother came back that evening. When I threatened to beat him, he admitted that he took the ten rupees and spent it all at the bazaar. You should see how much trouble I have, Muli. Tomorrow is the *sankraanti* day [holy day at the start of each lunar month]. I'll be performing fire ceremonies for my pilgrims. You should take two or three people with you and cut the Bamboo-Dam Land in my absence."

I heard all this but acted as if I had not heard. Jadu repeated his order. But I figured that the argument should go to the village and be public. So I simply said, "I've finished my work; I'm going." I took a couple of handfuls of paddy for making *menta* [a decoration] and walked home.

That evening Jadu came to my house.

"Give me some straw," he said. "My bullock needs it tonight."

I replied, "Where would I get any? We haven't started harvesting yet."

He said, "Your wife might have brought some. Give me at least two bundles."

I gave him two bundles and walked with him. On the way he said, "Are you ready to cut the paddy tomorrow?"

I said, "Yes, but let's go quickly; I've got to send news to a friend waiting at Dhadia's tea shop. Won't you go to the bazaar today?" I said this to delay talking about the field until we reached witnesses.

Jadu said, "Yes, I'll go to the bazaar later, after defecating."

Still delaying, I said, "I need some medicine for dysentery; I've been defecating four or five times a day. I thought that if I go with you I might get better medicine."

We reached Dhadia's shop; I suddenly said, "I don't want to wait; I want to go to the bazaar now. If you have anything to tell me about the paddy, tell me now. I may not see you later this night."

Jadu said, "How many people did you select to cut the paddy?"

I said, "Why should I hire and give wages to outsiders instead of keeping the wages inside my house? We've got lots of people in my family."

He said, "There's no difference. Whoever goes is paid a wage. Your family can go elsewhere to cut paddy."

"Why should I give my prepared paddy to others? And then beg others to eat [beg to be allowed to harvest another person's crop]?"

Jadu said, "What do you mean by 'your own prepared' paddy?"

I said, "It is not only my prepared paddy; it is my prepared rice in my pot. I've done everything for that crop except harvest it and eat it. I took that land as *hetaa*. Isn't it my own cooked rice? What does it matter to you what I do with that land?"

"What! Isn't it mine? You ask me, 'what's it to you' [a great insult]? You don't know what it is to me?"

"Yes, I ask you again. What's it to you? You told me three times to cut my paddy. And you mentioned you had no rice for yourself or straw for your bullocks. Why are you so greedy for my *hetaa* land?"

Jadu said, "Why should we talk on the road? Let's sit. Then I'll make you understand."

He went up the steps of the tea stall and sat down. I sat below on the road. Inside the tea stall sat six men of the Mallia temple servant caste—wealthy high-caste landowners of our village—and a Brahman priest. Outside near me sat three men of my caste who worked as farm servants.

Jadu said, "Oh, Muli, you agreed to take 2 rupees' wage for the days you work, 20 *gouṇii* of paddy at the end of harvest time, and 300 bundles of straw. How can you now say that you'll take *hetaa*?"

I replied, "You told your side of the story; now let me tell mine. I refused your offer. I told you I'd take 3 rupees' daily wage or *hetaa*. Then you gave me the land of Bamboo-Dam, which your previous farm servants had taken as *hetaa*. I agreed and continued to work for you for a wage of 2 rupees."

Jadu replied, "Paddy costs 1.5 rupees per *gouṇii*. If I gave you *hetaa*, why should I pay you 2 rupees per day instead of 1.5—60 rupees a month instead of 50?"

I shouted, "Does everybody give 2 rupees to their farm servants, or are you the only one? Ask other cultivators how much they pay their farm servants. Let's ask them! Ask them!" I stood up and pointed to the men in and around the tea stall.

Jadu said, "Muli, you *bhaaṇda saḷaa* [uncivilized wife's brother]! Why don't you listen to what I say? You say whatever pleases you, according to what you want to believe. Do you think I'll do what you tell, or what we both decided on?"

I replied, "Am I the uncivilized wife's brother or you? Come, tell the public! See how this man treats his farm servant. While we are talking, this Brahman calls me an uncivilized wife's brother. If I call him 'wife's brother,' whose prestige will be lost? Some landowners and some farm servants sit at this tea stall. Let them choose who the real uncivilized man is!"

I said to the Bauri men sitting on the road, "You all work as farm servants. What is your daily wage, 1.5 rupees or 2?"

One of the men said, "We get one *gouṇii* of paddy, and if that's not available, we get 2 rupees. But the money is not good for us [worth as much], because the paddy we boil into rice gives us more than 2 rupees' worth. The wage of 2 rupees is not profitable for us."*

---

*Historically, farm servants received a wage of one *gouṇii* of paddy a day. Since paddy is often unavailable these days, they receive cash instead. But they prefer payments in paddy, which they get cheaply; if they buy rice at the market they must pay more for it. That is why cash wages are 2 rupees, not 1.5, as Jadu claimed.

Pointing at Jadu to insult him, I said, "Tell that fellow. He gave me 2 rupees' wages. That's why he refuses to give me *hetaa*."

Then a thin, dark, sixty-year-old high-caste landowner named Jujia said, "Oh, Muli, why are you shouting? What's happening?" Because of his simple and straightforward character, the villagers respect Jujia's judgments.

I said, "All you *saa-aanta*(s) [respected masters] are sitting here. Some of the men of my caste and my street are sitting outside. You should judge my complaint."

Jadu said, "What will they judge?"

I said, "Why are you barking like this? You have no power to judge, no conscience. You don't know that others are here. Wait until I've finished. Then you can speak. Some of these masters employ or used to employ farm servants. They should hear this matter and judge. Oh, all my respected masters, you see, this fellow feels easier after the air passes through his anus. After he feels better, he forgets what his stomach felt like." When I talked to Jadu, I addressed him as an equal; when I talked to the gentlemen, I used the respectful form of address. I could see that Jadu was furious at this insult.

Old Jujia interrupted. "Why are you talking about other things [beating around the bush]? Get to the point."

I replied, "What can I say, my respected master? When this man's work stopped because another man quit working for him, this man requested me to work for him. At first I refused because he wouldn't give me *hetaa*. Finally he offered Bamboo-Dam Field as *hetaa* land. Under this condition I worked for him. Now that I've finished his work, he doesn't want to give me the *hetaa*."

A forty-year-old landowner named Pahali, short, heavy, and light-skinned, with a friendly face, said, "Nobody will give nor take anything from either of you. We'll listen. Don't quarrel on the road. Settle amicably."

I said, "What will I do? He offered me the *hetaa*. Now he won't give it. When he first promised me the *hetaa*, I worked for him, and I threw my efforts to luck. I didn't know how much the *hetaa* land would produce; it had been plowed late because of his quarrel with his previous farm servant.

"But I worked on that land anyway. I plowed it; I seeded it, paying for the seeds; I transplanted it; I weeded it; I collected sparrow excrement and threw it over the land—while Jadu neglected that field completely. He didn't spend a single pie on it [singular of paise], and even refused to let me plant lentils on it because he considered it my *hetaa* land—until the crop was good. Then he told me to cut it for him. How is this possible? That land belongs to Sankar now. He quarreled with Jadu at the time of transplanting. If I cut the crop and give it to Jadu, then Sankar will get his owner's share, Jadu will get his sharecropper's share, and I'll get nothing. Why did I work on that land as farm servant land? Now Jadu tells me he'll give me 20 *gouṇii* of paddy and that he never gave me *hetaa* land. What he says is false. Well, my respected masters, you should find out the truth from these facts."

The gentlemen asked Jadu for his side of the story. He said "I've already told you: Muli requested *hetaa* land, but I told him I'd give him 20 *gouṇii* of paddy and 300 bundles of straw, plus wages."

The gentlemen laughed, and one said, "How come Jadu says 300 straw bundles? Muli never said this. There is a difference of opinion."

Jadu replied, "It was our condition. He wanted to take *hetaa*. Who would give *hetaa* to him?"

Pahali said, "What do you say, Muli, another 300 bundles of straw are coming to you." The men laughed.

I replied, "What can I say? What you decide, I'll obey. I'm waiting for your decision."

Jadu shouted, "What decision will they give? I offered you 20 *gouṇii* of paddy and some straw. I'll give that to you. What decision will they give? A lime [sour] decision."

I said, "Why are you interfering? If the five men tell me to take the twenty *gouṇii* of paddy, I'll do so. Why are you not waiting for their decision? They asked me, and I replied. What's it to you?"

Jadu replied angrily, "Do you think I don't know what our agreement was? Am I a child? Do you think you'll change my mind? Do you think what you are telling is true? Can you touch my body and claim that what you say is true?"

I replied, "Why should I touch your body? You are a Brahman, the king of all the thirty-six castes. You are just like the deity Mahadeb, God. I am a small-caste man, far from God. If anyone touches the body of God he will sin, and God may curse him. I'll not touch your body. Why should I? Why aren't you telling the truth?"

Then Jadu spoke loudly, "I am taking an oath. If I speak falsely, no one in my line of descent will live to pour water for his ancestors!"

Rama, a tall, black, softspoken landowner with a long face, wide smile, and fluid gestures, said, "Oh, Muli, why are you complaining more? Why would God be displeased if you touched the Brahman telling an oath of truth? The Brahman has taken an oath on the lives of all his children, so we don't disbelieve him."

I replied, "Why do you believe this fire-eating man? Most people would fear to consume the property of Shiva and of Brahmans—a great sin—but he'd do it without a thought. He'd promise anything. I know many Cultivators who borrowed from him, paid their interest once, and then were compelled to pay again because they had no written receipt and he charged them again. Immediately after doing this he took oaths that he hadn't received any interest from these people. What do you know about him? He cheats people. His children break open locks inside his own house and take money and property because he earned this property unfairly. That's why he promises. He tells me to promise. I am not a man of his type. I used to show him respect, like a deity, because he's a Brahman. But I found that if I would touch his body, my hand got a bad smell because his body stinks like a mole in the ground!"

Jadu screamed, "This wife's-brother Bauri boy speaks like a king. Has your face gone up, as if proud, or what?"

I replied, "Yes, by your efforts."

Jadu replied, "Oh, wife's brother, by my efforts?"

I said, "Yes, because you behaved badly to me. In return you receive similar behavior from me. We worked together throughout the year. I never behaved like you, so why do I today? The causes of my bad behavior are your gift. Throughout your life you have been unable to be a good master." To call him incapable of being a good master was a great insult.

Jadu replied, "Oh, I'll learn everything that's good and bad from you. You are not a good man. I'll *see* you [I'll get my revenge]!"

I said, "Everybody in our village and on my street knows that Muli, Hata's eldest son, is very bad, and a liar, a cheater, and a tout [deliberate trouble-maker]; and that he takes many people's properties by lying and by creating litigation. So how can people judge Muli to be a good man? He is a very bad man."

Jadu replied, "Oh, wife's brother, why are you speaking indirectly like this? You are speaking just like a gentlemen, as if there were no fault with you."

I said, "Why should I speak indirectly? Actually, I am a man like that. Everybody in the village, from the lower castes to higher castes, calls me a liar. Confectioners, Bauris, Sweepers, Cultivators, Oilpressers, Brahmans—all call me a liar. And they call you a truthful man because you take the oath. I am not a gentleman; you are, because everybody calls you for compromising disputes. When you go to disputes, you increase them, just like showing and removing the plantain to cocks or bulbul birds to make them fight."

Facing old Jujia, I continued, "See, my Grandfather, this man told me to touch his body. How can I touch a Brahman's body? I know that it is bad. I am not a betrayer like this bad Brahman fellow. He is always in litigations and quarrels. Why did he tell me to touch his body without asking me to take other kinds of oaths? All of you respected gentlemen should listen to me. From my childhood I have never taken an oath, but now, because of this man, I am taking an oath on the life of my only child. If I am lying, my son should not survive until next year, and let the paddy I earn be as useless as the hair on my head! Who cares for it? Let that man take the paddy now and become richer and richer from it. He may get richer from me, but he is below me [morally]. He hired me for a year. He cheated me. Let it be.

"I am a laborer. Labor will be available for me elsewhere. But no laborer will be available for this man! What man has worked for him whom he hasn't cheated? Who will work for him? If any of you respected masters hire a farm servant and look after him properly, your farm servant will not quit his service unless you drive him out. Who has to appoint three farm servants in a year like this fellow? Ask this man, Jadu, has there ever been a farm servant who left his service happily? This wife's-brother Brahman today forced me to take an oath. Okay, I leave you everything. I don't want that *hetaa*, or even that twenty *gouṇii* of paddy. And he should never call me for any work. He should cut the paddy himself."

Old Jujia replied, "What Muli says might be true. He is a good boy."

Then Bhoia, a small-caste man like me, spoke. He is a short, talkative sixty-year-old, with a round face and thick, wavy hair. "Oh, Muli, you should be silent for a moment. You have talked too much. And the oath language you have used—wait. Our village masters will decide it. Why are you talking like this, using oath language? Oh, respected masters, this quarrel is over a piece of *hetaa* land. Muli wants it. Jadu refuses to give it. You have heard everything. You should give a decision that will please everyone. Since both have taken oaths, we cannot believe or disbelieve them."

I said, "You are all my respected masters. Whatever you decide, I'll accept and obey." I felt bad, very afraid and exhausted after taking the oath, and I wanted to get home immediately. I turned and left the tea stall.

Gunia Dash, a balding, light-skinned, forty-year-old Brahman, called me back. I replied that I didn't want to come back. Rama said, "Come, we'll decide your case. You wanted to take *hetaa*. We'll give it to you. Come back."

I returned. Pahali and Gunia told Rama and Jujia, "You are old men; you should decide this case so that this poor Muli should not be dissatisfied. In our opinion he should get his *hetaa* because no one gives paddy or straw instead of *hetaa*."

Gunia and Pahali stepped to one side of the tea stall. Rama said to Jujia, "You are the oldest of us. You should give the decision."

Jujia said, "Why should I? You give it." He was reluctant to make a judgment because it might not be followed.

Rama said, "There is no question about this decision. Everyone appoints a farm servant by giving him *hetaa*." Turning to Jadu, Rama spoke respectfully, "Oh, Babu, you can satisfy the Bauri, but the Bauri cannot satisfy you. You are offering twenty *gouṇii* of paddy; he wants the crops of that land. What good will paddy do you if your children die? And what good will paddy do Muli if his child dies? Nobody will die because of these oaths. You should give that land with the crop to Muli. It is his right to claim *hetaa*. If you hadn't decided to do it before, do it now. You are a man whom many people ask to compromise their disputes. Will you lose your own prestige by asking others to compromise your disputes? I give this decision as a mediator. You may accept it or reject it as you like. But you should give *hetaa* to him."

Jadu said, "How can I disobey a decision of five people? I offered twenty *gouṇii* of paddy. By taking the crop instead he'll get ten to fifteen *gouṇii* of paddy. When you give that decision, how can I disobey? Let it be. He should take the *hetaa*. I'm giving him the crop to make you five people happy."

Jujia said, "You should not think that way. Because your farm servant helped you all year, you got your entire crop. Usually the farm servant works for his master as he would work for himself. Sometimes working time is over but the work is not over; the farm servant keeps on working overtime and completes it. No outsider would do this. The farm servant works for you in many ways, and he receives a smaller daily wage than an outsider. You should happily give him what you owe him."

Jadu replied, "I agree with your decision, but that land doesn't belong to me. When Muli cuts that land he must call the *rajaa* [landowner], and he should give half the crop to him. I'll pay him back the half-share that the owner takes."

I replied, "Why should we have further quarrels? This man refused to give me *hetaa*. If you who are listening have decided that I'll take the crops of that land, then why should I give a half-share to the owner and ask for that half-share from this cheat here who is totally unwilling to give me the crop? Why should I give the fish in my hand to the bird and then run after that bird? I don't think such a decision is good for me. If a man takes an oath on his children over a trivial matter, do you think he will give me the owner's share of the paddy because of promises he makes? I beg of you. Tomorrow let me take all the crop and let the sharecropper pay the owner the share owed for that field. If I delay cutting, the paddy, which is already too dry, will wither. It should have been cut over a month ago."

Jadu said, "How can I give the owner paddy in substitution for that which you will take? I have collected none yet."

I said, "I don't know about that. You inform the owner. I'll cut the paddy tomorrow, you will count the bundles, and you can keep it where you like. When you are able to pay the share due the owner, we'll separate the paddy and the straw. You should tell me where I'll keep that paddy after it's cut."

He said, "At the threshing floor of Daitari the Confectioner."

I said, "Okay, tell your owner. Tomorrow, I'll cut the paddy while you and he watch."

He said, "No, I can't be there; my middle son will go instead."

I said, "That's okay."

I left the tea stall. A few minutes later I passed by it on the way home. Jadu was still sitting there, but the gentlemen had left. I stopped outside for a while; Jadu did not acknowledge my presence. After a while I walked to a food shop on my street owned by Marua, a friendly, talkative high-caste man. He put the shop on our street to get our business: we are allowed to enter that shop. Marua and several men from my street were discussing the quarrel.

When Marua saw me, he said, "Oh! Here's Muli!"

Chinta, a toothless, thin, seventy-one-year-old Brahman with a long nose and a shock of white hair, asked, "Well, what happened with Jadu?"

I described what had happened. It was the first time in the history of the village that an untouchable had dared to talk back to a Brahman. But Chinta was not angry with me. Although related to Jadu, he backed me. He said, "Why didn't you beat him? The day will come when you will beat him."

Marua said, "When the Bauris beat your cousin, you'll hold him for them?" The men laughed.

Chinta said, "Why, Muli, did you work for *that* man? You come from the same village. Didn't you know about his character, his reputation? At first I didn't realize, either, what sort of person he is."

I asked, "What happened to you?"

Marua said, "Jadu cheated Chinta in such a way that Chinta was without food."

I got my change and left. I didn't want to hear more.

I told my wife what had happened. The next morning, we went to my *hetaa* field with my mother, son, youngest brother, and his wife. We cut the entire crop. We were halfway through cutting the straw from the paddy when Jadu's middle son came out to the field.

I asked him, "Have you come here as the master? Where is your father?"

He said, "Father went somewhere else to do fire ceremonies."

I then asked, "What about your landowner?"

He said, "I don't know anything about that."

"What else did your father say?"

The boy replied, "Father said you should take the bundles to the threshing floor of Daitari the confectioner."

We continued cutting the stalks in half. A few minutes later I said to my son, "You, your aunt, and your grandmother should take some paddy bundles back. Eat something. Return, and take a couple of bundles more. Then we can finish our work faster."

We tied seven bundles together; my brother's wife carried four on her head; my son took three. Just before they left I whispered to them, "Take the bundles not to Daitari's house, but to ours." They left.

My wife and I continued cutting as Jadu's son watched. After a few minutes, he called to me, "Oh, Muli, see, see. Why are those two taking their bundles of paddy off their heads?"

I stood up and looked toward the village. In the distance I saw Sankar the Oilpresser-caste man talking to my sister-in-law and my son. My son stood with the bundles on his head, but my sister-in-law had dropped hers. Sankar was waving his arms wildly.

When I saw this, I shouted, "Oh, Sankar *daadi*, Sankar *daadi* [Uncle Sankar, Uncle Sankar], don't block their way! Don't make them drop the paddy! I'm coming!"

I ran, stumbling, over the dry fields to them. I asked, "Oh, Uncle Sankar, why did you force them to drop the paddy?"

Sankar said, "You don't know anything. I have several reasons."

I replied, "What?"

Sankar said, "Are you a thief or a gentleman?"

I said, "Why are you asking such a question?"

He replied, "Just now I'll call you a thief. I'm the owner of the land. Without asking me, why are you cutting my paddy?"

I replied, "I took this land as *hetaa* from Jadu because I am his farm servant."

Sankar said, "No, you are not his farm servant, and Jadu did not order you to cut the paddy. I just met him and asked him why someone was cutting the paddy. He replied, "I don't know who is cutting it.' I said to him, 'Muli, your farm servant, is cutting it.' He said, 'He wanted to take that land as *hetaa*. Last night I refused to let him take the crop. I don't know what has happened.' So, Bauri boy, how can you say it's your *hetaa*?"

I was dumbfounded. I asked, "Where did you meet him?"

He said, "Over by the river road cutting paddy."

I asked, "How is this possible? His son came to me and told me his father was busy doing fire ceremonies. Let's go to Jadu to prove whether he told me to cut the paddy or not. Several Mallias, a Brahman, and three Bauris heard him say I could cut the paddy today as my *hetaa*, and that he would pay you your share from his own pocket. Let's go to the village. Why are you making trouble? I can give you proof."

Sankar shouted, "I don't want their proof. I want to take them all with their paddy and straw to the police station! There I will get everything proved! Why should I, the owner, go here and there? Don't try to teach me! First come with me to the police station!"

I sat on the ground, put my head in my hands, and remained silent without moving for ten or fifteen minutes. Sankar stood there. Finally he said, "Why are you not answering? Come with me to the police!"

I stood and said, "Yes, let's go to the police. I am not a thief. If I am proven to be a thief, then I'll go to jail. I don't care. If I'm shown not to be a thief, then I'll get my crop. I don't care."

A temple priest named Artha stopped to hear the dispute. He said, "Look, Muli, if you go to the police, neither you nor Sankar will gain. It will cost both of you money. The police wait for quarrels like this to occur so they can make a profit out of them. So, do this. Take the paddy to Sankar's threshing floor. He is the claimant of 50 percent of the crop; but the sharecropper owns the other 50 percent. You cannot get the full crop because your master doesn't own the land. We live in one village; we always look into each other's faces. It is not a nice thing to quarrel. You are a poor man. If the quarrel goes to litigation, you won't get anything: Sankar and Jadu will each get half. So take the crop to Sankar's house. He'll give you 50 percent, and you can try to get the rest from Jadu. Don't take the crop to Daitari's house: Sankar and Daitari have been fighting a court case for the past five years. Sankar will surely take you to the police if you put the crop in Daitari's house."

What could I do? The police won't help a poor man, a small-caste man like me. I don't have money for bribes. I feared that I would be dragged into court. So I accepted Artha's suggestion. I carried the paddy to Sankar's threshing floor. Sankar went back with me to the field to see how much we had taken.

Sankar, a boastful, proud man, said, "Muli, you see, I suppressed my anger about what you did because I like you. My mother and grandmother used to feed me from what they earned from the people of your ward. You grandfather helped my mother and grandmother, stopping children from snatching puffed rice and cakes from the women as they sold them on your street. From that time your family and mine were like friends. When your grandfather died our ties broke. Even though I am now very high up, I recall my past. So I don't want to treat you badly, or take you to the police. But if, without you, that Jadu fellow had cut the paddy, I would have beaten him to death! That was my intention when I heard that someone was cutting the crop of my field. When I started out from my house today, I gathered together all my friends to beat the culprit. A man who cuts another's crop commits a serious offense; I'd be justified in beating the crop cutter from the field all the way to the village. I kept 1,000 rupees on the veranda of my tiled roof to be spent today for the litigation which would occur after I had killed the Brahman. But since you were cutting the paddy, I'll settle without killing you."

I remained silent. Then Sankar said, "Jadu is fortunate. He sent his child to the field. Otherwise I would have killed him."

Sankar told me to finish cutting the paddy. He left to oversee the harvesting of another crop.

My wife, said, "Much trouble has arisen. Bind the bundle for our wage. Why should we lose our wage? I'm cutting the other bundles; you cut ours, making it tighter and longer for ourselves." I did this.

Sankar returned to the field, and soon after, Jadu's son Indra also came. Indra said, "Oh, Muli, can you afford it if my father takes action against you?"

I said, "What great thing might happen that I can't afford?"

He said angrily, "If you can tolerate it, good. We'll see how you can tolerate a 379 case—theft from the fields."

"If I can't, what will happen will happen." I spoke bravely, but my heart sank. If I didn't do what Sankar wanted, he'd call the police; if I did what Sankar wanted, Jadu would call the police. What trouble I had!

Sankar interrupted. "What are you saying, Indra? Are you threatening Muli or me?"

Indra snapped, "Why should I talk to you? We've got no work with you." Then he left. Sankar and Jadu had quarreled several months before and were not on speaking terms.

My son and my brother's wife carried the paddy to Sankar's threshing floor. When Sankar saw that we kept three bundles as wages for three people, he asked, "What's this?"

I replied, "It's our wages. Since I worked like a sharecropper who takes shares, I'll take no wage here. But these other people worked as day laborers for a wage. Four people worked from my house: We'll take three bundles."

Sankar said, "I'm not your employer, Jadu is. He will give you your wages. Put the *mukula* [wage bundle] at the threshing floor with the other paddy. Then ask Jadu to pay you according to our custom."

I carried thirty bundles to Sankar's house. At his threshing floor, Sankar paid workers from other fields. An old woman tied up her wage bundle large and tight. Sankar took some back, as is his right. The old woman cried, "Why are you taking it away? We did not bind too much." Workers always quarrel about their wage, and demand more, even if the owner gives them a great amount.

Sankar smiled, and compromised. "Okay, let it be. Take it all, but give back one stalk." The old woman, grinning, gave him one stalk, then carried her bundle home, staggering under the weight.

I stood silently. There was no wage bundle for me or my household.

I went to Jadu's house. He wasn't there. I asked his wife where he was. She said he had gone to perform fire ceremonies, she didn't know where.

I said, "Jadu told me to take the crop of the *hetaa* field to Daitari's house, but Sankar forced me to take it to his place. What can I do? Jadu did not go to the field. He sent his son. Now Sankar won't give me my wage bundle; he tells me that my *nanaa* [brother] must pay it to me."

She said, "I don't know anything about that."

I started back to my house. On the way, I looked out over the fields that I had cultivated. At Lime-Paste Field near my house, Jadu's son Indra was directing several workers who were harvesting my crop. He had not called me to harvest the crop that I had grown! Jadu had hired me to work all year, in the hot sun, in the driving rain, and even in the night; but when the crops ripened the wages went to outsiders.

I passed by the tea stall where last night the gentlemen had mediated my quarrel. Diga, Jadu's old farm servant sat there, along with Dhadia, the tea stall owner. Diga called out, "What the men decided for you last night is already gone. Jadu has filed a case against you on rule 379 stating that you are not his farm servant, but just a thief. Go and get your good farm servant's wage!"

They laughed bitterly.

I went home and sat down on the front veranda of my house.

Cheated out of wages and rice, I faced jail, while my family faced starvation. I sat silently with my head in my hands, waiting for the police to come.

Muli's conflict with Jadu the Brahman miser occurred while he was narrating his life history to me. Despite the warnings of his wife, my assistant Hari, and myself, Muli insisted on working for Jadu. Invariably optimistic, Muli believed until the final quarrel that he would ultimately receive his share of the crop.

Most puzzling and disconcerting was Muli's refusal to testify to the truth of his claims while touching Jadu. By contrast, Jadu offered to take an oath while touching Muli. The villagers consider a touching-oath to be so powerful that if a person is not truthful he will suffer a terrible fate.

Muli's claim for remuneration was persuasive: all he asked was the standard payment given farm servants. Had he taken the oath, no one would have questioned his right to a share of the crop. His unbelievable refusal damaged his credibility in the eyes of the village elders, Hari, and myself. Since Jadu was a well-known cheater, the elders judged in favor of Muli; but significantly, they made no effort to enforce their decision, indicating that they also doubted Muli's story. They probably could not understand why anyone would agree to work for a man of Jadu's reputation, unless it was to take advantage of a shady deal.

Hari and I questioned Muli at length about his refusal to take the oath. "What did you have to hide?" asked Hari. "No one would have doubted you, but now no one believes you."

Muli insisted that he had told the truth, but that he feared touching the Brahman because it was such a great sin. In many incidents of his life history, Muli described himself as being forced to divulge information to or help Brahmans and other high-caste men who touched him while reciting an oath. Yet Muli never hesitated to eat meals with Brahmans or supply them with Bauri women. Only with oath-taking did he suddenly become fearful. Whether or not he feared the sin of touching more than the sin of lying, his refusal to take the oath sealed his downfall.

Part Five

Interpretations

30. Analysis of Muli's Life History

Although anthropologists have collected biographical data and life histories since the beginnings of the discipline, and have frequently used life history materials in their work, few have developed perspectives for the systematic use and analysis of life histories in their entirety.* Of such perspectives currently available, the most comprehensive is that of David Mandelbaum (1973:177-196). Mandelbaum distinguishes life passage or life cycle studies—which focus on how people socialize their young to make them viable members of society—from life history studies, which "emphasize the experiences and requirements of the individual—how the person copes with society rather than how society copes with the stream of individuals" (1973:177).

Mandelbaum uses three principles for organizing life histories: the *dimensions* of a life history—the biological, cultural, social, and psychosocial aspects of a person's life; the *turnings*—the major transitions that a person makes during the principal periods of his lifetime; *adaptations*—the personal changes that an individual makes that contribute to his survival. "The dimensions provide categories for understanding the main forces that affect a life. The turnings mark major changes that a person makes and thus demarcate periods of his life. A focus on adaptation directs our notice both to changes he makes and to continuities he maintains through his life course" (1973:180).

The Dimensions

Biological dimensions. According to Mandelbaum, "A dimension of a life history is made up of experiences that stem from a similar base and are linked in their effects on the person's subsequent actions." The biological dimension "is based on the person's organic makeup and somatic development" (1973:180).

*Dollard (1935) emphasizes the use of the concept of culture in analyzing life histories. Kluckhohn (1945) provides a comprehensive review of life history studies in anthropology up to 1945 and a brilliant analysis of their defects, as well as problems involved in collecting life histories. Langness (1965) reviews develop-

The information available on Muli's biological dimensions, although scant, is crucial for understanding his life history. Muli showed low resistance to disease and lack of stamina, both probably due to malnutrition. He feared pain and injury and in fact frequently injured himself. Accordingly, he avoided heavy physical work, preferring the life of a pimp to that of a stone quarry worker, preferring to narrate his life history rather than work in the paddy fields. Conversely, Muli's lack of enthusiasm for hard physical labor undoubtedly affected his physical development; while others worked, he sat, or wandered idly through the bazaar. Muli's father continually criticized him for being weak and clumsy; Muli often responded by accentuating the very behaviors his father wanted him to eliminate. Working in the stone quarries at various times, Muli broke pickaxes, split and ruined stone blocks, crushed his fingers carrying stones, and spiked his foot with the pickaxe.

Muli considered his skin dark and ugly, his body thin and unattractive. He recounted happier days in his youth, when he was better fed and therefore, by his definition, better looking. He complained that his body was "decreasing" as he was becoming older. At the age of 40, he idealized his youth; he never spoke of old age, or of his becoming older.

Muli often contrasted his own physical appearance and condition with that of others close to him: his grandfather, tall, stout, and immensely strong; his father, a smaller man, but also strong and hardworking; his wife, energetic, full of stamina, able to withstand pain, and physically stronger than himself; and his mother, weaker than her daughters-in-law. Muli's dominant recollection of his mother during the time of his childhood and youth was that she was frequently pregnant. She rarely worked outside the house; instead, she stayed at home bearing children and taking care of them.

Cultural dimensions. The cultural dimension of a life history, according to Mandelbaum, refers to "the mutual expectations, under-

---

ments in the study of life histories up to 1965 and outlines their uses, particularly in studies of psychological anthropology and social change. Mandelbaum (1973) reviews the study of life histories and attempts to formulate a perspective for their analysis. For the interpretation of Muli's life history, I have used Mandelbaum's perspective rather than Erikson's better-known one (see, for example, Erikson 1968, 1969) because I consider Mandelbaum's perspective to be both wider and more flexible than Erikson's.

standings, and behavior patterns held by the people among whom a person grows up and in whose society he becomes a participant" (1973:180). Cultural expectations provide a broad design, within which alternative paths exist for various persons (1973:193).

Muli's story portrays great divisions and tensions between his caste's ideals and expectations, and his own behavior. Much of the power of Muli's story results from his disregard of caste expectations. His family and friends expected him to follow caste rules, avoiding not only untouchables lower than himself, but also higher-caste people, except when working for them, borrowing money from them, or consulting them as teachers. The Bauris feared, not that they would pollute high-caste people, but rather that high-caste people would cheat and hurt them. Although more flexible than many of the higher castes, the Bauris nevertheless punished certain transgressors of caste rules, particularly women who were discovered to have lovers from other castes, whether higher or lower.

Muli frequently broke caste regulations. To convince a Goldsmith to hire him as a sharecropper, he took tea at the Goldsmith's house. He constantly tried to befriend high-caste men, even though his activities often led to disaster. He supplied women to high caste-men. He reported with relish how his Brahman friend, Dash Babu, ill with venereal disease, begged him to disregard food-handling taboos in preparing food for him. Nevertheless, Muli feared breaking certain caste taboos: he refused to touch Jadu the Brahman miser to take an oath, announcing that he feared the sin of touching a Brahman. On another occasion, feeling guilty as well as afraid, he ran away from home after discovering that he had eaten fish during a funeral mourning period when fish was prohibited.

Muli's family expected him to marry around the age of twenty, contribute earnings to the household, rear a family—preferably in his parental home—and take care of his parents when they became elderly. Instead, Muli became a reluctant householder who showed little filial piety and little commitment to his wife and son; he preferred touring with transvestites, wandering in the bazaar, having a good time. His wife became the main wage earner of the household. Whenever possible, Muli avoided the occupations expected of men: plowing, stone quarrying, and road construction. Instead, he became a pimp. Sometimes he helped his wife with women's work, such as cutting grass. Often he did nothing. Although his wife, mother, father, and grandfather criticized his poor work performance, Muli never changed his work patterns.

While he performed or participated in the life cycle rituals expected of him, both Muli, as well as his parents and grandparents, frequently departed from ideal ritual procedures. Muli was married even though his and his bride's horoscopes failed to match. At the death of his infant son, Anadi refused to invite his brother Muli to eat the bitter food that ends the period of funeral mourning. Muli's family and other Bauris showed great flexibility in adapting rituals to changed circumstances. When the ward leader refused to perform his obligatory rituals for them, Muli's family hired the deputy leader to perform the rituals. To marry Muli's divorced sister, a previously unmarried groom first symbolically married and divorced a tree trunk, thus equalizing his marital status with that of Muli's sister.

Like many people of his caste, Muli believed in and feared ghosts, spirits of the dead, and magic, which he used to explain the illness and death of his paternal grandfather, as well as his own infatuation with Tafulla. He also believed in fate as an explanation of events. Tafulla's family had put a love spell on him, said Muli, but in addition, it was fated in the stars that he would suffer at that time in his life. Muli sometimes explained that bad fate caused natural disasters. Despite his belief in fate, Muli never mentioned rebirth or reincarnation. When I asked him if he believed in rebirth, he replied, "Who knows about such things?" He focused on the past as well as present crises but never once expressed hopes for a better life in a future existence.

Similarly, Muli's belief in the concept of ritual pollution applied only to limited situations. While he believed that a corpse polluted immediate relatives, he ridiculed the idea that Bauris pollute higher castes, and he even questioned whether higher-caste people themselves really believe it, since he saw them disregard such notions when they became inconvenient.

Social dimensions. By constrast with cultural plans, which emphasize expectations and a schematic outline of a life history, the social dimensions of a life history, according to Mandelbaum, deal with "those acts of personal choice that are characteristic of the person's group and the common ways of working out the recurrent conflicts of life" (1973:180). The social dimension focuses on "social acts, conflicts, solutions, and choices. It includes the emotional experiencing of reward and penalty and the outcome of action in maintaining or changing behavior patterns" (1973:180). Social dimensions pertain to a "person's relations, choices, and decisions that are not culturally stipulated, yet are characteristic of behavior in his society" (1973:193).

Although Muli described very little of his childhood, he documented in great detail his changing relationship with his parents and relatives. During his childhood and youth, his mother appeared as a warm, forgiving, nurturing figure: she nursed him back to health when he was ill or injured, fed him special foods, gave him advice, and interceded when his father was angry at him. But after Muli's marriage, his mother appeared as an irritable, scolding, quarrelsome woman who used up their joint savings and then threw Muli and his wife out of the house. Muli's wife and mother, competing for Muli's affection, quarreled constantly. Muli further provoked his mother's resentment by refusing to work every day and by creating scandals involving the women of the ward.

Muli's father appeared as an authoritarian critic who continually found fault with Muli's behavior, from his eating habits to his poor work performance. Muli's father persistently urged his son to learn the skills of stone quarrying and cultivation, but to no avail. Muli was a constant embarrassment and burden to his father, Hata, who in Muli's account neither understood nor sympathized with Muli's problems. When he found out that Muli was working as a pimp, Hata prohibited Muli from ever returning home. Had he not done so, the other Bauri families would have outcasted Hata's entire family. Even though Muli and his father quarreled for years, Hata, only a few months before his death in 1971, tried to help Muli become a farm servant who would earn a steady income. Despite everything Muli had done, Hata still tried to help his errant son.

In theory, Muli's father, as head of the household, made important decisions for the family such as accepting betrothals for his children. In practice, his wife often influenced decisions and usually expressed her opinions quite forcefully. "Village brides have snot in their noses" (people know their neighbors too well) was her response urging rejection of a marriage proposal that came from a family in another Bauri ward of Kapileswar. Although Hata beat and kicked his wife, he was unable to control her quarrelsome behavior and in fact often gave in to her demands.

Muli portrayed his wife Kia as a hardworking, sharp-tongued woman who supported the family while he entertained himself at the bazaar, or sat and dreamed up slightly dishonest or off-beat schemes that invariably backfired on him. She ridiculed his schemes and urged him to abandon them in favor of working for low but certain wages as an unskilled laborer. Despite their frequent quarreling, Muli admired Kia's stamina, strength, and perseverance. Muli's life history indicates that Kia frequently expressed disappointment with her spouse. During the first year of their marriage, when Muli neglected to bring her back to his household, Kia became possessed by a demonic spirit that claimed it had been abandoned. When Muli announced that he planned to support both Tafulla and Kia, she rebuked him bitterly, saying that he was so incompetent that in an entire day he would be unable to separate a piece of straw. She attempted suicide when he beat her after an argument over his disregard for his family's welfare.

Why, then, did Muli's wife remain with him while other Bauri women left their husbands? Because she had a child, she would have had difficulty remarrying. Furthermore, her father had died just before her marriage, and her uncle was not anxious to let her return to her parental home. Muli's sisters, by contrast, had a refuge to return to when their marriages soured. Muli described how he and his parents actively helped his sisters to break away from unwanted husbands and return to their parental home between marriages. Finally, despite Muli's ill treatment of her, Kia at times revealed genuine affection for him. Seeing his impoverished condition after he had lived with Tafulla, Kia wailed, recalling earlier, happier days when she had fed her "king" and given him spending money.

Muli had little to say about his only son, Gopala, except for describing the ceremonies at his birth, the incident of sending him to school for the first time, and his strained reunion with Muli during the affair with Tafulla. Yet Gopala was truly an exceptional son, the first Bauri child from Kapileswar not only to complete three years of school, but also to enter high school. Muli never mentioned this remarkable achievement. Significantly, Kia's attempted suicide occurred after she had argued with Muli over who would pay the school expenses. Muli announced that as usual he had spent all of his earnings on his own pleasures and that Kia should pay. Muli's life history hinted that Gopala was close to his mother and distant from a father who not only showed little interest in him, but in fact abandoned him and his mother during nearly two years of his childhood. Muli's status-climbing did not extend to helping his son.

Muli's relationships with his uncles, aunts, grandparents, sisters, and two brothers-in-law were friendly and warm. He enjoyed visiting his maternal grandfather and maternal uncles, whom he described as hospitable and generous. When Muli broke a youth's knee during a rough game, causing a riot in his maternal grandfather's village, his grandfather, uncles, and their wives consoled him and told him to forget about it. Later in his life, these relatives lent Muli rice when he was without food. Muli often visited and consulted with his brothers-in-law Bisia and Damodar, whom he portrayed as responsible, supportive, and hardworking householders. Muli said little about his sisters except for their life-cycle rituals and times of crisis; but he described a number of incidents not included in this book in which he helped his sisters, who confided in him.

The person whom Muli admired most was Dharma, his paternal grandfather, who differed from him in character, behavior, and appearance. Muli's grandfather was the largest and strongest man of his caste, a good earner, an excellent drama performer and singer, and an outstanding and respected leader of his ward—a man with a gift for words and the ability to settle disputes. Muli's only likeness to his grandfather was his ability to speak well, and indeed, he said he had learned from his grandfather how to be clever with words. Grandfather Dharma, who dominated the first half of Muli's life, liked Muli and was tolerant of his indiscretions. Realizing this, Muli used his grandfather's authority to quash criticism of his own disreputable activities. Despite his admiration for his grandfather, Muli never forgave him for insisting that he marry a woman whose horoscope did not match his, thereby dooming the marriage.

Muli's relationships with high-caste persons were varied. Despite his quarrel with Jadu the miser, Muli portrayed Jadu's wife sympathetically. Although she followed caste rules of avoidance with lower-caste persons employed by her husband, she appeared as a generous mistress in a paternalistic employment situation; she wanted to feed the workers well and give them presents of cloth, and she bewailed the fate that had brought her in marriage to a miser's house. Similarly, Muli was friendly with Jadu's youngest son, who often followed Muli as he worked. Muli said he felt no anger or animosity toward the son of his oppressor. "It's not the child's fault that his father cheats everybody. Anyway, I like him; he's a good boy."

Muli's behavior toward high-caste employers depended on the way they treated him. He hoped to become a farm servant or a sharecropper, positions not only of job security, but of status compared to that of unskilled farm laborers. A landowning master ideally gave his farm servant or sharecropper meals and gifts from time to time in addition to the regular wages and crop shares. Muli indicated that he would have been happy to have been a servant to a generous master. Invariably, however, his expectations were not fulfilled; masters were not as generous as he imagined they should be; they in turn found fault with his work; the relationship soured; they dismissed him; and sometimes, said Muli, they cheated him. Only when Muli believed that a master had treated him with excessive unfairness did Muli attempt to fight for just compensation.

Muli admired and wanted to emulate the high-caste life style that included easy jobs, ample food, wealth, luxury items, and prestige. To associate with high-caste men, including his drama teacher, he supplied them with prostitutes and hoped, vainly, that they would therefore accept him as a friend. Many high-caste men humored Muli, taking meals with him and his prostitutes, making flowery speeches about friendship, and flattering him by telling him what a clever boy he was, but they always ending by saying that their friendship must remain a secret, never publicly announced or known. Muli, resentful of their double standard, at various times described these men as respected gentlemen, as friends, and as customers to be squeezed for money.

Muli said little about the men and boys of his drama troupe—his neighbors, with whom he had lived all his life. He also said virtually nothing about Bauri women outside his family except for those who became his prostitutes. His portrayals of them varied from sympathetic to resentful to unflattering, sometimes of the same woman. Thus he described genuine attachment and tenderness in the relationship of Koki with Dash Babu, but he also described his own angry refusal to sleep with Koki after Teacher had finished with her. After Dash Babu had slept with Koki, Muli referred to her as "used goods."

Muli gave a similarly varied account of his relationship with transvestites, whose effeminate life styles and speech patterns amused and intrigued him. At first, he described his transvestite acquaintances as friends, with whom he wandered around the market, embarrassing people by behaving scandalously. In these accounts Muli indicated a close identification with transvestites. Then suddenly severing his friendship with them, he denounced them as bad because they did not support him in an argument with another man.

Psychosocial dimensions. The psychosocial dimension, as Mandelbaum describes it, "focuses on the individual's subjective world, his general feelings and attitudes. These are individually experienced, but each individual's subjective experience is likely to be similar, in some considerable part, to that of others in his culture and society" (1973:180).

In his life history, Muli revealed several negative images of himself. Instead of describing himself directly, he often quoted others as saying that he was black and ugly, of low status, poor and powerless, clumsy, weak, unable to do men's work well, and a person who lacked leadership qualities. The boys as well as the men of his caste had no respect for him and often disliked him, while his parents and his wife viewed him as a lazy, incompetent, and untrustworthy man who lived on his wife's earnings.

While the people of Muli's own caste rejected him because of his personal failings, upper-caste people avoided him regardless of his individual qualities. Muli's life history thus provides an insider's view of the psychological effects of discrimination against people at the bottom of society. Like all Bauri males and females, he routinely experienced rejection on account of his alleged potential for polluting high-caste people. Muli, deeply resenting such discrimination, mockingly described how high-caste women avoided his presence so that he would not pollute them, how tea stall owners refused to allow him to enter their shops, and how, as long as he supplied them with Bauri women, high-caste men barely tolerated him. Muli expected to be insulted, avoided, and cheated in his everyday contact with higher-caste people, and he retaliated by cheating them.

Muli delighted in expressing self-deprecatory statements to a high-caste person precisely when he knew that that person desperately needed his help and would willingly deny the conventional high-caste stereotype that Muli was a pollutant. Muli, however, repeated the theme of his pollution numerous times, leaving the impression that he had internalized the very norms that he ridiculed. His own self-image was shaped by the very oppression that he rejected.

Muli tried to escape discrimination by emulating his oppressors, on whom he had to depend to survive. When they rejected him, he retaliated by trying to bring them under his control, often by supplying them with prostitutes; and when successful, he often described himself as laughing uncontrollably in their presence, reflecting the stress he felt at putting them at a disadvantage. Muli displayed a wide range of behaviors in different situations, with different and with the same high-caste people. He frequently played up to generous landowning masters, construction employers, or customers for his prostitutes, pretending loyalty but privately ridiculing their behaviors and ideals. Muli's acquiescence to his superiors did not mean that he accepted his lot.

The views that others had of him prompted Muli to exaggerate the very qualities that people criticized, and by doing so, he orchestrated his own disasters. He cultivated cleverness and dishonesty; he often described how he relied on quick wits and fast talking to evade crises that he frequently brought upon himself. Since he both admired and resented upper-caste persons, he tried to compete equally with them by being a big spender, while at other times he lied, cheated, and ridiculed them behind their backs, and they in turn cheated him. He had hoped that working as a pimp would bring him money, contact with higher-caste men, status, and friendship, but in fact his status remained unchanged. At forty he was as poor as he had been at twenty. He contrasted his unhappy life as a married man with his youthful years. He saw himself as a middle-aged failure whose youthful dreams had never materialized and whose future was bleak. Sometimes he held himself responsible for the acts which caused people to dislike him; at other times, he said that what had happened to him had been fated from the beginning.

Rejected by his family, his caste, and upper-caste people, Muli sought refuge in the company of transvestites drawn from many castes, who openly flaunted not only conventional sexual mores, but also rules of caste separation. People tolerated transvestites, but often made them the subject of coarse jokes. Muli, sensitive to stigma and ridicule, became insulted when a man seeing him with transvestites addressed him on the road with the intimate terms used for a wife. Although identifying with transvestites, Muli rejected them because he couldn't stand the arrogant ridicule.

The Turnings

Turnings, as Mandelbaum describes them, "mark major changes that a person makes and thus demarcate periods of his life" (1973: 180). Mandelbaum explains that a turning, or major transition in a person's life, takes place when a person takes on a new set of roles (a cultural dimension), enters into new relationships with new people (a social dimension), enters into a new self-conception (a psycho-social dimension). A turning may involve a single event, such as marriage, or it may develop gradually, such as a transition to old age. Some turnings, such as marriage, may be expected of all people in a group, while other turnings may represent an individual's personal choice, or reflect a response to a particular event. Often, however, an improvised turning "follows some established patterns" (1973: 181).

Muli's life showed four major turnings or transitions. The first was that he chose to become a pimp, and to befriend transvestites, irrevocably cutting himself off from the mainstream life style of Bauris that his parents expected him to follow. His transition was neither unprecedented nor revolutionary among Bauris, but rather represented an alternative life style choice that many Bauris followed. Most Bauri pimps and prostitutes also worked as day laborers; as long as they did not make a public spectacle of their prostitution activities, other Bauris pretended not to notice. But the Bauris expelled pimps and prostitutes who were open about their activities. Ultimately, Muli was expelled for this reason. Expelled prostitutes usually lived in huts a few yards outside the ward or village.

Muli's second turning, unlike the first, was prescribed by his caste: Grandfather Dharma arranged his marriage to Kia. Muli's parents and neighbors expected him to assume the responsibilities of a married householder, but he resisted and avoided them. His unhappy marriage was a major theme of his life history.

Muli's third turning became possible because he was a pimp: one of his high-caste clients set him up in the betel selling business. Unlike his first two transitions, Muli's change to businessman was a radical departure for the Bauris of his village (although Bauris elsewhere were businessmen). Muli had great fears and misgivings that he would not know how to run a business, and that high-caste people would ridicule him and refuse to buy from him. He found to his delight that his business was mildly successful.

Muli's fourth turning was the accidental termination of his business career. His one and a half years in the market became the high point of his life. For the first and only time he earned a steady income, and he also had status as a respectable businessman. Then, unwittingly, he engineered his own economic downfall by creating his messy affair with Tafulla, his second wife. Untouchables rarely receive opportunities to break away from poverty, but some extraordinary achievers, often with the help of their families, have improved their economic situation (Isaacs 1965[1974]:73–74). Muli was given a rare chance, but he failed.

Adaptations

Adaptations refer to the continuous adjustments or changes that a person makes during the span of a lifetime. "Adaptation," says Mandelbaum, "is a built-in process, because every person must, in the course of his life, alter some of his established patterns of behavior to cope with new conditions. Each person *changes* his ways in order to maintain *continuity*, whether of group participation or social expectation or self-image or simply survival. Some of these new conditions are imposed by his own physical development. Others arise from changing external conditions, whether of custom or climate, family or society" (1973:181).

Ironically, the very adaptative behaviors that Muli made use of to cope with poverty and discrimination also ultimately caused his downfall. Although he was an incompetent farm laborer and quarry worker, he found that he could earn easy money by pimping, which fit his physical abilities and psychological outlook. Most Bauris feared to associate with wealthy and powerful high-caste men. By contrast, Muli deliberately sought out such men, hoping to gain both money and prestige by his association with them. To keep a hold on them, he used deceit, and he put them in compromising positions. What was unique about Muli's approach, and ultimately disastrous for him, was that he also tried to befriend the high-caste men who visited his prostitutes. Muli's initial easy success prompted him to use deceit on everyone: his high-caste clients, his high-caste friend whose brother sold him the bullocks, the high-caste man who set him up in business, his two wives, his parents, his relatives, his neighbors, and his Bauri friends. Because he believed that others would cheat him, Muli usually pushed to gain further advantages at the expense of others.

To gain friendships with high-caste people, and status among people of his own caste, Muli became a big spender; he gave his oath-friend Bhima an expensive gold ring, creating the impression that he was wealthy; he offered to buy bullocks that he could not afford; he freely distributed betel and village cigarettes to the boys and men of his caste when he was a vendor in the market.

When Muli's deceitful behavior and big spending landed him in trouble, as often happened, he tried to extricate himself by attempting further deceptions, which usually worsened his condition. His downfall came when Tafulla's family, taking advantage of his good-natured generosity at the market, invited him to their house so that they could enjoy his earnings. Muli's betel business failed when he became embroiled in the scandal with Tafulla, which consumed his time and capital. After his business failure, his fortunes plummetted: a goldsmith whom he generously lent money cheated him out of the money plus harvest wages; high-caste clients for his prostitutes abandoned him; his wife attempted suicide; and Jadu the miser-landlord cheated him out of another harvest wage. Muli, seeking easy ways out of day labor, helped to precipitate all of these disasters by his own behavior.

Muli's identification with transvestites fitted his adaptive behavior of pimping. Because he acted in an effeminate manner and used women's dialect, he mingled easily with women, and they talked to him openly. While high-caste people and the men of his caste rejected him, transvestites and prostitutes accepted him and encouraged his behavior.

Muli's adaptations enhanced his abilities to be a life history narrator. As a marginal member of his society, he became a detached, ironic critic of it, while his contact with high-caste men helped him to become more articulate than most Bauris.

Consequences

Muli's life history portrayed conflicts between the ideals of his caste, his own expectations, and his actual behavior. Muli's thwarted expectations led him to idealize his youth. His attempted adaptations were in the long run unsuccessful. He failed to solve both his internal problem of negative self-image and the external problem faced by almost all untouchables of his village: poverty, discrimination, and failure to benefit from the growth of the new city. Pimping brought Muli no improvement over the other available life style choices: hard physical labor and religious healing. No Bauri laborers or healers in the village have improved their economic or social situation in the past decade, while high-caste people have benefited enormously from urbanization. Of some 456 Bauris in Muli's village, only two young men (one of them Muli's brother Sarala) have improved their economic condition, combining extraordinary talents and exceptional good fortune. Muli's life history thus is representative of the condition of most Bauris, who try to improve their situation but fail.

Mandelbaum observes that "at no stage is a person merely an inert recipient of the cultural and social stamp, but in childhood he has less scope for choice, less capacity for social manoeuvre" (1973: 193). The importance of the life history approach, suggests Mandelbaum, is that it enables the observer to study and assess the relation of freedom to determinism in a person's life. "Each person is a bound actor and a free agent. In the study of life history we can consider the degree to which he is either and the importance of both. This approach enables us to see that an individual has some opportunity for self-direction within the unwritten scenario of his culture and the open-ended drama of his society. It is a means of understanding his point of view, the choices of which he is aware, the indeterminacy that he perceives" (1973:194).

Muli's life provided an excellent example of the interplay between the bound and the free. At one extreme, external economic and ecological constraints provided a limited range of choices. A person could choose to work or not work; and those who worked could choose between a few unskilled, low-paying jobs with low risk, or slightly more remunerative but higher-risk (of being outcasted) jobs of pimping and prostitution.

To become a pimp or prostitute, a person had to disregard cultural norms prohibiting such activities. Muli disregarded the norms of his group, not overtly, but covertly. Overtly, he went through the motions that represented "respectable" behavior. Covertly, he broke the rules, showing no guilt whatsoever in doing so. He portrayed his prostitutes similarly: while giving the appearance of respectability, in fact they slept with higher-caste men because they enjoyed it and wanted the money. Throughout his life history, Muli depicted how he, his family, and his friends creatively manipulated, adapted, or disregarded rituals to fit their needs. Social relations were similarly varied, from founding and abandoning drama troupes to forming a household consisting of a Bauri woman, her Bauri husband, and her Brahman lover—while appearing to comply with the norms of society.

Although the broad outline of Muli's life was determined by the cultural norms and the socioeconomic conditions of his caste group, he exercised great flexibility of choices within the limited context in which he found himself. But the extraordinary luck and success of his youngest brother, Sarala, who became an automobile mechanic, highlights another important aspect of people's lives brought out by life histories. The choices and adaptations that people make are tied to situational circumstances, often chance accidents.* Had Sarala not had a brother-in-law who was an automobile mechanic, he would have had no one to train him and find him a job repairing automobiles. Had his brother-in-law Bharata not had a Brahman patron who found *him* a job in a service station, Bharata, however talented and determined, might never have become an automobile mechanic.

Given the events that occurred in Muli's life, he was doomed to fail. But what if those events had been different? He was on his way out of poverty until Tafulla's family dragged him back down. Must we assume that he inevitably would have failed had he not met Tafulla? What would his life have been like if he had married a different woman—one who would have left him, or refused to support him, or complied with his demands as Kia rarely did? Did Kia's behavior prompt Muli to turn to transvestites? Conversely, what sort of woman would Kia have become if, instead of marrying Muli when she was fourteen, she had married a hardworking good provider? Must we assume that she would have developed into the

---

*In their comments about Mandelbaum's perspective, Lloyd and Suzanne Rudolph particularly emphasize the importance of situational circumstances, chance events that might affect a person's adaptations (Rudolph and Rudolph 1973:201–203).

bad-tempered, sharp-tongued shrew who lived with Muli? Given the economic and social position of all Bauris, Muli's chances to succeed undoubtedly were infinitesimally small. But the chance success of his brother, plus his own temporary success, shows that his failure, however likely, may not have been inevitable.

31. Conclusions

The Editor's Role in Muli's Life History

In biographical accounts of semiliterate or nonliterate people, the distinction between biography and autobiography is often difficult to make, given problems of editing, translation, and directing of narrations. Consequently, as Langness has observed, some anthropologists prefer to use the term "life history" to cover the extensive account of a person's life, whether written or narrated by that person, by others, or by both (Langness 1965:4–5).

If the life histories of semiliterate and nonliterate people are the result of the combined efforts of narrator and translator-editor, then how much of a completed life history reflects the narrator's efforts and how much reflects the editor's contributions? What aspects of a life history are independent of the investigator who collects it?

Allport, recognizing this problem in 1942, cautioned against excessive editing, while at the same time he claimed that personal documents take their meaning from the investigator's comments and interpretations (Allport 1942:83–86, 142; also see Blumer 1939: 77–81). More recently, Devereux has argued that "a rat experiment, an anthropological field trip or a psychoanalysis contribute more to the understanding of behavior when viewed as a source of information about the animal psychologist, the anthropologist or the psychoanalyst, than when it is considered only as a source of information about rats, primitives or patients." The data of behavioral science, according to Devereux, is threefold: "1. The behavior of the subject. 2. The 'disturbances' produced by the existence and observational activities of the observer. 3. The behavior of the observer: his anxieties, his defense maneuvers, his research strategies, his 'decisions' (=his attribution of a meaning to his observations)" (Devereux 1967:xix). The data of the observer that need study, says Devereux, include not only the observer's cultural and social background, but also the process of "countertransference," that is, how an observer reacts as a person to his own observations (1967:xvi–xx,

41–47, 83–126). In summary, to quote La Barre's comments about Devereux's perspective, "field ethnography (and indeed all social science) as presently practiced, may be a species of autobiography" (La Barre 1967:viii).

I do believe that Devereux's insight on the observer as a datum of behavior is an important one. However, I also believe that La Barre's evaluation of its importance, if taken literally rather than metaphorically, would carry it to such an extreme as to reduce it to an absurdity. For example, I am quite convinced that Muli's life history is not the autobiography of James Freeman.

I have no doubt that in certain subtle and significant respects, Muli's account of his life history, as elicited by my promptings and as affected by my translations and editing, constitutes a rearrangement if not an actual alteration of the raw data of the facts of his life. But I believe that the portrait of Muli which emerges is a faithful one in all essential respects. My own contributions can be compared with those of the photographic artist who produces a portrait of his subject by controlling the lighting and background in his studio and modifying the composition of the portrait in the darkroom by selective cropping, that is, editing.

I would grant that Muli's life history might well have been recognizably different had it been collected by a different person with a different personal background and different categories of reference to guide his directing of Muli's narration and editing of Muli's account. Nevertheless, I am convinced that Muli would have been recognizable as the subject of the life history, just as he would be recognized as the same subject if he were to sit for a portrait by two different photographic artists with their own distinctive styles. To elaborate the example: Karsh's portrait of Churchill, while instantly recognizable as a Karsh photograph, is nevertheless a portrait of Churchill and not of Karsh.

A life history like Muli's does not exist as an external datum, independent of time, place, and person, waiting to be recorded. Rather, it is the joint production of two or more persons with the right combination of personalities, interests, and biases who happen to come together at the right time and place for creating a life history.* The

*My views on the nature of life history are paralleled by Richard Schechner's views on rituals and performances. Schechner (influenced by Victor Turner's studies of rituals, especially his metaphors of liminal and liminoid) emphasizes that anthro-

role of the observer thus is a crucial component of a life history. No comparison of life histories is possible without knowledge of the editor's perspectives and values that influenced the final form of the history. Failure to assess or at least recognize the observer's or editor's role leads to an image of a life history that is distorted and incomplete, since each editor, though not consciously, is necessarily influenced by his own perspectives.

In describing my relationship with Muli and my influence on him, I also deliberately discussed my own values and my reactions both to his behavior and to my own behavior. Since I may well be unconscious of the extent to which my own frame of reference and biases influenced my editing of Muli's narration, the reader must himself consider more fully what in the narrative appears to be more a reflection of the observer than the narrator. If I were to attempt to trace out in detail my own unconscious biases, I would need to write an entire volume—as indeed Devereux has done—a Herculean task that could not be included in this limited space.

Nevertheless, to the reader who might wonder not only about my conscious biases, but about their origin—the extent to which my own background might need to be taken into account in separating my contribution from Muli's in the production of his life history—I offer the following brief summary of personal background which I brought to the study and which led me to do it. Any self-analysis may simply be self-delusion, but as I see it now, besides collecting information on social change, my motivations for collecting Muli's life history were twofold: first, to describe the world of meaning of a person from a culture other than my own; and second, to document a life history of oppression.

While my interest in other cultures and world views originated in early childhood, my focus on India, untouchables, and life histories was inspired by accident rather than by choice. When I entered graduate school at Harvard in 1958, I had no narrowly focused interest, but rather several interdisciplinary ones concerning symbols, ritual, and myth. My selection of a geographical area came, as it does

---

pological reports are not an imitation of nature, but a creation of it. Muli's life history provides an excellent example. The process of creating a life history might itself be interpreted using the metaphor of the liminoid (Schechner:lecture at the University of California at Los Angeles, February 17, 1978; Turner 1974:14–17, 255–261).

for many anthropology graduate students, because I had to choose a thesis topic and do field research in a culture other than my own. What initially drew me to India was not its village life or its social problems, but rather its philosophy and religion; and indeed, my first publication, which appeared in a journal of philosophy, dealt with the distinction between myth and metaphysics in Indian thought (Freeman 1966:517–529). I soon learned, however, that philosophical speculations were not the stuff of Harvard doctoral dissertations in anthropology. One professor told me to quit dabbling; another asked me what my philosophical bubble-blowing had to do with anthropology; and a third suggested that I transfer to the Divinity School.

I felt, however, that what I was doing belonged in anthropology, for my focus in that article on metaphysics was on how people attribute meaning to their universe, and what consequences follow from losing the belief in a meaningful universe. In retrospect, the study of meaning in world views is the main thread that connects my early philosophical writing, my subsequent studies of Hinduism, including firewalking, my study of Muli's life and world view, and my current ongoing life history studies of other Indians.

But why was I fascinated with questions about meaning, and why in particular with meaning in a culture other than my own? What was there about such questions that absorbed my attention, that made them interesting to me?

Of the many possible influences that led me to my present studies, surely those exerted by my mother and father were particularly formative. My mother, uprooted as a child from her native village in Hungary, an immigrant to the United States, where she became an academic editor, idealizes family and village life from her childhood recollections; but at the same time, she has developed an acute sense of the relativity of different social settings. She sees herself, not as attached to a particular place, but as an outsider ready to move on, an inhabitant of two cultural worlds. My father, an American-born citizen whose parents came from the same village as my mother's, actively rebelled in his youth against the religious and cultural traditions of his parents, to which he has remained a hostile critic. He became a university professor of philosophy, a Peircean pragmatist impatient with social and religious customs that he considers nonrational nonsense. From my mother, I developed my curiosity about other cultures, my desire to experience living in a close-knit social group with a meaningful world view, and also my empathy and respect for village life styles, without committing myself to those life styles. Thus I was particularly attracted to Muli's description of his drama troupe because of the sense of community that it revealed. From my father, I developed an outsider's skeptical attitude toward people's explanations of their own behavior, and a penchant for scrutinizing such statements critically. Muli's life history intrigued me intellectually because it tested my ability to wrestle with the paradox of which statements were "true" in the narrative of a man who proudly proclaimed himself a liar.

As members of a minority religious group, my parents (and I to a much lesser extent) experienced various forms of discrimination that heightened my sensitivity to the emotional plight of people like Muli and motivated me to seek an oppressed person and portray his sufferings. I recognized in Muli's accounts of discrimination, exploitation, and stigma a common bond that he shared with me and my relatives. While my personal experiences may not be a necessary prerequisite to taking the life history of an oppressed person, they undoubtedly guided my decision to highlight the psychological effects of discrimination in Muli's life.

In 1962, I selected Bhubaneswar, Orissa, as a research site because one of my professors, Cora DuBois, had begun a long-term study there. The site interested her because it featured an old Hindu pilgrimage center adjacent to a newly built administrative town. The new town, squat, ugly, traditionless, and bureaucratic, turned me off immediately. By contrast, the village where Muli lived, a minor pilgrimage center, intrigued me with its distinctive caste of temple priests and their strong sense of identity and rootedness in this one community that reminded me in many ways of the village of my mother and grandparents. My doctoral dissertation (1968) focused on certain aspects of the religious life style of those priests, while my subsequent book (1977a) described many contrasting life styles within the same village.

While I included life history materials in these two studies, I focused mainly on the broad features of village, caste, economic, and religious organization rather than on the personal experiences of the villagers. With this material as necessary background, I then turned to what had become over the years my primary interest, a focus on the villagers as persons, on their recollections of the events and experiences that gave meaning to their lives or forced them to question the meaning of their existence.

By recording the lives and sufferings of Muli and his people, I hope that I have helped to hasten the day when such sufferings cease, not only for Indian untouchables, but for all victims of social inequality.

Significance of Muli's Life History

The story of Muli's life may move others, as it did me, to ponder their own experiences in ways they had previously neglected. An authentic life history confronts us with an immediacy and concreteness that compels our involvement, that causes us to discover within ourselves something about human predicaments everywhere in the face of which our cultural differences become insignificant. Muli presents such a life history. The cultural idiom in which he operates may be foreign to us, but his aims are not: he strives for dignity; he seeks to be respected by the people around him; he questions why fate has brought him to his present circumstances; he wants a good life for himself. As he approaches what he thinks of as old age, Muli sees his dream of achieving a good life slipping by; a bleak end awaits him. He expresses no hopes of salvation or a better existence in a future life. His particular beliefs are guided by his cultural setting, but his predicament is not.

The unique contribution of a life history is that it helps the reader to understand the abstract principles of behavioral science as reflected in the lived experience of the narrator. A life history at its best transforms the lifeless abstractions of behavioral science into vivid personal accounts. Abstract discussions of the concept of stigma provide a necessary basis for generalization, but the high-caste tea stall boy's humiliating caste insults of Muli bring the concept of stigma to life in a way that no abstraction can convey.

The life history of Muli also gives us an insight into the nature of oppression in any caste society. His history stands as an indictment, not merely of the caste system as an Indian phenomenon, but of stratified systems of inherited inequality everywhere, which invariably produce effects similar to those described by Muli. In his comparison of stratified societies, Berreman contends that "the Black in America and in South Africa, the Burakumin of Japan, the Harijan of India, the barber or washerman of Swat, the Hutu or Twa of Ruanda, have all faced similar conditions as individuals and they have responded to them in similar ways" (1972:405).* On the basis of evidence from many stratified societies, Berreman concludes that "no group of people is content to be low in a caste hierarchy—to live a life of inherited deprivation and subjection—regardless of the apparent stability of the system and regardless of the rationalizations offered by their superiors or constructed by themselves" (1973:17).

Berreman's words are particularly apt when applied to India. Untouchables throughout India rarely claim to be proud of their place in society; instead, individually or in groups, many attempt to pass as "clean" high castes by changing their names, customs, occupations, and dress to those of the "clean" castes.† Others deny their caste by converting to anticaste religions such as Buddhism, Islam, or Christianity. Still others join political groups that cut across caste lines. In the anonymity of cities, untouchables usually can blot out more of their past than those who reside in villages, but the process, slow and painful, often takes generations. In Muli's village, where untouchables depend for their livelihood on higher-caste employers, denials of untouchability provoke severe high-caste economic retaliation, if not physical violence. Thus external conditions have doomed Muli and most of the people of his caste to failure no matter what they choose to do, and Muli's adaptations reflect this situation. Muli and other Bauris have failed, not because they embody expectations of failure or accept their lot, but rather because the Bauris face social and economic disabilities that they are presently powerless to change.

*Many incidents in Muli's life history show striking similarities with events recorded in other cultures. For example, he often quotes himself as saying to his masters that he is dark, dirty, and polluting; but his tone suggests that, like the slaves of the antebellum southern United States, he plays up to his masters by telling them what he thinks they believe or want to hear. He often pretends loyalty to a high-caste master while privately ridiculing his master's ideals (see Osofsky 1969:9, 21–24). Muli's description of the double standard of high-caste men who treat him familiarly in private and disavow him publicly finds its exact parallel in a passage describing a high-status Japanese woman's treatment of her low-status friend (see Norbeck 1972:195–196).

†See Isaacs (1974:143–149, 157–160) for a discussion of "passing" by Indian untouchables. See also De Vos and Wagatsuma (1972:245–248) for a discussion of passing among Japanese Burakumin.

Significance of Life Histories

Four implications follow from my account of Muli's life history. While these implications are drawn from a particular life history, they reveal universal characteristics that to a greater or lesser degree are found in all life histories.

1) By its nature, a life history involves the creation of the very data that are analyzed. Muli's life history came into being, not as an integral or historical part of Muli's culture, but because an American outsider provoked and guided its creation. In this sense Muli's life history derives both from American culture and Indian culture: it translates an untouchable's life style into an American idiom.

2) A life history does not just happen, but is indeed staged and directed by the investigator, even when the investigator tries to be nondirective.

3) The outcome of a life history is unpredictable: neither Muli nor I had any way of knowing what would be revealed to us during the process of taking the life history—about each one of us or about the other.

4) The process of taking a life history involves what Richard Schechner, influenced by Victor Turner, calls "theatrical liminality": a situation in transition.* Schechner, a professor of drama, likens the anthropological fieldworker to the theater director, "who does not author the script, but somehow guarantees its realization before an audience. Similarly, the fieldworker doesn't create the society he studies, but his presence gives these cultures a special significance, a reverberative importance both to those he studies and to those he reports back to" (Schechner 1977a:12; see also Schechner 1977b).

The fieldworker, observes Schechner, works in a liminal and transitional mode, for he is neither simply a performer nor just a spectator, but rather a person between two societies. The fieldwork process itself, Schechner suggests, involves the three-phase process essential

---

*Turner uses the term liminal in a special sense: "The attributes of liminality or of liminal *personae* ('threshold people') are necessarily ambiguous, since this condition and these persons elude or slip through the network of classifications that normally locate states and positions in cultural space. Liminal entities are neither here nor there; they are betwixt and between the positions assigned and arrayed by law, custom, convention, and ceremonial. As such, their ambiguous and indeterminate attributes are expressed by a rich variety of symbols in the many societies that ritualize social and cultural transitions" (Turner 1969:95).

to ritual structure as elaborated by van Gennep and, more recent-ly, by Victor Turner: *separation*—the stripping away of one's culture-habits; *initiation*—the finding out of what is new in the society one is temporarily part of, plus the deeper revelations about oneself that emerge from this process; and *reintegration*—the translation of an investigator's findings into a form comprehensible to the world he returns to (Schechner 1977:12). My account of taking Muli's life his-tory exemplifies this ritual process.

For the past several decades, investigators have spoken of the potential that life histories hold, yet many writers have observed that their promise appears not to have been fulfilled; and there appears to be no clarity about what that promise is (Langness 1965:18; Mandelbaum 1973:179).* As Mandelbaum observes, the investigator becomes "uncomfortably aware that his description and analysis have omitted something of great importance . . ." (Mandel-baum 1973:178). Life histories have been used quite effectively to focus on or answer particular kinds of questions concerning culture, culture change, theoretical issues in culture and personality, and such specific aspects of culture as women's views. Life histories have also been used for literary and humanistic purposes. Historically, life histories, like other data in the behavioral sciences, have been evalu-ated in terms of the issues of generalizability and representative-ness, or, failing that, they have been seen as pilot studies needing further validation. Possibly these have been, if not wrong criteria, then at least misleading criteria by which to evaluate them.

Life histories contain three distinctive characteristics that are over-looked if investigators focus on generalizability:

They have a configuration of experiences conveyed by a contin-uous narrative made vivid by concrete detail.

They have a compelling quality that may be absent in statistical concerns about generalizability. What drew me to Muli was some-thing compelling about him. The compelling dimension, although not unique to life histories, is best or most effectively represented by them.

The process of taking the life history is an important part of the

---

*I am indebted to David Krantz for pointing out in many conversations what he terms the unfulfilled promise of life histories, their compelling nature, and the problems involved in evaluating them according to conventional behavioral science criteria.

life history. This aspect of life history studies is virtually unreported by others, yet it is here, in this liminal phase where narrator and observer meet, that the creative process begins and brings the development of insight and deepening understanding, both for the narrator and the observer. Not only the details of the life history, then, but also the process of creating it may be where we should look if we are to further our understanding of life histories.

 *Reference Matter*

Appendix A: Bauri Rituals

Muli's life history includes several lengthy descriptions of life-cycle rituals which I have omitted from this book. Others I have summarized in my introductions; examples of these are the rituals described here.

Although Bauri life-cycle rituals differ in details from those of the high castes, they focus, as do high-caste rituals, both on the general themes of purification and elimination of pollution and on themes peculiar to each ceremony. For example, at the birth of his youngest brother, Sarala, Muli describes the rituals for family members, their house, and their household items that remove the pollution believed to occur at the birth of a child. Other rituals at that time focus on the welfare of the newborn infant: for example, he remains near a fire for seven days, and the women of the household keep him warm by placing their hands near the fire and then on his body. On the seventh day, after further purification rituals, a ward leader, the child's maternal aunt and uncle, and seven women of the ward cook a meal, offer it to a grinding stone considered to be the deity of birth, ask the deity to bless the child, and then name the child.

The funeral of Dungi, Muli's paternal step-grandmother, involves not only purification of the deceased person's relatives, house, and household articles, but also many rituals designed to free the dead person's spirit from the family. According to Muli, if these rituals are not performed properly, the spirit will become a malevolent ghost who harms people at night or possesses and kills them.

Each day for ten days, Muli's father, Hata, offers the spirit of his stepmother some food and water at the crossroads leading into the ward. On the tenth day, Hata, surrounded by relatives and ward leaders, makes a mud figure of his stepmother at the bank of the Gangua River near his village, gives offerings of food to the figure, carries a pot of food into the river, breaks the pot, and drops it into the water. Muli says that the image of the deceased person becomes visible beneath the water at that time.

After having his head shaved to purify him, Muli's father leads his relatives toward the village. He carries a bone of his deceased stepmother, representing her body, in a covered box. At the cross-roads outside the ward, Hata scratches three lines with an iron stake, believing that this will prevent the dead spirit from following people into the village and harming them.

In the room where Grandmother Dungi died, a family priest creates a turmeric-powder image of a human figure that represents the spirit of the deceased, and figures of plants, birds, cows, and trees that represent new life. Hata places the bone of his stepmother on the sacred eastern side of a purifying sacrificial fire and offers sacred nectar to the bone, then to himself, his guests, and his relatives, thus purifying them of all death pollutions.

At midnight, five men from the ward carry a clay oil lamp to the crossroads where Hata had scratched three lines. Placing the lamp on the road, they throw offerings of food and water across the lines. Because they fear the spirit of the deceased, they avoid stepping over the lines. Muli says that the flame from the oil lamp is the living spirit; when it expires, the spirit has gone to heaven. This ritual invites the spirit to return to the village the next day in the form of an ant. As the men return from the crossroads, they keep their mouths closed to prevent the spirit from entering them, causing dysentery, bleeding, and death. To frighten the spirit away, the men hum loudly while beating iron nails together.

Meanwhile, Hata has remained in the room where his stepmother died. He forms a small mound of sand, which he covers with a basket. When the men return, he removes the basket, catches an ant running over the mound, and places it in a small shell securely covered with a cloth. The ant represents the spirit of the deceased person. If no ant appears, the five men return to the crossroads to repeat their rituals.

The following morning, the eleventh day after Grandmother Dungi has died, the family priest makes a turmeric-powder image of her that is her last representation. Hata places on the image the last food offerings that Grandmother Dungi will receive. Then he carries the ant in the shell to the edge of a pond, where he releases it, thus freeing the spirit forever.

In many respects, the rituals described by Muli are similar to those described by Babb for the community he studied in central India: a focus on the problems of "intense pollution and a potentially malevolent ghost," and the "obligation on the kin of the deceased to cut his spirit free from this world and to see it safely and comfortably on to the next" (Babb 1975:90–91). This is done, as Babb observes, by giving offerings to the spirit. While notions of rebirth figure in the ceremonies, the main problem faced by kin is that a spirit does not automatically become free after death, but hovers in a marginal existence, with the potential of becoming a malevolent ghost "until it is transformed by ritual means into an ancestral spirit" (Babb 1975:92; see Babb pp. 90–98 for further details).

Appendix B: Bauri Marriage Rites

I have omitted Muli's lengthy account of his sister's marriage and most of the details of his own marriage, since Babb adequately describes and interprets such rituals in his study of popular Hinduism in central India (Babb 1975:81–90). Babb observes that getting married involves an elaborate sequence of rituals which varies with family and caste circumstances. The activities include complex procedures for the selection of spouses, elaborate gift-giving, and what Babb terms the purely ritual aspect of marriage.

Babb's brief summary of the selection process applies in most cases to the castes of Kapileswar, Orissa: "Among lower ... castes it is the bride, not the groom, who is sought, and accordingly it is the groom's father who typically initiates the search and proposes the match. The reverse obtains among higher castes. After the proposal there is a period of mutual examination between the two families. In higher castes this includes matching of horoscopes. The final settlement of the marriage usually hinges on a satisfactory financial arrangement between the two fathers. Among the upper castes this is a matter of dowry; among the lower castes a matter of brideprice ... The sums involved (in brideprice) can be quite substantial, often in the hundreds of rupees, and clearly play an important role in easing the financial burden of the bride's father, who bears the main expense of the marriage ceremony itself" (Babb 1975:82).

With some exceptions, Muli's descriptions of his wedding and that of his sister resemble the general patterns described by Babb. The day before the wedding, female relatives anoint the deities of the ward shrines with oil and turmeric and then similarly anoint the bride and groom. Babb (1975:84) interprets these rites as treating the bride and groom as goddess and god. "In fact, from this point forward, the bride and groom are treated quite literally as deities, as objects of worship in their own right. In the ritual sense the marriage represents the high point in both of their lives (however ephemeral the marriage might actually turn out to be) and this is expressed in their treatment as living manifestations of divinity."

In his own ceremony, Muli refers explicitly to this worship: "Next, the priest performed the *bandana* [worship of the bride and groom as deities]. He did this by performing a ritual called *aarati* [waving a lamp or light before an image to honor it]. Then we returned to the altar. Our hands and cloth remained tied together. The cloth would remain joined for seven days."

Bibliography

Aggarwal, Partap C., and Mohd. Siddique Ashraf 1976. *Equality through Privilege: Study of Special Privileges in Haryana.* New Delhi: Shri Ram Centre for Industrial Relations and Human Resources.

Allport, Gordon 1942. *The Use of Personal Documents in Psychological Science.* Bulletin 49, New York: Social Science Research Council.

Babb, Lawrence A. 1975. *The Divine Hierarchy.* New York: Columbia University Press.

Bailey, F. G. 1957. *Caste and the Economic Frontier.* Manchester: Manchester University Press.

———— 1963. *Politics and Social Change: Orissa in 1959.* Berkeley: University of California Press.

Barber, Bernard 1968. "Social Mobility in Hindu India." In *Social Mobility in the Caste System in India,* ed. James Silverberg, pp. 18–35. The Hague: Mouton.

Bartlett, Sir Frederic C. 1932 (1967). *Remembering: A Study in Experimental and Social Psychology.* Cambridge: Cambridge University Press.

Berreman, Gerald D. 1964. "Brahmins and Shamans in Pahari Religion." *Journal of Asian Studies:* Aspects of Religion in South Asia, ed. Edward B. Harper, 23 (June): 53–69.

———— 1965. "The Study of Caste Ranking in India." *Southwestern Journal of Anthropology* 21, no. 2: 115–129.

———— 1972. "Race, Caste, and Other Invidious Distinctions in Social Stratification." *Race* 13, no. 4 (April): 385–414.

———— 1973. *Caste in the Modern World.* Morristown, N.J.: General Learning Press.

Blumer, Herbert 1939. *Critiques of Research in the Social Sciences: I. An Appraisal of Thomas and Znaniecki's The Polish Peasant in Europe and America.* Bulletin 44, New York: Social Science Research Council.

Carstairs, G. Morris 1967. *The Twice Born: A Study of a Community of High Caste Hindus.* Bloomington: University of Indiana Press. First published 1957.

Census [for 1961] of India 1966. *Orissa: District Census Handbook, Puri.* Cuttack: Orissa Government Press.

Census [for 1971] of India 1971. *Orissa: Provisional Population Totals.* Cuttack: Orissa Government Press.

Chaudhuri, Nirad 1968. *The Autobiography of an Unknown Indian.* Berkeley: University of California Press. First published 1951.

408

Cohn, Bernard 1955. "The Changing Status of a Depressed Caste." In *Village India*, ed. McKim Marriott, pp. 53–77. Chicago: University of Chicago Press.

DeVos, George, and Hiroshi Wagatsuma, eds. 1972. *Japan's Invisible Race: Caste in Culture and Personality*, rev. ed. Berkeley: University of California Press.

Devereux, George 1967. *From Anxiety to Method in the Behavioral Sciences.* The Hague: Mouton.

Dollard, John 1949. *Criteria for the Life History.* New York: Peter Smith. First published 1935.

Erikson, Erik H. 1968. "Life Cycle." *International Encyclopedia of the Social Sciences*, IX, 286–292.

―――― 1969. *Gandhi's Truth: On the Origins of Militant Non-Violence.* New York: Norton.

Freed, Stanley A., and Ruth S. Freed 1967. "Spirit Possession as Illness in a North Indian Village." In *Magic, Witchcraft, and Curing*, ed. John Middleton, pp. 295–320. Garden City, N. Y.: Natural History Press. Reprinted from *Ethnology* 3, no. 2(1964): 152–171.

Freeman, James M. 1966. "Myth and Metaphysics in Indian Thought." *The Monist* 50, no. 4: 517–529.

―――― 1968. *Power and Leadership in a Changing Temple Village of India.* Ph.D. dissertation, Social Anthropology, Harvard University.

―――― 1974. "Trial by Fire." *Natural History* 83 (January): 54–63.

―――― 1977a. *Scarcity and Opportunity in an Indian Village.* Menlo Park, Calif.: Cummings.

―――― 1977b. "Rites of Obscenity: Chariot Songs of Eastern India." *Journal of Popular Culture* 10, no. 4: 882–896.

Harper, Edward B. 1964. "Ritual Pollution as an Integrator of Caste and Religion." *Journal of Asian Studies*: Aspects of Religion in South Asia, ed. Edward B. Harper, 23 (June): 151–197.

Hazari 1969. *Untouchable.* New York: Praeger.

Isaacs, Harold 1974. *India's Ex-Untouchables.* New York: Harper and Row. First published 1965.

Kane, Pandurang Vaman 1974. *History of Dharmaśāstra (Ancient and Medieval Religious and Civil Law)*, 2nd ed., V, pt. I. Poona: Bhandarkar Oriental Research Institute.

Karve, D. D., and E. McDonald 1963. *The New Brahmans: Five Maharashtrian Families.* Berkeley: University of California Press.

Kluckhohn, Clyde 1945. "The Personal Document in Anthropological Science." In *The Use of Personal Documents in History, Anthropology, and Sociology.* Bulletin 53, pp. 79–173, New York: Social Science Research Council.

Kuper, Hilda 1960. *Indian People in Natal.* Natal: At the University Press.

410   Bibliography

La Barre, Weston 1967. "Preface." In *From Anxiety to Method in the Behavioral Sciences*, by George Devereux, pp. vii–x. The Hague: Mouton.

Langness, L. L. 1965. *The Life History in Anthropological Science*. New York: Holt, Rinehart, and Winston.

Mahar, Michael, ed. 1972. *The Untouchables in Contemporary India*. Tucson: University of Arizona Press.

Mamdani, Mahmood 1972. *The Myth of Population Control*. New York: Monthly Review Press.

Mandelbaum, David G. 1973. "The Study of Life History: Gandhi." *Current Anthropology* 14, no. 3 (June): 177–196.

Mayer, Adrian 1960. *Caste and Kinship in Central India*. Berkeley: University of California Press.

Meier, August, and Elliot Rudwick 1976. *From Plantation to Ghetto*, 3rd ed. New York: Hill and Wang.

Mishra, K. C. 1971. *The Cult of Jagannatha*. Calcutta: K. M. Mukhopadhyay.

Norbeck, Edward 1972. "Little-Known Minority Groups of Japan." In *Japan's Invisible Race: Caste in Culture and Personality*, eds. George De Vos and Hiroshi Wagatsuma, rev. ed., chap. 9, pp. 183–199. Berkeley: University of California Press.

Norman, Donald A. 1969. *Memory and Attention: An Introduction to Human Information Processing*. New York: John Wiley and Sons.

Opler, Morris 1958. "Spirit Possession in a Rural Area of Northern India." In *Reader in Comparative Religion: An Anthropological Approach*, eds. William Lessa and Evon Vogt, pp. 553–566. Evanston, Ill., and White Plains, N.Y.: Row, Peterson.

Osofsky, Gilbert, ed. 1969. *Puttin' on Ole Massa: The Slave Narratives of Henry Bibb, William Wells Brown, and Solomon Northrup*. New York: Harper and Row.

Panigrahi, K. C. 1961. *Archaeological Remains at Bhubaneswar*. Bombay: Orient Longmans.

Rosaldo, Renato 1976. "The Story of Tukbaw: 'They Listen as He Orates.' " In *The Biographical Process: Studies in the History and Psychology of Religion*, eds. Frank E. Reynolds and Donald Capps, pp. 121–151. The Hague: Mouton.

Rosner, Victor 1966. "Fire-Walking the Tribal Way." *Anthropos* 61: 171–190.

Rudolph, Lloyd, and Susanne Rudolph 1967. *The Modernity of Tradition*. Chicago: University of Chicago Press.

Rudolph, Susanne Hoeber, and Lloyd H. Rudolph 1973. "Comments" [on "The Study of Life History: Gandhi," by David Mandelbaum]. *Current Anthropology* 14, no. 3 (June): 201–203.

Schechner, Richard 1977a. "Field-Work and an Aspect of Theatrical

Structure/Process." Unpublished paper for Burg Wartenstein Symposium no. 76, *Cultural Frames and Reflections: Ritual, Drama and Spectacle*. New York: Wenner-Gren Foundation for Anthropological Research.

———— 1977b. *Essays on Performance Theory*. New York: Drama Book Specialists.

Sharma, Hari P. 1973. "The Green Revolution in India: Prelude to a Red One?" In *Imperialism and Revolution in South Asia*, eds. Kathleen Gough and Hari P. Sharma, pp. 77–102. New York: Monthly Review Press.

Sinha, B. N. 1971. *Geography of Orissa*. New Delhi: National Book Trust, India.

Srinivas, M. N. 1966. *Social Change in Modern India*. Berkeley: University of California Press.

Stein, Burton 1960. "The Economic Function of a Medieval South Indian Temple." *Journal of Asian Studies* 19, no. 2: 163–176.

Tandon, Prakash 1968. *Punjabi Century*. Berkeley: University of California Press.

Times Weekly, Bombay 1973. "Dalit Literature." *Times Weekly* 4, no. 17 (November 25). Special eight-page issue.

Turner, Victor 1969. *The Ritual Process*. Chicago: Aldine Publishing Company.

———— 1974. *Dramas, Fields, and Metaphors*. Ithaca and London: Cornell University Press.

Tyler, Stephen A. 1973. *India: An Anthropological Perspective*. Pacific Palisades, Calif.: Goodyear.

Vidyarthi, L. P. 1961. *The Sacred Complex of Hindu Gaya*. Bombay: Asia Publishing House.

Yalman, Nur 1964. "The Structure of Sinhalese Healing Rituals." *Journal of Asian Studies*: Aspects of Religion in South Asia, ed. Edward B. Harper, 23 (June): 115–150.

Zelliot, Eleanor 1972. "Bibliography on Untouchability." In *The Untouchables in Contemporary India*, ed. Michael Mahar, pp. 431–486. Tucson: University of Arizona Press.

Glossary-Index